INTERRELIGIOUS AND INTERCULTURAL INVESTIGATIONS

12

Collana diretta da
Laurent Basanese, SJ

Centro Studi Interreligiosi

BITRUS TENEU MAIGAMO

Islamic Extremism and its Challenges to the Catholic Missionary Activity in Northern Nigeria Since 1999: A Missiological Study

Pontificia Università Gregoriana
Pontificio Istituto Biblico

Vidimus et approbamus ad normam Statutorum Universitatis
Roma, Pontificia Università Gregoriana
Die 21 mensis maii anni 2019

Prof. Laurent BASANESE
Prof. Tang ABOMO

Cover e impaginazione: Yattagraf srls - Tivoli (RM)

Gregorian & Biblical Press
Piazza della Pilotta 4, 00187 - Roma
www.gbpress.net - books@biblicum.com

ISBN 978-88-7839-**427**-8

This work is dedicated;
To my parents Zachariah Maigamo, now deceased,
and Elizabeth Nchepteh Dodo.

To Leah Sharibu (who is still held in captivity by the Boko Haram
for refusing to denounce her Christian faith).

To all victims of Boko Haram terrorism.
To all persecuted Christians
who suffer religious extremism across the globe.

Acknowledgement

As the saying goes in Akurmi, *"Sano dote wa ciye ti te ne ubosa"*, undertaking a doctoral research is neither a day's job nor a one man's effort. It is often successfully done with the collaboration and dedication of others particularly those who desire to see one's progress in life. It is to this end that I wish to express my sincere gratitude to all those who made all inputs to the success of this research. But important to note first and foremost is the magnanimity of the Almighty God for the good health of mind and body granted to me and the grace to remain resilient through thin and thick to complete this study. My gratitude also goes to my family; James, Abraham, Jacob, Emmanuel, and Dominic (brothers), and all relations for their constant support, love and words of encouragement. I particularly remain ever indebted to my first professors: Zachariah Maigamo Dodo (father-late) and Elizabeth Nchepteh Nna (mother) for teaching me the values of life to resiliently remain focused amidst difficulties in the pursuance of success in life through hard work and dedication.

I thank in a special way my Bishop, Most Rev. Dr. George Jonathan Dodo, the Priests, Religious and Lay Faithful of Zaria Diocese for giving me the opportunity to undergo my studies (both License and Doctoral) in the Gregorian Pontifical University, Rome (2011-2019). The same thanks go John Cardinal Olorunfemi Onaiyekan (Abuja Archdiocese - Emeritus), Arch/Bishops Peter Yaryock Jatau (Kaduna Archdiocese – Emeritus), Matthew Man-Oso Ndangoso (Kaduna Archdiocese), Ignatius Ayau Kaigama (Abuja Archdiocese), Matthew Ishaya Audu (Jos Archdiocese), Joseph Danlami Bagobiri (Kafanchan Diocese - Late), Oliver Dashe Doeme (Maiduguri Diocese), and Julius Yakubu Kundi (Kafanchan Diocese), for their words of encouragement and the materials made available to me at the course of this research. In the same vein, I also thank Bishops Thomas James Olmsted and Eduardo Alanis Nevares (Bishop and Auxiliary Bishop of Phoenix Diocese, USA respectively) for their warm welcome and fatherly care during my summer breaks and thereafter my stay in the States.

Further still, I want to appreciate the friendship and moral support of Rev. Frs. Victor Yakubu, David Kelash, David Samphilippo, Keith Kenny,

Dindo B. Cuario, Ishaya Samaila, Henry Atuma, Samuel Ameh, Alphonsus Bakyil, Cletus Dauya, Solomon Yaryock, John Izuala, Raymond Ogboji, Peter Wazimtu, Peter Bakwap, Christopher Damina, Michael Kagarko, Vincent Achi, Jonathan Yabiliyok, Augustine Isek, Everest Baniyet-Njei, Moses Ma'aji, and Emmanuel Ezema. In the same vein, I humbly appreciate the prayerful support of Rev. Sisters Augustina C. Efunechi, Beatrice Danladi, and Mary Sidi. I also appreciate the love and encouragement of my nephews and nieces Job, Jesse, Harriet, Joyce, Jerry, Jennifer, Daniel, Juliet, Judith, Jude Maigamo, Agnes Apaa, Magdalene Dashe, Hailey, Rose, Barbara & John Wade, Dora & Jose Pedrego, Randolph & Shawn Gear, Richard & Michelle Zahner, Felicia & Emmanuel Ezeigwe, Sue Moravec, Sue Schindel, Lucia & Lucila Rodriguez, Rita Poindexter, Mary Jewett, Dixie Hart, Jon & Teresita Cox, Sandra & Russell Mocker, Jeff & Yun Hui Beech, Daisey Toal, and the families of Anthony D. Weber, Victor Datuwei, Vincent Obialor, Raphael Obioma, and Simon Ibonine (late).

In the area of academics, I remain highly indebted to my principal supervisor, Prof. Laurent Basanese, for his patience, love and invaluable contributions to the success of this research. Your belief and confidence in me to execute an excellent work is highly appreciated. In like manner, I am also grateful to Profs. Zust Milan SJ, Bryan Lobo SJ (Dean), Paul T. Abomo SJ, Maria, DeGiorgi, Francis Oborji, Jacquineau Azetsop SJ, Steven Nkom (late), Muhammed Gwadabe, Rotgak Gofwen, Enoch Oyedele, Joseph Mamman, Peter B. Tanko, Musa Balarabe, and Drs. Victor Anyagu, Lumumba Dodo, Paulinus Nweke, and Ms. Wilma R. Hoffman for their various inputs at different stages of my studies. Thanks too to my research assistant, Peter Orpin for the transcription of my interviews. In the same vein, I thank Andrew Haruna, Esther Peter, Hannatu Moses, Esther Yakubu, Hannatu John, Rebecca Stephen, Simon Vitalis (late), Alhaji Ibrahim Kufena, Marcus, Revs. Sunday Ibrahim, Abraham Nake, Matthias Adugba, Rev. Frs. John Bakeni, Gideon Obasogin, Matthew Sukada, Denis Kaye, Basil Kassam, Boniface Nkom, and John Wumboli for their respective contributions.

The sacrifices and financial contributions of Missio Aachen cannot be quantified. Thanks a million for sponsoring my studies both at Licentiate and Doctoral levels. So also, I sincerely appreciate the Superior Generals of SMA Very Rev. Frs. Jean-Marrie Guillaume (past) and Fachtna O'Driscoll (present), their respective Councils and the entire SMA Generalate, for their hospitality in my first two years in Rome. Special thanks to the Society of Jesus' Fondo Sostegno Studi al Consorzio, Domus Interprovinciales Romanae for the one-year scholarship support. I also appreciate in a special way the financial support of Dr. Brian Duggan & Family, Joseph & Alma Nackard, Bill, Kim & Joseph Trinh, Dcn. Ron & Linda Martinez,

Juan Rodriguez, Gabrielle Klein, John & Olivia McCormick, Barbara & Jim Trost, Paul & Edith Woll, Barsha Shepherd, Juan & Alicia Ayala.

My special gratitude also goes to Don Agostino (Parroccho di Sta. Manria Assunta, Sgurgola), Andrea Cassali (Capo di Azione Cattolica Sgurgola), Angela, Lina, Annunziata, Romeo and Uriah for their love and encouragement. Thanks also to the Nigerian Community in Sgurgola, the members of the Joint Alumni Association of Jos, Makurdi and Kaduna Major Seminaries (JOMAKA) in Rome, and members of the association of the Nigerian Priests, Religious, Seminarians (NIPRELS) in Rome. To all those whose names could not be mentioned here due to time and space constrain, I sincerely assure you that your respective contributions and words of encouragement are highly appreciated and you are all in my prayers.

General introduction

1. Introduction

Since the 9/11 Al-Qaida terrorist attack in America, terrorist activities have been on the increase with alarming rate around the globe. Most parts of the world, especially Africa have been bedevilled by the acts of terrorism from Egypt to Sudan down to Kenya and Central Africa Republic (CAR), across Mali and down to Nigeria and her neighbouring countries that include Cameroon, Chad and Niger. According to the report of the Institute for Economics and Peace (hence, IEP) in the Global Terrorism Index of 2014 (henceforth GTI), there has been over a five -fold increase of the number of people killed in terrorist act since 2000, and examining closely the terrorists' activities, there was an overwhelming increase of deaths from terrorism, rising from 3,361 in 2000 to 17,958 in 2013[1].

But shockingly, the year 2014 became worse as a result of the series of attacks launched by the barbaric terrorist groups. It is to this end, that the Global World Index (hereafter GWI) observes that the high rise of terrorism in 2014 was a result of the frequent activities concentrated within five countries across the globe. The countries in question, were ranked as the highest impact of terrorism all over the world. They are named according their respective ranking; Iraq, Afghanistan, Pakistan, Nigeria, and Syria[2]. Hence, their inhumane activities have been a global subject of criminology[3], and have raised a global alarm.

The attacks of the Islamic State for instance, in Iraq and the Levant (ISIS/ISIL), in Syria (now known as Islamic State – hereafter IS) in which hundreds of thousands of people were displayed, maimed and killed, with particular attention to the attack on the Iraqi's second largest city – Mosul, in which Christians[4] whose history is traced back to the 1ˢᵗ Century AD were almost wiped out of the face of the earth; the February 2015 execution of

---

[1] IEP, *Global Terrorism Index* 2014, 2.

[2] Cf., IEP, *Global Terrorism Index* 2015, 2.

[3] M.F. AJIBOYE-DARE, *Terrorism. The Nigerian Perspective*, 12.

[4] L. MOGAN, "Iraqi's Christians Persecuted by ISIS".

the dozens of Ethiopian Christians in Libya[5]; the beheading of an Egyptian Christian group; the recent Al Shabaab attack on Christian students in Garissa University College, Kenya in which 147 students were killed and several others injured[6]; the sporadic bombing of Churches in northern Nigeria and the kidnapping of over 276 young School girls in Chibok town of Borno State in 2014[7], and *ipso facto* (by that very fact) the abduction of the 110 Dapchi girls in Yobe State in 2018 (barely after four years)[8]; the numerous cases of sexual harassment and gang rape of Christian women by some gangs of Islamic extremists in Sudan[9]; the crushing to death of five Christian men by a bulldozer for refusing to take part in the national cult of North Korea; the killing of Catholic priests and missionary workers in Colombia[10]; and the series of coordinated terrorist attacks across Europe, United Kingdom and America just to mention but few, all and many others are proves to the aforementioned that violence committed in the name of religious ideologies is always on the increase from one region of the globe to another, and has thus arouse the interest of the world.

Bearing in mind therefore the statistical records of the terrorists' activities, they obviously suggest that terrorism is constantly on the rise day by day, and Christians are often affected across the globe. It is to this end that the 2015 Open Door World Watch List (ODWWL) opines that the Middle East remains the most violent while Africa experiences the largest increase in Christian persecution, and approximately 100 million Christians are persecuted worldwide, making them one of the most persecuted religious groups in the world[11].

This reality is succinctly captured in the letter of the Holy Father Pope John Paul II – *Tertio Millennio Adveniente* – when he examined the reality of martyrdom of the first millennium Christians alongside with the martyrdom of the second millennium. For him, as the Church was born out of the blood of the martyrs of the first millennium, so also the Church of the second millennium which he described as the Church of the martyrs. This is as a result of the present persistent persecution of Christians across the globe.

The Church of the first millennium was born of the blood of the martyrs: *"Sanguis martyrum - semen christianorum"*. The historical events linked to the figure of Constantine the Great could never have ensured the development

---

[5] J. CASPER, "More Martyrs. ISIS Executes Dozens of Ethiopian Christians in Libya".

[6] M. CUDDIHY, "Kenyan University Attack. 149 Killed and 79 Wounded.

[7] F. CHOTHIA, "Will Nigeria's Abducted Schoolgirls ever be Found?".

[8] S. BOLAJI, "Dapchi Girls Abduction. Some Unanswered Questions.

[9] K. ALLEN, "South Sudan. Women Raped under the Noses of UN Forces".

[10] J.L. ALLEN Jr., *The Global War on Christians*, 47-153.

[11] DANIEL, "Persecution of Christians Reaches Historic Levels".

of the Church as it occurred during the first millennium if it had not been for the *seeds sown by the martyrs and the heritage of sanctity which marked the first Christian generations.* At the end of the second millennium, *the Church has once again become a Church of martyrs.* The persecutions of believers —priests, Religious and laity—has caused a great sowing of martyrdom in different parts of the world. The witness to Christ borne even to the shedding of blood has become a common inheritance of Catholics, Orthodox, Anglicans and Protestants, as Pope Paul VI pointed out in his Homily for the Canonization of the Ugandan Martyrs[12].

From the observation of the Holy Father, it is obvious that the persecution of Christians is not new to the Church. However, its presence in our new millennium of great civilization is unthinkable. Hence, the persistence of the menace of terrorism that sweeps across the globe in our modern society under the auspice of religion, necessitates a new strategy for the survival of Christians and Christian missionary activities in Muslim dominated societies. It is on this note that the northern part of Nigeria is not in isolation.

In Nigeria for instance, the role of religion in the life of its people cannot be overemphasized. Within the political arena of the country, it plays a vital role in the socio-political development of the country, so much that nothing essentially can be said of Nigeria without recognizing this reality. But sadly, enough however, religion is often mentioned with negative connotations in respect to some historical events such as:

> The Jihad, the civil war propaganda, the Shari'a law controversy, the tensions provoked by the Nigerian accession to the Organization of Islamic Countries (OIC) and the incessant religious crises that have engulfed the Northern part suggest that religion cannot be ignored or be simply waved off in the Nigerian political development[13].

More so, religion has also become a readily weapon of manipulation in the hands of some greedy politicians in order to achieve their selfish political ambition of "divide and rule". Should one be right thus to infer that religion is responsible for the violence in the northern Nigeria? This is, however, debatable since scholars' opinions differ. In this regard, chapter two will shade more light on this issue and hence examines some religious violence.

Nevertheless, it is pertinent to state that in recent times, there has been a growing concern about Nigeria's continued survival as a nation in the face of the ever-increasing growth in violent conflicts, especially in the northern region of the country. Prior to its general elections of 2015, a lot of speculations permeated almost every nook and cranny of the country that

---

[12] JOHN PAUL II, "Tertio Millennio Adveniente", §37.

[13] N.D. DANJIBO, "Islamic fundamentalism and Sectarian Violence", 3.

Nigeria has finally reached its crossroad of being one nation. Fear and anxiety mounted so high that seem to suggest proves to the aforementioned, but its successful and peaceful concluded elections proved the opposite. Notwithstanding, the northern region remains a volatile area to many Nigerians who desire to make it a home for themselves, and the minority indigenous groups who desire not be evicted from their ancestral homes. To this effect, the struggle for survival becomes unavoidable.

It is against this backdrop that it becomes imperative to note that since the return of Nigeria to civil rule in May 1999, the northern region has been the theatre of many forms of violence perpetrated by some armed Islamic religious fanatics called in Arabic *Jama'atu Ahlis Sunna Lidda'awati Wal-Jihad* (JASLWJ) which is translated as "People committed to the propagation of the Prophet's Teaching and Jihad"[14] but inappropriately popularly known as *Boko Haram*[15] which literarily means in Hausa language "Western education is prohibited", who gradually transmogrified into a terrorist group and whose terrorist activities have greatly affected the socio-economic, political, and religious activity of the region.

While violent conflicts could hardly be described as something new in Nigeria and particularly in the north[16], the constant bombing of Churches, mosques and government institutions, and the ever-increasing rise of suicide bombers that sporadically detonate bombs at rampant amidst innocent civilians by the Islamic extremists give birth to a new trend of violence that thus pose serious security challenges to the nation's security outfit, socio-economic development of the region, and *vis-à-vis* (in relation to) the missionary activities of the Church in northern region.

2. Statement of the Problem

Nigeria, being a secular state with multi-ethnic, cultural and religious background, finds issues of conflicts complicated puzzles to break. Since her independence in 1960, the issues of insecurity and instability appear to have been the major challenges of her political historical development. Hence, there

---

[14] J. ISHAKU, *The Road to Mogadishu. How Jihadist Terrorism Tears Nigeria Apart*, 21-32. Also see J. ADIBE, *Nigeria Without Nigerians*, 30.

[15] A name that was commonly attributed to the Islamic fanatical group and promoted by the media. But it was later rejected by its leader. We shall however, come to know the preferred name of the group in question as we deal with the group deeper in chapter one of the study.

[16] Following very closely the history of events, violent conflicts have occurred in virtually all the 36 states of the federation since the return to civil rule in 1999. Few that deserve mention here is the peaceful demonstration of Christians all over the twelve adopted sharia states in the north.

14

has never been a single decade that passes without experiencing at least one major cataclysmic crisis in the country. For instance, the country experienced the Western region political crises in 1960s, the incessant military coups, a bloody civil war that lasted for almost three years (1967-70) which is popularly known as Biafra Civil War (hence BCW), and some chain of sectarian crises that predominantly preoccupied the activities of the last four decades[17].

Sadly, to note that most of these crises took place in the northern region of the country. While other regions therefore were developing due to the existence of relative peace, the north on the other hand was preoccupied with one crisis or the other ranging from socio-political to ethno-religious crises. To this end, it is an understatement to say that these forms of violence have created a lot of socio-economic, religious, political, and environmental lacuna in the holistic development of Nigeria as a nation, and particularly in the northern region since the nation's independence. They have further threatened the Nigerian efforts toward achieving her sustainable political and economic desired goals like every nation around the globe.

Suffice to say that since the civil war, nothing has ever claimed many lives in Nigeria like these so-called sectarian crises which are directly linked to the crises surrounding the issues of relations between Christians and Muslims[18] due to the existing tension of struggle for survival among the two major religions (Christianity and Islam). Although this tension may be traceable to the 1978/9 Shari'a debate which began to manifest itself in the 1980's *Maitatsine* religious crisis, such tension was never at any time as volatile as it is today.

The 1987 Kafanchan riot of Kaduna State for instance, which started by the Muslim students' society of the College of Education due to a claim inciting preaching by a Muslim convert invited by the Christian students' fellowship during their annual "Christian revival" buttresses the above point. The religious tension of the crisis reared its ugly head even at the Panel of investigation into the crisis. During the roll-call of the representatives of different religions at the Panel for instance, while the Muslims acknowledge their presence with *Allahu-Akbar*! Christians on the other hand opted for "Praise the Lord!" response[19].

---

[17] Some of these sectarian crises include; the 1980 Maitatsine riot in Kano which sporadically spread to other northern part of the country, the 1987 Zangon Kataf, the June 12, 1993 post elections crisis, 2001 Jos riot, 2002 Miss World crisis, 2004 Yelwa massacre. In summary the period between 2000 and 2008 was characterized by series of religious crises which became worse with the appearance of the Boko Haram on the scene.

[18] K. MCGARVEY, "Gender, Peace and Religious Coexistence", 57.

[19] M.H. KUKAH, *Religion, Politics and Power in Northern Nigeria*, 191.

Thereafter, other violent skirmishes took place. For example, the 1988 Kaduna Polytechnic Chapel riots, and the Ahmadu Bello University (hence ABU) Zaria riots, the 1991 Bauchi violence, Katsina, and Kano riots, just to mention but few. But notably, with the introduction of Shari'a law[20] in 1999 by the then governors of twelve states in northern Nigeria that include; Bauchi, Borno, Gombe, Jigawa, Kaduna, Kano, Katsina, Kebbi, Niger, Sokoto, Yobe, and Zamfara, Nigeria reached once again another landmark in its history of religious tensions owing to the fact that the introduction of the Shari'a law directly contravened the Nigerian constitution on freedom to religious belief and worship of all citizens[21] which clearly states that:

> Every person shall be entitled to freedom of thought, conscience and religion, including freedom to change his religion or belief, and freedom (either alone or in community with others, and in public or in private) to manifest and propagate his religion or belief in worship, teaching, practice and observance[22].

While this was perhaps done out of the sense of responsibility to duty, and to fulfil their political campaign promises, the complexity of the nature of some of the northern states was neither considered by these key actors of the respective states, nor did they take into cognizance of the rights of the minorities who are non-Muslims (Christians and the indigenous traditional religionists popularly known as African Traditional Religionists – hence ATRs). Notably too, the said governors lost the sense of their responsibilities as custodians and enforcers of the law as a result of their quest for political power. Hence, the reaction to the introduction of the Shari'a law by the non-Muslims became eminent in some of the above "so-called" stated Shari'a-states.

In each of these crises, the impact was always beyond imagination. Lives and properties were always destroyed. As a result, these in no measure, affected directly the existing fragile relationship between Christians and Muslims. It became more fragile and soured than ever. Tension increased, violence reached its peak and Christians became the proverbial endangered spe-

---

[20] It is imperative to note that the Introduction of the Shari'a law started by the then governor of Zamfara State Alhaji Ahmad Sani Yerima (27th May 1999 – 27th May 2007). In order to fulfil his political campaign promises made in 1999 at his political campaign rallies for chief political popularity, Yerima re-introduced the Shari'a law in his State on 27th January 2000, and thereafter other 11 State governors followed in the same manner.

[21] It is imperative to note that the above mentioned "so-called" Shari'a States were ruled by Muslims who were the majority. Being therefore at the hem of affairs, decisions were taken without necessarily considering the feelings of the minorities. Hence, Islamic agenda are often promoted at the detriment of other existing religions.

[22] CONSTITUTION OF THE FEDERAL REPUBLIC OF NIGERIAN 1999, article 38, §1.

cies. This became obvious when Christians within the aforementioned States protested against the introduction of the Shari'a law as an infringement of their human right to freedom of worship as stated above. The February and May 2000 Christian peaceful demonstration in Kaduna metropolis in protest against the strong debate to introduce Shari'a law in the State, for instance, saw the killing of over 2,000 people by the Islamic extremists. It is against this backdrop, that some commentators described the riot as the single worst outbreak of violence in Nigeria since the BCW[23]. It is in this light, that the introduction of the Shari'a law into practice therefore, paved the way to the rise of the Islamic extremists – the Boko Haram.

For the reason above, the Boko Haram took the advantage of the Shari'a law and subjected Christians in the north to a lot of untold hardships. At socio-cultural level for instance, Christians in some parts of the northern states are often falsely accused of either blasphemy or violating the traditional values of Islam. As a result, they are tried and charged under the Shari'a law that in most cases they are subjected to all sorts of humiliation and torture. The Christian indigenous youth in most Muslim dominated states are often denied of their rights of indigenization and job opportunity base on religious affiliation, and the Christian young girls are forced into Islamic marriage through abduction and intimidation. In the area of religion, Christians are often denied the right to acquire land for the erection of religious structures such as Churches, hospitals and schools as we shall see in chapter two as the work progresses.

A vivid example is the Catholic Dioceses of Maiduguri and Sokoto which were created as dioceses in 1966 and 1964 respectively under the then Kaduna province but remained the dioceses with the highest number of total areas of diocesan territory but with least parishes. While Maiduguri led with 132,000 km^2 and only one parish in existence, Sokoto diocese had 109,507 km^2 with 9 parishes in existence prior to the creation of Abuja and Jos provinces[24]. This is mostly as a result of the restrictions on land acquisition for the erection of religious structures and other religious activities. In the same vein, Christians in general within the northern region, are often denied of the right to job opportunity, the right to freedom of worship, and in most cases, they are confronted with religious violence in which their women and sometimes young girls are abducted, tortured, raped and sold out to slavery. The April 14-15, 2014 Boko Haram's abduction of the Chibok girls and the Dapchi girls on February 19, 2018 are clear examples to the aforementioned.

---

[23] HUMAN RIGHTS WATCH, "The Miss World Riots".
[24] ANNUARIO PONTIFICIO PER L'ANNO (AnPont), 419 & 682. Also see Appendix N.

Further still, from 2009 till date, majority of Christians in the north are confronted with the constant sporadic detonation of bombs while observing their religious obligations in their respective places of worship. Bombs are also detonated at business centres and other public places where most often Christians are suspected to be the majority. As a result of the Nigerian government inability to curb the situation and provide enough security for her citizens many were left to the mercy of their oppressors, thereby adding unto them more frustration, fear and anxiety. Hence, the inferno destroyed not only the Christians' sources of livelihood but also separated them from their beloved ones and evicted most of them from their ancestral homes.

Therefore, these variances imperatively call for an in-depth study. It is in view of this scenario that this research seeks to examine the existing tension in the relationship between Christians and Muslims with the view of understanding the challenges posed to the missionary activity of the Catholic Church in such volatile region, and the Church's role amidst these challenges while exposing the ways that could bring the realization of an enabling environment that will enhance peaceful coexistence between Christians and Muslims within the geographical location of the northern region and the entire country at large.

3. Motivation of the Study

In respect to the state of events in the northern region of Nigeria, my primary motivation to engage into this work is my personal experience of the soured relationship that has come to exist among the Christians and Muslims in the region. As a growing child, I lived in an environment that was characterized by cordial and peaceful atmosphere. Both Christians and Muslims could study, play, go to farm, and eat together especially during religious festivities, but today such a relationship has been curdled due to suspicion, mistrust, and hatred of one another. As the Christians suspect and distrust the Muslims so also the Muslims do same. One's religious beliefs and ideologies are often perceived with disgust by members of the other religion.

In the same vein, my curiosity towards understanding the plight of other Christians from other parts of the region as regards the continued expression of Islamic extremism that is perpetrated by the adherence of the major religion in the region over the adherence of the minor religion is also a motivating factor to this study because in the past only Kaduna state and sometime Benue state that were known as volatile states. But now almost all the states within the region are volatile. As a result, the constant unrest seems not to have only retarded the socio-economic development of the region, but also poses challenges to the missionary activity of the Church.

It is therefore hoped that by the end of the research work, efforts will be made to offer some suggestions toward finding possible ways that could bring the realization of the desired enabling environment for a better peaceful co-existence of the members of both religions, that could enhance the missionary activities of the Church. This, however, will be examined by considering the documents of the Church in respect to Christian's relations with other religions, and dialogue. *Hitherto*, we will take into consideration the efforts of the Catholic Bishops Conference of Nigeria (hereafter CBCN) particularly their discourses toward realizing a peaceful community issued in various communiqués.

4. Originality and Importance of the Study

Since this study concerns violence perpetrated by a particular extremist group of one religion over the other, it is an overemphasis to say that it is a common phenomenon that is known and experienced in every part of the world particularly at this era of terrorism. The recent terrorist attacks around the globe for instance, the Russian plane crash in Sinai Peninsula in Egypt, the Paris and Saint Denis series of attacks in France, San Bernardino shooting in USA, Manchester and London Bridge attacks both in UK, and the Burkina Faso attack, just to mention but few, confirm the above.

Although there are times that such conflicts or rather terrorists' attacks could be profitable to some individuals, groups or organizations, violence however is generally destructive and regressive in nature. Hence, the search for peace becomes inevitable. In this regard therefore, everyone in the society is a stake holder because security is not only the duty of the uniformed personnel or security agents, but it is the duty of all members of the society that ought to be security conscious. Thus, all parents, teachers, students at all levels, politicians, traditional and religious leaders, community leaders, managers, doctors, lawyers, civil servants, government, NGOs, security agencies, private and cooperate organizations, young and old, men and women *et al* (and others), must become inevitable stakeholders in the search for a peaceful society, thereby becoming our brothers and sisters' keepers.

Scholars like Toyin Falola, Shedrack G. Best, Akintunde E. Akinade, Isidore Nwanaju, Muhammad S. Umar, A. Christian van Gorder, Jan H. Boer *et al* have all written and several researches have been conducted in the effort to proffer solutions to the numerous conflicts and violence in Nigeria, but no study of this nature nevertheless, has ever been carried out as regards the challenges posed by such violence on the Catholic missionary activities in northern Nigeria since 1999. Thus, this is another contribution to the field of knowledge and the on-going search.

Further still, this research combines both primary and secondary sources in analysing the phenomenon. With regard to primary sources, it relies mostly on the analysis of information gathered through qualitative interviews as its primary source. To the best of my knowledge, a comprehensive study of the theme in question has never been conducted on the study population. This in-depth study will therefore make a significant contribution to the field of missiology.

As regards the originality of the study, the primary sources are derived from the empirical fieldwork research which generated the first-hand information of the theme under investigation, while the library research formed its secondary sources. Although, scholars, have made immense scholarly contributions in the area of the study, but such well-articulated and published contributions, focus mostly on the general overview of terrorism and its socio-economic impact on the development of the Nigerian state, without taking into account the challenges that such terrorists' violence pose on the missionary activity of the Church within the northern region of Nigeria. The works of scholars such as; Gus Martin, Bruno S. Frey, Adibe Jideofor, Jacob Zenn, *et al*, are all bolsters to the aforementioned.

It is against this backdrop therefore that this research is important because it will contribute towards finding enabling environment that could enhance a mutual relationship among the Christians and Muslims in the region under review, thereby enhancing the missionary activities of the Church within the region.

5. Goals and Objectives of the Study

The goals of this thesis are:
1. To examine the missiological implications of Christian witness in a violent prone society.
2. To explore and evaluate the foundations and root causes of Islamic extremism and intolerance in Northern region of Nigeria.
3. To understand the underlying factors responsible for the soured relationship, suspicion, and hatred that exist among the Christians and Muslims in the northern Nigeria.
4. To understand the link between the Nigerian Boko Haram extremist group with the international terrorist groups in line with the desire of achieving a socio-political power.
5. To make recommendations on ways of realizing the enabling environment that could enhance religious tolerance and peaceful co-existence in northern Nigeria with the view to boosting missionary activities in the northern region.

6. Research Questions

The research questions are posed in order to be the precursor of this study. It is hoped that the pattern of argument will follow along the research questions in order to arrive at a logical conclusion. It is for this reason that the study thus begs the following questions:

1. What are the missiological implications of Christian witness in a violent prone society such as the Northern region of Nigeria?
2. What are the foundations and root causes of Islamic extremism and intolerance in Northern Nigeria?
3. What are the factors responsible for the soured relationship, suspicion, and hatred that exist among the Christians and Muslims in the northern Nigeria?
4. What is the link between the Nigerian Boko Haram extremist's group with the international terrorist groups such as Al-Qaida, Al-Shabaab, IS, etc., in line with the desire of achieving a socio-political power?
5. What are the ways of enhancing religious tolerance and peaceful co-existence among Christians and Muslims in northern Nigeria?

7. Scope and Limitation of the Study

As the title of the dissertation indicates, the scope of this study is basically the Northern Nigeria. Even at that, it lays emphasis on Christian-Muslim relationship in northern Nigeria with particular attention to the present era of democracy in view of the activities of the Boko Haram Islamic extremists. This basically covers the period under review since the rise of Boko Haram Islamic militancy in the region. Hence, the study focuses on violent crises that are socio-politically manipulated but with religious undertone. With regard to the study population, it is focused on the Catholic Church and its missionary activities in northern Nigeria. This study is basically limited by time and what it can cover being a doctoral dissertation which has to be submitted within a given time frame.

8. Methodology

The method of the research is historical, expository and evaluative. It is historical because it identifies the major events in Christian-Muslim relationship in northern Nigeria. It is expository because it examines the terrorist activities of the Boko Haram. In the same vein, it is evaluative because it analyses the Boko Haram terrorism in respect to the Christian-Muslim relation in the region and *vis-à-vis* the role of the Catholic Church as regards her response to religious violence in northern Nigeria. For data collation, it uses both primary and secondary data that involves an empirical fieldwork and a library research.

Regarding primary data, I conducted a qualitative interview in order to get the various opinions of Christians with particular attention to the Catholic faithful and their leaders on the menace of the Islamic extremism, and their respective responses toward it. To have a balance view, Muslims were also interviewed as regards their perception of the existing relationship with their Christian counterparts. Then the Church's documents that include, *Nostra Aetate, Ad Gentes Divinitus, Dignitatis Humanne, Ecclesia in Africa, Africae Munus et al*, and the communiqués of the CBCN were also consulted. The data collated was analysed and integrated into the main body of the work. The secondary data generated from published materials on the phenomenon. These range from the theological foundations of the study, socio-political, psychological and to other published materials regarding the research problem.

9. Clarification of Terms

This section deals with the concept of key terms that are the thrust of this research. We define and clarify some of these terms within the context of their application in this study in order to avoid ambiguity. However, we do not claim that these definitions are exhaustive and conclusive because they can be understood and defined differently by different scholars and disciplines. The definition of these terms within the context of this study therefore becomes relevant for a better comprehension of the argument of the study. Terms are defined in an alphabetical order.

9.1 *Extremism*

According to Martin Gus (an American specialist in terrorism and juvenile justice) the word "extremism" is characterized by intolerance toward opposing interests and divergent opinions, and it is the primary catalyst and motivation for terrorist behaviour. However, extremists who cross the line to become terrorists always develop noble arguments to rationalize and justify acts of violence directed against the enemy nations, people, religions, or other interests. Extremism for him, therefore, cannot be better comprehended without its basic elements such as; style and content which constitute the fundamental factor of the definition of the concept.

Laird Wilcox (an American specialist on political fringe movement) on the other hand holds that extremism is more an issue of style than content because people may hold either radical or orthodox views but the style of their expression of such views is what makes the difference[25]. Thus, extremism could be described as the precursor to terrorism because it leads to the violent expression of a person's beliefs. As such, an extremist that is liable to become terrorist is bound as observed by scholars and experts to exhibit the following characteristics; intolerance, moral absolutes, broad conclusion, and new language and conspirational beliefs[26]. It is against this backdrop that the term "extremism" can be defined within context as an expression of belief that is motivated by intolerance, moral absolutism and violent behaviour toward the so-called perceived enemy with the intent to achieve self-religious or political interest as we shall see in the development of the thesis.

9.2 *Fundamentalism*

The use of the word 'fundamentalism' has become wide spread, especially in the media, and is increasingly penetrating the academic circles. Due to its indiscriminate usage scholars find it difficult to accept and use it as a concept rather than a label. Defining it within its original context therefore, the term 'fundamentalism' takes us back to the nineteenth century when it was used by Christians to refer to the American ultraconservative protestant Christians Biblical Literalists and inerrantists who propounded a list of 'fundamentals' that all true Christians should follow[27]. By implication, the use of the word involves two tendencies; first, the tendency to take the Holy Scripture literally in its inerrancy, and second, the tendency of adhering to a few elaborated fundamentals as the line of demarcation between true believers and the rest[28].

Applying therefore these features to the Islamic fundamentalists, the use of the word within context of this research would refer to the Islamic revivalists and reformers of the nineteenth and twentieth centuries who found

---

[25] Cf., L. Wilcox, "What is Extremism?", 54.

[26] M. Gus, *Understanding Terrorism*, 42.

[27] The term is generally understood as an interdenominational movement that originated in American Protestantism toward the end of the 19th century. It came into existence as a reaction against the liberal and modernistic currents of theology that infiltrated the seminaries and universities especially in the Northern and Eastern parts of United States. Niagara Bible Conference for instance, drew up fourteen fundamentals of faith in 1878 which were later reduced to five. These include; the inspiration and inerrancy of the Bible, the virgin birth and full deity of Christ, Christ's death as a sacrifice to satisfy the divine justice, Christ's bodily resurrection, and Christ's return in bodily form to preside at the Last Judgment. See A. Dulles, "Fundamentalism", 27. Also see F.M. Denny, *An Introduction to Islam*, 345.

[28] Cf., T.A. Collins, "Fundamentalism, Biblical", 29.

it important to reinterpret the Qur'an in the light of new circumstances and in respect to the new message they sought to emphasize for Muslims of their own generation whose ideologies have given rise to the present Islamic extremists that continue to perpetrate violence in the name of Islamic religion. Few of these outstanding fundamentalists include: Sayyid Qutb (1906-1966) and Abul Ala Maududi (1903-1979). While Sayyid, holds that 'all activities of life, including social and political life, are to be carried out in accordance with God's commands as found in the Qur'an because all activity is *ibada* (worship), either of God or of *taghut* (idol/ despot)', al-Maududi on the other hand, was more concerned with political power by emphasizing on the segments of the Qur'an that serve their purposes (which sometimes the exercise is reduced to extensive quoting of verses) than the interpretation of the text itself in its totality. It is therefore imperative to note that this literalistic attitude toward the interpretation of the Qur'an, thus, draws a line of demarcation between the fundamentalists from their coreligionists[29]. Hence, the term "fundamentalism" refers to the Islamic extremists who are popularly known as Islamic terrorists. It is against this background that the two terms "extremism" and "fundamentalism" are used interchangeably within the context of this study.

However, the term 'fundamentalism' within the framework of this study does not refer to the fundamentals of Islam which is known as the five pillars of Islam[30], and also the six articles of faith (imam)[31]. In the same vein, the term does not refer to the Islamic scholars who are specialized in the Islamic discipline called *"ilm usul al-fiqh"* (that is science of the fundamentals of jurisprudence) which is conceived mainly with the genesis and sources of the general jurisprudential rules.

9.3 *Religious Violence*

Within the general domain, the term 'violence' may not seem problematic, but we should realize that in the Western world the meaning of the term has expanded in such a manner that we use the term 'violence' to describe emotional, intellectual, and verbal confrontations as well as mere misrepresentation of another person's opinion; consequently, we now sometimes feel the need to

---

[29] See the works of: O. LEAMAN, ed., *The Qur'an*, 568-571; A.S. SIDAHMED – A. EHTESHAMI, eds., *Islamic Fundamentalism*, 3, respectively.

[30] The five pillars of Islam include; the pronouncement of the shahada (that is to testify explicitly that there is no other God, but Allah and that Muhammad is his messenger), prayer, fasting, almsgiving, and Hajj (pilgrimage to Mecca).

[31] The six articles of faith (*imam*) include; the belief in Allah, His messenger, the Holy Books, Angels, the Day of Judgment, and Destiny.

speak of 'physical violence'[32]. This has conditioned us by experiences to refer to the term 'violence' as physical violence that is linked with ethnic crises, civil wars, mass murders and suicide bombings. Qualifying therefore, the term 'religious violence' within the context of the study, it refers hence, to both physical and psychological violence unleashed by a religious terrorist group with the intent to forcefully convert its so-called perceived enemy within a given geographical area to the group's religious affiliation. However, this does not exclude the term from its problematic definition because defining it within a historical perspective remains a difficult task since the ancient world never had a specific term for religion as it is defined today.

9.4 *Terrorism*

From a common understanding, the term would seem to be an easy concept to define. This is because, instinctively the term may be narrowed down to the understanding of politically motivated violence which is usually directed against "soft targets" (that is the innocent civilians) with the intention to affect (terrorize) a targeted audience. But technically it is beyond such an oversimplified presumption. Experts, scholars, government administrators, and other interested agencies have for some time grapple with designing and agreeing on a clear universal definition of the concept "terrorism" but it remains an ongoing debate around the globe. As a result, there is a remarkable variety of approaches and definitions.

In this regard, the Arab Convention for the Suppression of Terrorism defines terrorism as any act of threat or violence, whatever its motives or purposes, that occurs in the advancement of an individual or collective criminal agenda and seeking to sow the panic among people, causing fear by harming them, or placing their lives, liberty or security in danger, or seeking to cause damage to the installations or property or to occupying or seizing them, or seeking to jeopardize national resources[33]. Nevertheless, the United States summarizes the definition of terrorism under the Federal Criminal Code as "activities that involve violent… or life-threatening acts… that are a violation of the criminal laws of the United States or of any state and… i) appear to be intended to intimidate or coerce a civilian population; ii) to influence the policy of government by intimidation or coercion; or iii) to affect the conduct of government by mass destruction, assassination, or kidnapping[34].

---

[32] J.N. Bremmer, "Religious Violence" 10.

[33] The Arab Convention for the Suppression of Terrorism, Cairo, April 22, 1998.

[34] The United States Federal Criminal Code, Definitions.

In the same vein, scholars like Christopher C. Harmon (an expert in the fields of terrorism and counterterrorism, insurgency and revolutionary warfare, counter-insurgency, and international relations) on the other hand, defines terrorism as "the deliberate and systematic murder, maiming, and menacing of the innocent to inspire fear for political ends"[35]. So also, Bruce Hoffman (a political analyst known for his views on terrorism and insurgency)[36] defines it as the deliberate creation and exploitation of fear through violence or threat of violence in the pursuit of change[37]. To further illustrate the range of definitions, David J. Whittaker (a prolific writer on terrorism) gives a list of many different definitions[38].

However, from the above varied definitions, we can identify certain common features that run through each of them such as; the use of illegal force in instilling its desired fear on the public, it is most often perpetrated by sub-national actors, it involves the use of unconventional methods, it is often politically motivated, and in most cases, its attacks are often directed against the "soft" civilians and passive military forces in order to influence the government, and finally, it is often aimed at purposefully affecting an audience.

Within the context of this study therefore, the term "terrorism" refers to the group of some religious extremists who deliberately perpetrate violence against "soft" civilians, religious institutions, governmental institutions and agencies associated with government in order to achieve its desired religious goal within the disguise of political aspiration. This implies that, although the violence in northern Nigerian can easily be conceived as politically motivated, but its undertone seems to suggest that is more of religion than politics. Nevertheless, it is important to state here that terrorism is not to be placed at the same pedestal with "guerrilla warfare. For guerrilla warfare aims at harassing and sabotaging the efforts of the larger "so-called" enemy troops – who are well experienced, well trained, and well equipped – by a small and usually independent forces that are less experienced, less trained, poorly equipped – through irregular military actions. Hence, while the former (terrorism) most often concentrates on the "soft" civilians as its target of destruction, the later (guerrilla warfare) concentrates on the military as its target.

---

[35] C. HARMON, *Terrorism Today*, 1.

[36] Bruce Hoffman is the Director of the Centre for Security Studies and Director of the Security Studies Program at Georgetown University's Edmund A. Walsh School of Foreign Service. He is a specialist in the study of terrorism and counterterrorism and insurgency and counter-insurgency.

[37] B. HOFFMAN, *Inside Terrorism*, 43.

[38] D.J. WHITTAKER, ed., *The Terrorism Reader*, 8.

10. *Status Quaestionis*

The expression of Islamic extremism in the region has been well documented by many scholars as a result of its persistence within the region. In order to address the situation, the studies of Christian van Gorder, Isidore Nwanaju, Jan Boer give an excellent examination of the interactable interfaith violence that have been reoccurring in the country with particular reference to its northern region. The scholars evaluated these crises alongside the nature of the relationship that exists between Christians and Muslims who formed the major population of the region. Their works: *Violence in God's Name; Christian-Muslim Relations in Nigeria; and Nigeria's Decades of Blood* respectively, exposed the existing soured relationship between Christians and Muslim, and the suspicion and hate that characterised their relationship in the country. In this regard, Boer went further to trace some factors that could be responsible for such riots in his second volume titled, *Muslims Why the Violence?*[39]. Although such factors were not exhaustive enough, the contribution of his work, however, cannot be overlooked.

But in understanding the composition of the northern region (our study population) Matthew Kukah in his work *Religion, Politics and Power* gave an in-depth analysis of the complicity of the northern region with particular attention to its socio-political and religious development from the emergence of the Hausa political class to the end of the military regime. He examined the heterogenous nature of the region in which both Christians and Muslims co-exist side by side with one another thereby giving rise to the existing tension among the two major religions. Fear of domination by the Hausa/Fulani paved the way to the oppression of the Christian minority group in the region thereby perceiving Islam not only as a threat but also "the political future of the non-Muslims in the north was uncertain"[40]. Hence, Christians had to struggle for identity. Although, the above authors never treated our research topic, but rather gave a general insight to the problem, their enormous contributions however to the study cannot be underestimated.

While nothing significant has changed as regards the position of the above scholars, it is interesting to note that with the emergence of the Boko Haram, the existing fragile relationship has been more weakened. It is against this backdrop that the intractable terrorist activities of the Boko Haram attracted the attention of many scholars across the globe.

---

[39] J.H. BOER, *Muslims. Why the Violence?*, 77-130.
[40] M.H. KUKAH, *Religion, Politics and Power in Northern Nigeria*, 49.

Jideofor Adibe in his work, *Nigeria Without Nigerians: Boko Haram and the Crisis in Nigeria's Nation-Building* gave a phenomenological analysis of the emergence of the Boko Haram terrorist group from its evolution to radical stages. In *Terrorism: The Nigerian Perspective*[41], Mary F. Ajiboye-Dare presented however, the account of the emergence of the Boko Haram in a different perspective thereby noting its modus operandi within the north-eastern region and the legal implications that confront both the Nigerian government and its citizens as a result of the sporadic bombings and attacks of the terrorist group on innocent Nigerians. Her work is an eye opener toward understanding the teething problems in the northern region that perhaps provided the fertile ground for the emergence of the Boko Haram terrorist group. This she did by assessing the root cause of the intractable insurgency via exploring the historical background of the region within its educational, economic, socio-political and religious perspectives. However, being a lawyer by profession, her work though focused on Boko Haram and the havoc caused to the northern region, and particularly the northeast, she however, gave more credence to the legal implications of the terrorist group than its effects on the growth of the Church within the region. To this effect, Ajiboye-Dare reiterated that the struggle of the Boko Haram to establish the Shari'a law across Nigeria will not be realistic owing to the democratic and pluralistic nature of Nigeria[42]. Nonetheless, both mentioned authors on the menace of the Boko Haram terrorist activities did not treat the research topic in question. Their works however, contributed immensely to the general understanding of the group's terrorist activities within the region under study.

In the same vein, there were many articles published in this respect. Among others is the *Boko Haram and the Recurring Bomb Attacks in Nigeria: Attempt to Impose Religious Ideology through Terrorism?* in which Ali S. Yusufu Bagaji *et al*, identified the primary objectives of the Boko Haram terrorist group by tracing the emergence of the group from its initial stage of development to its stage of transmogrification into terrorism. They carefully examined the ideology and philosophy of the group whose core mission was to establish an Islamic State where orthodox Islam could be practiced across the nation[43].

Andrea Brigaglia however, went a step further to trace not only the emergence of the Boko Haram but also discussed the influence of *salafism* on the group. Owing that the thrust of *salafism* is centred on theological

---

[41] M.F. Ajiboye-Dare, *Terrorism. The Nigerian Perspective*, 52-81.

[42] M.F. Ajiboye-Dare, *Terrorism. The Nigerian Perspective*, 72-73.

[43] A.Y. Bagaji – al., "Boko Haram and the Recurring Bomb Attacks in Nigeria", 70.

purity, this theology is reinforced by the belief that all *salafis* especially those of the *Wahhabi* persuasion are "entrusted with a mission to revive the original creed of the forebearers (*Salaf*) of Islam, purportedly lost at some point in the history of Islam"[44]. Hence, they see themselves as the "save sect". This type of exclusivist attitude greatly influenced the Boko Haram that informed their attacks on not only Christians but also other Muslims, Shiites and the Sunnis inclusive as they hold onto the principle of *sola scriptura* and de-centralization of religious authority that are in direct contrast with the traditional Sunnis. Nevertheless, the authors neither examined the impact of the terrorist activities particularly on the existing fragile relationship of Christians and Muslims in the region nor did they bring to limelight the challenges of the Church in line with the activities of the terrorist group.

Since the inception of the Boko Haram the notable research that has been intensively carried out to my knowledge is the study that was done by the African Studies Centre (hence, ASC) sponsored by the Institut Français de Recherche en Afrique (hereafter, IFRA-Nigeria) titled, *Boko Haram: Islamism, Politics, Security and the State in Nigeria*, edited by Marc-Antonie Pérouse de Montclos, which made an in-depth examination of the terrorist group *vis-à-vis* the Nigerian state. The study x-rayed the possible fertile ground that led to emergence of the group and its radical metamorphoses. The work gave an insight on the effect of the terrorist group on both Christians and Muslims and *vis-à-vis* the Nigerian government[45]. But it, however, did not expose the challenges that confronted the Church or perhaps the Mosque (inclusive).

Nonetheless, due to the intervention of Nigerian government in collaboration with the neighbouring countries, the strength of the terrorist group has been reduced to a very minimal level. All captured territories have been re-captured back by the Nigerian forces.

11. Structure of the Thesis

The thesis is divided into five chapters with general introduction and conclusion. There exists a gradual progression of thought from each preceding chapter to the proceeding chapter due to their interconnectedness. On the general note, the work begins with a general introduction by stating what the problem is and its motivation. It brings out the significance of the study and its contribution to the field of knowledge and to the region of the

---

[44] A. BRIGAGLIA, "The Volatility of Salafi Political Theology", 181.

[45] G. CHOUIN – al., "Body Count and Religion in the Boko Haram Crisis, 234.

study in view, thereby stating its aims and objectives. As precursors to the study, the general introduction, proceeds to state some research questions that are pertinent to the study while noting the limitation of the research and gives a definition of some key terms that are used within context.

The first chapter begins by attempting to trace a brief historical background of terrorism with the view to have an idea of the trend of terrorism. It then examines the modern terrorism that gives birth to Al-Qaida, Al-Shabaab, IS and the Nigerian Boko Haram. Thereafter, it establishes the correlation between terrorism and religion while exposing some relevant theories of terrorism with the view to serve as parameters in understanding the terrorist activities of the Boko Haram in the northern part of Nigeria. Nevertheless, it is, however, imperative to note that the chapter discusses extensively the emergence of the Boko Haram, its activities and source of survival.

Bearing in mind that the violent crises within the northern region mostly revolve between Christians and Muslims, the relationship between these two keys actors therefore forms the basis of the second chapter, while we examine in brief the historical background of Nigeria. But it is important to note that as vast and diverse Nigeria is, its detailed description is beyond the scope of this study. However, attention is given to some relevant events particularly within the northern region. To this end, tracing the brief origin of both Christianity and Islam in the region under study becomes pertinent. This is to unravel the present existing suspicion, hate and mistrust among Christians and Muslims especially within the region, while at the same time stating the factors that serve as fertile ground to the soured relationship that finally led to the expression of extremism by the Boko Haram.

Noting however, the principle of cause and effect in every given violent situation, the chapter goes further to expose some few violence among others that took place in the northern region which are believed to have some religious undertone. In the discussions of these violence, attention is given only to some relevant areas that pertain this study. Thereafter, the chapter exposes the challenges that confront the growth of the Catholic Church and Christianity at large within the region due to the persistence of the intractable violence and the expression of extremist behaviours perpetrated at all levels.

Chapter three on the other hand, serves as a buffer to the entire work as it focuses on the empirical aspect of the research. Its main thrust is the scientific methodology of the study. This chapter is designed to give an elaborate account of the research design or rather the plan on how the research was conducted[46], and the justification for the choices made before

---

[46] B.L. BERG, *Qualitative Research Methods for the Social Sciences*, 28.

and during the fieldwork. To this end, the issues involved are discussed under four broad sections that include; methodology, sampling, data collection, and ethical issues.

Chapter four focuses on the data generated by presenting the various contributions of the respondents and analysing it where necessary while maintaining the originality of the respondents. Chapter five on the other hand, makes an evaluation of the work and recommends certain possible ways that could lead to the realisation of the desired enabling environment for both Christians and Muslims to live harmoniously within the northern region with the view to boosting the missionary activities of the Church. Thereafter, the work is concluded with a recap of the major points of the study while noting the recommendations put forward. A comprehensive bibliography and appendices are presented at the end of the research.

CHAPTER I

Terrorism in the 21st Century: The Nigerian Narrative and Theories

1. Introduction

This chapter sets to examine the historical background of terrorism in perspective with the view to understanding the development of the violent acts perpetrated against humanity from antiquity to the present modern age particularly to Christians in northern Nigeria. In this regard, it explores the gradual evolution of terrorist acts that were perpetrated based on "victim selection" within a society to the indiscriminate attacks of innocent civilians. Thereafter, it also explores the swift change of ideologies from radical socio-revolutionary to radical nationalism (especially separatist ethno-nationalism) and religious extremism that have thus become the two most influential ideological pillars of terrorism today. It is therefore along this line of thought that the chapter further seeks to examine the existing link of terrorism with religion, with particular attention to religious extremism while bearing in mind the proliferation of the rise of terrorist groups in the 21st century under the auspices of religion. By way of summary, religious extremism became internationally, the most powerful motivational and ideological basis for groups to engage in terrorism.

Having established the above link, the chapter goes further to examine the rise of modern Islamic extremism taking into cognizance the establishment of Al-Qaida terrorist group as the first multinational terrorist group of the twenty-first century that confronts the world with a new kind of threat and thus set the pace for the present proliferation of Islamic extremist groups at both local and international levels. Hereafter, the chapter proceeds to examine the Nigerian situation of terrorism championed by its local terrorist group and explores the needed parameters that could assist in the understanding of terrorism particularly within the Nigerian context. Finally, it draws its conclusion by giving a recapitulation of the chapter.

2. **Terrorism: Historical Background in Perspective**

The first manifestation of organized terrorism recorded in history, was in the Middle East Palestine in the first century. The Zealot sect[1] (who were referred to as *sicarii* – a generic Latin term derived from *sicarius* which means "dagger-man") was one of the very first groups to practice a systematic terror that was recorded as a result of a census taken by the Roman authorities that was perceived by the Jews as a humiliation by their submission to a foreign power. Hence, the need for political and religious emancipation arose[2].

As time passed by, the term in its various forms evolved maintaining a nature of "victim-selection" – that is a situation whereby terrorists preferring to target specific individuals. In most cases, the high-profile political or security figures in the society, such as government ministers, or the 'tyrants'— kings and presidents — were their targets. This can be clearly seen from the activities of the Sicarii between 66 and 70 C.E, and the Assassins in the twelfth and thirteenth centuries[3]. This method of selection continued up to the second half of the 19th century. This singular act of "victim-selection" was to some extent partly justified by its advocates and

---

[1] The Zealots were reformers who believed that they had to account to God alone, they had an unquenchable thirst for freedom. As a religious organization, they sought, often by force, to impose a degree of rigor in religious practice. For instance, they attacked other Jews whom they felt to be insufficiently scrupulous in their piety. They took up terror as an instrument. As a political organization, they sought to wrest their country's independence from Rome. The party's religious aims were inseparable from its political objectives. For more information, see the works of: R.A. HORSLEY, "The Sicarii. Ancient Jewish 'Terrorists'", 435-458; M.A. BRIGHTON, "The Sicarii in Acts. A New Perspective", 547-558.

[2] Cf., G. CHALIAND – ARNAUD, eds., *The History of Terrorism*, 55-58.

[3] The Assassins were radical Shi'ite Ismali brothers/sect, commanded by Hassan-Dan-Sabah, the Old Man in the Mountains" (the son of a Twelver Shiite of Yemeni origin who had settled in Persia), who waged a campaign of murder against 'servants of the unrighteous' in Persia and Syria in the twelfth and thirteenth centuries. Taking up arms of terrorism was a logical choice for the Assassins, as it had been for the sicarii in the first century. As a result, they co-opted the use of terror to psychological end and targeted, among others, a foreign, Christian power (the Crusaders). It is imperative to note that the terrorists themselves were animated by an unshakable faith that allowed them to sacrifice themselves willingly in the course of a mission in the certainty that they would ascend directly to paradise. An ideology that lays the foundation of today's terrorists' ideologies. However, it is worth noting that the Assassins did indeed carry out political murders with as much publicity as possible and thus were terrorists, but they were selective in their killings and not like their modern counterparts who kill everybody even the innocent bystanders. In other words, the Assassins were highly selective in their terrorist activities. For further studies see the works of: A. CAMPBELL, *The Assassins of Alamut*; F. DAFTARY, *The Assassin Legends*.

perpetrators in 'humanitarian' terms because it was viewed as causing fewer innocent and accidental victims than, for instance, mass uprisings. As time passed by this development changed and from the early 20th century, terrorism became less and less selective and eventually became a form of violence dominated by indiscriminate attacks on civilians. As a result, it paved the way for the perpetrators (both individuals and groups – and their leaders) to provide ideological justification of their actions[4].

In the 19th and much of the 20th centuries the ideologies of groups involved in terrorist activities were dominated by various radical socio-revolutionary, leftist and anarchist concepts. For instance, the ideologies of left-wing terrorists[5] of the second half of the 20th century (such as the West German Red Army Faction and the Italian Red Brigades) did not include many motives and ideas beyond the 'classic' ideologies of radical revolutionary and anarchist groups of the 19th century. But prior to World War II and in the first post-war decades, terrorism was widely employed by anti-colonial and other national liberation movements in the Middle East, North Africa and parts of Asia. It was at this stage that several national liberation and nationalist groups that combined terrorist means with other violent tactics managed to achieve all or most of their declared goals. Some even came to power in their newly established states. A vivid example is the Algerian Front de libération nationale – National Liberation Front (hence FLN).

The FLN led the armed struggle for independence from France after 1954 and at a certain point decided to turn to terrorist tactics in urban areas. It became the ruling party after Algeria's independence in 1962[6]. At

---

[4] For an in-depth history of terrorism in the 19th and 20th centuries see the works of: W. LAQUEUR, *A History of Terrorism*; G. CHALIAND – ARNAUD, *The History of Terrorism*, 55-58.

[5] Left-wing terrorism refers to the use of generally indiscriminate and unlawful violence against civilians and non-combatants by political forces adhering to Marxist, Leninist, Stalinist, Maoist or other left-wing theory or practice, seeking to undermine or obtain state power by acts of targeted violence against representatives of the state and the capitalist economic system.

[6] Others who used terrorism means to gain political power include: the underground Jewish organization Irgun (Irgun Tseva'i Le'umi, National Military Organization, also known as Etzel), which fought for almost two decades for the creation of the state of Israel; and the Greek Cypriot insurgency movement Ethniki Organosis Kyprion Agoniston (EOKA, National Organization of Cypriot Fighters), which fought British rule in Cyprus in the mid-1950s and gained independence in 1960. Puerto Rican nationalist terrorist groups were also active in the years following World War II – launching terrorist attacks against US officials in the early 1950s and attempting to assassinate US President Harry S. Truman in 1950 – but were not successful in advancing the goal of independence.

this juncture, it is important to stress that these two centuries in question (19th and 20th), which marked the rise of socio-revolutionary and anarchist terrorism may seem to be the first historical peak of left-wing terrorism[7] with particular reference to the Irish Republican Army (IRA) who could be described as one of the 20th century's most prolific and dangerous terrorist groups. In the same vein, following the end of the cold war, communist, radical socialist and other leftist ideologies suffered an overall decline as a result of the disintegration of the Soviet bloc, the end of the East-West ideological confrontation and the collapse of the bipolar world system. The role of these ideologies as a basis for groups involved in terrorist activity thus, decreased. As a result, in the 1990s the ideological currents of radical leftism were increasingly replaced by radical nationalism (especially separatist ethno-nationalism), and by religious extremism[8], which became the two most influential ideological pillars of terrorism. It is from this foregoing that we can argue that ideologies incorporating radical nationalism (including ethno-separatism) or religious extremism form a more favourable basis for inducing and 'justifying' the use of terrorist means than purely secular socio-political ideologies.

3. Terrorism in the 21st Century

Today, most people have a vague idea or impression of what terrorism is, but they lack a more precise, concrete, and truly explanatory definition of the word. This imprecision has been abetted partly by the modern media, in the effort to communicate an often complex and convoluted message in the briefest amount of airtime or print space possible has led to the promiscuous labelling of a range of violent acts as "terrorism." For instance, flipping through the pages of a newspaper, or browsing through the pages of the social media networks, or rather turning on the television and radio transistor, and – even within the same broadcast or on the same page of a newspaper or social media networks – one can easily find such

---

[7] E. STEPANOVA, *Terrorism in Asymmetrical Conflict*, 32.

[8] A good example of the aforementioned scenario is the coming into existence the Al-Qaida terrorist group between 1989 and 1990, after the IRA which was divided into two factions. While the first IRA was formed in 1919 during the Irish War of Independence, it was however, later split into two factions at the signing of the Anglo-Irish Treaty (December 1921). While the Pro-Treaty IRA faction agreed and recognized the self-governing Ireland under the British sovereignty, the Anti-Treaty IRA faction on the other hand disagreed and were determined to remove all vestiges of British rules that led not only to the bloody Irish Civil War (June 1922-May 1923) but also to the bombings of some government targets in England in 1939.

disparaging acts as the bombing of a building, the assassination of a head of state, the massacre of civilians by a military unit, or the deliberate poisoning of a public drinking water, all described as incidents of terrorism.

In summary, virtually every abhorrent act of violence that is perceived as directed against society – whether it involves the activities of anti-government dissidents or governments themselves, organized-crime syndicates, common criminals, rioting mobs, people engaged in militant protest, individual psychotics, or lone extortionists – is often labelled "terrorism." As a result, the term becomes so popular among the varied strata of our modern society and thus devoid of a definite definition. Against this backdrop, close examination of the concept therefore becomes necessary as already noted in the general introduction of the thesis.

As rightly observed from the above, the 19th and 20th centuries marked the first historical peak of the left-wing terrorism. Hence, towards the end of the 20th century, there was a sharp change of ideologies as already argued above, because national liberation, especially anti-colonial movements were replaced by radical ethno-nationalist movements that was often with separatist aims. As a result, this new ethno-nationalism was thus rarely tied to left-wing ideology, but it was instead more often linked to religious extremism. A vivid example is the IRA who later broke into two factions (the Pro-Treaty IRA faction who seem to align with the protestants and the Anti-Treaty IRA faction who on the other hand seem to align with the Catholics as the world was made to believe in the 1969 Battle of the Bogside riots in Derry). At the end of the 20th century therefore, radical ethno-nationalism and ethno-separatism moved to the fore as the ideologies that were most commonly employed by terrorist organizations. The wind of this change therefore manoeuvred itself into the 21st century thereby paving the way for the radical ethno-nationalism, and especially ethno-separatism, to retain its importance as one of the most widespread ideologies of groups employing terrorist means.

This however, gradually yielded primacy to religious, especially Islamist extremism. But this is not to exonerate the Christians because the IRA terrorist acts is an example of the Christian act of terrorism as noted above[9]. It is imperative to note that the use of Islamist here refers to the group of

---

[9] Although the struggle for independence seemed to have been over, the struggle to get Ulster back from the British control however continued irresistibly. The biggest obstacle was that the majority of people in the northern region did not want to be liberated, they were Protestants and were happy as citizens of the United Kingdom. But in the 1960s the confrontations between Catholics and Protestants hardened and the revolutionary spirit that swept across Europe and the USA affected the green island as well. While the Catho-

Muslims who are committed to political action to implement what they regard as an Islamic agenda within the context of the modern nation-state[10]. In other words, the Islamists are actors who use a variety of strategies in order to achieve a variety of goals, including the recognition by the state of the right to form Islamic political parties, the implementation of Shari'a-inspired legal reforms and, in some cases, overthrowing the government to establish an elusively defined "Islamic State"[11]. As a result, religious extremism became the ideological basis for terrorist groups active in more localized settings and, above all, for the emerging transnational violent Islamist movement. For example, in the case of the Islamic Movement of Uzbekistan (IMU), violent Islamism has served as a counterbalance and an alternative to nationalism. In the same vein, in Kashmir or Chechnya, it has been employed in combination with radical ethno-separatism.

It is however, imperative to note that the advent of what is considered modern, new or international terrorism as some scholars may describe it, could be traced back on the July 22, 1968, a day when three armed Palestinian terrorists, belonging to the Popular Front for the Liberation of Palestine (hereafter, FLP), one of the six groups that then constituted the Palestine Liberation Organization (hence, PLO), hijacked an Israeli El Al commercial flight en-route from Rome to Tel Aviv. However, it is pertinent to note that this does not in any way suggest that terrorism or hijacking of commercial aircrafts never occurred before then[12] but the El Al hijacking differed significantly from all previous ones.

---

lics felt suppressed and demonstrated for civil rights and equal treatment with the Protestants, the Protestants on the other hand, saw the Catholics' action as a provocation against them as a group and the situation ran out of control. Hence, this period of confrontations particularly the period after the 1960s was called the 'Troubles'. To this effect, the British soldiers came in 1969 to bring order to the society, but unfortunately, they took sides and the discrimination against Catholics went on. Nevertheless, it is important to note that terrorism and murder were carried out both by extreme Catholics and extreme Protestants whereby a lot of civilians were hurt or killed. People suspected of being terrorists could be kept in internment (in practice the same as jail) for years without a trial. Most people who were brought in were Catholics. The soldiers' presence in Northern Ireland today is extremely provoking to the Catholic side. Cf., "Thirteen Questions About Northern Ireland" in *Passage-engelsk laereverk for Vg1*.

[10] Schmid describes Islamist as adherence to Islamic fundamentalist ideology. It is often applied to members of groups advocating armed struggle against non-believers and heretics (jihad). See A.P. SCHMID, ed., *The Routledge Handbook of Terrorism*, 649.

[11] Cf., J. PISCATORI, "Islam, Islamists, and the Electoral Principle", 2.

[12] It is imperative to note that within the year 1968, eleven incidences of hijacking prior to the El Al flight hijack had already taken place at different locations within the globe. The hijack of the El Al flight was thus the twelfth incident that occurred within the same year.

In this respect, Bruce Hoffman points out some reasons that suggest that the period in question was an epoch which marked the beginning of modern terrorism. He stated thus:

> First, the purpose of the hijackers was not simply the diversion of a scheduled flight from one destination to another, as had been the case in the past, but the hijacking was a bold political statement. The terrorists who seized the El Al flight had done so with the express purpose of trading the passengers they held hostage for Palestinian terrorists imprisoned in Israel. Second, unlike previous hijackings, in which the origin or nationality of the aircraft that was being seized did not matter so long as the plane itself was capable of transporting the hijacker(s) to a desired destination, El Al – as Israel's national airline and by extension, therefore, a readily evident national "symbol" of the Israeli state – had been specifically and deliberately targeted by the terrorists. Third, by engineering a crisis in which the consequences of a government's ignoring or rejecting the terrorists' demands could prove catastrophic, leading to the destruction of the aircraft and the deaths of all people on board, the terrorists succeeded in forcing their avowed enemy, Israel, to communicate directly with them and therefore with the organization to which they belonged, despite the Israeli government's previous declarations and policy pronouncements to the contrary. Finally, through the combination of dramatic political statement, "symbolic" targeting, and crisis-induced *de facto* (in fact) recognition, the terrorists discovered that they had the power to create major media events – especially when innocent civilians were involved[13].

This singular event of the El Al hijacking brought a drastic change in the nature and character of the history of terrorism. For the first time, terrorists began to travel regularly from one country to another to carry out attacks. They also began to target innocent civilians from other countries who often had little or nothing to do with the terrorists' cause or grievance. But since the desire of the terrorists is to endow their acts with the power to instil fear on the minds of the public, and to attract attention and publicity, the attacks on the innocent civilians become obvious.

It is against this backdrop, that the intent of the hijackers of El Al flight was to shock and, by shocking, to stimulate worldwide fear and alarm. To buttress this point therefore, John Horgan (a psychologist)[14] succinctly opines that instilling fear on the mind of the public is the goal of terrorism.

> Very often, it seems that the goal of terrorism is simply to create widespread fear, arousal and uncertainty on a wider, more distant scale than that achieved

---

[13] B. HOFFMAN, *Inside Terrorism*, 63-64.

[14] John Horgan is a College Lecturer at the Department of Applied Psychology, University College, Cork. He is widely published in the areas of forensic psychology and terrorism. His research and teaching have taken him to many countries, where he lectures to police, intelligence, military and public audiences on terrorism and political violence.

by targeting the victim alone, thereby influencing the political process and how it might normally be expected to function[15].

With the fast-technological advancement that transformed the speed and ease international commercial air travels and vastly improved both the quality of television news footage and the promptness with which that footage could be broadcast around the globe paves the way for the dramatic tactical changes in terrorism. Such an ample opportunity was quickly appreciated by the terrorists and as a result, they could perpetrate violent acts in countries other than their own and directly involve or affect the foreign nationals so much so that such acts could attract global attention to themselves and their cause. With regard to this, Hoffman suggests that the PLO is at the forefront of this transformation due to their high record of attacks between 1968 to 1980[16].

In view of the above, Ekaterina Stepanova[17] opines in the Stockholm International Peace Research Institute (hence SIPRI)[18] Research Report no. 23, that the PLO among others ranked the six deadliest nationalist group in the world:

> The six deadliest nationalist groups of this period were all Palestinian organizations. The resort to terrorist means, including international terrorism, by the Palestine Liberation Organization (PLO) and other Palestinian militant groups from the late 1960s until the 1980s demonstrated how to internationalize – and draw international attention to – a local asymmetrical armed struggle…. In sum, radical nationalism came to the fore alongside extreme left-wing ideologies as an ideology of groups that employed terrorist tactics[19].

Owing therefore to the PLO success achieved in publicizing the Palestinians' plight through the "internationalization" of its struggle with Israel their modus operandi has since become a model for similarly aggrieved

---

[15] J. Horgan, *The Psychology of Terrorism*, 1.

[16] Between 1968 and 1980, Palestinian groups were responsible for 331 incidents, compared with the 170 incidents attributed to the next most active group, the anti-Castro Cuban terrorist movements, and Irish and Turkish groups were in third position with 115 incidents each. See B. Hoffman, *Inside Terrorism*, note #2, 309.

[17] Ekaterina Stepanova (Russian) is a member of the editorial board of Terrorism and Political Violence and Security Index. She led SIPRI Armed Conflicts and Conflict Management Project, and also led a research group on non-traditional security at the institute of World Economy and International Relations (IMEMO), Moscow. She authored Anti-terrorism and Peace-building During and After Conflict.

[18] SIPRI is an independent international institute for research into problems of peace and conflict, especially those of arms control and disarmament. It was established in 1966 to commemorate Sweden's 150 years of unbroken peace.

[19] E. Stepanova, *Terrorism in Asymmetrical Conflict*, 36-37.

ethnic and nationalist minority groups around the globe, demonstrating how longstanding but *hitherto* ignored or forgotten causes can be resurrected and dramatically thrust onto the world's agenda through a series of well-orchestrated, attention-grabbing violent acts. For this reason, the insignificant group (the Boko Haram) as it was conceived by some Nigerians and tagged by the Nigerian government as a group seeking for recognition and thus ignored has finally emerged on the international news headlines and newspapers as a terrorist group.

Against this backdrop therefore, the close examination of the Nigerian terrorist group (Boko Haram) becomes expedient. Nevertheless, it is pertinent to understand the link between terrorism and religion in order to ascertain whether or not the violent act of the Boko Haram is purely political or there exist some religious undertones.

4. Terrorism and Religion

With the collapse of the Soviet Union, the end of the cold war and the decline of leftist movements, a global vacuum in secular protest ideology emerged. This vacuum quickly started to be filled with radical currents – the explicitly extremist ethno-nationalist or religious ideologies. Religious extremism has internationally indeed become the most powerful motivational and ideological basis for groups engaged in terrorist activity[20]. It is however important to note that these extreme religious ideologies can be found in every religion and not pinned down to a particular religion as we have noted above in the case of the IRA.

In the late 20th and early 21st centuries the main terrorist threat to international security and to the security of many states – such as the USA and its Western allies, India, Russia, China and many Muslim countries – has been posed either by Islamist terrorism or by ethno-nationalist terrorism that has been Islamized to varying degrees. For instance, out of the 67 foreign terrorist organizations identified across the globe by the United State Bureau of Counter Terrorism, 61 organizations on the US State Department's list of foreign terrorist organizations (as of Oct. 2018) are Islamist groups[21].

Nevertheless, it is necessary to point out that when discussing the ideology of violent Islamism[22], it is pertinent to distinguish between religious and quasi-religious extremism. 'Purely' religious terrorism has been main-

---

[20] E. STEPANOVA, *Terrorism in Asymmetrical Conflict*, 57.

[21] UNITED STATES DEPARTMENT OF STATE: Diplomacy in Action, "Foreign Terrorist Organizations". Also see E. STEPANOVA, *Terrorism in Asymmetrical Conflict*, 58.

[22] "Islamism" is a term that refers to a broader political category.

ly practiced by a limited number of marginal, closed religious groups and totalitarian sects. The religious extremism that provides the ideological basis for many broader movements usually goes far beyond religion and theology as such to encompass socio-political and socio-economic protest and issues of culture and identity. Quasi-religious on the other hand, stems its character partly from the quasi-religious nature of Islam in its fundamentalist forms. Fundamentalist Islam provides a comprehensive concept of a social, political, ideological and religious order which has become a way of life and societal organization where religion, politics, state and society are inseparable.

To identify therefore, a religious terrorist group, Ekaterina Stepanova postulates certain general features that are shared by most of the terrorist groups that are guided by an ideology with a strong religious imperative. The first feature is the presence of a religious leader. A religious terrorist group usually necessitates a formal blessing by some spiritual authority or guide who may not necessarily hold any senior or leading position in the group, and they do not necessarily possess solid theological credentials or clerical education[23]. This usually points to the group's quasi-religious, rather than purely religious, character – that is, to its goals and agenda being highly politicized. A vivid example is, of course, bin Laden, who lacks any proper theological credentials, education or reputation but effectively poses as a spiritual leader and an oracle for the Muslim world.

It is important to bear in mind that the formal blessing usually takes the form of a special religious and legal pronouncement – *fatwa*[24], which legitimizes the use of terrorist means and may either precede or follow the act of terrorism. By this singular act of issuing *fatwas*, the group spiritual leader thus, uses an Islamic religious and legal instrument to convey essentially political manifestos. In fact, one of the main formal criteria for identifying an armed group as the one whose ideological basis is predominantly religious is precisely the presence of clerical figures in a group's leadership. This is especially so if this presence is combined with the consistent use of religious rituals or sacred texts for the inspiration and justification of violence, including terrorism, and for activities such as attracting and re-

---

[23] Examples of spiritual guides with a leading position within their group include the late Ahmed Yassin, founder of Hamas, Muhammad Hussein Fadlullah and Hassan Nasrallah of Hezbollah, the Sikh leader Jarnail Singh Bhindranvale, the pseudo-Shinto 'messiah' Shoko Asahara of Aum Shinrikyo, Osama bin Laden of Al-Qaida, Yusuf Muhammed of Boko Haram *et al.*

[24] "*Fatwa*" is an opinion or ruling on Islamic law (Shari'a), traditionally made by highly esteemed Islamic scholars to settle difficult or unclear cases.

cruiting new members. This extends to movements with multiple leaders and networks with an even more dispersed, diversified or even 'virtual' leadership – a pattern that characterizes the post-Al-Qaida transnational violent Islamist movement.

The second feature is the making of direct references to sacred texts with the view to justifying its armed violence. When a group is essentially guided by a strong religious imperative, as opposed to organizations that are merely formed on an ethno-confessional or sectarian basis, the common characteristic that is easily notifiable is the explicit justification of armed violence, which includes terrorism, by making direct references to sacred texts. These texts are not necessarily apocryphal or heterodox but may include the holy books or traditional writings that are fundamental to a certain religion or confession, such as the Qur'an or the *Hadith*[25] for Islam.

Third feature is the perceived of self-sacrifice via suicide bombing as an act of martyrdom or faith. Both religious and quasi-religious terrorist groups do not limit themselves to the use of sacred texts. They actively employ and adjust religious and quasi-religious rituals and cults, such as self-sacrifice and the cult of martyrdom, for their purposes. In this way, those who carry out a terrorist act see themselves and are perceived by their group and its supporters as martyrs for faith. In contrast to many secular militant organizations, for terrorist groups whose ideology is strongly influenced by religious extremism, the upgrading of a terrorist attack to an act of faith (especially when carried out as an act of self-sacrifice) effectively removes some of the basic constraints on incurring mass casualties. It thus facilitates the perpetration of deadlier, large-scale attacks.

Worthy to note is that, religious extremists identify, interpret and see 'the enemy' in broader and universal terms more than secular or ethno-confessional groups that religion is not their focal point. Although the enemies may be personalized to some extent by certain key figures, but they are however, used as examples of the more generalized notion. The new trend among radicals for example after the Al-Qaida attack is to 'fight all the infidels, whether believers or non-believers. Unlike socio-revolutionary terrorists of the late 19th century and ethno-nationalist radicals, the enemy is not reduced to either a handful of individuals nor to a certain social class or ethnic group but is rather generalized and most often personalized as evil. The enemy may, for example, range from the West to the entire world of unbelief, ignorance and materialism (*jahiliyyah*[26] in Islam) or 'all injustice

---

[25] The Hadith are narrations about the life, actions and sayings of the Prophet Muhammad.

[26] Jahiliyyah is a traditional Islamic notion referring to the state of lawlessness and ignorance in the pre-Islamic period; it literally means 'ignorance' in Arabic and is used

on earth'. To this, the replacement of religious extremist ideology over the secular radical socio-revolutionists became necessary.

The fourth feature is always geared toward a divine witness of God. It is the believe of every religious terrorist that the ultimate effect of any terrorist act guided by a strong religious imperative is to bear witness to the divine and higher being. Hence, suicide bombing is perceived as the highest act of bearing witness to God.

The last feature focuses on the little or no distinction between religion and politics. Most religious armed extremist groups (regardless of their confession) do not as a rule, draw a clear distinction between religion and politics. This trend is most developed in Islamist organizations, both those that do not use violence and those that engage in violent activity. This is in large part due to the holistic, all-embracing nature of Islam, where legal and normative aspects of life are developed in far greater detail than in other religions[27]. At this juncture, we now examine closely the rise of modern proliferation of Islamic extremism.

5. The Rise of Modern Islamic Extremism

In order to do justice to the theme in question, the need to examine in brief the historical development of Islamic fundamentalism cannot be overemphasized. Following the fall of the 'last Caliphate' – the Ottoman Empire (which was formally abolished by the Turkish President Mustafa Kemal Atatürk in 1924[28], and the end of World War I, the Islamic fundamentalist movement – *Salafism*[29] – came to the limelight. From the

---

to denote ignorance of divine guidance. It is also employed by radical Islamists to denote the current state of unbelief, ignorance and materialism in the world that is not governed by norms of fundamentalist Islam.

[27] E. STEPANOVA, *Terrorism in Asymmetrical Conflict*, 66.

[28] See the work of S. UNSAR, "A Path-Dependent Analysis", 104-105

[29] The *Salafist* movement or *Salafism* is an ultra-conservative reform movement found within the Sunni Islam that advocates a return to the traditions of the "devout ancestors" (the Salaf). It was developed in Arabia in the first half of the 18th century in order to confront the European colonialism. It is pertinent to note that *salafism* is a concept that has been used in western scholarship on Islam since the early twentieth century, but only employed by the media in the twenty-first century. However, within the academic literature the term "*Salafism*" is derived from the expression *al-salaf al-salih* which means the pious ancestors. The salafis believe that the Qur'an and the *hadith* (the prophetic tradition) are the only legitimate sources of religious conduct and reasoning. But the general understanding of the term is that *salafism* represents a more literalist and more puritan approach to Islamic doctrine and practice. Speaking therefore of the "salafis" or "the salafi movement" refers to the actors or a movement of Islamic group whose practice of Islam is more

19th century, the theory and practice of Islamism[30] started to develop. It should be kept in mind that, factors like modernization, and its power of secularization in the post-World War II, nationalist, left-wing and other ideologies associated with it within the ambience of socio-political, economic and culture spheres contributed greatly to the rise of the fundamentalist movements such as the anti-colonial movements that were guided by secular nationalist ideologies in the 20th century that include for instance; Baathism in Iraq and Syria, the Neo-Destour movement (or Bourguibism) in Tunisia, as well as the FLN in Algeria and the PLO in Palestine[31]. In other words, this century experienced the broad national liberation movements that often-had extremist factions that alongside other tactics employed terrorist means, both against the colonizers and against the more moderate nationalists.

It is against this backdrop, that in the mid-20th century, both prior to World War II and in the first post-war decades, terrorism was widely employed by anti-colonial and other national liberation movements as earlier stated. However, it is imperative to stress that not all Islamist movements were violent. Such fundamentalist non-violent movements are today referred to as the moderate (legalist). These include the Jamaat-e-Islami movement, founded in 1941 in British-ruled India by Maududi and now based in Pakistan, and the Muslim Brotherhood movement that was established by Hassan al-Banna in Egypt in the late 1920s and early 1930s and was actively opposed to secular Nasserism in the post-World War II

---

of puritan and more rigorous than other Muslims. Cf., T. HEGGHAMMER, "Jihadi-Salafis or Revolutionaries", 249.

[30] Islamism is referred to the political activity to advance the fundamentalist agenda, with the re-establishment of the Islamic Caliphate as the rhetorically ultimate goal.

[31] Baathism is another version of a pan-Arab nationalist, Arab socialist ideology. The Baath Party was founded in Syria in 1947 and a branch was established in Iraq in 1954. It came to power in both countries in 1963. Baathists remain in power in Syria but were deposed in Iraq in 2003 by the US-led invasion. The Tunisian Neo-Destour (New Constitution) Party succeeded the nationalist Destour Party in 1934 as a secular, modernist national liberation movement against French colonial rule. It was founded and led by Habib Bourguiba, who became the first president of independent Tunisia in 1957. For a brief period, from the mid-1960s until the early 1970s, the movement experimented with socialism. The FLN was one of the several national liberation and nationalist groups that combined terrorist means with other violent tactics as already mentioned above and managed to achieve all or most of their declared goals in Algeria. It led the armed struggle for independence from France after 1954 and at a certain point decided to turn to terrorist tactics in urban areas. It became the ruling party after Algeria's independence in 1962. The PLO – a multi-party Palestinian political confederation of a nationalist and mostly secular character – was founded in 1964 as a national liberation resistance movement.

period[32]. Subsequently, many other Islamist groups were formed within these broad movements of the violent fundamentalist groups or in association with them. One among others is the Al-Qaida[33] violent fundamentalist movement founded by Osama bin Laden.

Al-Qaida is the first multinational terrorist group of the twenty-first century that confronts the world with a new kind of threat. Since the contemporary wave of terrorism which began in 1968, no fundamentalist groups resembling it have previously emerged. Al-Qaida has moved terrorism beyond the status of a technique of protest and resistance and turned it into a global instrument with which to compete with and challenge Western influence in Muslim world. It is thus a worldwide movement capable of mobilizing a new and *hitherto* unimagined global conflict.

The incident of US 9/11 is a vivid example that cannot be ignored. It is therefore imperative to state that in the recent years of the 21st century, we have seen an increased and spread of Al-Qaida, and other organizations that are linked to it and adopt its beliefs and ideology. These organizations all descend from radical Political Islam, whether they are recognized as part of Al-Qaida or are simply compatible with its foundations based on ideological Islamic rhetoric, within what has become known as the Salafi Jihadi movement[34]. This movement became remarkably strong in the internal Syrian conflict and regained its power and presence in Iraq, as it entered into a military confrontation with the Iraqi military. Furthermore, it was able to reinforce its presence in other areas, such as Yemen and Somalia, where it enjoys huge capabilities despite the strikes it has received over the past years.

The paradox lies in the fact that Al-Qaida itself was seriously concerned when the Arab revolutions erupted, especially after the success of the Tunisian and Egyptian revolutions. Al-Qaida's organizational and intellectual

---

[32] The Jamaat-e-Islami and the Muslim Brotherhood called for the gradual transition to Islamic rule and the creation of Islamic states through peaceful means as an alternative to secular, Western-style socio-political development and modernization.

[33] "Al-Qaida" is an Arabic word that refers to as "the base".

[34] *Salafism* is a term that is derived from the expression *al-salaf al-salih* which refers to "the pious ancestors" and the *Salifis* believe that the Qur'an and the *hadith* (Prophetic tradition) are the only legitimate sources of religious conduct and reasoning. But however, the general conception of the term refers to the practice of Islam that is more puritan and rigorous than any Islamic practice. The Salafi Jihadi movement therefore could refer to the movement of a group of Muslims whose desire is to change what is considered wrong and un-Islamic that is outside *Shari'a* and it is a deviation from Islam. This movement considers *jihad* as an inescapable obligation on every Muslim and as the summit of Islam. However, there are nuances as regards the general accepted definition of the concept. For an in-depth knowledge, see the work of T. HEGGHAMMER, "Jihadi Salafis or Revolutionaries", 249.

leadership therefore feared that these revolutions could create a huge set-back for the group, as Arab societies would be adopting democracy and opting for peaceful change. However, the situation witnessed a complete turnaround. Instead of the fears and concerns of losing popularity that occupied the group's members, the organization actually found a vast space to operate in Syria, Egypt and Iraq, and managed to attract many new members and supporters[35]. At this juncture, it is pertinent to note that with the 9/11 terrorist attacks the radical Islamic Al-Qaida thus became ever more internationally popular and thereafter paved the way to the present proliferation of Islamic extremist groups[36]. We now examine the Nigerian terrorist group.

6. Terrorism: The Nigerian Narrative

As we have just seen from the foregoing, terrorism, arguably, is the biggest threat to global peace and stability in the contemporary times. It is an oversimplification to therefore say that since the dawn of this millennium, the incidence of terrorism has been on a steady rise globally, particularly from the barbaric incident of September 11, 2001, that razed down to ashes the Twin Towers in New York which claimed to death almost 3,000 lives of different nationalities around the world[37], and not to mention the loss of properties. Against this backdrop, the worldwide manifestation of terrorism has thus been evident not only within the Africa continent, but also within the Nigerian soil. This ugly phenomenon found its expression in the country as a result of the emergence of the Islamic extremists' group popularly known as Boko Haram. It is imperative to thus note that since its advent, the sectarian insurgency has wrecked immense havoc in the country, thereby challenging the stability of its peace and development, and above all posing a threat to the collective survival of the Nigerian citizens. It is on this note we shall explore below the nature of the terrorist group, how it came about, its ideology, what it desires to achieve, its link with other international bodies and *vis-à-vis* its sponsors.

6.1 *Boko Haram*

The "Boko Haram" phenomenon has become a major source of worry and consternation in Nigeria and beyond. The name "Boko Haram" has become a household name in most local and international media houses

---

[35] F.E. STIFTUNG, *The Rise of Religious Radicalism in the Arab World*, 9.

[36] For a more study on Al-Qaida, see the following works: R. GUNARATNA, *Inside Al-Qaeda*; S.S. SHAHZAD, *Inside Al-Qaeda and the Taliban*.

[37] Cf., Cnn Library, "September 11, 2001".

and has become one of the factors that made Nigeria famous around the globe, however, in a very negative manner due to their constant violent attacks. How they came into existence still remains a matter of debate because there are varied narratives to this effect. Being a strong proponent of the Boko Haram's ideology and an ardent critique of Western civilization in the 60s, we can say that this organization could be the outcome of one Mallam Yusuf from Gashua, Yobe state (a father to Mohammad Yusuf known as the leader of Boko Haram)[38].

Another narrative is that it is an extension of the 1980s *Maitatsine's* group owing to their modus operandi, except that they became more sophisticated and technologically advanced due to the difference in period of operation. Nevertheless, the bone of contention here is not necessarily how it is developed – although it is an essential element – but the havoc it caused to Nigerians particularly Christians in the north and the nature of the dented image it presents internationally about Nigeria. It is therefore impotant to closely examine some basic elements of this group in question.

6.2 *Etymology*

The name "Boko Haram" is a compound name comprising of Hausa and Arabic words. These are coined together by the residents of Maiduguri city the capital of Borno state – where their headquarters was based[39] – and later employed by the media, and *vis-à-vis* the public. The common usage of the name simply means "western education is prohibited". This is too simplistic to convey the original meaning of the coiners. In order to have therefore a better understanding of what "Boko Haram" means the necessity to examine its etymology becomes essential.

Etymologically the word "Boko" was derived from a Hausa traditional joke at wedding to mean "deceit"[40], while "Haram" is an Arabic word adapted into Hausa language to mean 'something unacceptable' or 'forbidden' in Islam. Combining these two words together "Boko" (deceit) and "Haram" (something unacceptable/forbidden or prohibited), to refer "Boko Haram" would therefore mean "westernization or rather western civilization, education inclusive is a deceit to Islam or is prohibited by Islam". Anything outside this may suggest a downplay of the original meaning of the coiners' and perhaps may change the course of the group's

---

[38] J. BAKENI, *Understanding the Enigma of Boko Haram*, 2.

[39] See Appendix A.

[40] Cf., M.H. KUKAH, "Boko Haram. Some Reflections on Causes and Effects", 3-4.

ideology. It is thus, worthy to note that this notion is still held till date among many Muslim fundamentalists in the north. In other words, there is a common perception among most of the people of the northern Nigerian Muslims that western education is the product of Christianity, a tool used for conversion by the early Christian missionaries, and western civilization is thus synonymous to Christianity. This explains why the *"Almajiri* School[41]" is preferred in the north to the western education which has thus posed a setback as regards the socio-economic development of the region.

6.3 *Historical Background*

During the colonial era, the typical fanatical Muslim conceived western education and westernization in general to be a deceit. Thus, fanatics like Mallam Yusuf as stated above, spearheaded the opposition of the western education as early as 60s and propagated that it is forbidden in Islam. As a result, the fruit of his campaign started manifesting itself when in 1980s an immigrant from northern Cameroon and Islamic spiritual leader – Alhaji Muhammadu Marwa – mobilized some Muslim youths across the northern region and posed a serious national security threat under the name *Maitatsine*[42] which started from Kano and spread to other five northern states within a twinkle of an eye. It was from the Maitatsine inferno that Nigeria as a nation started witnessing the rise of Islamic extremist movements particularly within the northern region.

In the 1980s after the Maitatsine incident for instance, there was another Islamic group that was established shortly by Ibraheem az-Zakzaky called the Muslim Brotherhood (known in Hausa as "Yan Brothers"). Many Muslim youths join this movement and Muhammad Yusuf was inclusive. The Muslim Brothers were known of their emotional rhetoric and enthusiasm

---

[41] *Almajiris* (plural of *Almajiri* means disciples) are the pupils of Islamic Qur'anic School whereby the *Mallam* (master) collects some pockets of Muslim children most often from poor family backgrounds and educates them on the Qur'an. These children remain under his watch until they are properly schooled in the way of Islam and grounded in the knowledge of the Qur'an. While fending for themselves and their master through begging from house to house and street to street during the day, at evenings they gather round the *Mallam* and learn the Qur'an by memorization. As the *Almajiris* grow to maturity and are well-informed in the Qur'anic knowledge, the master sends them forth into the society as propagators of Islam. While others become *da'awa* (preachers) and *mallams* (masters) of other *Almajiris*, others on the other hand become easy tools for political tugs to manipulate for their selfish political aggrandizement and also cohorts of Islamic extremists. It is imperative to note that this system of school has no connection in whatever way with the western education and it is an informal way of learning.

[42] The Maitatsine saga will be discussed elaborately in the next chapter.

ideology against the Nigerian government in the name of Islam. However, within the same group, there emerged *Tashayyu* (Shi'ism) in 1994 with an inclination to serve the Iranian interest under the leadership of Zakzaky. As a result of this development, the group of the Yan Brothers fractured into various groups such as the Shi'ites under the leadership of Zakzaky and the Salafi under the name *Jama'at ut-Tajdeed ul-Islami* which remained on a similar course as the Muslim Brothers.

6.4 *Origin*

The Boko Haram movement led by Mohammed Yusuf came to light in a form of resurgence in 2009 but its initial existence could be traced back to the years 2001 -2004[43]. Unlike Al-Qaida and its affiliates, Boko Haram is a local organization that focuses specifically on Nigeria and few adjacent countries (Cameroon, Niger and Chad) that share boundary with Nigeria rather than international jihad. Within its gestation period however, the group was virtually not known, although it was linked to the group that was operating in Yobe state who called themselves "Nigerian Afghanistans". But from the early stage, the Boko Haram group was busy mobilizing itself and recruiting its members. As a result, its violent activities never attracted much needed attention not until the year 2009 when the Nigerian police force clamped down on them due to the breakdown of law and order[44] and couple with some skirmishes of conflicts within the north-east region.

2009 was a very historical year in the whole world not only in Nigeria. It brought about the emergence and the first out show of the Boko Haram insurgency. Later than 2009, they were still gathering members. Those of us who have been here before 2009, we use to see the group like a political thing that has metamorphosed into Boko Haram now with the former leader Mohammad Yusuf who was killed, and they were very religious. Before we knew what was happening, they became dreaded with a goal to Islamize Nigeria and they had a goal of enforcing their religious teachings and practices to even their fellow Muslims and Christians alike[45].

---

[43] As regards the exact year of their existence, there exist various literatures. See: M.A MAMBULA, *Nigeria. Ethno-Religious and Socio-Political Violence*, 47; A. BRIGAGLIA, "The Volatility of Salafi Political Theology", 180; J. CAMPBELL, "Boko Haram, Origins", 2; A. MURTADĀ, *Boko Haram in Nigeria*, 4-26.

[44] The breakdown of law and order was as a result of a law that was recently enforced by the Nigerian government within the period under review, stating that "all motor cycle users must use their helmet while riding on any of the Nigerian major roads". See A. MURTADĀ, *Boko Haram in Nigeria*, 8.

[45] DURSA, "Interview".

From the foregoing, it is suggested that Boko Haram is essentially an anti-establishment group that is against government institutions like the police and other agencies. In other words, it is a radical Islamic sect opposed to Western education and its civilization. But could there be any underlying factors that constituted the fertile ground for this insurgency? We shall attempt to answer this question in the next chapter. Nevertheless, while the group is widely referred to as Boko Haram, it originally called itself *Jamā'at Ahl al-Sunna li'l-Da'wa wa'l-Jihād 'ala Minhāj al-Salaf* (Association of the People of the Sunna for Preaching and Jihad According to the Salafi Method) in line with the earliest generation of Muslims"[46]. However, with the success recorded in capturing some major urban centres of the northeast and establishing the short-lived Boko Haram's "so called" Islamic State, as it was officially declared by its leaders in August 2014[47], and having officially pledged its allegiance to Islamic State (hence IS) in March 2015, the terrorist group *ipso facto* changed the above original name to *al-Dawla al-Islāmiyya Wilāyat Gharb Ifrīqiyā* (The Islamic State, West African Province – hereafter ISWAP)[48]. This implies that since March 2015 till date, the Boko Haram is officially known with the later name.

However, before the group's publicity by the media, it claimed that it was out to seek the proper understanding of Islamic faith as stated by Abdullah (a Boko Haram member). "We started as a small group of faithful who wanted nothing to do with politics"[49]. But shortly after the crackdown of their cell in Maiduguri, and the killing of their spiritual leader by the security force in 2009, they became angry over the fact that their own Islamic religious leaders (and their so – called Muslim political leaders) have come under the control of the state and are unable to give voice to their pains and sufferings.

As a result, they took to violence for *"an eye for an eye"* revenge believing that western education is fake, because it is responsible for the corrupted minds of their Islamic religious leaders and their Muslim political leaders, and above all for the pollution of the public morality that paves the way to corruption. This thus, explains why their first targets of violence were the State and Federal governments and their institutions[50]. But the extension of their inhumane acts on the Christians and their fellow

---

[46] A. BRIGAGLIA, "The Volatility of Salafi Political Theology", 176. Also see, J. BAKENI, *Understanding the Enigma of Boko Haram*, 3.

[47] ___, "Boko Haram Declares 'Islamic State".

[48] ___, "Nigeria's Boko Haram Pledges Allegiance to Islamic State".

[49] ABDULLA, "Nigeria Crisis A Threat to the Entire Country", 39.

[50] A. BRIGAGLIA, "The Volatility of Salafi Political Theology", 184. Also see, M.H. KUKAH, "Boko Haram. Some Reflections on Causes and Effects, 8.

Muslims (who opposed them), and religious institutions remains a hard nut to crack. One of the tasks of this study therefore is to find out the motive of this extension of the attacks on Christians. Nonetheless, the above given reason of vengeance by the group seems to be very weak to explain the magnitude of their violent acts. In this light, it is opined that it could be out of their believe in the ideology of *salafism*, owing to the fact that their spiritual leader Muhammad Yusuf was a diehard member of the Islamist movement known as *Jamā'at Tajdīd al-Islām* (JTI), – a protest movement that had been active in the late military era, especially under the Abacha junta (1993-1999)[51].

6.5 *Reorganisation of Boko Haram*

After the destruction of the Boko Haram's headquarter in Maiduguri and the death of their spiritual leader Muhammad Yusuf via the extra-judicial killing by the Nigerian police, the official spokesman of the movement announced that it would not change a thing in their planned agenda and they will never give up. But what happened to their members and their leader was a source of strength and perseverance to implement their plans. Against this backdrop, on August 16, 2009 the British Broadcasting Corporation (hereafter BBC) reported that there had been a new proclamation that the group had reorganized itself. This was based on the words of Thānī Umar – self acclaimed deputy leader of Boko Haram – who stated that: "The movement had joined up with Al-Qaida and thus intends to launch series of bombings starting in August in both Northern and Southern Nigeria so as to make Nigeria ungovernable"[52].

It is important to note that from this period the group went into a comatose for some months, and just to resurface in the month of June 2010 on the internet with Abū Bakr Shekau as its leader dressed in army uniform with face masked and an AK47 in the background, refuting the claim that he had been killed alongside with other members in 2009 clash. From this appearance, Abū Bakr Shekau remains the leader of the group up to December 2015 at the time the Nigerian government declared that Boko Haram has been technically conquered. Worthy to note here is Shekau's manifesto: prison break[53], attacks against Nigerian

---

[51] M.H. Kukah, "Boko Haram. Some Reflections on Causes and Effects", 180.

[52] A. Murtadā, *Boko Haram in Nigeria*, 10.

[53] The Bauchi prison break that took place on September 7, 2010 in which more than 700 prisoners were released by the Boko Haram was the most significant of all prison breaks by the group. See J. Zenn, *Northern Nigeria's Boko Haram*, 54.

armed troops and police force[54], against Christians[55] and against whistle-blowers of the movement[56].

6.6 *Ideology*

Owing to the Return of democracy in Nigeria that has finally come to stay, its aftermath is a necessary story that must be told. After the 1999 democratic transition, Nigeria as a nation never witnessed the creation of any Islamic party or mass movement that would violently adhere to the implementation of Shari'a by law or by force. However, there were some Islamist networks in the country who were involved in the agitation for the implementation of the Shari'a-inspired by the penal code in the majority Muslim states of the north.[57] At the forefront of the pro-Shari'a agitation, however, was not an organized Islamist network with a political vision, but it was out of the selfish interest of some political leaders who saw the agitation for the implementation of the Shari'a as a viable tool to be employed for the success of their political career. Against this backdrop, the intensity of the agitation came from the Muslim community only after the elections as a result of the ardent need to begin to benefit from the dividends of democracy. The case of the then governor of Zamfara state[58] – who was the first northern governor to implement Shari'a law in his state[59] – is a good example of the aforementioned.

> After 1999 with the return of democracy, the first phase of extremism we witness was the clamour on the demand for Shari'a law and that started in most states. This was in itself a political motivated because it was the political elite who wanted cheap popularity and then also to score cheap political points. They motivated that in the sense that they wanted to endear themselves to their people and they thought that will be a faster way of getting political capital. So, it resulted in that, so people were excited and encouraged that they were going to do that and create that, so it became quite easy for people to now demand those things they promised when the political elections were over[60].

Owing to the fact that there existed the network of salafi actors, the demand for the fulfilment of the political promises made during the 1999

---

[54] The bombing of the Nigerian Police Head Quarters in Abuja on June 16, 2011 was the peak of their foresaid attacks on the Nigerian troops and Police Force. See Y. OLOMO-JOBI, *Islam and Conflict in Northern Nigeria*, 233-234.

[55] We will elaborate more on the Christian attacks in the next chapter.

[56] A. MURTADĀ, *Boko Haram in Nigeria*, 11.

[57] We shall examine closely the issue of Shari'a in the next chapter.

[58] Ahmad Thānī Yarimabakura (popularly known as Ahmad Sani Yerima)

[59] A. MURTADĀ, *Boko Haram in Nigeria*, 11.

[60] MALLAM, "Interview".

electioneering campaigns could be an ample opportunity that presented itself at the disposal of the *salafis*. Against this backdrop, *salafism* which is an increasingly important school of thought within modern Sunni Islam, of which the Wahhabi movement[61] (the official religious doctrine of the modern Saudi Arabian kingdom), has gradually become the most influential manifestation. In order to have a better understanding of the Boko Haram's ideology is necessarily therefore to understand the central thought of *salafism* which is characterized by its sharp emphasis on theological purity as already mentioned above[62].

In other words, the champions of *salafism* are reinforced by the belief of being entrusted with a mission to revive the original creed of the fore bearer (Salaf) of Islam that was purportedly lost at some point in history of Islam. The Salafis, especially those of the Wahhabi persuasion, believe that they constitute the historical embodiment of the "saved sect" (*al-firqa al-nājiya*) mentioned in a famous statement attributed to the Prophet Muhammad, which they interpret in an exclusivist sense[63]. Such an exclusivist attitude is directed not only towards Shiite beliefs, but also towards much, if not most, of the historical manifestations of Sunni religiosity and theological thought, which Salafis variously categorize as spurious (*bid'a*) or as outright unbelief (*kufr*)[64]. The doctrine of salafi finds therefore a strong

---

[61] *Wahhabism*, considers itself to be the true Salafist movement. It started as a theological reform movement, having the goal of calling (*da'wa*) people to restore the 'real' meaning of *tawhid* (oneness of God or monotheism) and to disregard and deconstruct 'traditional' disciplines and practices that evolved in Islamic history such as theology and jurisprudence and the traditions of visiting tombs and shrines of venerated individuals whereby they classified such disciplines and practices as *shirk* (polytheism), *kufr* (unbelief in God), *ridda* (apostasy), and *bida'* (innovations). Its founder, Muhammad Bin Abd al-Wahhab (1703-1792), forced people to adhere to a very strict and literal interpretation of "monotheism" and to fight *shirk*. His followers, who called themselves *al-muwahhidin* (the monotheists -- as if others, especially Muslims, are not), are labelled by others as *Wahhabis*. It is imperative to note that *Wahhabism* prohibits many practices in which other Muslims engage, such as listening to certain types of music, drawings of human beings or other living things that contain a soul, praying while visiting tombs (including Prophet Mohammed's tomb), following any *madhahib* (schools) of Islamic jurisprudence, which in fact constitutes Sunni orthodoxy. However, most sheikhs of his time and after rejected Abd al-Wahhab's view and some of them even judged the sheikh as an apostate (*murtad*), making his *takfir* (accusing others of unbelief) of Muslims invalid and illegitimate. For more study on *Wahhabism* see the works of: A. MOUSSALLI, "Wahhabism, Salafism and Islamism"; D. COMMINS, *The Wahhabi Mission and Saudi Arabia*.

[62] See above notes #28 & #33, on *Salafism*.

[63] A. BRIGAGLIA, "The Volatility of Salafi Political Theology", 181.

[64] For more insight see A. BRIGAGLIA, "The Volatility of Salafi Political Theology", 181. Also see above notes #28 & #33, on *Salafism*.

consideration appeal to Muhammad Yusuf who built the ideology of his terrorist group around its theology.

Nevertheless, it is imperative to state that the salafi trend is relatively of recent introduced in Nigeria, which was primarily represented by two partly overlapping networks of *Izala*[65] (*Jamā'at 'Izālat al-Bid'a wa-Iqāmat al-Sunna*) and *Ahlus Sunna*. While Izala represents an earlier Salafi leadership in Nigeria, Ahlus Sunna on the other hand represents the later (modern/contemporary) salafi leadership. It emerged around a generation of younger Nigerian Salafis, many of whom had studied at the Islamic University in Medina (Saudi Arabia) and could boast of a more robust grasp of the Wahhabi theological corpus than their Izala counterparts, as well as a closer link with the global network of the students of Saudi Arabia-based Salafi religious establishment. It was this later Salafi movement therefore that Yusuf Muhammad was absorbed in around 1999[66]. But his (Muhammad Yusuf's) radicalism as exhibited by his group (Boko Haram) portrayed in the media as a characteristically anti-modern one, is an apparent irony that even the Ahlus Sunna's supporters could not explain. His radicalism includes; the rejection of the Nigerian constitution; the rejection of public, secular education and of the "human theories" it promotes; finally, the preparation for jihad. Hence, he broke away from them and formed his radical terrorist Boko Haram.

At this point in time, the radical ideas of Muhammad Yusuf started to resonate within a sector of the young Muslims almost in an unconscious way, and these ideas appealed not only to the rural and uneducated Muslim youths but also to the urban and even university students who most of them have already engaged in circulating the classical jihadi propaganda videos portraying militants training in Afghanistan or Chechnya. At some point it was also known among Nigerians that some of the graduated students and workers among Yusuf's adherers brought out their school certificates and other valuable credentials and burnt them to ashes as a sign of total rejection of westernization[67], and thereafter, they started promoting their master's radicalism. It will be of interest to know that there was even a song that was in circulation among the Muslim youths in both secondary and tertiary schools and later became a ringing tone:

---

[65] Izala was established in 1978 by the students of Abu Bakr Mahmud Gumi (d. 1992). Its main goals were to promote and popularize Gumi's critique of the traditional religious scholars (which are for the most part Ash'ari and Sufi) and to encourage the "eradication" (this is the meaning of the word *'izāla*) of spurious practices (*bid'a*).

[66] A. BRIGAGLIA, "The Volatility of Salafi Political Theology", 182.

[67] Cf., TELL, 2009, 34.

> I pledge to Islam, my religion / to be faithful, loyal and honest / to serve Islam with all my power / and I pray for Allah's assistance. / I have promised to be a Muslim / I have promised to work for Islam / I have promised to serve for [sic] Islam / so that I may get eternal bliss. / We want Qur'an as constitution / we want Hadith as constitution / we want Qur'an as constitution / we will no more accept the theories. / Human theories are barbaristic [sic] / human theories are barbaristic / human theories are aimless theories / we will no more accept the theories. / Oh, you brother, Jihad is coming / oh my brother, jihad is coming / oh my sister, jihad is coming / we will no more accept the theories![68].

This song was produced by one Ibrāhīm al-Barnāwī KSA (i.e., Kingdom of Saudi Arabia), seemingly a Nigerian resident in Saudi Arabia. The above text mimics and ridicules the Nigerian official national pledge that is recited by all school children at the beginning and end of each school day. The wordings of the National pledge are as follows:

> I pledge to Nigeria, my country
> To be faithful, loyal and honest,
> To serve Nigeria with all my strength,
> To defend her unity and uphold
> Her honour and glory.
> So, help me God.

To add to its intended effect of mockery, on the internet it circulates in the form of a video clip in which the song is superposed to the images of a group of Nigerian schoolboys and schoolgirls dancing during a school recital. Of recent, the initial lines of this "Boko Haram pledge" have been solemnly quoted by Abū Bakr Shekau before histrionically burning a Nigerian flag, in one of his internet videos[69].

6.7 *Motive*

Following closely their trend of events, it is difficult for one to state clearly that this is exactly what they want. As a result, there exist various narratives to this regard. However, we can deduct from the speculation of few sources. For instance, a narrative opines that Boko Haram seeks a complete and immediate implementation of Islamic Shari' a law across the country[70].

---

[68] I. AL-BARNĀWĪ KSA, "I Pledge to Islam my Religion".

[69] A. BRIGAGLIA, "The Volatility of Salafi Political Theology", 183-184.

[70] M.E. OKEMI, "Boko Haram. A Religious Sect or Terrorist Organization", 2-3. Also see Economist, "Nigeria Crisis", 39.

The mission of the sect was to establish an Islamic State where 'orthodox Islam' is practiced. Orthodox Islam according to him (Mohammed Yusuf, leader of the sect) frowns at Western education and working in the civil service because it is sinful. Hence, for their aim to be achieved, all institutions represented by government including security agencies like police, military and other uniformed personnel should be crushed[71].

By implication, they want all Nigerians to submit and to convert to Islam beginning with the then President Jonathan Ebele Goodluck (a Christian from the south-south region of the country) or resigns because only Muslims rule the Muslim *Umma* (community). In like manner, the constant arrest of their leaders, family members and all their relations must stop immediately, and the Government must release all their arrested members from prisons across the country. Another source contends that it is an outgrowth of social, economic, and political challenges in northern Nigeria that led them to such acts[72]. They advocate for an end to corruption and injustice and a return to the ways of Allah where justice and equity are the watchwords.

Furthermore, not until a few years ago, all political violence was limited to the Niger delta region. This narrative has it that owing to the presidential amnesty deal granted and concluded in June 2009 and duly signed by the then president of Nigeria, late Umaru Yar'adua which brought relative peace when $68 billion was to be spent for both allowances and training at home and overseas of ex-militants[73] in order to lay down their arms, the Boko Haram on the other hand desired such a "slice of the amnesty cake" just like their counterparts in the Niger Delta region. Hence, they are fighting not really because they want to establish an Islamic State but rather to also enjoy a presidential amnesty"[74]. But the plausible narrative that could be considered strong enough and convincing owing to the magnitude of their violent act is that Boko Haram can only be understood as local promoters of the global (radical) *salafism*[75] as stated above.

Owing to aggrieve factor, another narrative contends that Boko Haram was aggrieved by the Nigerian government in respect to the crackdown of their cells, arrest of members and their families and above all the extra

---

[71] TELL, 2009, 34. Quoted in N.J DANJIBO, "Islamic Fundamentalism and Sectarian Violence".

[72] J. ZENN, "Nigeria Al-Qaidaism", 113.

[73] NSRP., "Policy Brief". Also see S. OJO, "Amnesty Programme".

[74] J. BAKENI, *Understanding the Enigma of Boko Haram*, 13.

[75] See the works of: A. KASSIM, "Defining and Understanding", 173-200; A. THURSTON, "Nigeria's Mainstream Salafis", 109-135.

judicial killings of their members and their charismatic religious leader. As a result, they needed a vengeance since terrorism exists when there is an aggrieved group that is denied of its privileges and rights and the opportunity to be listened to or heard, a supportive group and an oppressive or suppressive group[76].

6.8 *International Link*

Given the persistent frequency and sporadic attacks of the Boko Haram and their resilient in withstanding the Nigerian government counter-terrorism policies, that seem to have proved ineffective or counterproductive, it is suspected that the group must have been linked with some of the international terrorist groups like Al-Qaida, Al-Shabaab, IS and the like as back-ups. In attempt to unravel the mystery behind their wild inferno therefore, we find some plausible reasons that seem to suggest international influence(s) on the group.

For instance, the group's deliberate fashion of its name after the Taliban in Afghanistan as "Nigerian Taliban" and "Black Taliban" sends a signal of an international linkage[77]. Another reason is the meeting of the group's key figures with the leadership of Al-Qaida in the Islamic Maghreb (hence AQIM) in neighbouring Niger, and in like manner, the group's claim to have sent its members for military training to Afghanistan, Lebanon, Pakistan, Iraq, Mauritania and Algeria[78].

Evidence also emerged that the Boko Haram has ties with the Somali militant group Al-Shabaab[79]. The claim of the group's spokesman buttresses the aforementioned when he states that "Boko Haram fighters had been sent to Somalia and Yemen for further training"[80]. In the same vein, he went on to say that "We want to make it known that our jihadists have arrived in Nigeria from Somalia where they received real training on warfare who [*sic*] made that country ungovernable.... This time round, our attacks will be fiercer and wider than they have been"[81]. There is also the evidence that at least one hundred Boko Haram fighters are part of the Movement for Unity and Jihad in West Africa (hence MUJAO). The MUJAO group

---

[76] M.E. OKEMI, "Boko Haram: A Religious Sect or Terrorist Organization", 4.

[77] ECONOMIST, "A Taste of the Taliban: Islamist Attacks in Nigeria" (August 1, 2009) 44.

[78] D. BLAIR, "Does Nigeria's Taliban Have the West"; I. MANTZIKOS, "The Absence of the State in Northern Nigeria", 60.

[79] T. JOHNSON, "Boko Haram", 4.

[80] C. ERO, "Bombing in Abuja'.

[81] K. ZIMMERMAN, "From Somalia to Nigeria"; H. SOLOMON, "Counter-Terrorism in Nigeria", 194.

split off from the AQIM in order to focus on the jihad in West Africa and the Sahel regions[82].

Having received the needed training in the above stated camps, it is obvious that the modus operandi of their attacks sharply changed from the use of knives, machetes, bows and arrows, and petrol bombs to the use of suicide car bombers and Improvised Explosive Devices (hereafter IEDs). For instance, the adoption of the Al-Qaida's tactics of suicide bombings which was never known in the history of Nigeria demonstrates the afore-mentioned[83]. It is worthy to also note that the quality of explosives used also demonstrates the group's increasing sophistication and its linkage with the international terrorist bodies. This is proven by the group's change in choice of targets. From the local target of police stations, Churches, markets and other soft targets to the bombing of the United Nations (UN) headquarters in Abuja[84].

The public declaration by one of the group's spokesmen Mūsā Tankū in a BBC Hausa service that Boko Haram had joined up with Al-Qaida is a bolster to the above. This thus seems convincing owing to the evident of the Al-Qaida's interest in Nigeria when Osama bin Laden enlisted Nigeria in 2003 as one of the oil countries that must be liberated by Al-Qaida from the shackles of America[85]. In another development, the declaration of Shekau in March 2015, makes the group's link with the international bodies clearer than ever when he declared their allegiance to the IS[86].

The unavoidable struggle to establish Shari'a law by Al-Qaida, al-Shabaab and Hezbollah who have posed threats to the peace and security of their host countries as well as their neighbours seems to suggest the possibility of Boko Haram international linkage. Since it is said that 'birds of the same feather flock together', it could be that Boko Haram's interest in establishing Shari'a law in Nigeria might have attracted the attention of its international terrorist groups for their support toward the realization of this common interest in Nigeria. Against this backdrop, therefore, the probability of Boko Haram alliance with Al-Qaida, al-Shabaab, Hezbollah, IS and other Islamic terrorist groups in order to realize their common desired goal in Nigeria may be high[87].

---

[82] H. SOLOMON, "Counter-Terrorism in Nigeria", 194.

[83] A. MURTADĀ, *Boko Haram in Nigeria*, 22.

[84] H. SOLOMON, "Counter-Terrorism in Nigeria", 194.

[85] J. ZENN, *Northern Nigeria's Boko Haram*, 6.

[86] ___ "Nigeria's Boko Haram Pledges Allegiance to Islamic State".

[87] Cf., M.F AJIBOYE-DARE, *Terrorism. The Nigerian Perspective*, 72.

6.9 *Sponsorship*

Given the poor nature of the socio-economic background of the *almajiris* who formed the membership of the Boko Haram, and who perpetually live from hand to mouth for survival, to have suddenly been seen constantly moving about with sophisticated machine guns like the AK47 and the like, thus, calls for attention. Common sense would suggest that there must be some societal elites or international organization(s) that are funding their survival and weaponries when we carefully examine side by side the cost of the weapons and the *almajiris'* economic status in the society. In this regard, there are varied narratives of speculations.

Some speculated that due to the group's link with international terrorist groups, the likelihood of the group's funding by such organization is high. Given that the group's leader Yusuf was charged by the Nigerian court in 2006 for receiving funds from an Al-Qaida's linked organization, it is speculated that the group was thus being funded by the Al-Qaida. In the same vein, in March 2010 it was alleged that AQIM which operates in North Africa offered to assist the group with training in weapon handling, men, arms and ammunitions to enable them to defend themselves and to destabilize the Nigerian State[88].

The active involvement of prominent Nigerians is another narrative. For example, it was advanced that the chairman of Petroleum Drivers Association in Kaduna, one Nuhu Muhammad was arrested on the grounds that he supplied the group with rocket launchers, IEDs materials, soldier uniforms, army belts, cartridges and AK-47 assault rifles[89]. In like manner, the confession of an immigration official (who was arrested in September 2012 after being caught posing as an army officer) to have partaken in the Boko Haram training of handling weapons, special operations and assassinations in Niger state and his mentioning of other government officials as conspirators with the terrorist group suggests the narrative of local supporters[90].

The porous nature of the Nigerian borders is a good factor to this regard. It could have allowed a free movement of weapons from outside into the country through the borders especially in the northern part where the sentiments of the "Islamic Brotherhood" seem to be very strong. To this regard, some Nigerians speculated that the Boko Haram used such ample opportunity to smuggle in weapons after toppling Libyan government led

---

[88] Cf., Y. Olomojobi, *Islam and Conflict in Northern Nigeria*, 223; J. Adibe, *Nigeria without Nigerians*, 73.

[89] J. Zenn, *Northern Nigeria's Boko Haram*, 34.

[90] J. Zenn, *Northern Nigeria's Boko Haram*, 35.

by Muarmman Gadhafi since a lot of the members of the group were partakers in the fight in Libya. Nevertheless, this speculation has no strong basis despite its existing trace.

From the foregoing, it becomes important to shift our attention to the theories of terrorism. This section aims at exposing the parameters that scholars used in analysing the phenomenon of terrorism around the globe. Can these theories be applicable to the Nigerian situation?

7. Theories of Terrorism

The quest toward understanding the persistent terrorists' violent acts is what has preoccupied the minds of many scholars at the different levels of research and fields of expertise. In this respect, experts have delved into deep research at various respective fields of knowledge in order to find possible solutions to the inferno in question.

Nevertheless, theories of terrorism do not come from a single branch of discipline, but rather they come from a variety of disciplines such as international relations, political science, history, psychology, sociology, criminology and criminal justice, law, victimology, military science, communications studies *et al*. Each of these disciplines, however, draws on a particular research tradition with its goals and scholarly criteria. In like manner, it is essential to equally point out that as there exist multiple definitions of the term "terrorism", so also there exist varieties of theories of terrorism due to the lack of a universally accepted theory by scholars of various disciplines. Nonetheless, let us examine closely few of the theories that are directly related to our study.

7.1 *Psychological Theories*

Within the social science perspective, "violence" though with multiple definitions, is generally perceived as an act that intentionally cause physical harm or injury to another person. But however, this perhaps seems too narrow and restrictive to provide any meaningful description of violence because psychological and emotional harm is also as relevant as physical harm, and that injury is merely an outcome and not a descriptor of the act. Hence, threats as well as overt acts are necessary to be included in the description of violence[91].

---

[91] Cf., R. BORUM, *Psychology of Terrorism*, 9. Dr. Randy Borum is Associate Professor in the Department of Mental Law & Policy University of South Florida. He is a licensed psychologist and is Board-Certified (ABPP) in Forensic Psychology. He is currently a consultant to the US Department of Defence, Department of Homeland Security, Advisory Board

Randy (a psychologist) proposes two major general ways that violence can be caused. First is by multiple factors due to the present of a complex interaction of biological, social/contextual, cognitive, and emotional factors that occur over time. Then secondly, it is caused by a deliberate choice of an action as a strategy that is goal-directed and intended to achieve certain valued outcome for the actor. In this case it is free of any instinctual drive and inevitable psychological and social forces[92]. Despite the elusiveness of the term "terrorism" the discipline of psychology has developed some theories that could be applied to the understanding of terrorist violence. It is against this backdrop that the need to examine closely the following psychological models becomes vital.

7.1.1 Instinct Theory

The word "instinct" refers to an innate pattern of behaviour[93] while Webster's Dictionary refers to it as a natural or acquired tendency[94]. We can thus simply say "instinct" is behaving in a natural way or rather having a tendency of desiring to do something in a particular way. This theory is sub-divided into two approaches; the psychoanalytic and ethology.

The first approach, Psychoanalytic approach is perceived as the most widely recognized theory that addresses the roots of all forms of violence. In this model, Sigmund Freud – an Austrian neurologist that was best known for developing the theories and techniques of psychoanalysis – viewed aggression more generally as an innate and instinctual human trait, which most should outgrow in normal course of human development. It is in this regard, that the psychological motivation of a terrorist is derived from the terrorist's personal dissatisfaction with his life and accomplishments. As a result, he finds his raison d'être in dedicated terrorist action. Having no trace of psychopathy (mental disorder) among the terrorists, they generally see themselves as "true believers" – thereby viewing themselves to be right while others are wrong. As a result, they tend to project their antisocial motivations onto others, creating a polarize "we" versus "they" outlook. The terrorists attribute only evil motives to anyone outside their own group which enables them to dehumanize their victims and thus

---

Member for the FBI's Behavioural Science Unit, an Instructor for the BJA's State and Local Antiterrorism Training (SLATT) Program, and the Principal Investigator on the "Psychology of Terrorism" initiative for US government agency.

[92] R. BORUM, *Psychology of Terrorism*, 11.

[93] CONCISE OXFORD ENGLISH DICTIONARY, 736

[94] WEBSTER'S DICTIONARY AND THESAURUS, 196.

remove any sense of ambiguity from their minds[95]. Freud however, later suggested that humans have the energy of life force called "Eros" and the death force called "Thanatos" that seeks internal balance[96]. From the perspective of Freud's theory therefore, violence is seen as the "displacement" of the death force (instinct) "Thanatos" from self and onto others[97].

Another psychoanalyst from the Neo-Freudian group is Carl Jung[98] who identified the process of shadow projection and scapegoating as the source of violence because the personal unconscious that seeks to repress and hide all those aspects of the self that we don't want to acknowledge, like our fears, feelings of fallibility etc, if not integrated well into the conscious ego, is commonly then projected outward, in the form of violence[99].

The second approach, Ethology is alternatively defined as the scientific study of animal behaviour, especially as it occurs in a natural environment and as the study of human ethos, and its formation[100]. This model holds that aggression arises from a very basic biological need – a "fight instinct" that has had adaptive value as humans have evolved. This is advanced by the ethologist, Konrad Lorenz (an Austrian zoologist, ethologist and ornithologist) who argued that the drive from aggression is innate and that in humans only its mode of expression is learned through exposure to, and interaction with the environment[101].

7.1.2 Drive Theory (Frustration-Aggression)

The drive theory can also be referred to as frustration-aggression hypothesis (FAH hereafter). Frustration here means "being prevented from attaining a goal or engaging in behaviour. In other words, it is a response to frustration as opined by John Chowing Davies (a political psychologist)[102], or blockage of one's goal attainment. The response to this denial or blockage may emerge as a 'fight or flight' situation-as either an aggressive, defensive reaction, or none at all (i.e. either physically or psychologically

---

[95] Cf., D.J. WHITTAKER, "Motivations for Terrorism", 13-14

[96] R. CORRADO, "A Critique of the Mental Disorder", 293-309. Quoted by R. BORUM, *Psychology of Terrorism*, 11.

[97] R. BORUM, *Psychology of Terrorism*, 11.

[98] Carl Jung was a Swiss psychiatrist and psychoanalyst who founded analytical psychology. His work has been influential in many fields of disciplines such as psychiatry, philosophy, anthropology, psychobiology, neuroscience *et al.*

[99] Cf., C. JUNG, *Civilization in Transition*.

[100] Cf., American Heritage Dictionary.

[101] Cf., R. BORUM, *Psychology of Terrorism*, 12.

[102] J.C DAVIES, "Aggression, Violence, Revolution and War", 251.

fleeing, or attempting to ignore the problem, or at least attempting to reduce its perceived importance through dissonance).[103]

This is to say that the main explanation that FAH provides is that aggression is not just undertaken as a natural reaction or instinct as realists and biological theorists assume, but that it is the outcome of frustration and that in a situation where the legitimate desires of an individual is denied either directly or by the indirect consequence of the way the society is structured, the feeling of disappointment may lead such a person to express his anger through violence that will be directed at those he holds responsible or people who are directly related to them[104]. In order to buttress this point, Randy Borum, opines that the frustration-aggression hypothesis is based on the basic premise that aggression produces frustration, and *ipso facto* frustration produces aggression.

However, there is a lacuna because in Borum's opinion, frustration does not inevitably lead to aggression even though it results in problem solving or dependent behaviour, since aggression is known to occur even in the absence of frustration. From the foregoing therefore, it is not justifiable to see frustration alone as a necessary and sufficient causal factor[105]. It is against this backdrop that Leonard Berkowitz[106] in his reformation of the FAH, held that it is only "aversive" (strongly opposed) frustration that leads to aggression[107].

7.2 *Cultural Theory*

In general, cultures shape values and motivate people to actions that seem unreasonable to foreign observers since all human beings are sensitive to threats that are against the values by which they identify themselves. These values include; language, religion, ethnicity *et al.* The possibility therefore of losing any of these values can easily trigger defensive and even xenophobic reactions. The cultural theory therefore emphasizes the role of culturally induced conflict; it shows how enemy images are created from deep-seated attitudes about human action that are learned from early stages of growth in the explanation of conflict.[108] It thus contends that even though there are different forms of identities, the one that is based on

---

[103] Cf., J. HORGAN, "The Search for the Terrorist Personality", 10.

[104] S.A. FALETI, "Theories of Social Conflict", 47-48.

[105] R. BORUM, *Psychology of Terrorism*, 12.

[106] An American Social Psychologist that was best known for his research for altruism and human aggression.

[107] L. BERKOWITZ, "Frustration-Aggression Hypothesis", 59-73.

[108] R. MARC, *The Management of Conflict*, 18.

people's ethnic origin and culture that is learned on the basis of that ethnic origin is one of the most important ways of explaining violent conflict. Identity is thus seen to be the reason for social conflicts that take long time to resolve. Nevertheless, this does not mean that conflict is unavoidable where there are ethnic differences.

The psycho-cultural conflict theorists argue that social conflicts that take long time to resolve become a possibility when some groups are discriminated against or deprived of satisfaction of their basic (material) and psychological (non-material) needs (as these needs are identified in Maslow's theory of "motivation")[109] on the basis of their identity. Religion for example, may be the most volatile of cultural identities because it compasses values deeply held. A threat, therefore, to one's religion puts not only the present at risk but also one's cultural past and the future. Thus, terrorism in the name of religion can be especially violent because the terrorists with religiously motivation view their acts with moral certainty and even divine sanctions.

7.3 *Raw Empirical Theory*

This is more of a statistical theory applied by psychologists in order to explain violence and to identify its predictors. This is also referred to as Risk Factors theory (hence RF). It is a borrowed term from the field of public health, specifically from the discipline of epidemiology (i.e the study of causes and course of diseases). The Risk Factors is technically defined as "... an aspect of personal behaviour or life style, an environmental exposure, or inborn or inherited characteristic which on the basis of epidemiological evidence is known to be associated with health-related condition(s) considered important to prevent[110]. Applying this concept therefore to this study, it implies to any factor of this kind that when present it makes the probability of violence higher than when it is absent.

---

[109] Abraham Harold Maslow was an American psychologist who opined that in humans there are certain needs that are desirable by every human and denial of these needs can easily attract violence. He referred to these needs as "Human Basic Needs" in his Human Motivation Theory. These needs include; psychological, safety, belongingness and love, esteem, and self-actualisation needs. However, he noted that these human basic needs can only be realised or achieved when certain preconditions are met. These preconditions include; freedom of speech, freedom of action that is devoid of others' harm, freedom of expression, freedom to investigate and seek for information, freedom of self-defence, justice, fairness, honesty, and orderliness in a group. Interesting to note is that an attack or threat to these preconditions is an attack or threat to the human basic needs. Hence, it is reacted with a threat (or violence). Cf., A. MASLOW, *Motivation and Personality*, 35-48.

[110] J.M LAST, ed., *A Dictionary of Epidemiology*. Quoted in R. BORUM, *Psychology of Terrorism*, 15-16.

It is imperative to note that risk factors have been classified into two major categories that include; static and dynamic factors. While static factors are factors that are historical, for example, early onset of violence; or dispositional in nature and are unlikely to change over time for instance, gender. Dynamic factors on the other hand, are factors that are typically individual, social or situational factors that often do change. For example, attitudes, associates, and high levels of stress, and, therefore might be more amenable to modification through intervention[111].

However, it is worth noting that these factors may not be the likely predictors when applying them in determining the risk for terrorism because risk factors tend to operate differently at different ages, in different groups, and for different – specific – types of violent behaviour with regards to terrorism. For example, the factors that predict violent behaviour in the urban gang member with a drug addiction often differ from those that predict violence among predatory child molesters or perpetrators of domestic violence[112].

7.4 *Anomie Theory*

This theory was introduced by Émile Durkheim[113] in his book "The Division of Labour in Society in 1893". The concept "Anomie" describes the condition of societal breakdown in respect to the societal breakdown of France in the late 19th century. Due to variety of causes, for Durkheim, some people experienced a perceived collapse of societal rules on how people ought to have behaved with each other. This breakdown of an individual's "construct" – how they perceive their environment – caused them to not know what to expect from one another. The term "Anomie" is thus defined as a state where societal norms (expectations on behaviours) are confused or unclear. For those norms are individual's construct. In this regard, the failure or absence of such societal norms, for Durkheim results to one's engagement in deviant behaviour such as terrorism.

To make distinct his theory, Durkheim proposed two concepts regarding societal interaction. This includes mechanical and organic societies. For him, all societies evolve from a simple (non-specialized form) which he referred to as "mechanic", toward a highly complex and specialized form called "organic". In a mechanical society (i.e a simple and non-specialized form of society) people generally are able to follow simple rules of

---

[111] Cf., R. BORUM – al., "Assessing and Managing Violence Risk", 205-215

[112] Cf., R. BORUM, *Psychology of Terrorism*, 16.

[113] David Émile Durkheim was a French sociologist who rose to prominence in the late 19th and early 20th centuries, and was credited as being one of the principal founders of modern sociology along with Karl Marx and Max Weber

interaction, and the expectations of the simple society are not too taxing on the individual. Social bonds between individuals in the society are likely to be personal. People behave and think more or less alike, and also more or less perform the same work tasks such as hunting, fishing, fathering, farming et cetera, with the same group-oriented goals such as to provide for their family needs, groups or clan.

Whereas, in the organic society (i.e a complex and specialized form of society), the work, norms, and expectations of the individuals become more complex than that of the mechanical society. In the organic society, people are no longer tied to one another by close bonds necessary for their survival. Social bonds are attenuated and impersonal, and in the event that these bonds are attenuated, they become so fragile that the individual's social construct becomes more at risk to external factors that are beyond the individual's control. For example, such external factors like economic, political, joblessness, misfortune et cetera can easily trigger him and cause his social construct to collapse[114]. For Durkheim therefore, social disruption such as economic depression, lack of job opportunity or high rate of unemployment and other pressures that adversely affects family lives can cause greater anomie at the individual level. As a result, individuals easily engage themselves in high rate of deviance crime and violence.

Contextualizing Durkheim's theory of anomie within the modern terrorism, it will mean that some people engage themselves in violent extremist behaviour due to a high sense of a perceived collapse of the societal norms. The society is no longer matching up to the individual's or group's political, economic, or moral expectations. As a result, violence becomes the last option which in most cases it is directed at the symbol of authority or directed to those related to the authority.

7.5 *Labelling Theory*

Advancing on and building upon the Durkheim's anomie theory, academics in the first half of the 20th century began considering other potential causes of deviant and violent behaviour. "Labelling" was one of the most potent of these theories. The term "labelling" is defined as an act of society attaching pejorative (condemnatory/derogatory) names to certain acts exhibited by certain members of the society or by a sub-group. By implications, the very act of labelling such acts or sub-groups as deviant, serves as a causative factor in promoting anti-social behaviour. Here, we shall examine few of the leading champions of this theory.

---

[114] Cf., G. KHALIL, "Etiology of Deviant Behaviour", 24.

7.5.1 Frank Tannenbaum

Frank Tannenbaum[115], in his theory contended that when a society defines a particular act as "evil" such act is actually transformed into the definition of the actor as evil. This happens, when it undergoes a process that is divided into three stages: In the first stage, Tannenbaum held that an individual finds himself engage in deviant and violent behaviour when he fails to integrate himself into the society. It is at this first stage that the individual in question is labelled (tagged), and this drives him towards (or away from) options for his future life[116]. In other words, the individual is conceived to be what the society has labelled his act.

While the second stage shifts gradually from the definition of the individual as evil, and as result, every act of his either ordinary or extraordinary is looked upon with suspicion. The third stage on the other hand, is the stage that the individual himself begins to have a different concept of his own self. In other words, the individual has gone slowly from a sense of grievance and injustice, of being unduly maltreated and punished, to a recognition that the definition of him as a human being is different from that of other boys in his neighbourhood, his school, his street and wherever he finds himself within the society. Thus, the change of his self-concept *vis-à-vis* changes his worldview of life[117].

Aligning his theory alongside with terrorism, Tannenbaum applied the same three stages as he contended that once the individual is associated with deviance or even with a deviant group from the society's perspective, he is labelled as deviant and thus viewed as a bad and "unredeemable" human being. In other words, when the society labels the individual and/or the group he is associated with as "terrorist" anything he and/or the group does is seen through that lens of terrorism, and at the same time from the perspective of the individual and/or the group, there exists a simultaneous shift of recognizing his status as a human being as different from others and thus identifies himself and his acts as being aligned with the labelled group.

---

[115] Frank Tannenbaum was an American academic that concerned primarily with delinquency as a learned behaviour, and much of his work focused on why and how young boys deviate from societal norms. See G. KHALIL, "Etiology of Deviant Behaviour", 25.

[116] Cf., F. TANNENBAUM, *Crime and Community*, 20.

[117] Cf., F. TANNENBAUM, *Crime and Community*, 17.

7.5.2 Edwin Lemert

Lemert[118], held that "only human beings define, regulate, and control the behaviour of other human beings"[119]. In stating his theory of labelling, Lemert made a distinction and linkage between primary and secondary deviance. For him, primary deviance can be explained by various models while secondary deviance is explained by labelling[120]. Primary deviation is assumed to arise in a wide variety of social, cultural, and psychological contexts in which one may be seen as an outsider as a result of the variety of factors which include; race, gender, religion, nationality et cetera. These for Lemert cannot be causative factors of deviant behaviour but rather the society's reaction to those elements of primary deviance defines one's behaviour as deviant.

In respect to modern terrorism and extreme violence, Lemert opined that when individuals follow the simple basic rules of the society such as "work hard, get an education, and you will be successful" and yet they are denied meaningful participation in the society, or when paths to success in the society are not predictable, transparent, or reliable for them because of their status as outsiders (i.e. due to elements that constitute primary deviance which are beyond the individual's control, such as race, ethnicity, religion, gender et cetera, then friction occurs and can lead to a deviant behaviour).

7.5.3 Howard S. Becker

Becker's[121] concept of deviance is best seen in terms of society's reactions to the conduct and individuals in question. In other words, the idea of deviance is always a label affixed to acts and persons by social audiences to the behaviour in question. "The deviant is one to whom that label has been successfully applied, deviant behaviour is the behaviour that people so labelled"[122]. For Becker therefore, labelling is especially causative when applied to an "outsider". Society seeks to label outsiders, so it may better understand the outsiders in question. However, such applied label could be inaccurate, misleading or even patently false. To put it in clear terms, Becker primarily looked at the deviance from a perspective of "insider"

---

[118] Edwin McCarthy Lemert, was a leading sociologist of his time. He taught primarily at the University of California, first in Los Angeles, then in Davis.

[119] E.M LEMERT, *Human Deviance, Social Problems*, 29.

[120] E.M LEMERT, *Human Deviance, Social Problems*, 48.

[121] Howard Saul Becker is a widely published American sociologist known for his studies of occupations, education, deviance, and art.

[122] H.S BECKER, *Outsiders' Studies in the Sociology of Deviance*, 9.

and "outsider" relationship. For him, it is the insiders who make the rules, and judge the outsiders based on the extent they deviate from those rules. As a result, such judgment by the insiders of the outsiders could block certain opportunities to the outsiders. He thus further stressed that the dynamic relationship between the insiders and the outsiders is on-going because the outsiders today may find themselves through a social shift to the insiders tomorrow and vice versa, and outsiders, if successful, may become tomorrow's bureaucrats (the ultimate insiders).

7.5.4 Edwin Schur

Schur[123] in the process of criminal trial referred to as "status degradation ceremonies" for example, it allows the society to label someone who was previously innocuous/innocent to now be labelled as a criminal. He opines that once the person has gone through that "ceremony of status degradation" and he is labelled as a criminal, the society gets to re-examine his past events and behaviour, and then interprets such past events and behaviour to fit its new label of that person. For him therefore, "deviance is viewed not as a static entity but rather as a continuously shaped and re-shaped outcome of dynamic processes of social interaction[124]. In succinct terms, Schur's concept of "retrospective interpretation" means that once the society has applied its label, it will reconsider the actor, and where the label is negative (or deviant), the society is likely to deem that the actor was deviant all along (whether that labelling is accurate or not will not stop the society from its reconsideration). As a result, the society's reconsideration will discount previous evidence, and evaluates the individual based on his new label as deviant. The society's view of the entire actor's previous acts or conduct will thus be skewed by this new label.

In applying Schur's labelling theory to terrorism, a two-way street is thus involved:

a. The terrorists engage in labelling in order to dehumanize their intended targets. For example, when a violent extremist labels his intended target as an "other", it justifies his action to destroy his target without a remorse bearing in his mind that those individuals within his target do not deserve any protection but destruction.

---

[123] Edwin Schur is another leading American sociologist who reevaluated and expanded the application of labelling theory in the 1970s. He introduced the concept of "retrospective interpretation that involves the mechanisms by which reactors come to view deviators or suspected deviators in a totally new light". Cf., E. SCHUR, *Labelling Deviant Behaviour*, 52-56.

[124] E. SCHUR, *Labelling Deviant Behaviour*, 8.

b. On the other hand, the authorities can engage in labelling an individual or group what he/it is not. This is possible because labelling makes it easier for authorities to identify and discriminate against the targets of their operations. It also allows the authorities to rally popular support both locally and internationally for the particular target/label in question. This kind of labelling occurs mostly when it is applied in haste, haphazardly, or inappropriately[125].

7.6 *Structural Conflict Theory*

The structural conflict theory is divided into two main sub-orientations; radical structural theory and liberal structuralism. The radical structural theory was championed by scholars such as Karl Marx (a German economist and sociologist), Friedrich Engels (a German philosopher and social scientist), Vladimir Ilyich Lenin (a Russian political theorist) *et al.* While the liberal structuralism is championed by Ross who is currently known as William Rand Kenan Jr. – a professor of political science that is specialized in conflict theory and management), Scarborough and John Galtung (a Norwegian sociologist, mathematician, and the principal founder of the discipline of peace and conflict studies). The main argument of the structural conflict theory is that conflict is built into the particular way societies are structured and organized.

The theory looks at social problems like political and economic exclusion, injustice, poverty, disease, exploitation, inequity et cetera as sources of conflict. For the structuralists, the conflict occurs because of the exploitative and unjust nature of human societies, domination of one class by another et cetera. This case is made by scholars such as Friedrich Engels, Karl Marx, Joseph Lenin, and Mao Tse Tung, who blame capitalism for being an exploitative system based on its relations of production and the division of society into the proletariat and bourgeoisie. The exploitation of the proletariat and lower class under capitalism creates conflict, and as a result, such exploitation causes conflict.

Structural theory, therefore, lays its emphasis on how the competing interests of groups tie conflict directly into the social, economic, and political organization of society as well as the nature and strength of social networks within and between community groups. It is in this light that Ross noted that in situations for instance, where economic and political discrimination and weak kinship ties are the defining characteristics of a society, the chances that negative forms of conflict will be higher than

---

[125] G. KHALIL, "Etiology of Deviant Behaviour", 31-32.

in situations where the conditions are exact opposite[126]. In other words, when social, political economic and cultural processes are monopolized by a group, it creates the enabling conditions that make people to adopt adversarial approaches to conflict.

In another perspective, Kothari (a former Director of the United Nation's University's Programme on Peace and Global Transformation,) opines that resource control is a major cause of conflict between individuals and groups within political systems and between nations. In his words, he succinctly states that "the control and use of (natural) resources lies at the heart of the deepening crisis in the world today"[127]. Kothari describes this crisis as separating the world into axes of material comfort and of deficiency with a concentration of poverty and scarcity and unemployment and deprivation in one large sector of mankind (underdeveloped countries) and of overabundance and overproduction in another much smaller section (developed countries)[128].

Scarborough on the other hand, examines situations for instance, where existing structures are tilted in favour of one group while putting the other(s) at a disadvantaged positions; where cultures are seen as exclusive; where holders of certain powers or privileges are unwilling to acknowledge the rights of others to be different; or where people find it difficult to identify with political and economic ideas of a political regime, the chances are that conflict will emerge and escalate if nothing is done to correct such anomalies. In respect to internal conflict however, Faleti observes that problems of overpopulation, economic underdevelopment, unintegrated social and political institutions, as well as demographic factors that put pressure on human settlements and available resources are the main factors responsible for the emergence of internal conflict[129].

7.7 *Economic Theory*

Economic factor of conflict aggravation in most cases is misconceived by people because people in conflict zones are often assumed to be fighting over, and not about, something that is material when especially such a volatile zone is within an underdeveloped country or within an area of scarce resources. In this case, the question that must be asked is, what is the nature of the conflict, is it as a result of greed (deliberate intention to 'corner' something for the public to be private) or is it as a result of grievance

---

[126] R. MARC, *The management of Conflict*, 4.

[127] K. RAJNI, "The North-South Issue", 6.

[128] Cf., S.A. FALETI, "Theories of Social Conflict", 44.

[129] Cf., S.A. FALETI, "Theories of Social Conflict", 44.

(anger arising over some feelings of injustice perpetuated)? Bearing this in mind, it is observed that some people (commonly referred to as 'conflict entrepreneurs') actually benefit from chaos: while the overwhelming majority of the population are affected by the negative impacts of conflict; the leaders of armed formations that are actually perpetrating the violence often profit from the chaos; (and) that while the prospect of pecuniary gains is seldom the principal incentive of rebellion, it can become for some insurgent groups, a preferred state of affairs[130].

Examining closely the economic motivating factor in conflict or violence, Breda and Malone hold that across the ages, conflicts have come to be seen as having a "functional utility" and are embedded in economic disparities. War, the crisis stage of internal conflicts, has sometimes become a vast private and profit-making enterprise. They further contended that even though issues in conflict may later be packaged as resulting from ideological, racial or even religious (value) differences; these represent at the most basic level, a contest for control over economic assets, resources or systems.[131] Economic theory thus highlights resources, and to that extent, is close to the structural theory already examined above.

7.8 *Relational Theory*

The relational theory attempts to provide explanations for violent conflicts between groups by exploring sociological, political economic and historical relationships between such groups. Thus, the believe here is that cultural and value differences as well as group interests all influence relationships between individuals and groups in different ways. At sociological level, differences between cultural values are a challenge to individual or group identity formation processes and create the tendency to see others as intruders who have to be prevented from encroaching upon established cultural boundaries.

In the arena of political economy for instance, it identifies power and the advantages that it confers as a key source of tension between different interest groups within a political system. In situations where multiple groups share a common resource that is fixed in nature, the chances that each will attempt to eliminate, neutralize or injure the 'other', or monopolize such a resource is as high as the tendency to enter into a negative relationship[132].

---

[130] S.G. BEST, *Introduction to Peace and Conflict Studies in West Africa*, 45.

[131] Cf., S.G. BEST, *Introduction to Peace and Conflict Studies in West Africa*, 46.

[132] See the works of C. LEWIS, *The Functions of Social Conflict*, and Z. MAOZ, *Paths to Conflict*, respectively.

Within the perspective of history, conflicts grow out of past history of conflict between groups that has led to the development of negative stereotypes, racial intolerance and discrimination. Such a history of negative exchanges between groups may make it difficult for efforts to integrate different ethnic and religious groups within the society to succeed because their past interactions make it difficult for them to trust one another. In like manner, in the light of favouritism, the fact that 'others' are perceived as different make us feel they are entitled to less or are inferior by reason of cultural values or skin colour. This, therefore, disrupts the flow of communication between us and them and to the extent, twists perceptions that we have about each other. In the same vein, the acknowledgement that two or more groups have to compete for the same resource (whatever it may be) creates an enabling condition for the increase of the chances of conflict whereby interaction between the groups in question on the nature of resource sharing may fuel the crisis/conflict.[133]

7.9 *Systemic Theory*

Systemic theory provides a socio-structural explanation for the emergence of violent social conflicts. This theory holds that reasons for any social conflict lie in the social context within which it occurs. It is against this backdrop that it is observed, "any analytic penetration of the behaviour characterized as 'purposive political violence' must utilize as its tool a conception of the social context in which it occurs"[134]. In this regard, our attention thus is focused on the social factors and effects of large-scale changes in social, political and economic processes that would usually guide against instability. It is therefore worthy to note that the systemic factors that lead to changes in people's material comfort include environmental degradation that reduces access to source of livelihood, uncontrolled population growth especially in urban centres, resource scarcity and its allocation through lopsided political processes and competition, the negative effect of colonial and cold war legacies, breakdown of cherished values and traditions that play crucial social control functions, widespread poverty in the midst of plenty, the domination and marginalization of minority groups by the majority, and ethnicity. These all constitute systemic causes of conflict in a society.

Furthermore, this theory, also seeks to explain the relationship between modernization and political disorder and see movements between different

---

[133] S.A. FALETI, "Theories of Social Conflict", 53.

[134] S.A. FALETI, "Theories of Social Conflict", 53.

periods of economic and political history as containing large amounts of 'pull factors', tension and crises that create conditions of internal conflict and instability. It is against this backdrop that Lucian Pye[135] observed the following as the six key issues within modernization projects that generate conflicts. These include; identity crisis, legitimacy crisis, penetration crisis, participation crisis, integration crisis, and distribution crisis. In the effort therefore to cope with these different challenges and crises of modernization, most governments that find it difficult to gain the legitimacy needed to attract support from the people usually resort to unconditional means and force rather than processes that are in line with the rule of law, in an effort to suppress the legitimate demands of the people, prevent opposition and civil society groups from criticizing policies that they do not agree with, and generally attempt to dictate the terms on which peace will be attained[136].

8. Conclusion

From the foregoing, this chapter tried to explore the historical development of terrorism in brief from the first century when it was officially put into record to the present age. This development did not only bring a metamorphosis of the tactics of "victim selection" – which was justified by the perpetrators due to its minimal impact with the regard to humanitarian – but it also brought the tactics of modern soft target and indiscriminate attacks on the innocent civilians thereby giving it a new face from the dimension of conventional war to the dimension of unconventional war of terrorism.

It also unravelled the shift of interest from radical socio-revolutionary, leftist and anarchist ideologies to radical nationalism (especially separatist ethno-nationalism), and religious extremism which today have become the two most influential ideological pillars of terrorism of the twenty-first century, that *ipso facto* gave birth to the present religious extremists whose constant violent activities continue to pose serious threats to local and international security.

---

[135] Lucian Pye was a political scientist, sinologist and comparative politics expert considered one of the leading China scholars in the United States. Educated at Carleton College and Yale University, Pye chose to focus on the characteristics of specific cultures in forming theories of political development of modernization of Third World nations, rather than seeking universal and overarching theories like most political scientists. As a result, he became regarded as one of the foremost contemporary practitioners and proponents of the concept of political culture and political psychology.

[136] Cf., S.A. FALETI, "Theories of Social Conflict", 53-54.

It is to this effect that Ekaterina Stepanova postulates five general features that are shared by most of the terrorist groups that are guided by an ideology with a strong religious imperative. These include; the presence of clerical figures in a group's leadership, the use of sacred text to justify armed violence, the use of religious rituals such as self-sacrifice and the cult of martyrdom as acts of faith, the acceptance of those who witness only to Allah as the only believers, and lastly the conception of religion and politics as inseparable entities. This implies therefore, that the presence of these factors in any terrorist group defines the terrorists' aim and objective. Against this backdrop, the Al-Qaida is a vivid example from which emanated other Islamic extremists' groups such as al-Shabaab, Hezbollah, IS, Boko Haram *et al.*

Owing to the ideology and philosophy of the Boko Haram whose intent is to replace modern state formation with the traditional Islamic state, believing that western values run contrary to Islamic values and westernization is the mother of evil, the destruction of the modern state institutions becomes therefore a necessary duty for its members. As a result, the establishment of the Shari'a law becomes inevitable. This has placed Nigeria as a circular state into a tight corner that its image has been dented as a result of the perpetrated terrorist activities of the group which in no doubt have affected the nation and its citizens in all ramifications. Lives and properties worth trillions of dollars have been destroyed and thus brought a drastic retardation in the nation's socio-economic, political, cultural and religious growth particularly in the northeast. Against this backdrop, it is an over simplification to say that the Boko Haram extremist activities also pose a serious security challenge *vis-à-vis* a threat to Nigerian national unity as a state, and *ipso facto* to the missionary activities of the Church in the northern region of the country.

While the Nigerian government therefore continues to confront the inferno relentlessly, it is imperative to ask the following disturbing question; what provided the ample opportunity which served as a fertile ground that necessitated the emergence of the Boko Haram monstrous group? In response to this question, the need to understand the historical development of Nigeria becomes thus expedient. Hence, this constitutes the focal discussions of the second chapter, with the view to examine the nature of the existing relationship between Christians and Muslims.

However, the above stated theories are strong pointers toward the understanding of the persistent terrorist violent acts in the region. In this regard, it is obvious that the theories in question are intertwined with one another and they vividly give reasons for the expression of terrorism. Although, all

76

the parameters are valid, but analysing each of them side by side with the peculiarity of the reality in northern Nigeria, the cultural theory explains distinctively the persistent terrorist violent acts of the Boko Haram in the region. Owing to the fact that Islam being the religion to have come into existence before the advent of Christianity in the region, the presence of any religion particularly Christianity is therefore a great threat to its Islamic values. As a result, persistent religious friction or conflict abounds.

CHAPTER II

Nigeria: A Historical Overview and an Encounter of Christianity and Islam in Its Northern Region

1. Introduction

The thrust of this chapter is basically on Nigeria. It focuses on the historical development of the country, with special attention to its socio-economic, political and religious growth. However, it is essential to quickly state here that bearing in mind the vast and diverse nature of Nigeria, its full details of historical development are beyond the scope of this work. But attention will be given to some key areas that are significance to the study.

Being a pluralistic state, much attention will be given to the influence of the colonial administrators on the emergence and development of the country's northern region. Some considerations will also be made regarding the role and strategies of missionaries in the establishment of both the Christian and Islamic religions. Against this backdrop, efforts are made toward examining the existing relationship between Christians and Muslims living side by side with each other in the region, from the pre-colonial era down to the present age.

The chapter also seeks to explore the underlying factors responsible for the constant intractable violence that continues to menace the peace and socio-economic and religious development of the region. As a result, the exploration of possible factors that serve as fertile ground becomes expedient. Bearing in mind however, that Islamic extremism and its challenges is the thrust of this work, the chapter therefore goes further to expose with scholarly objectivity some religious crises that obviously took place in the northern region as a result of the expression of religious extremism by adherents of the religion in question. It then examines the factors responsible for the religious crises. By way of doing justice to the work, the chapter further seeks to understand the possible challenges that such religious crises pose on the life of the Church with particular interest on the missionary activities of the Church within the region under review. Thereafter, a résumé of the chapter is made by way of conclusion.

2. **Nigeria***: A Historical Overview from Pre-Colonial to Post-Colonial Era*

The history of Nigeria is characterized by so many significant events. One of such events is the activities of the European explorers that led to the coming of the colonialists and their subsequent taking over the control of the vast landscape of the most populated black African country called Nigeria. With the exploration of the British explorers; Mungo Park (1805), Hugh Clapperton (1820), the Lander brothers (1830), Eduard Vogel and Eduard R. Flegel (1850), the mysteries of the interior pathways of the river Niger was finally unravelled and proved that the Niger was one of the longest and the most promising trading rivers in the world. As a result, it paved the way for the European traders who were completely unfamiliar with the complicated series of rivers, streams, and inlets that made up the Niger Delta to start exploring such a new adventure. With their presence on the Niger however, the role of the African middle men who were solely in charge of controlling the trade in hinterlands goods was gradually taken over, and at the end of the day, they (African middle men) were by-passed by the Europeans[1].

Nigeria, being a multi-ethnic, cultural nation and a religious fertile ground, was colonized by the British at the turn of the 20th century, although evidence of its habitation, dates back to the tenth century B.C[2]. It is one of the West African countries, below the Sahara Desert, that has a long Atlantic Ocean coastline[3].

Being a colony of the British government, with three protectorates north, south and east which were amalgamated in 1914 to constitute what is called "Nigeria", it gained its independence on October 1, 1960. It is divided by two navigable main rivers, the River Niger (third longest river in Africa which runs for 730 miles through Nigeria that enters the country via the present Kebbi State in the northwest and pours into the Gulf of Guinea through its many branches in the Niger Delta in southern Rivers and Delta States) and then River Benue (the Niger's main tributary) which comes from the northeast, and confluences at its centre known as Lokoja, Kogi State.[4] These two rivers as it were, naturally divided the country into three geo-political regions with twelve states that include; north, west and east[5], with a high concentration of three major ethnic groups; Hausa in the north, Igbo in the east, and Yoruba in the west[6].

---

[1] Cf., T. Falola – M.M. Heaton, *A History of Nigeria*, 90-93.

[2] T. Falola – M.M. Heaton, *A History of Nigeria*, 16.

[3] See Appendix B.

[4] See Appendix C.

[5] See Appendix D.

[6] See Appendix E.

After the independence, Nigerians took full responsibility of its governance, making it a federal republic with its capital territory at Lagos which was however, relocated to Abuja (the centre of the country) in 1991 as its new Federal Capital Territory (hence FCT). It has three tiers of government bureaucracy – federal, state and local – with each tier guaranteed certain responsibilities by the constitution of the nation. To this effect, Nigeria constitutionally is a secular democratic nation that guarantees the right to the freedom of religious beliefs and worship[7].

The above stated three geo-political regions have today been further subdivided into six geo-political zones that comprise of 36 states and the FCT (Abuja). These include: North Central (known as the "middle belt" which is made up of 6 states: Benue, Kogi, Kwara, Nasarawa, Niger, Plateau and the FCT – Abuja); North East (the flashing point of the Boko Haram. It is made up of 6 states: Adamawa, Bauchi, Borno, Gombe, Taraba and Yobe States); North West (made up of 7 states: Jigawa, Kaduna, Kano, Katsina, Kebbi, Sokoto and Zamfara States); South East (comprises of 5 states: Abia, Anambra, Ebonyi, Enugu and Imo States); South-South (made up of 6 states: Akwa Ibom, Cross River, Bayelsa, Rivers, Delta and Edo States); and South West (made up of 6 states: Ekiti, Lagos, Ogun, Ondo, Osun and Oyo States.

Being the most populous Blackman nation in the world, it is estimated in 2017 to have an approximate population of 190 million people[8], with over 350 ethnic/linguistic groups[9]. To this effect, it ranks the number 7 in the world list of countries with high population density. Geo-linguistically, three national languages are officially recognized and spoken in each of the three regions; Hausa in the North, Yoruba in the West and Igbo in the East, while the English language is generally spoken in all the regions as the official national language since 1960. The Pidgin language – a combination of indigenous languages and English developed through a long time of contact with British traders and later with colonial authorities – is also commonly used in all the regions especially among the commoners[10].

---

[7] The 1999 Nigerian Constitution, section 38, paragraph 1, states: "Every person shall be entitled to freedom of thought, conscience and religion, including freedom to change his religion or belief and freedom (either alone or in community with others) and in public or in private, to manifest and propagate his religion or belief in worship, teaching, practice and observance".

[8] This figure was based on the United Nations estimates of the year in question. See NIGERIAN POPULATION.

[9] See Appendix E.

[10] T. FALOLA – M.M. HEATON, *A History of Nigeria*, 4.

Although, agriculture forms the basis of the economic activity and life-style for most Nigerians it also provides the nation with surplus food crops for both domestic and export purposes. The nation is blessed with abundant mineral wealth which includes coal, iron, tin, columbite, lead, copper, zinc and small amount of gold, silver and diamonds. However, since the 1970s to the present day the nation has rely heavily on petroleum as its major source of income thereby neglecting other resources. As a result of this over-reliance on petroleum, it has paved the way to the high political struggle for resource control thereby giving room to greed and corruption whose end result is injustice and poverty amidst plenty.

With regard to religion, the religious landscape of Nigeria is complex, and its religious demography remains undetermined due to its sensitivity as regards Christian-Muslim relationship. To this effect, religion and ethnicity were excluded from the year 2006 in the national population census. Although, in most situations, figures are always manipulated based on the user's interest of religious affiliation, it is however, commonly accepted that Christianity and Islam are the two major religions while the adherents to the indigenous traditional religion (ATR) form the minority. While the Hausa/Fulani region is chiefly Islamic, the Igbo region is Christianity, and the Yoruba region has a mixture of both Islam and Christianity, but in all regions the ATR exist in small number[11].

The navigation between religion and politics in Nigeria has greatly centralized the place of religion in the development of the nation. This is replete in the virulent contest for the sharing of the 'national cake'. As such, government moves are closely monitored by both Christians and Muslims and any perceived favouritism of one religious' group over the other is often challenged with disdain by the aggrieved religion. This political significance of religion, coupled with the growing uncompromising Muslim and Christian activism, has thus led to the increasingly damaged cordiality between the adherents of the two major religions, thereby producing a growing culture of intolerance, distrust, suspicion, hate and religious violence, predominantly in Northern Nigeria[12].

Against this backdrop, it is important to note that religious conflicts have therefore revolved mainly around the activities and relationships between Christians and Muslims. These conflicts have increased in number, frequency and intensity, resulting in the loss of lives, destruction of property, fears, distrust, suspicion, displacement of people, and constituting a major hindrance to the development of the nation. To this effect, we shall

---

[11] P. JENKINS, *The Next Christendom*, 173.

[12] A. ADOGAME, "Nigeria," 329-330.

examine below some of these religious conflicts that have heinously threatened the process of Nigerian nationhood, peace and unity. But nonetheless, it is imperative to first look at the nature of the northern Nigeria and the advent of these two major religions in Nigeria but particularly in the north, bearing in mind their respective methods of evangelization.

3. Advent of Christianity and Islam in Nigeria

As noted above and depending on the region, Nigeria is a home to a variety of religions. This situation accentuates regional and ethnic distinctions and has often been seen as a source of sectarian conflict amongst the population. Even though, the country is apparently divided equally between Islam and Christianity in the north and south respectively, whereby Christians are said to be 40% in population, Muslims 50% and Indigenous Beliefs 10%,[13] it is evident that across its regions, there is widespread belief, albeit suppressed for political reasons, in traditional religious practices. Going down memory lane however, Islam has a long history in the country. Established in the seventh century Arabia, it spread at a remarkable pace in the Middle East and North Africa, then to the Western Africa[14]. Finally, it arrived in Nigeria in the eleventh century through the Northern region when the king of Kanem, Humai, is said to have converted[15].

Although, there was a contact made as far back as the eighth century by the traders plying the trans-Saharan routes with North African Muslims and West Africans resulted to the emergence of a small Muslim community in Kanem-Borno Kingdom[16] (the oldest Islamic community in Nigeria) in the northeast. During the reign of Dunama Dibbalemi in the thirteenth century (who led *jihads* – holy wars), Islam further made substantial inroads into the hinterland of the Empire. Thereafter, it spread out to the

---

[13] INDEX MUNDI, "Nigeria Demographics Profile 2016".

[14] M. IWUCHUKWU, *Muslim-Christian Dialogue*, 2-4.

[15] T. FALOLA – M.M. HEATON, *A History of Nigeria*, 29.

[16] The Kanem-Borno Empire around the Lake Chad basin existed from the 9th until the 19th century. It had a large territory and extended into areas of present-day countries that include Niger, Chad, Cameroon and Nigeria. The Borno part was created in the 14th century. Kanem-Borno functioned as an independent Islamic state until the 19th century when warlord and slave trader Rabih Zubayr, a fleeing Sudanese rebel, conquered large parts of Central Africa including Kanem-Borno. In 1900 however Rabih was defeated in present day northern Cameroon by the French who wanted to extend their influence into the interior of Africa. The remnants of the Kanem-Borno Empire were divided between the British (Nigeria) and French (Niger, Chad) colonial parts of West and Central Africa. Cf., ENCYCLOPAEDIA BRITANNICA, "Rābih az-Zubayr".

main Hausaland[17] during the reign of the ruler of Kano Empire Ali Yaji (1349-1385) and became institutionalized in 1500[18]. The success of this spread however, is often attributed to three common factors that include; commerce, missionary evangelization, and political expansionism[19].

In another development, the massive trading and commercial activities of the period under review also saw the spread of Islam in the other regions. For instance, during the reign of Mansa Musa (1312-1337) of the Mali Empire, Islam was introduced to the Yoruba land in the west while in the east (the Igbo land) it was introduced in the 1930s, notably in Nsukka[20]. At this juncture, it is necessary to state here that with the massive jihads carried out, the seed of hatred was hence sown between Muslims and other minority tribes who refused forceful conversion. To this effect, important to note thus, is the Jihad of Uthman dan Fodio[21] in the nineteenth century (a

---

[17] The Hausaland according to legend, refers to the seven states named after the seven sons of Bawo (the son to Bayajida); Biram, Daura, Katsina, Zazzau (Zaria), Kano, Rano, and Gobir. These sons of Bawo became the eponymous founders of the "legitimate seven" which was commonly known as Hausa Bakwai (seven Hausa). It was these seven states that constituted the Hausaland. However, the historiography of the cultural and political hegemony of the Hausaland assigned the title Banza Bakwai (illegitimate seven). They were called Banza Bakwai because they were not originally/authentically Hausa, but they were adopted into the household of the Hausa people. These include; Zamfara, Kebbi, Gwari, Yauri, Nupe, Ilorin (dominated by Yoruba tribe), and Kwararafa (Jukun). They formed part of the Sokoto Caliphate. It is interesting to note that Bayajida came from Baghdad via Kanem-Borno to Daura. According to legend, while in Daura, Bayajida exhibited an act of heroism by killing a very big snake at the city well which prevented the Daura people from accessing its water. By way of appreciation, his heroism earned him the queen of Daura's hand in marriage, and thus had the son Bawo. See the work of: C.C. IFEMESIA, *States of Central Sudan*, 72-112.

[18] It should be noted that at this period of 1500, Islam was not generally accepted by all the Hausa/Fulani. It was however, a religion of the elites.

[19] M. IWUCHUKWU, *Muslim-Christian Dialogue*, 1.

[20] Y. OLOMOJOBI, *Islam and Conflict in Northern Nigeria*, 2-3.

[21] Uthman dan Fodio was a Fulani Islamic scholar and leader of the Islamic revolution that established the Sokoto Caliphate in northern Nigeria in the nineteenth century. He was born in 1754 and educated in the Hausa state of Gobir. Although dan Fodio subscribed to the Sufi Qadiriyya order, his major spiritual and religious mentor was a Tuareg from Agades, Mallam Jibril ibn Umar, who held radical and extreme views, including the use of *jihad* (a holy war) to achieve a just government. He was disturbed by the widespread syncretism and paganism afflicting Islam in Hausaland at his time. Hence, reformation became imperative to him as a matter of duty. To achieve this reality, dan Fodio developed a group of followers known as "the community" by late 18th century, who subscribed to his vociferous calls for a purification of the political and religious make-up of the region. Relations between dan Fodio and the King of Gobir deteriorated over the King's refusal to institute sweeping Islamic reforms. In 1804 dan Fodio fled from Gobir after an attempt had been made on his life. His followers went with

Fulani scholar and the founder of the Sokoto Caliphate)[22], which became the focal point of Islam in Nigeria, and particularly in the north[23].

Christianity on the other hand, came much later despite the aborted attempts made in the past. With regard to history, Christian missionary activity in Nigeria in general dates back to over five hundred years ago, given the impetus by the Papal Bull of demarcation of 1455 by Pope Nicholas V, which eventually empowered Portugal to take control of all commercial and spiritual influences over Africa[24]. To this effect, it suggests that the Catholic Missionaries were the first missionaries to have arrived in Nigeria. The efforts started in Benin Kingdom when the Portuguese opened a trading centre at Benin Port of Givato. As a result, the first Portuguese priests from the diocese of Lisbon were sent by the king of Portugal in 1472 in the company of some Portuguese merchants to evangelize and trade with the Benin Kingdom (the present Edo state of the south-south geopolitical zone of Nigeria) but it ended a fruitless mission due to little or no impact on the Edo people, and the inability of the missionaries to understand the indigenous religion which was closely attached to the Benin kinship[25].

---

him and organized a revolution against the king. Later in the year dan Fodio declared a *jihad* against the heretical Hausa rulers. Over the next decade dan Fodio and his followers toppled the Hausa dynasties in most states in northern Nigeria (stretching from Gobir to present-day Cameroon – excluding cities of Kanem-Borno Empire – and from Agades in present-day Niger Republic to Ilorin – the Northern axis of South-Western Nigeria). He replaced them with Fulani emirs, thus bringing into existence the Sokoto Caliphate, which ruled the region for the next century. It is important to note that after the *jihad*, the Islamic leadership he set up was a Sunni. In 1812 dan Fodio divided the administration of the territories under his control between his brother Abdullahi and his son Muhammadu Bello and retired from public life and thereafter he died in 1817. Cf., R.A. Adeleye, *Power and Diplomacy in Northern Nigeria*, 31-33; T. Falola – M.M. Heaton, *A History of Nigeria*, xxiv.

[22] The Sokoto Caliphate was one of the largest Empires of West Africa in 19th century. It covered parts of present-day Burkina Faso, Niger, northern Nigeria and Cameroon. The Empire was founded by Uthman Dan Fodio, its first Sultan and a radical Fulani Muslim cleric as just mentioned above. He gathered disenchanted Hausa and Fulani behind him and conquered large parts of the region. After Dan Fodio's death in 1817 the Caliphate was divided into Western (Gwandu as capital) and Eastern (Sokoto as capital) parts, but eventually Muhammad Bello, Dan Fodio's son was recognized as second Sultan and gained control over all of the Caliphate. The Caliphate became the centre of power in the region but disintegrated by the 1880s through internal rivalry. French and British colonial troops conquered its territory in 1903. See A. Mulders, "The Impact of Persistent Violence on the Church", 53.

[23] M. Iwuchukwu, *Muslim-Christian Dialogue*, 1. Also see: Y. Olomojobi, *Islam and Conflict*, 4; J.B. Bakeni, *The Encounter of The African Traditional Religion*.

[24] See I. Nwanaju, *Christian-Muslim Relations*, 88.

[25] J.F.A. Ajayi, *Christian Missions in Nigeria*, 2; I. Nwanaju, *Christian-Muslim Relations*, 89.

With the establishment of the office of the Sacred Congregation for the propagation of Faith in 1622 by Pope Gregory XV (1621-1623), as an arm of the Vatican Curia for the supervision of all missionary activities around the world, strong reports were given to the *Propaganda Fide* which drew its serious attention to the situation of the Benin mission. Against this backdrop, the Benin Prefecture was created in 1648, and the Spanish Capuchins of the province of Valencia and Aragon were saddled with the responsibility to manage it[26].

In the middle of the seventeenth century, the office of the *Propaganda Fide*, Rome made another effort by sending the Spanish and Italian Capuchins led by Fr. Angel Valencia who was made the Apostolic Prefect and arrived in Benin on February 12, 1651 with other twelve priests to assist him. They in turn made a determined effort by adopting the method of converting the king *vis-à-vis* his subjects, but they equally failed in their missionary adventure because they were denied free access to the *Oba* (the Benin King). Several relentless efforts were however, made but never yielded wonderful results not until late nineteenth century.

Within the period under review, the Niger Expedition of 1841 marked the beginning of a new missionary enterprise in the country due to the presence of some protestant missionaries who accompanied the Niger Expedition group led by Thomas Fowell Buxton[27]. At this period, the establishment of colonies in Africa and particularly in West Africa coincided with the establishment of the Protestant missions to Africa such as the Church Missionary Society (hence CMS), the Basel Mission, the Wesleyan, the North German Missionary Society, etc[28]. These missions were focused on reaching out to Africans and bringing them into Christianity. As a result, they (missions) paved the way for the arrival of the CMS and the Wesleyan Methodist in Yoruba land.

In 1842, a group of the CMS landed at Badagry, and its members found their way to Abeokuta in 1846, where they were joined later by the Wesleyan Missionary Society. Thereafter, the American Southern Baptist Mission set up a mission in Abeokuta as well in 1850[29]. Bearing this in mind, one could see the reason of the Protestant missionaries' prosperity in Nigeria prior to the arrival of the Catholic missionaries like the Society of the Mis-

---

[26] I. NWANAJU, *Christian-Muslim Relations*, 89. Also see, A. LOPES, *The Popes*, 88.

[27] J.F.A. AJAYI, *Christian Missions in Nigeria*, 13. Also see, A.B. LAMIDO, *The CMS in Wusasa*, 55.

[28] It is interesting to note that prior to this period of expedition, the course of the Niger River had already been discovered as already stated above.

[29] T. FALOLA – M.M. HEATON, *A History of Nigeria*, 87.

sions of Africa (hence SMA) in September 1863 in the West (Lagos)[30], and the Holy Ghost Fathers (hereafter Spiritans) in December 1885 in the East (Onitsha)[31]. It is worth noting that, the detailed account of the missionary endeavours of both the Protestant and Catholic missionaries is beyond the scope of this work[32]. Hence, we now focus our attention toward examining the geographical region called the "North" in order to present to us a clearer picture of the region under study.

4. The Setting: Northern Nigeria

From a cultural standpoint, the north is far more heterogeneous than the south due to the existence of many varied cultures that live side by side with the Hausa and the Fulani[33]. For instance, the Birom and the Angas in Plateau State; Shuwa and Kanuri in Borno State; Gwagi, Baju, Kataf and Akurmi in Kaduna State; Tiv, Idoma, and Igede in Benue State, to mention just a few. Talking therefore about the Northern Nigeria certain historical facts necessarily need to be put into right perspectives. For instance, with the arrival of the Islamic missionaries and traders from the Northern part of Africa (the Berbers and Arabs) in Kanem-Borno Kingdom Islam was thus introduced, and later spread around to most of the Southern Sahara, including the Hausa states and the entire West African region as we have already seen from above. However, prior to the arrival of the British Colonial Administrators the Sokoto Caliphate had already been established by the conquering force of Uthman dan Fodio thereby bringing into existence two powerful independent Islamic empires, namely; the Sokoto Caliphate and part of the Borno Kingdom, each having its organized and centralized system of authority[34].

---

[30] A.O. MAKOZI – G.J.A. OJO eds., *The History of the Catholic Church in Nigeria*, 15.

[31] A.O. MAKOZI – G.J.A. OJO eds., *The History of the Catholic Church in Nigeria*, 38.

[32] However, an in-depth studies can be made in reference to the works of: E.P.T. CRAMPTON, *Christianity in Northern Nigeria*; _ *Christianity in Northern Nigeria*; M. CROWDER, *The Story of Nigeria*; F.K. EKECHI, *Missionary Enterprise and Rivalry*; A.O. MAKOZI – G.J.A. OJO, eds., *The History of the Catholic Church in Nigeria*; E. O'CONNOR, *From the Niger to the Sahara*; A.B. LAMIDO, *The CMS in Wusasa*; M.E. EZEH, *Archbishop Charles Heerey*; and the work of T. FALOLA, *The History of Nigeria*.

[33] CF., A.C. van GORDER, *Violence in God's Name*, 6.

[34] As a result of the exploration of the British explorers; Mungo Park, Hugh Clapperton, and the Lander brothers as already stated above, the British had earlier gotten a quasi-knowledge of the North. Although limited and sparse it may be, the one thing they were, however, certain about was the significant control and influence of the Fulani hegemony over the territories administered at large from Gwandu and Sokoto by both the Emir of Gwandu and the Shehu of Sokoto.

Upon the formal meeting of the world leading capitalist nations at Berlin in 1885 at the request of Portugal in 1884, German Chancellor Otto von Bismarck called together the major western powers of the world to negotiate questions and end confusion over the control of Africa. It was under the chairmanship of Von Bismarck, that the British government thus set the process of taking Nigeria. To this effect, the larger part of the Northern Nigeria that had earlier come under the control and influence of the Royal Niger Company (hence RNC)[35] at the time it got its Royal Charter in 1886, finally came directly under the control of the British government after the revoke of the charter in 1899[36].

The revoke became necessary as a result of the French occupation of Bussa on the Niger in 1897 – very close to the RCN treaty zone but not technically within it. The threat of the French became eminent to the British and they needed to act fast or they would stand the chance of losing the Northern territory. The revoke of the RNC's charter thus paved the way for the British government to take total control of the affairs and management of Nigeria. As a result, this new development saw the division of the RNC into north and south. While the company's northern territories (Ilorin inclusive) became the Protectorate of Northern Nigeria under the leadership of Lord Lugard on January 1, 1900[37], the southern territories (palm oil zone on the Niger delta) on the other hand were amalgamated into the Niger Coast Protectorate, and thus formed the Protectorate of Southern Nigeria[38]. Hence, it is interesting to note that the years 1900 and 1914 are very significant in this study because in the year of 1900 the governments of the North and South were officially formed and in 1914 the two protectorates in question were merged to form one nation called Nigeria.

At this juncture, it is worth noting that the most significant and symbolic feature of the creation of Northern Nigeria as noted by Rotgak Gofwen (a sociologist) was the extension of the Hausa-Fulani hegemony[39] that could better the commercial relationship of the British with the Caliphate (bearing in mind

---

[35] The Royal Niger Company was the first company established by George Goldie under the name, United African Company which was later renamed as National African Company. But in 1887 it was officially given some political privileges to oversee all British territories in Nigeria called the Royal Charter under the new name "Royal Niger Company.

[36] T. FALOLA – M.M. HEATON, *A History of Nigeria*, 98-100.

[37] It should be noted that it was at this period (1900, with the defeat of Rabih by the French as seen in the footnote number 15 in page 7) that the Kanem-Borno Kingdom was thus conquered by the French and divided among the French, British, and German colonial authorities, resulting the kingdom becoming parts of four different countries, namely; Republic of Niger, Chad, Cameroun, and Nigeria. It was therefore the part of the kingdom annexed to Nigeria that was merged with the Sokoto Caliphate to become the present Northern Protectorate.

[38] T. FALOLA – M.M. HEATON, *A History of Nigeria*, 98-100.

[39] Cf., R.R. GOFWEN, *Religious Conflicts in Northern Nigeria*, 13.

the testimony of the three British explorers), who had the control of the large part of the north, without necessarily taking into consideration the existence of the minority tribal groups that largely formed the central part of the region. Against this backdrop, the merger between the Sokoto Caliphate and the part of the Borno Kingdom annexed to Nigeria thus became expedient.

To better understand the complexity of the Northern region therefore, it is essential to bear in mind that the North, although emerged as a monolithic bloc within the context of socio-political affairs in the country, it was however, composed of three major religious groups; Islam, Christianity and ATR which were made up of hundreds of linguistic and ethnic groups with conflicting historical legacies and the struggle for identity and survival[40]. While prior to the advent of colonialism the northern part of the region was dominated by the Hausa-Fulanis and the Kanuris who were organized in various city states with centralized government and Islam playing a central role in their social organization particularly after the Uthman dan Fodio's jihad conquest, the southern part of the region on the other hand was largely inhabited by several minority groups who were predominantly animists[41] without any centralized authority. It was therefore among these minorities that Christianity found its roots in the northern region. Hence, it is within this context that talking about the North will clearly refer to a complex and heterogeneous region whereby the Muslims are predominantly in the far north and the Christians are predominantly in the south of the region. The demography below is a bolster to the fore.

Religious Adherence	Numbers and percentages
Christians	26,194,969 (34.8%)
Muslims	44,876,405 (59.6%)
African Traditional Religionists[42]	4,198,348 (5.6%)
Total Northern Population	**75,269,722 (53.6%)**

Table 1: Religious Adherents in Northern Nigeria per 2014[43].

---

[40] R.R. GOFWEN, *Religious Conflicts in Northern Nigeria*, 13.

[41] The "animists" refer to the other tribes (or rather the minorities) in the north who refused islamisation by their Muslim counterparts and were independent of one another, therefore, not under one unifying authority of the Emirs, but were forcefully placed with the adjacent Emirs as their traditional leaders for a convenient administration of the Colonial Administrators. This is to say that while under the direct rule of the Emirs, they were ruled indirectly by the British. Hence, the emergence of the *indirect rule system*. More will be said on this type of system as the work progresses.

[42] Adherents of ATR plus < 1% adherents of other religions and non-religious.

[43] Cf., A. MULDERS, "The Impact of Persistent Violence on the Church, 9.

Consequently, this explains the massive land mass of the region over the western and southern regions of the country where its geographical location forms the nation's three quarter of landmass[44].

4.1 *The Advent of Christianity and its Approach to Conversion in the North*

In the North, as already stated above, Islam existed for more than three centuries prior to the arrival of Christianity. The North came to light in January 1900 when Sir Frederick Lugard, the first British High Commissioner assumed responsibility over its vast land known as Protectorate of Northern Nigeria as we have earlier noted above. He introduced the system of *Indirect Rule* (i.e. the protectorate was administered by indirect rule in which native authorities – chiefs and emirs – under the supervision of British staff ruled the people)[45].

It is interesting to note that in the *indirect rule system*, Lugard retained in office any defeated emir willing to accept his conditions, while any unwilling emir was simply deposed. This was consistent with Lugard's overall strategy of avoiding any coordinated resistance by all the emirates at once. He always assured his appointed emirs that he would be guided by the usual local rules if such rules were acceptable to him. However, the emirs would then have to obey and carry out the laws of his own administration in accordance with the 'advice' of a Resident as his political officer in each local area.

Local administration of justice and appointment to local political offices would, however, continue subject to certain restrictions. But the right to land, mineral resources, taxation and monetary exchange, firearms, and "other minor matters" would no longer be under the control of emirs[46]. However, this system failed woefully because it was applied artificially and as a result, it caused endless tribal wars between the Emirates and the "animistic island" (minority tribal groups) which continued till 1959 when the North attained self-government. It is very important to state here that with this system of indirect rule the seed of hatred was once again sown among the animistic island and the Emirate.

---

[44] Cf., R.R. GOFWEN, *Religious Conflicts in Northern Nigeria*, 13.

[45] An *Indirect Rule* was a system introduced by the British Colonial Administrators as an easy access of ruling the North indirectly through the direct leadership of the traditional leaders over the northerners for a convenient administration of the region by the British government. This system of administration empowered the emirs and the chiefs to lord their power over the minority tribes whose authority was independent of each other and any centralized power.

[46] M.S. UMAR, *Islam and Colonialism*, 24-25.

Nevertheless, the first attempt of planting the seed of the Gospel in the North was made by the Franciscan missionaries between 1688 and 1850 by a Franciscan brother by name Peter Farde (a native of Belgium) who was captured at sea and became a slave of a wealthy Muslim master, and was brought from Algeria to Agadez[47]. While with his master, Peter succeeded in converting him and his household to Christianity. This made possible for other Franciscans to follow suit. For example, after twenty-three years, Frs. Carlo Maria from Italy and Severino from Czechoslovakia made another attempt but could not succeed due to illness. Thereafter, several attempts were made by different Catholic missionaries at different periods of time, but all proved unsuccessful as we have seen from the foregoing, until the arrival of the SMAs in the region in 1907.

Prior to the arrival of the SMAs however, there was already a Christian mission in Lokoja established by Samuel Ajayi Crowther in 1866 known as "Anglican Niger Mission. Then the SMAs arrived in 1884 wherein they started the establishment of Catholic Churches through the missionary zeal of Frs. Jules Poirier and Fiorentini. As these efforts went unnoticed, a vigorous attempt was made to penetrate the interior of the north in its entirety in the first decade of the twentieth century. Suffice it to note here, that it was during this period that protestant activities flourished greatly. For instance, Dr. Bingham's establishment of the first Sudan Interior Mission (hence SIM) at Pategi (a small Muslim emirate in Nupe land) in 1901; Dr. Kumm and the first Sudan United Mission (hereafter SUM) at Wase (now Benue State) in 1902; Dr. Miller and the Anglican Hausa Mission to Kano and Zaria, and then the SMAs who later joined the race in 1907 by opening the first Catholic mission station north of the rivers Niger and Benue at Shendam by Fathers Oswald Waller, Ernest Belin and Joseph Mouren[48].

It is thus from this missionary zeal that today Christians are found in all hinterlands of the north and most especially among its natives known as *Maguzawa* but now preferred to be called *Masihiyawa*[49]. Hence, Chris-

---

[47] R. HICKEY, *The Growth of the Church in Northern Nigeria*, 9.

[48] E. O'CONNOR, *From the Niger to the Sahara*, 9; R. HICKEY, *The Growth of the Church in Northern Nigeria*, 15.

[49] The term "Maguzawa" was a derogatory term that refers to somebody as a pagan, archaic, unenlightened. Its usage was employed by the Hausa/Fulani in order to humiliate the Hausa minority group who vehemently resisted the forced conversion of the Islamic jihads weighed against them throughout history. In contrast however, the Hausa minority group prefer to be called "Masihiyawa" in order to be identified as believers of Christ and not pagans. The term "Masihiyawa" is derived from an Arabic word *Masi* which means Saviour. *Masihi* (singular) therefore means a follower of Christ the Saviour while *Masihiyawa* (plural) means followers of Christ the Saviour. Consequently, the rejection of the

tianity started flourishing, but it should be noted that the Colonial Administrators never allowed the missionaries to penetrate the far north (where Islam had already made great impact) for their commercial interest. It is, however, these areas that have formed the large portion of today's basis of evangelization in the Northern region that today Christianity is present in all nooks and crannies of the region. We now examine the approach of the Christian missionaries in respect to the conversion of their converts.

With regard to the Christian missionary approach, the missionaries had the backing of the Colonial Administrators. They were not only negative and judgmental of the indigenous religion but also uncompromising in their approach since they had no prior knowledge of the new cultures they were to meet. Although they tried, with varying degrees of success, to impose their categories of thought on the Africans, but the sincere realization of the need to accept the African customs, rites and tradition, that were not conflicting with the divine laws could not be ignored[50]. In respect to missionary approach, the Holy Father Pope Pius XII in his address to the directors of the Pontifical Mission in *Evangelii Praecones* was very clear on this when he stated that:

> The specific character, the traditions, customs of each nation must be preserved intact, so long as they are not in contradiction with the divine law. The missionary is an apostle of Jesus Christ. His task is not to propagate European civilization in mission lands.... Rather it is his function so to train and guide other peoples, some of whom glory in their ancient and refined civilization, as to prepare and dispose them for the willing and hearty acceptance of the principles of Christian life and behaviour...[51].

Without mincing words, the Holy Father's message vividly states the ardent need of taking into cognizance the traditional values of the local culture of the people to be evangelized. But how many missionaries especially in African continent adhered to this message? African converts were rather forced to throw away their works of arts and sculptures as a mark of total and sincere conversion to Christianity despite the traditional values they attached to them. Although, the indiscriminate throwing away of such works and arts might have filled the hearts of the missionaries with Christian joy of missionary success, but it did however, incalculable harm to the people's cherished heritage.

The tragedy, as Obaro Ikime (a renowned historian) observed, was that carvings which were purely for artistic and decorative purposes were con-

---

derogatory term "Maguzawa" implies the rejection of their misplaced identity as believers of Christ and not pagans, archaic or unenlightened people as it was earlier promoted by the Hausa/Fulani.

[50] C.D. IsIzoh, ed., "Christianity in Dialogue", 3-4.

[51] POPE PIUS XII, "Evangelii Praecones", 60.

nected with '*Juju*' and so often destroyed in the fervour that characterized nascent Christianity[52]. A good example of the destruction of such artefacts is the hacking down of the Ikenga statue that adorned the city of Owerri, Imo State in the present South-eastern part of Nigeria and a giant cross was replaced as a sign of Christianity in action. While the use of persuasion was employed, the establishment of schools and hospitals by the missionaries also served as baits in their missionary approach.

4.2 *The Advent of Islam and its Approach to Conversion in the North*

From the above exposition, much has been said on the advent of Islam in the northern region[53]. It is to this effect that we come to understand that Islam came to Nigeria through the north, and there it spread as far as the west and little part of the east as already seen above. As it spread, it was slowly transformed into a religion of the elite – specifically rulers and merchants. Its spread, however, became more rapid than ever during the Jihad of Uthman dan Fodio (1754-1817), as earlier stated in which many people were forced into the religion. However, undue emphasis on its centrality and dominance has become a source of consternation among other Muslims and scholars in what made up former Northern Nigeria. Reasons offered for this include cultural, theological, historical, social and political factors, all aimed at challenging the Fulani and Anglo-Fulani tendencies in the presentation of the Jihad history and the Islamisation of Northern Nigeria[54]. We cannot get into a detailed account of this controversy over its centrality, nevertheless, further study could be made[55].

But with regard to Islamic approach to conversion, it was more of violence than persuasion, even though persuasion was first used at its initial stage of establishment. The Arab itinerant traders who introduced Islam to the Hausa/Fulani in the north were careful not to demand a sudden break with the traditional religion of the people. They won their converts progressively, and they made sure that they first enlisted the interest of their leaders. The rulers, in turn, influenced their subjects and encouraged them to say the Muslim confession of faith (*Shahada*): "*Là Ilàha Illallàh Mu-*

---

[52] O. IKEIME, *The Isoko People*, 61-62.

[53] See subtitle 3 above.

[54] Cf., M.H. KUKAH, *Religion, Politics and Power in Northern Nigeria*, 1; J.B. BAKENI, *The Encounter of The African Traditional Religion*, 40.

[55] T.G. GBADAMOSI, *The Growth of Islam Among the Yoruba*. For more information see also the following works: J. HARNISCHFEGER, *Democratization and Islamic Law*; J. KENNY, "West Africa and Islam"; M.H. KUKAH, *Religion, Politics and Power in Northern Nigeria*; F. SALAMONE, *Gods and Goods in Africa*.

hammadur Rasulullàh". Thus, the gradual penetration of Islam was made possible because of its tolerance to the indigenous religion of the people.

However, with passionate interest in respect to this study it is pertinent to note that a radical change came in the 19th century when Uthman dan Fodio, an enthusiastic Fulani Muslim teacher as already stated above, felt disgusted at the way his fellow Muslims were compromising with the adherents of the African Traditional Religion whom he perceived as the enemy of Islam that must be converted or destroyed. To hasten this, he adopted the path of no compromise toward a lax and prevaricating Muslims and the corrupt political leaders.

For him it was only the act of reformation and renewal that would bring religious profession from the shadows of compromise and make public virtue of it that in the end the contrast with the African heritage would be sharper[56]. He quickly organized some of his followers into a fighting force and waged a Jihad against those who did not accept Islam, or those compromising with the traditional religion[57]. He forced many Hausas to boycott the traditional religion and to accept Islam. Nonbelievers were however, forcefully converted while war was constantly waged against those who refused conversion. His jihad (as he was convinced) therefore "purified" Islam.

The forceful and violent methods of Islamic expansion and campaign continued by his descendants, not until the time of Sir Ahmadu Bello (1910-66). At this time in question, there was a new dimension to the campaign as we shall see later in his conversion campaigns and islamisation programme in northern Nigeria. One of the methods of conversion he adopted for instance was the use of physical gifts: correlating conversions with economic and political benefits for the converts. We shall elaborate more on this point as the work progresses. Nevertheless, it is important to note that by accepting the gift of money implies an automatic conversion to Islam. It is not surprising therefore, that the use of the elements; force (jihad), violence, and persuasion through the gift of materials as baits, are still employed by the present-day Islamic fanatics in the north as a way of expanding their religion. The uprising of the 1982 Maitatsine and the 2011 insurgence of Boko Haram are clear parameters of the aforementioned.

From the foregoing, we have seen how these two major religions came into existence in the country, and *ipso facto* in the north. The question we may ask is that; how do these religions since their inception in the country affect the relational life style of Nigerians especially within the region under investigation? In this regard, the need to examine the existing relationship between Christians and Muslims both before and after the colonial rule becomes essential.

---

[56] L. SANNEH, "The African Christian and Islam", 8.

[57] M.L. FITZGERALD – R. CASPAR, *Signs of Dialogue*, 6-7.

5. The Relationship between Christians and Muslims in Northern Nigeria

Under this subheading, the nature of the Christian-Muslim relationship will be treated under three categories. These include pre-colonial, colonial, and postcolonial periods. Each period takes into consideration the factors that influenced the nature of the existing relationship at the time under review.

5.1 *Pre-Colonial Era 1200-1800*

In discussing the relationship between Islam and Christianity, the need to examine the relationship that existed between Islam and the indigenous religions (ATR) prior to the advent of Christianity cannot be overemphasized. Prior to the jihads of Dunama Dibbalemi in the thirteenth century and Uthman dan Fodio in the nineteenth century, as earlier stated, there existed a great deal of similarity and continuity with the religions of Africa. Islamic practices were carried out almost in *pari passu* (side by side) with ATR. In other words, there was cordial understanding and relationship among the adherents of both religions[58]. This was perhaps possible owing that the Muslim traders and particularly the Mamelukes and the Turks, at the time under review seemed to be more interested in their trade – the unwillingness to lose their Mediterranean trade as well as Trans-Saharan trade in Africa – rather than being concerned with affairs of religion[59].

Nevertheless, it does not in any way suggest that the values of Islam were completely compromised. But however, it is pertinent to point out that the incessant jihads championed from one period to the other played a great influence in the existing relations. As a result of the jihads the existing cordiality among the adherents of both religions was thus disrupted. Hence, the minority tribes found themselves in constant war with the jihadists in order to avoid forceful conversion. It is to this effect that factors such as religious tolerance, economic pursuance, and religious expansionism cannot be overemphasized as regards the existing relationship between Muslims and the traditionalists.

5.2 *Colonial Era 1840-1960*

With the arrival of Christianity however, there came a new trend in the existing relations between Islam and ATR. As the pre-colonial era was characterized by hatred and war after the jihad of Uthman dan Fodio, the Colonial era was rather characterized by suspicious, distrust, hatred, reli-

---

[58] See the subtitle 4.2 above.

[59] I. Nwanaju, *Christian-Muslim Relations in Nigeria*, 122.

gious bigotry, and tension. Let us now examine some of the factors that sowed the seeds of the aforementioned feelings. Although the European Colonialists came to Africa with no hostility whatsoever towards Islam (there were, however, exceptions), there is no gain saying that many Christian missionaries especially in Northern Nigeria who were fired by the zeal to rescue the Africans from the claws of paganism and Islam came with a mind set about Islam.

A vivid example was the burning enthusiasm that pushed the pioneering missionaries to undertake the study of African languages for the conversion and civilization of the non-Christians and Muslims. Sigmund Wilhelm Koelle (a German missionary that was recruited for the CMS) was said to have written about his inspiration and conviction received in his great dream to have evangelised even the Muslims. He dreamed that he entered the empire of Borno from Tripoli in modern-day Libya arguing that 'the time will at length come when also in such entirely Mohammedan countries as Borno the banner of the Cross will be unfurled'[60].

Another factor was the technological transfer that accompanied the early missionaries such as flashlights, match sticks, and hurricane lamp, which created in the minds of most traditional Africans the notion that these material benefits were necessary accompaniment of conversion to Christianity. On the part of the African Muslims they were not accepted as evidence of Christian European superiority, but on the contrary, the Euro gadgets were perceived as the works of the Devil in collaboration with the European[61]. To this effect, this mental attitude of the African Muslims might have also contributed to their non-acceptance of the western education for a long time that led the region to socio-economic and education backwardness.

In another development, the instructions received by the colonial agents to promote religion and education among the native inhabitants of the colony... to take care, to protect them and their persons and in the free enjoyment of their possessions, and by all lawful means to prevent and restrain all violence and injustice, which may in any manner be practiced or attempted against them, became to some extent part of the missionary goals of some missions. For instance, Joseph Shanahan's (Prefect of the Apostolic of Lower Niger) view of the missionary goal of his Congregation did not differ greatly from the above instructions.

In like manner, and with regards to the preconceived mind-set of the Missionaries about Islam, it was said of Missionaries like W. Kumm (a leading evangelical missionary of SUM) to have warned other missionaries that un-

---

[60] I. NWANAJU, *Christian-Muslim Relations in Nigeria*, 127.

[61] I. NWANAJU, *Christian-Muslim Relations in Nigeria*, 127.

less they did their duty, 'these wards of ours will find their nemesis in the cul-de-sac of Islam'. By implications, the general perception of the Missionaries was rooted in the belief that Islam was not the right religion to save Africa, and the question of its long existence and domination in the continent was seen as a retardant factor of civilization and progress since the religion was rooted in economic exploitation of the people, expressed in the drive for slave trade.[62] Against this background, Islam was accused to be a religion without the knowledge of the divine fatherhood, a religion without compassion for those outside its pale, a religion without love. And since only love can redeem Africa, Islam was seen as having no vision for Africa[63].

Another area of great importance in understanding the nature of the relationship between Christians and Muslims is the Colonial policies. It was generally perceived by the Missionaries that the existing colonial policies were in favour of the Muslims. As a result, Islam enjoyed preferential treatment and protection over Christianity. For instance, the outright rejection of the presence of the missionaries within the Sokoto Caliphate by the Colonial Administrators, the Sultan and the Emirs of the emirate is a bolster to the aforementioned.

It was said of Bishop H. Tugwell (of Hausa Party Mission) and Walter Miller (who came to preach in Kano) that the Emir rejected them and in clear terms he told them; "we do not want you: you can go, I give you three days to prepare: a hundred donkeys to carry your loads back to Zaire, and we never wish to see you here again"[64]. However, the motive of the rejection of the missionaries in the Muslim emirates remains an issue of debate within the field of scholarship[65] owing to the fact that it contributed in defining the nature of the relations that existed between the Christians and Muslims within the colonial era.

Further still, the non-approval of applications by Christian missions to build up centres of worship in the emirates was another contributing factor. The cases of Borno, Bauchi, and Kano emirates are bolsters to the aforementioned. For example, the applications made by SIM for the site at Birma (in Borno emirate), another at Darazo in (Bauchi emirate), and then a site at Garko (Kano emirates) were all rejected because the residence of Borno had raised objections, and while in the second and third cases,

---

[62] I. NWANAJU, *Christian-Muslim Relations in Nigeria*, 151.

[63] I. NWANAJU, *Christian-Muslim Relations in Nigeria*, 129.

[64] I. NWANAJU, *Christian-Muslim Relations in Nigeria*, 128.

[65] See the works of: A.E. BARNES, "Evangelisation where it is not wanted", 412-441; E.A. AYANDELE, "The Missionary Factor in Northern Nigeria", 133-158; C.N. UBAH, "Problems of Christian Missionaries", 351-371; E.P.T. CRAMPTON, *Christianity in Northern Nigeria*.

the simple reason was because the places were predominantly Muslim in population. In summary, with regard to the process of applications, the Colonial Administrators always had a lot of sympathy for the Muslims[66].

Interestingly however, infrastructures such as dispensaries – which were conceived by the emirs as non-utilitarian in their approach to evangelization – were always welcomed but with astute diplomacy and suspicion of their religious implications. It is pertinent to note that most of the hospitals and schools established by the Christian missionaries remain today among the best in the country. For instance, the eye hospital in Kano which was established by the SIM in 1943 still ranks the best in the country.

From the foregoing therefore, it is obvious that the above stated factors created the atmosphere of suspicion, disgust, and distrust among the adherents of the two foreign religions (Christianity and Islam).

5.3 *Post-Colonial Era 1960-1998*

The post-colonial era experienced a crisis of identity by both Christianity and Islam due to factors such as the islamisation of northern Nigeria, implementation of Shari'a law by the Muslims, and Christian fundamentalism. At the independence in 1960, Nigeria was launched into a new era of its historical development toward a national maturity in its entire socio-political, economic and religious sphere. The post-independence excitement for instance, seemed to have created an atmosphere of national unity which found its expression in the Nigerian national anthem "… *One nation bound in freedom, Peace and unity*"[67], and the political slogan "bridge the gap" that became the catchwords between the Northerners and the Southerners.

The romance of this cordiality seemed to gain root among the adherents of the two religions in question, but how long would this last? Just for a little moment. With the independence, the emirs began to feel the impact of their reduced authority, especially over the Christians and other non-Muslims in the North. It was clear that the transfer of power and the control of police, courts, prisons and taxes to the political groups, reduced them to the position of ceremonial leaders. By implication, Islamic power began to be a shadow of its old-self, and Northern Muslims felt threatened by the Southerners who were predominantly Christians and the fast-growing number of northern minority Christians.

---

[66] Cf., I. NWANAJU, *Christian-Muslim Relations in Nigeria*, 130-133.

[67] The Nigerian National Anthem goes thus: Arise, O compatriots; Nigeria's call obey; To serve our fatherland; With love and strength and faith; The labour of our heroes past; Shall never be in vain; To serve with heart and might; One nation bound in freedom; Peace and unity.

It is interesting to note that at the time under review the southern Christians had been empowered by western education which paved for them the way to migrate from south to the north for the needed public service skills in the region and *vis-à-vis* the northern Christians minorities. The threat that lack of western education posed to the northern ruling class was thus captured by a poet who had warned that the northerners must wake up or else they would be left far behind because:

> Those we met sitting on the floor,
> Are today the top men of modern times.
> Status is now based on modern education,
> The talk of the son of so and so is over[68].

Hence, fear of domination began to build up among the Muslim dominated Northerners. The issue of northernisation and islamisation became obvious.

Against this backdrop, some highly conservative Muslims in the North viewed the departure of the Colonial Administrators as an opportunity to regain and pursue vigorously the programme of islamisation of Nigeria that had begun in the early jihads as we have earlier seen from above. In this regard, with the movement of political leadership from South to North in 1963 (when Nigeria became a republic), Sir Abubakar Tafawa Balewa became its first Prime Minister under the umbrella of Northern People's Congress (hence NPC)[69] while Sir Ahmadu Bello remained the first and only Premier of Northern Nigeria since its inception (1954-1966), and was doubled as the Sardauna of Sokoto and promoted to the Sokoto Native Authority Council – titles that automatically made him the chief political adviser to the Sultanate. With this development as the Premier of the northern region, the islamisation programme was thus ripe.

It is to this end that Ahmadu Bello saw his manifest duty as the continuation of the work of his great-great grandfather Sheikh Uthman Dan Fodio[70]. As a result, he embarked on massive conversion campaigns toward the realization of the gigantic project of the northern islamisation in 1963. The salient motive of this islamisation is best described in the words of

---

[68] M.H. KUKAH, *Religion, Politics and Power in Northern Nigeria*, 18-19.

[69] The NPC was a party that was dominated by the Muslims ruling class also referred to as Native Authority (NA). It was perceived by both Christians and Muslim commoners (the *talakwa*) as an oppressive party. This was demonstrated when appointments were only given to Muslims without a single Christian. The ministerial appointments of the 1951 in which no single Christian was appointed as a minister during its first period of governance is a bolster despite its motto, "One North, One people" irrespective of religion, rank or tribe. Cf., I. NWANAJU, *Christian-Muslim Relations in Nigeria*, 162.

[70] L. RASMUSSEN, *Christian-Muslim Relations in Africa*, 55.

Matthew Hassan Kukah (a Catholic Bishop, a prolific writer, and a political analyst) as he opines "the chivalrous campaigns by Sardauna to transform Northern Nigeria into a new caliphate exposed the fact that in reality, the NPC's motto of *One North, One People Irrespective of Religion*, was only waiting to be translated into *One North, One People, One Religion*[71].

In his conversion campaigns, the Sardauna among others employed the method of material gifts and political promotion to new converts as baits. In other words, new converts would be lavished with material gifts at their conversion ranging from money, clothes, and food. Those who were jobless, were given employments and those with jobs were automatically promoted without merits. Political appointments were equally offered as signs of warm welcoming. It was recorded that the Sardauna would give even traditional titles that never existed to new converts, and in another development would give money to communities in order to have mosques built[72].

As a buttress, it is said of one Mr. Jack Muggeridge (a colonial officer who worked in Northern Nigeria at the time in question) who recalled that the Sardauna would go to a place and say, "take money, you must have a mosque"[73], and in another development, he would gather people and then sprinkled water over them. Thereafter, he would asked, "who among you water has touched?' Those who raised their hands, he would ask them to go to his right side and those who did not were asked to remain at his left-hand side. Then, he would admonish those at his right-hand side that they were the only chosen ones that *Allah* has favoured and as such they stand the chance to benefit a lot of divine blessings. As a proof of *Allah's* favours upon His chosen people, the Sardauna would offer to each convert a bundle of new wrapper and an amount of money which served as baits[74].

Although the Sardauna's conversion drive sowed the seed of division and hatred among the Northern Muslims and Christians, his campaign further saw the establishment of the Jama'atu Nasril Islam (hence JNI)[75] in 1961 which became the Islamic all-purpose institution for the channelling of finances, the propagation of Islam in the North in all its ramifications, including the building of Koranic schools, and overseeing the propagation

---

[71] M.H. KUKAH, *Religion, Politics and Power in Northern Nigeria*, 20.

[72] M.H. KUKAH, *Religion, Politics and Power in Northern Nigeria*, 20-22.

[73] M.H. KUKAH, *Religion, Politics and Power in Northern Nigeria*, 22.

[74] Personal discussion with one of the first converts of Sardauna in the 60s (Yahaya) in Maiduguri, who returned back to Christianity shortly after his conversion to Islam.

[75] By the virtue of the existence of JNI, it implies that every Muslim in Northern Nigeria, male and female, young and old was deemed a member of it. But to be an active member remained a matter of personal choice.

and practice of Islam which were all sponsored by the millions of dollars that flowed from Saudi Arabia. Nevertheless, it is pertinent to note that the above developments obviously show that the Sardauna was not only seen as a political leader (the Premier of the Northern Region) but also as a religious leader. His elevation as the Vice President of the World Islamic Council is a bolster to the aforementioned[76].

In reaction to the establishment of the JNI and to resist strongly the islamisation mission of the Sardauna, the Christians in turn established the Christian Association of Nigeria (hereafter CAN) in 1964 in order to unify them in fighting their "so called" common enemy. It should be noted however, that what is known today as CAN is an adopted name from Northern Christian Association (NCA). An Association formed by the northern Christians in response to religious and political activities of the northern region at the time under review. As a national body, CAN technically came into existence on 27th August, 1976, at the meeting held in the Catholic Secretariat by the Christian leaders in response to Brigadier Shehu Yar'Adua (the then Chief of Staff of the Supreme Military Headquarters), when he demanded of their opinion during their meeting at Dodan Barracks — the seat of the military government — as regards the recitation of the "National Pledge" that was recited in the schools[77].

It is important to note that the two religious' bodies (JNI and CAN) of the respective religions have been the two main religious bodies that represent the interest of their respective religions at the political platform. Against this backdrop, as the JNI ("Group for the Victory of Islam") was established to be the social, political, and religious mouthpiece for Muslims in northern Nigeria that seeks to encourage Islamic literature in Nigerian vernacular languages, to build mosques and encourage Islamic centres of learning, and in like manner, to unify northern Muslims and to promote their interests in religious and political matters, the CAN on the other hand, was also established in order to unify the Christians toward resisting political oppression and islamisation.

Just like the JNI, CAN could also be seen as the social, political, and religious mouthpiece for Christians in Nigeria that seeks to serve as a basis of (action for) the unity of the Church, especially as (intended) in our Lord's pastoral prayer: 'That they all may be one'; (Jn 17:21) to act as a liaison committee by means of which its member Churches can consult together and when necessary, make common statements and take common action; to be a watch-dog of the spiritual and moral welfare of the nation; to propagate the Gospel; and

---

[76] M.H. Kukah, *Religion, Politics and Power in Northern Nigeria*, 21.

[77] For more information on CAN see the work of I.M. Ebwerem, "A Dangerous Awakening", 75-100.

to promote understanding among the various people and strata of society in Nigeria. From here, we now turn our attention to the present moment.

5.4 *The Return to Democracy 1999-till date*

Nigeria was ruled by military dictators for almost four decades since the aftermath of the 1966 coup[78]. The era of the military dictators lasted from 1966 to 1999. It was however, punctuated by civilian democratic rule of the "so-called" second republic from 1976 to 1983. Considered highly corrupt, the second republic was cut short by the military coup of 1983 that saw General Muhammadu Buhari into power (the present democratically elected president). With the return to democracy, a new leaf of politics was turned over and this *ipso facto* influenced the existing relationship between Christians and Muslims. However, it is interesting to note that for the first time since 1966 the northern region lost control of the political power of Nigerian at its centre. As a result, the fear of domination became more heightened than ever.

In order to deal decisively with this monstrous political challenge, the northern region saw the need of designing new strategies for regional self-assertion in the federation. Consequently, the issue of implementation of Shari'a law became necessary. But bearing in mind that the post-colonial era as described above was a time bomb period waiting for the right opportunity to explode, the realization of democracy thus paves the way to such awaiting

---

[78] The year 1966 was a historic year in the history of Nigeria. It was a year that experience two coups d'état. The first coup was led by five majors (Kaduna Nzeogwu, E. Ifeanjuna, D. Okafor, C.I. Anuforo, and A. Ademoyega) in the early hours of January 15, 1966. The five majors claimed that their goal was to bring an end to the tribalism and corruption that had characterized the First Republic. To achieve their objective, the coup leaders arrested all the regional premiers, and killed the Federal Prime Minister Tafawa Balewa, Premier S.L. Akintola of the Western Region, and Premier Ahmadu Bello of the Northern Region, and many northern military officers were also killed during the coup. With their success, power quickly devolved to the commanding officer of the Nigerian army, Major General John Aguiyi-Ironsi, who immediately swung into action of restoring order, eradicating regionalism and tribalism, and ending corruption. But at the course of executing these projects, Ironsi found himself in deep trouble with the northerners especially when he enacted the Decree no. 34 in May 24, 1966, in which he officially abolished the federal system and replaced it with a unitary system. Implying the end of regional structures. The Northerners perceived Ironsi's (an Igbo) action as Igbo domination over the Northerners. To fight back for their "rights" the Northerners staged a countercoup on July 29, 1966 capturing and killing Ironsi. Thereafter, Lieutenant Colonel Yakubu Gowon (a Christian northerner) became the supreme commander of the armed forces and the new head of state. To fulfill the mandate of the northerners' wish, he immediately announced the repeal of Decree no. 34 implying that Nigeria remains a federal system nation with respect for regional differences. Cf., T. FALOLA – M.M. HEATON, *A History of Nigeria*, 172-175; T. FALOLA, *Colonialism and Violence in Nigeria*, 183-184.

opportunity. In other words, the contemporary era marks the manifestation of terrorism in northern Nigeria which is characterized into two phases.

The first phase is as already noted, was characterized by the clamour on the demand for the implementation of Shari'a law in the northern region. This demand may seem not to be out of place noting that during the 1998/99 electioneering campaigns, some northern political elites who wanted cheap popularity and to score cheap political points, employed the service of religious sentiments. At their respective campaigns, they promised the people the implementation of Shari'a law if elected, the building of more Koranic schools, the boosting of their economy by providing more job opportunities to the youths and others alike.

Recalling the abortive efforts made during the 1978 and 1998 Shari'a debates, such political promises therefore excited the people and were encouraged to vote such politicians into power. Being a democratic government, it is expected that the promises made during the electioneering campaigns must be fulfilled. For this reason, the people began to demand for those things that were promised to them after the elections as part of their dividends of democracy. In an attempt to please their people and then gain more political favours and recognition, a lot of states implemented the Shari'a law without taking into consideration of the multi-cultural and multi-religious nature of the Nigerian society, and particularly the northern region in which the three religions as earlier stated exist side by side.

On the other hand, the second phase is characterized by the activities of the Boko Haram terrorist group in order to bring to reality the implementation of the Shari'a law. This was possible due to the global rise of Muslim revivalism which paved way for the proliferation of Islamic movements of fundamentalists whose focus has been on the creation of theocratic states as we have already pointed out in chapter one. In the same vein, the romance of the northern political elites with the members of the Boko Haram was also a contributing factor because in this type of political business, religious clerics become power brokers since they control a lot of people in their mosques and had influence over them. The case of the then governor of Borno state, Ali Modu Sheriff who used the Boko Haram to win the 2003 elections is a bolster to the aforementioned.

By way of reward, some followers of Mohammed Yusuf, for instance, Alhaji Buji Foi was promoted to Minister of Religious Affairs while Abubakar Adam Kambar was released from jail, where he had been held for armed robbery[79]. To this effect, it is worth noting that such religious clerics

---

[79] M.P. De Montclos, "Boko Haram and Politics", 148.

then became political consultants so much so that politicians would consult them in order to succeed in their political career. With this development, it thus gives room to some kind of consciousness that state, power, politics and religion could go together. As a result, the religious clerics have hence become an influential group and political stakeholders.

Arising from the above development, the religious clerics in no doubt have now become very powerful political contestants since they could make and unmake, as well as enthrone and dethrone political leaders. Conscious of their weapons therefore, the demand for the control of the state by the religious leaders became expedient. The argument might go thus; 'you leaders are corrupt, you are not ruling well. We install you there, but you are not living according to Islam. There is no justice, and moral decadence is on the increase. Let us therefore create a state where the *Mallam* (religious cleric/ teacher) will be the head of government who will govern by the divine law of *Allah* (Shari'a) in order to sanitize the society'. Bearing in mind however, that political leaders will not be lured into this kind of political colloquy, they thus employ the use of force. In this regard, it becomes a matter of survival of the fittest. Terrorism therefore becomes the possible effective weapon to achieve their desired goal bearing in mind that either they become victors, or they become the victims. But the burning question deep within is, what went wrong, that Nigerians particularly the government were taken unaware by the insurgence of the Boko Haram being its first kind ever experienced in the country? We shall try to address this question in the next section.

6. The Fertile Ground

Following the above expositions of the existing nature of Christian-Muslim relations, it is obvious that the expression of extremism in northern Nigeria did not start overnight or rather the emergence of the Boko Haram did not appear from nowhere. It however, manifested itself as a result of certain salient issues that have been in the pipe line without proper redress. To address the above question therefore, we shall consider certain factors that formed the bedrock of the contemporary expression of the Islamic extremism which has manifested itself in the extreme activities of the Boko Haram in the north-eastern region.

6.1 *The Colonial Conquest of the Sokoto Caliphate*

As earlier mentioned above, it will be recalled that, as Islam was introduced into Nigeria in the eleventh century, the Islamic religion had been mostly superficially adopted by the rulers of the various states[80]. Some of the Hausa kings

---

[80] See subtitle 3 above.

often repudiated the religion by returning to indigenous religions for their spiritual guidance, and for political reasons, owing that they had no problem in allowing Islam to co-exist alongside with the indigenous religions. Since one of the principal beliefs of fundamental Islam is that society and government should be ordered solely upon the teaching of the Prophet Muhammad, the Fulani clerics of the 18th century accused the ruling elites of their time of the western and central Sudan of illegitimacy because of their inability or unwillingness to adopt wholesale Islamic governing principles and social orders[81].

Against this backdrop, Islamic reformists movements led two successive jihads in the western Sudan in 18th century. The jihad led by Alfa Ba in Futa Jallo region of Senegambia in 1727-1728, and that of Abd al-Qadir in Futa Toro region in 1770s. It was within this same period that another reformist movement was growing in the central Sudan in the area of the Hausa states led by Sheikh Uthman Dan Fodio who succeeded in establishing the Sokoto Caliphate as stated above.

It is, however, interesting to note that while Sokoto remained the Caliphate (i.e the headquarters of all the conquered emirates), Islam remained the basis of creation and governance of the Caliphate. Through it (Islam), justice, equity, egalitarianism and fair play were dispatched and dispensed. To this effect, Shari'a law was extolled as the means to inter-personal, governmental relationship, and thus became the legal principle of governance of the Caliphate[82].

With the taking over of power from the RCN by the British government in 1900 and the establishment of the Northern Protectorate as already mentioned, the hand writing on the wall was clearly gearing towards the fall of the Sokoto Caliphate under the rule of the British colonialists. Prior to the 1900 events, the British in 1898 had established the West African Frontier Force (hence WAFF) with headquarters at Lokoja, who would be used to conquer and control the peoples and nations located in the region around the Niger-Benue confluence and beyond. It is interesting to note that at the establishment of the Northern Protectorate, the northern kings and chiefs were neither consulted nor was their consent sought. As a result, the application of force became inevitable in order that the colonial government could become a reality, and to stamp its authority on the newly established protectorate.

Between 1900 and 1906, the colonial army attacked the emirates of Bida, Yola, Kontagora, Kano, Bauchi, Sokoto, Borno, Zaria, and Katsina. Within the same period, the Sokoto Caliphate was brought to its knees un-

---

[81] Cf., T. FALOLA – M.M. HEATON, *A History of Nigeria*, 63.
[82] Cf., A.A. OKENE – S.B. AHMAD, "Ibn Khaldum, Cyclical Theory", 84-86.

der the rule of the British imperialists. Although faced with stiff resistance by the leaders and followers of these emirates, in 1901 and 1902 key emirates such as Yola, Bauchi, and Kontagora were conquered by the British, and a year later, the powerful and most industrious emirate of Kano also fell. The emirates fell one after the other due to internal skirmishes and squabbles, lack of modern technology, and trained army. Their old tactics of cavalry charges and defending walled cities could not prevent the British devastation wrought by their heavy artillery and machine guns[83].

The seat of the Caliphate, however, was the British biggest prize that must be conquered. As a result, all efforts were made in order to achieve this desiring goal. But it is pertinent to state that the Sokoto leadership was not ignorant of the motives of the British, and it was familiar with the resistance wars in some of its emirates and the wars between the French and Tukulor west of Sokoto, and above all, Lugard had also indicated to the Sokoto leadership that he would use all the force necessary to overthrow the Caliphate[84].

Against this backdrop, on March 15, 1903, the British invading forces appeared and attacked the Caliphate. Due to the use of modern technology and weapons such as Maxim guns, 75-mm canons, and magazine riffles against the single-short rifles, dane guns, bows and arrows of their opponents, the battle did not last for more than two hours and the Caliphate fell to its knees[85]. Hence, by this conquest, the Caliphate had obviously lost its sovereignty, political authority and independence, and auras to the British.

The British conquest of the Caliphate was thus a hard blow on the face of the northern Muslims. Although, Lord Lugard tried to keep to the status quo the socio-economic, political and religious life of the Caliphate, the wound however, was never healed because the northern Muslims perceived that it was a direct attack on Islam by non-believers. It is thus, the hope of the common northern Muslim to see that the demised Islamic state (the Sokoto Caliphate) is resurrected to its full scale of power and domination in the country. To this effect, the conquest of the Caliphate has established the bedrock of today's expression of Islamic terrorism in the region.

---

[83] Cf., T. FALOLA, *Colonialism and Violence in Nigeria*, 14.

[84] T. FALOLA, *Colonialism and Violence in Nigeria*, 15.

[85] T. FALOLA, *Colonialism and Violence in Nigeria*, 15.

6.2 *The Clash of Civilizations*

This could also be argued that the Islamic terrorism of the Boko Haram could be a manifestation of the clash of civilizations as argued by Samuel P. Huntington[86] in his article "The Clash of Civilizations?". In his work, Huntington opines that the fundamental source of conflict in the Post-Cold War will no longer be primarily ideological or economic as it were during the cold war but it will be on culture because culture today is the greatest divisions among humankind and the dominating source of conflict[87]. During the cold war as he argued, the world was divided into the first, second and third worlds. But today these division are no longer relevant. It is however, far more meaningful now to group countries not in terms of their political or economic systems or in terms of their level of economic development but rather in terms of their culture and civilization. For instance, as the culture of Italian village in the south differs from that of the north but both Italian regions share the common Italian culture that differentiate them from German culture, so also the European communities will share common cultural features that distinguish them from Arab, Chinese or African cultures[88].

For him therefore, civilization identity will be increasingly important in the future, and the world will be shaped in large measure by interactions among seven or eight major civilizations. These include; Western civilization primarily led by North America and Western Europe, Confucian civilization led by the Chinese, Japanese civilization, Islamic civilization led by the Arab world, Hindu civilization led by the Indians, Slavic-Orthodox civilization led by the Russians, Latin America civilization and possibly African civilization. The most important conflicts of the future will hence occur along the cultural fault lines separating these civilizations from one another[89]. This is necessary because for him, the fault lines between civilizations are speedily replacing the political and ideological boundaries of the Cold War as the flash points for crisis and bloodshed[90]. As the ideological division of Europe has disappeared, the cultural division of Europe between Western Christianity, on the one hand, and orthodox Christianity and Islam, on the other, has re-emerged. In Italy, France and Germany for instance, the racism is increasingly open, and political reactions and

---

[86] Samuel P. Huntington is the Eaton Professor of the Science of Government and Director of the John M. Olin Institute for Strategic Studies at Harvard University.

[87] S. P. HUNTINGTON, "The Clash of Civilizations?", 22.

[88] S. P. HUNTINGTON, "The Clash of Civilizations?", 24.

[89] S. P. HUNTINGTON, "The Clash of Civilizations?", 25.

[90] S. P. HUNTINGTON, "The Clash of Civilizations?", 29.

violence against Arab and Turkish migrants have become more intense and more widespread since 1990. This scenario shows that the interaction between Islam and the West is seen as a clash of civilizations[91].

Going down history lane, Huntington postulation of the future of the world may hold water. Although some Westerners have argued that the West does not have problems with Islam but only with violent Islamist extremists. Fourteen hundred years of history however demonstrate otherwise because there were through centuries a continuing and deeply conflictual relation between Islam and Christianity. At times, peaceful coexistence has prevailed; more often their relation has been one of intense rivalry and of varying degrees of hot war[92].

While we share the same opinion with Huntington to some degree that the clash of civilizations could be a possible fertile ground for the expression of the Islamic extremism in the northern region as a result of the influence of the Western culture owing to the five factors outlined in page 211 of his book[93] and that the West took the lead in the acquisition of the culture of modernity, and thereafter spread it across the globe, it is obvious that within this context, the Nigerian constitution can be perceived as the product of the Western culture. Hence, it must be replaced by the Shari'a law, and opposition against it attracts Islamic provocation.

But the lacuna in Huntington's argument is that nations today are driven not only by cultural lines but also by nationalistic interest owing to the fact that nations could share the same culture but differ in national interest. A vivid example is the US' threat to withdraw from the membership of the North Atlantic Treaty Organization (NATO) in 2018 – an intergovernmental military alliance formed in 1949 to protect North American and European member countries[94]. By implication, this scenario could be a pointer that the interest of US as a united nation supersedes the common interest of NATO before its president.

---

[91] S. P. HUNTINGTON, "The Clash of Civilizations?", 32.

[92] S. P. HUNTINGTON, *The Clash of Civilizations*, 209-218.

[93] These factors include; 1) the Muslim population growth which has generated large numbers of unemployed youth that become recruits to Islamic causes, 2) the recent resurgence of Islam that has given Muslims a reaffirmation of the relevance of Islam compared to other religions, 3) the West's attempt to universalize values and institutions, and maintain military superiority has generated intense resentment within Muslim communities, 4) without the common threat of communism, the West and Islam now perceive each other as enemies, and 5) increased communication and interaction between the West and Islam has exaggerated the perceived differences between the two societies. Cf., S. P. HUNTINGTON, *The Clash of Civilizations*, 211.

[94] J.E. Barnes & H. Cooper, "Trump Discussed Pulling US from NATO".

Most importantly, his argument seems to suppress the reality of religion expansionism. In other words, it is the desire of every religion to grow, spread across the globe and dominate the world. Islam is therefore not excluded from this reality. This reality manifested itself in the northernisation campaign of Sir Ahmadu Bello as already noted above.

6.3 *The Rise of Pentecostal and Charismatic Movements*

The 1970s experienced a dramatic proliferation of new forms of Pentecostalism and the movement of Charismatic renewal which made a significant presence in the African continent. This type of explosion of Christianity was at first identified with young men and women who labelled themselves as pastors and evangelists despite their insufficient knowledge of theology and pastoral experience. Their proselytizing activities, which largely occurred within existing Christian Churches and public places, were remarkable and daring as they called on other Christians to repent from all kinds of evil associations. To this effect, their common slogan was *you must be born again*, and they always advance to their listeners with rhetoric question *Are you born again?*

The young vibrant puritan preachers were grossly involved in what we may describe as "aggressive evangelization". They offered prayers for deliverance from every kind of malevolent spiritual force. They held crusades, camp meetings, Holy Ghost night vigils, healing and deliverance services, and they promoted their new evangelism through literatures such as fliers, posters and pamphlets. In addition, the new evangelists erected their sign boards in conspicuous places in the cities with obnoxious writings such as "Jesus will claim this city tonight" or "Operation win them for Jesus". They would move from street to street announcing publicly their scheduled activities using loud speakers that in most cases become a public nuisance.

In these movements, the role of the media cannot be overemphasized. The Pentecostal for instance, are very powerful in their preaching and the use of the Media in order to propagate their ideas. Media healings, for example, accompanied by miracles are relayed on Television and transmitted by Radios[95]. The use of the media is a clear tool of expansion, a reflection of globalizing aspirations, as well as a calculated attempt to transform and Christianise popular culture so that it is safe for consumption by 'born again' Christians[96]. As a result, unlike the traditional Churches, the Pente-

---

[95] I. NWANAJU, *Christina-Muslim Relations in Nigeria*, 261-262.

[96] R.I.J. HACKETT, "Charismatic/Pentecostal Appropriation of Media", 258.

costals invest heavily on the media owing to the fact that they can easily impact a wider audience within a given short time.

Interestingly, by the late mid-1980s, this new phenomenon had been institutionalized in new independent Churches which most often go by descriptions of 'ministries' or 'fellowships'. In another development, the Pentecostal and Charismatic movements became the fastest growing religious endeavour in Africa between 1980s and 1990s. The number has grown from about thirty independent Charismatic organisations in the mid-1970s located in Nigeria, Ghana, and Malawi to more than ten thousand groups across the continent by the year 2000. The membership has become substantial with about 8 million of the estimated 52 million Christians in Nigeria, about 2 million of the Christians in Ghana, about half a million in Cameroon, and Cote d'Ivoire, and about 300,000 each in Benin and Burkina Faso. In like manner, in Togo it was about 150,000 Christians, and about 2,000 in Niger Republic. In Southern Africa, the new movements equally added greatly in the demography of independent Churches. To this effect, the Charismatic movements have within three decades moved into a position of power in many African countries[97].

To this end, the impact of the Pentecostals and the Charismatic movements over the spiritual and socio-political sphere of the society is something that is worthy of note. Their enthusiasm in their respective services, the relative novelty of their messages and the proliferation of large number of new Churches advertising themselves widely in the print and electronic media in a competitive religious landscape were sources of inspirations that attracted a lot of membership into the movements. Members found the Pentecostal and Charismatic movements unique modern doctrines imbued in their 'can-do' spirit, market-oriented, success-directed, prosperous gospels and charismatic styles more appealing than the traditional Churches.

With the relative number of members, the Pentecostal began to sense they could have impact on the socio-political life of the nation. In the late 1980s for instance, Pentecostals and Charismatics started to be more politically active to protect their rights against Islam. Their significant involvement in politics followed the pronouncement of the late Sheikh Abubakar Gumi (the Grand Khadi of Northern Nigeria), in late 1987 that Muslims would never allow non-Muslims to rule the country as head of state or president. He also said that in the event of this happening, Muslims would seek to divide the country[98].

Consequently, in Kaduna, the Charismatics in 1988 joined with other Christians to field candidates, who eventually won majority seats in the

---

[97] M.A. OJO, "Competition and Conflict, 151.

[98] QUALITY (1987), 35-39, cited in M.A. OJO, "Competition and Conflict", 169.

city elections, and eventually installed a Baptist minister as the chairman of the local government in the city that had been considered a Muslim stronghold[99]. Important to note is the fact that the rise of the Pentecostals' interest in politics also coincided with the rise of radical Islamic reformists that also claimed interest in the political sphere. As a result, the clash of interest among the two fundamentalist groups of the two religions in question paved the way for religious animosity that serves as a bedrock to the present manifestation of extremism.

6.4 *The Shari'a Debates*

To set the tune for the transition of government from the military regime to the civilian rule, the then military head of state General Murtala Mohammed set up a Constitution Drafting Committee (hereafter CDC) in 1976 as part of the programme of the return to civil rule after ten years of military dictatorship without recourse to constitutional provisions. By August of the same year, the draft of the constitution was ready. Worthy of note in the drafted constitution, was the provision made – for the first time in the history of the nation's judiciary – for the establishment of a Federal Shari'a Court of Appeal, which was to have equal powers to those of the existing High Courts and Federal Courts of Appeal[100]. In order to have a popular opinion on the subject, the government having received the drafted constitution, then threw it open for debates around the country.

The Northern region quickly swung into action. This was because of the perception by the northern Muslims that the Islamic political order established by Uthman dan Fodio according to Shari'a law, had been spoiled with the coming of the British. Hence, it must be restored back[101]. The following words capture succinctly the destruction of the Islamic political order:

> The dynamic policy towards the administration of Islamic law advocated by Uthman Fodio and others has become stagnant and static under the influence of colonialism and neo-colonialism. The emphasis has shifted from the "social relevance" and "public good" of laws, a hallmark of Maliki jurisprudence, to their so-called "modernization", which simply means their conformity to Western legal values. It was indeed mischievous that Islamic law was allowed to be applied only so long as it was not found "repugnant to natural justice, equity and good conscience…" without any regard to the fact that the English statute… could itself be "repugnant…"[102].

---

[99] M.A. Ojo, "Competition and Conflict", 169.

[100] M.A. Ojo, "Competition and Conflict", 165.

[101] J.H. Boer, *Muslims: Why the Violence?*, 18-19.

[102] J.H. Boer, *Muslims: Why the Violence?*, 18-19.

In this regard, the northern region for example, spurred into action by organizing seminars in Zaria, Minna, Kano, and in Ilorin at different times within the same year of 1977. As a pointer to the political undertone of the Shari'a law, the Director of the Institute of Administration and the host of the first seminar held in Zaria, Dr. Suleiman Kumo observed that the Shari'a law necessarily should remain the law of the land because the English law was an imposition of the Colonial Administrators. "Why should the translated English law which, let it be recalled, was imposed on the country by the colonial regime, be allowed to remain the common law of Nigeria?" To this effect, Suleiman called for the total demolition of the legal structure because for him "… it has been an architectural eyesore"[103]. In the same vein, Maaji Baba Shani (a colleague of Dr. Kumo) opined that:

> "The law of the land is the law which commands the approval of the majority alone. Minorities have a right to demand safeguards for their legitimate rights and interests and we are bound to concede this demand as Islam enjoins us to do so. But it is not fair for minorities to ask us to throw our ideology overboard and introduce laws which are against our convictions merely for the sake of appeasing them. When we were helpless because of foreign domination, we tolerated the supremacy of un-Islamic laws. But we are now the Administrators of our destiny[104].

The above views were clear pointers to the radical opinion of the northern Muslim representatives to the Constituent Assemblies of 1978 and 1998 respectively in respect to the Shari'a debates.

At this juncture, it is pertinent to point out the thrust of the Shari'a debates. In the drafting constitution presented to the Nigerian government, there were the following provisions:

1. There shall be a Federal Shari'a Court of Appeal which shall be an intermediate Court of Appeal between the States' Shari'a Courts of Appeal and the Supreme Court of Nigeria.
2. The Court shall be composed of the Grand Mufti and such a number of Muftis (not less than three) as the National Assembly may prescribe.
3. In each State of the Federation that so desires, there shall be a Shari'a Court of Appeal to be established by the Constitution of the State[105].

During the 1978 Constituent Assembly (henceforth CA), these provisions became one of the centres of discussion of the assembly. The Shari'a issue divided the assembly into two opposing camps. Most Muslims from

---

[103] Quoted in M.H. KUKAH, *Religion, Politics and Power in Northern Nigeria*, 120.

[104] M.H. KUKAH, *Religion, Politics and Power in Northern Nigeria*, 120.

[105] M.H. KUKAH, *Religion, Politics and Power in Northern Nigeria*, 118.

the Northern Nigeria favoured the proposed role for the Shari'a arguing that it would help protect the rights of Muslims who have been disenfranchised over the years. In the opposing camp were the Christians both from the north and the south who opposed the expansion of the scope of Shari'a, arguing that it would undermine the secular nature of the nation and encourage discrimination based on religious grounds[106].

Despite the warning and appeal made to the members of the CA by the then Head of State, General Olusegun Obasanjo[107] that "the African genius is a child of moderation not given to unnecessary intellectual inflexibility. It prefers to arrive at a consensus through compromise … the African mind accepts that only God alone is perfect and that human beings can only give their best and no further," and the appeal of the CA chairman, Justice Udo Udoma that, "our contribution will unite the country, promote the rule of law, justice, peace, harmony, and integration…, neither religion and regional interests was pushed aside, nor compromise could easily be reached.

While the Muslims conceived Shari'a as a legal duty that must be observed by all Muslims, Christians on the other hand perceived it as the suppression of their human rights. Owing to this complexity and the uncompromising attitudes of both actors, both the 1978 and 1998 Shari'a debates were thus fruitless. The move was vehemently opposed by the Christians in the north and some Muslims in the west. In the response of Wilson Sabiya of the then Gongola State he was quoted to have opined that:

> "It is criminal to make non-Muslims in this country, slaves of Islam and be forced to pay tribute for the protection, application, promotion and enforcement of Islam. We have had enough of this crime. We want to be free and we will go to any extent to gain that freedom… The issue, put bluntly, is the *declaration of Islam as state religion to be enforced, propagated and maintained by the State* at the expense of non-Muslim taxpayers. It is in this light do we understand some state Government systematic confiscation of Church Institutions, the Inauguration of Pilgrims Welfare Boards, appointment of Grand Khadis, the establishment of only Islamic Institutions in some of our universities, the appointment of only Islamic teachers in many of our primary and post-primary institutions, all paid and maintained by the State at the expense of non-Muslims[108].

---

[106] Cf., M.A. Ojo, "Competition and Conflict", 165.

[107] Although the move towards the transition of government from the military rule to civilian rule was initiated by General Murtala Mohammed in 1976, the call for the Constituency Assembly however, was made by Major General Olusegun Obasanjo who took over the mantle of leadership after the assassination of General Murtala in February 1976.

[108] Cf., M. Iwuchukwu, *Muslim-Christian Dialogue*, 61.

In order to reach a consensus however, a sub-committee was inaugurated consisting of people who believe in Shari'a and those who do not and were thus saddled with the responsibility of devising a way whereby anybody aggrieved by the judgement of an Appeal Court in the State dealing with Islamic law will be able to appeal to the Federal Court of Appeal. In his report to the members of the CA, the chairman of the sub-committee Chief Adebo reported how the committee had arrived at a consensus by both sides shifting grounds from their initial hard positions. He therefore stated that:

> The sub-committee agreed that, "whenever there was a Shari'a case on appeal, the Federal Court of Appeal would be constituted by three judges learned in Islamic law. They are not called a Panel. They are not called a division. They are called a Federal Court of Appeal and for that purpose, they are the Federal Court of Appeal[109].

The above recommendation of the sub-committee generated another phase of intense debate that lasted for three days as to whether a Panel or a Division should be the right appellation for the recommendation. To this effect, the political interest of the northern Muslims especially the ruling class was thus laid bare because they sensed the recommendation of the sub-committee as a battle lost. As a result, on the 10th April 1978 they officially registered their protest through their representative Alhaji Kam Salem who told the house: "We beg to formally submit to you this notice and confirmation to you that as from the deliberations of the Assembly on Section 180 (1) (c), we cease to participate in the work of the Assembly and do hereby withdraw." Thereafter, they immediately staged a walkout from the CA.

It is interesting to note that this action did not succeed in halting the debate of the CA but rather as opined by Kukah it smoothed the way for the adoption of the recommendation of the sub-committee which deleted the controversial provisions of Section 180 (1) (c) in the CDC draft. Hence, the sub-committee recommendation became the constitutional provision on Shari'a in the final document[110]. Although the pro-Shari'a group finally returned back to the floor of the Assembly after some weeks of indecision, threats, and statements accusing the house of "distorting the balance of democratic representation", their action however, spurred the desperate members of the Muslim Students' Society (hence MSS) to send unpleasant words to

---

[109] Constituent Assembly Proceedings. Quoted in M.H. KUKAH, *Religion, Politics and Power in Northern Nigeria*, 125.

[110] M.H. KUKAH, *Religion, Politics and Power in Northern Nigeria*, 126.

the Assembly to either stop the opposition of Shari'a or take the full responsibility for putting the entire nation in chaos. To demonstrate their readiness to keep to their words, pro-Shari'a protesters took to the streets in Zaria and Kaduna with banners boldly written: *No Shari'a, No peace; No Shari'a, No Constitution; No Shari'a Muslims, No Nigeria et al* [111].

In the CA of 1998, the scenario of 1978 repeated itself. It was once again an imposed compromise that saved the situation. The Shari'a controversy marked a fundamental change for the worse in Christian-Muslim relations because public hate speeches started filtering in many northern cities, and inciting sermons were done in the public with the view to ignite the anger among the Christians. In the political arena, religion became a viewable tool in the hands of politicians whereby religious differences were deliberately fanned for political purposes[112]. Against this backdrop, such deliberate discriminatory and inciting statements thus provided the fertile ground for the expression of terrorism that is today experienced in the country. At this point, it is therefore, imperative to examine few of the religious crises that took place as a result of the expression of religious extremism particularly from the first-time Nigeria experienced the rule of democracy to date.

7. Islamic Extremism: An Overview of Religious Crises in Northern Nigeria

There were numerous crises that took place within the geopolitical region of the north. While some were politically motivated, others were triggered by ethnic identity. However, the following are examined base on their religious undertone as a result of the expression of religious sentiments and extremism.

7.1 *The Kano Maitatsine Riots of 1980-1985*

The year 1979 was a pivotal year in the historical development of Nigeria bearing in mind that it was a year that saw the end of military rule and coming into existence the new constitution of the country, coupled with the first bud of democratic promise that brought the reality of the civilian rule. Although, there had been some internal squabbles among the Muslims (between the Tijaniyya and the Qadiriyya sects)[113] due to some

---

[111] M.H. KUKAH, *Religion, Politics and Power in Northern Nigeria*, 127.

[112] M.A. OJO, "Competition and Conflict", 166.

[113] The Tijaniyya is a Sufi tariqa (order, path) within Sunni Islam. It originated in North Africa and then spread to West Africa. Its adherents are called Tijani. The order attaches

doctrinal issues, the situation worsened in the 1980 when the first volley of damnable clashes shattered a fragile peace that existed among the inhabitants of one of the Nigerian's oldest and industrious cities called Kano[114]. Interestingly, it is also one of the oldest Islamic cities that is known as a religious stronghold.

On December 18 & 19, 1980, the people of Kano experienced some skirmishes between a mystical sect called *Maitasine* (led by Alhaji Muhammadu Marwa)[115] and the Nigerian police force that led to the destruction of lives and properties. The name *Maitatsine* is a Hausa word coined to mean "someone who curses or damns". It was derived as a result of his (Marwa) abusive preaching in which he constantly used the phrase "*Allah ya Tsine...*" (may God curse/damn...).

While in Kano, Marwa preached a radical creed which called for jihad and an end to the use of all western consumer goods and luxuries such watches, televisions, radios, automobiles, and buttons. However, he did not condemn the use of modern weaponries[116]. In his preaching, he mocked the wealthy Muslims as infidels, and all those who peruse other books other than the Qur'an. He instigated his followers never to patronize the modern hospitals. He told them that it would be better for them to die from the infection of a small cut than to go to a secular hospital and receive medical aid from a godless *kafir* (pagan).

While he scorned the police as agents of Satan, he also admonished his followers to reject all forms of constituted authority that was not Islamic. This was as a result of the corrupt nature and decadence of the Nigerian government which the Maitatsine group believed that such government

---

a large importance to culture and education, and emphasizes the individual adhesion of the discipline (murid). While Qadiriyya is a Sufi tariqa (Sufi order). It derives its name from its founder Abdul-Qadir Gilani (1077–1166) of Gilan. The order relies strongly upon adherence to the fundamentals of Islam. These two orders in question were instrumental in the transition of Islam in the 18th century from a class religion to a religion of the whole people (the commoners). Cf., M. IWUCHUKWU, *Muslim-Christian Dialogue*, 7.

[114] A little about the city, Kano has been in existence for more than a thousand years. It is renowned for its industrial activities such as leather and metal crafts. It is a city that has kept its pre-eminent place as the largest city and most important city of sub-Saharan Africa, well known as the centre of the groundnut, hide and skin trade, and as the hub of the largest network of road, rail and air routes linking Northern Nigeria with other parts of African Continent.

[115] Alhaji Muhammadu Marwa (popularly called Maitatsine) hailed from the northern part of Cameroon. He migrated to Nigeria in 1962 and settled in Kano where he attracted a lot of Muslim followers as a result of his eloquence in preaching.

[116] A.C. van GORDER, *Violence in God's Name*, 231.

was constituted by "infidels" and must be resisted[117]. For this reason, Marwa's intransigence angered the authorities in Kano in 1962 which led to his deportation from Kano[118]. But he later found his way back to Nigeria in 1975, and once again resettled in Kano till his death.

Nevertheless, it is pertinent to state here that the 1979 scuffle that broke out in Mecca had great influence in the Maitatsine riots. A riot that was organized by the supporters of Ayatollah Khomeini in Mecca, led to scores of believers being killed. To this effect, the Maitatsine rose in support for those who had been killed. Marwa concurred with Khomeini's revolutionary assertions that Shari'a needed to be established throughout the Muslim world and that the evils of society were flourishing because too many Muslims had compromised their faith to serve the western gods of lascivious, materialism and capitalistic greed[119].

Against this backdrop, Marwa proclaimed that *Allah* ((God) had shown him that he had a special role to fulfill in bringing a pure expression of Islam to power. The turning point came when in 1980 Marwa's son was murdered mysteriously. Tension rose, and Islamist banners foisted in the streets of Kano written in Hausa, Arabic, and English that: "Democracy is unbelief! We do not want a constitution! We want government by the Holy Qur'an alone!"[120]. Meanwhile the activities of Maitatsine and his followers became a threat and a source of worry to the people of Kano to the extent that the then Governor Abubakar Rimi issued a letter on November 26, 1980 giving the sect two weeks to quit Kano state. But the governor's notice fell on deaf ears.

The riot began on December 18, 1980, when the Maitatsine sect took a number of police hostage and then barricaded themselves into their headquarters. They were armed with swords, dane guns, bows and arrows, and clubs, and prepared to serve Allah even if it meant their death. Marwa brainwashed his followers that those who embraced his revelations would become invincible to the police bullets. This however, proved not to be the case because Marwa himself was among the first casualties that were killed by the Nigerian police. But surprisingly, the death of Marwa became a source of inspiration to his followers to follow in his "holy" and suicidal discipline[121].

The writings found on the breast plate of their military leader Saidu Rabilu bolsters the aforementioned as it is read "If I were cut into pieces and I die, I

---

[117] T. FALOLA – M.M. HEATON, *A History of Nigeria*, 206.

[118] M.H. KUKAH, *Religion, Politics and Power in Northern Nigeria*, 154.

[119] A.C. van GORDER, *Violence in God's Name*, 232.

[120] A.C. van GORDER, *Violence in God's Name*, 232.

[121] A.C. van GORDER, *Violence in God's Name*, 233.

will return back to life again. There is no worthless person like Muhammadu Allah (Prophet). I prefer to die than to live in this world. It is better for him. If I die, animosity ends, madness ends. At the time I am dead, I am dead, but I will return to this world a second time"[122]. Although the police quelled the riot within ten days, the surviving devotees took to their heels to other neighbouring states and further staged battles. With regard to the level of destruction, both Christians and Muslims were killed and countless houses and other properties, mostly owned by the Muslims were equally destroyed[123].

7.2 *The Kafanchan Riot 1987*

Kafanchan, a settlement outskirt of Kaduna is known of its centrality as regards the Nigerian railway. It is the railway junction that links the north with other parts of the country[124]. It has been a place of rebellions, dating back to series of tax-uprisings against the British in 1922 and 1946[125]. The 1987 incident of Kafanchan is always difficult to verify, based on the fact that most accounts describing the events are based on the author's religion affiliation or sympathy[126].

Nevertheless, the Kafanchan crisis of 1987 erupted at the Kafanchan College of Education during the annual celebration of "Evangelical Week" organized by the Fellowship of Christian Students (hence FCS) of the campus. The event was tagged "1987 Mission on Campus". As part of the preparations, fliers, posters, fez caps, and banners were printed in order to publicise the programme and attract participation within and outside the campus. Some of the captions read: "secret revealed" come to the convocation square, March 6 – 8th, 1987 at 6.pm daily"; "Dead or Alive"; "Are you an Agnostic?"; "Welcome to Jesus Campus"[127].

The last caption 'Welcome to Jesus Campus' served as the first antecedent to the conflict that later ensued because such statement within the Nigerian context, is always perceived as an invitation to war[128]. More to it,

---

[122] M.H. KUKAH, *Religion, Politics and Power in Northern Nigeria*, 154.

[123] A.C. van GORDER, *Violence in God's Name*, 233.

[124] Tracing its historical background, Gofwen states that the town is believed to have got its name from a Hausa word "Kafa" meaning build or set-up, and "Chan" meaning over there. Bringing the two words together, "Kafanchan" would therefore mean build it over there. Its existence came to be as result of the British search for a site to establish the railway station in the area. Cf., R.R. GOFWEN, *Religious Conflicts in Northern Nigeria*, 83-84.

[125] A.C. van GORDER, *Violence in God's Name*, 235.

[126] A.C. van GORDER, *Violence in God's Name*, 235.

[127] Cf., R.R. GOFWEN, *Religious Conflicts in Northern Nigeria*, 85.

[128] Cf., A.C. van GORDER, *Violence in God's Name*, 235.

the welcome banner was strategically placed at the main entrance of the institution. At the complaint of the Muslim students to the school authority that the banner and its position gave the impression that all members of the institution were Christians, the FCS were asked to remove the banner, and they complied a day prior to the commencement of the activities.

While the school authority was settling the complaint over the banner, the FCS observed that some of their placed posters around the school had been torn off by unknown persons, and on arriving to the venue where they normally hold their Sunday fellowships, in order to break their fasting in preparation for the forthcoming event, they discovered that it was deliberately occupied by the Muslim students for their own programme. This was perceived by some of the Christian students as a deliberate predetermined act of provocation since the Muslim students knew that classroom block F was the usual venue for the FCS fellowships.

However, on March 6, the situation took a forceful turn when the Reverend Abubakar Bako, a convert from Islam and one of the invited guest speakers of the event, delivered an exposé where he compared his bankrupt life as a Muslim with his new-found faith in Christ[129]. His use of the Qur'an in comparison with the Bible was perceived to be offensive to the MSS. Among others were the following verses Bako quoted:

"(God) show us the straight path, the path of those whom you have favoured, not the path of those who earn your anger" (Q. 1:6-7) ... "And remember when Allah said, O Jesus I will raise thee to myself and cleanse thee of those disbelieve. I will make those who follow you superior to those who disbelieve, and unto me you will all return, and I will judge between you in the matters wherein you dispute. As for those who disbelieve, Allah will chastise them with heavy chastisement, here on earth and in the hereafter. But as for those who believe, Allah will reward them in full for Allah liveth no wrongdoer" (Q. 3: 55-57)[130].

From this Qur'anic vision of Jesus, Bako concluded that the Qur'an itself testifies that only Christians follow the right path[131].

---

[129] It is interesting to note that Abubakar was both an itinerant preacher based in Kano (a Muslim dominated city) and a research fellow at the Centre for Social and Economic Research at Ahmadu Bello University, Zaria. The title that seem to be the cause of the crisis is "Wondrous Ways" in which he dealt on his past life experience as a Muslim in comparison with his new life as a Christian. In the effort to do justice to his theme, he cited the Qur'an alongside with the Bible many times which led to the claim by the MSS that he was taking certain Qur'anic passages out of context.

[130] O. KANE, *Muslim Modernity in PostColonial Nigeria*, 191.

[131] O. KANE, *Muslim Modernity in PostColonial Nigeria*, 191.

The response to the Reverend's talk that sparked off the crisis varies. While the MSS claimed that they were first attacked by the FCS when some of their members were sharing their dissatisfaction with regard to the wrong interpretation of the Qur'an by the Reverend, some of the FCS started throwing stones on them[132]. On the other hand, the FCS claimed that one Aisha, a member of the MSS, stormed the crusade venue, seized the microphone from the speaker and shoved him. A free-for-all began: both Muslims and Christians took up whatever was at hand (sticks and stones) and tried to pummel either Bako, or to punch those who were attacking him. FCS fended off their MSS visitors and barricaded themselves inside a classroom[133]. Although the school authority was able to curtail the uprising within the campus and closed down the school, the crisis had already spilled over in the town.

Thereafter, it escalated to other parts of the state due to the propaganda of the media. The Radio Nigeria, Kaduna reported in both English and the local language (Hausa) news bulletins every hour that in Kafanchan, Christians had started killing Muslims, that Muslims had fled into hiding and that two mosques had been burnt and also copies of the Qur'an had been burnt in public[134]. Although the riot was finally brought under control after the destruction of lives and properties, it however seemed to be very clear that the riot expressed deep-seated feelings of resentment, prejudice and all forms of frustrations between Muslims and Christians on the one hand, and the people of the area against the government on the other[135].

7.3 *Evangelist Reinhard Bonnke's Crusade Riot of 1991*

In the autumn of 1991, less than five years after the Kafanchan crisis, anxieties and tensions began to build-up in the largest Islamic city of the African Sub-Sahara. In October 1991, CAN organized a five-day crusade and invited a German-born evangelical crusader, preacher and healer, Reinhard Bonnke. It was scheduled to take place at the Kano Race Course. Few weeks to the crusade, the Local Organizing Committee (hence LOC) had mounted serious publicity in order to draw the attention of the public to the event. Various mechanisms were used for the publicity. Announcements were made on both television and radio media; a motorcade went

---

[132] Cf., R.R. GOFWEN, *Religious Conflicts in Northern Nigeria*, 86-87.

[133] Cf., A.C. van GORDER, *Violence in God's Name*, 236-237.

[134] Cf., R.R. GOFWEN, *Religious Conflicts in Northern Nigeria*, 91.

[135] M.H. KUKAH, *Religion, Politics and Power in Northern Nigeria*, 188.

120

through parts of the city including the walled city advertising the crusade and its venue. In a summary, the city was conspicuously covered with handbills and posters written boldly in *A'jami* (Hausa language written in Arabic letters) that "Jesus for all by the year 2000" and "Capturing Kano for Christ"[136].

The tone of advertisement and the use of the term "crusade", a word that immediately rankles Muslim ears and reminds them of the crusades of the past centuries, led some Muslims to rush to the bizarre conclusion that Christian troops were being marshalled for a military attack[137]. Worse still, they were equally angered by the fact that they sought for a similar permission to bring in one Sheikh Ahmed Deedat from South Africa for a religious revival for the Muslims in Kano but were denied[138].

In like manner, the venue which was given to the Christians for the hosting of their crusade, was denied of them (the Muslims) in one of their celebrations[139]. Against this backdrop, the perceived double standards of the government and the triumphalist messages of the Christian advertisements, thus, spurred the Muslims to rise up in the defence of their faith. They protested that Christians should not be allowed to hold the crusade, and the permission granted to the Evangelist Bonnke should be withdrawn. In this regard, over 8,000 youths protested over the presence in town of Reinhard Bonnke, whom they accused of planning to blaspheme Islam[140].

On the demand of the protesters, the Christians were denied of the venue earlier given to them. As a result, they rescheduled the event to take place at St. Thomas /St. Louis School in Sabon Gari, an area carved – outside the Muslim dominated walled city – for the strangers that is dominated by the Christians. Despite the denial of the Race Course venue by the state government and the security agents as demanded by the Muslims, they (Muslims) still resolved to use force in preventing the crusade from holding.

As Bonnke arrived in the city on 13th October 1991, violence broke out. The Muslims left the mosque amidst the battle cry of *Allah Hu akbar* (God is Great), they detoured to Galadima street and specifically towards the Sabon Gari area (Christian settlement) and started destroying handbills, posters and banners. Those who stood on their way were attacked. The multi-million-naira Sabon Gari market was ransacked and looted. While people were killed, businesses and homes were equally set ablaze. By way of self-de-

---

[136] O. KANE, *Muslim Modernity in PostColonial Nigeria*, 199.

[137] J.H. BOER, *Nigeria's Decades of Blood*, 41.

[138] A. TAIYE, "Religious Fanaticism and Fundamentalism in Nigeria", 148.

[139] J.H. BOER, *Nigeria's Decades of Blood*, 41.

[140] Cf., R.R. GOFWEN, *Religious Conflicts in Northern Nigeria*, 103.

fence, Christians quickly organized themselves and retaliated with an attack[141]. This reprisal however, led to more destruction of lives and properties.

The Christians living around Sabon Gari, Rimi Kebe, and Tudun Murtala areas suffered the greatest human and material losses[142]. Although the police intervened and assured the citizens of their safety by claiming that they had everything under their control, however, the violence did not end until after two days of fighting and killing. Statistically, while government figures recorded 8 deaths, other eye witnesses recorded 200, and CAN claimed 2,000 deaths, and 22,000 people displaced. The people took refuge in Bukavu army barracks and Bompai police station[143].

However, it is worthy to note that the visit of the Evangelist Reinhard Bonnke to Kano was not the first in Nigeria. He had earlier visited and held similar crusades in the cities of Lagos, Enugu, Jos, Ilorin, and Kaduna. Yet, in these other cities, violence was never recorded, except for the displacement of banners and posters that clearly told the story that Bonnke had miraculously healed the sick, cleansed the lepers, and gave sight to the blind through the power of spirit-led prayer[144].

7.4 *Kaduna Shari'a Riot of 2000*

The year 2000 was one of the most violent years that the people of Kaduna state would ever remember. It was a year that the city experienced an outbreak of the worst religious violence in the history of the country that was occasioned by the introduction of Shari'a law by the then civilian governor Ahmed Makarfi. What triggered the Shari'a conflict of 2000, however, was the impression of the Christian citizens that the action of the government will turn the state into a Muslim state which is a heterogeneous and multi-religious in nature[145]. In order to have a better picture of the crisis and understand better its magnitude in terms of destruction of both lives and property, it is imperative to digress a little and expose the composition of the state in question.

Prior to the Colonial conquest, the present-day Kaduna town was traditionally inhabited by the Gbagyi people who were pushed to the outskirts and their land was taken from them. The name "Kaduna" comes from the Hausa word "Kaduna" which means "crossing the river of Snails"[146]. The composition of the entire state is however better described in the following words:

---

[141] R.R. GOFWEN, *Religious Conflicts in Northern Nigeria*, 104.

[142] A. TAIYE, "Religious Fanaticism and Fundamentalism in Nigeria", 148.

[143] O. KANE, *Muslim Modernity in PostColonial Nigeria*, 201.

[144] A.C. van GORDER, *Violence in God's Name*, 244.

[145] Cf., O.E. ALAO – A.G. MAVALLA, "Kaduna State Shari'a Crisis" 8.

[146] R.R. GOFWEN, *Religious Conflicts in Northern Nigeria*, 110.

Officially British perspectives on the growth of Kaduna may be summarized as follows. In 1913 Kaduna was selected by Lugard to be the Capital not just the north, but of the whole of Nigeria. For practical reasons, including cost, Lagos continued to be the capital. At the time, Kaduna was Savanna bush and a resting place for Crocodiles (Kada, in Hausa). Hence the name "Kaduna". Zungeru had been the seat of government in the early days, but in 1917 government activities were shifted to Kaduna. It was near to Zaria, where the military headquarters was located at the time. The railway line to Zaria passed through Kaduna, which was more congenial to expatriates because of its climate and water supply. By 1956, Kaduna is a town of about 30,000, and serves as an administrative and military base... Kaduna is also the major centre of rail traffic in the north, with the largest junction, handling about 250 trains a week. This facilitates the large influx of southerners... In short, by 1956, Kaduna is a town of soldiers, railway men, administrators, educational institutions and southern migrants[147].

Against this backdrop, it is obvious that Kaduna as a city is strategically positioned with its rich antecedents. Today, it is the third largest state in the country with a population density of over 2 million people in 2014. More than any other city in Northern Nigeria, Kaduna city occupies the most important political position in the region following its historical development of politics[148]. Furthermore, it is one of the states in Nigeria with the largest number of ethnicities. It has over 50 ethnic groups living side by side and each struggling for identity[149]. In this regard, the Hausa/Fulani dominates the northern part of the state and the Christians who are of different ethnicity dominate the southern part. It is also interesting to note that the British indirect rule policy worsened the situation pertaining to the struggle for survival of these numerous ethnics. Hence, the heterogeneous and pluralistic nature of the state always serves as a fertile ground for any un-averted conflict. At this point, we now examine the crisis.

Since the departure of the British Colonialists after independence, there has been a longstanding contention over the introduction of Shari'a in the country. Shari'a is seen by many Muslims as an entire system of guidelines and rules which encompass criminal law, personal status law, and many other aspects of religious, cultural, and social life[150]. The Dictionary of Islam succinctly states that Shari'a is: "The way or road in the religion of Mohammed, which God has established for guidance of His people both for the

---

[147] R.R. GOFWEN, *Religious Conflicts in Northern Nigeria*, 110.
[148] O.E. ALAO – A.G. MAVALLA, "Kaduna State Shari'a Crisis of 2000, 9.
[149] WIKIPEDIA, "Kaduna State".
[150] ___, "'Political Shari'a'?", 1.

worship of God and for the duties of life"[151]. Shari'a within this context is thus viewed as the basis of *Umma* (Islamic community). It is in this regard that the protagonists of Shari'a in Nigeria have argued that given its crucial significance in Islam, no Muslim can be said to be fully practicing Islam without being guided by the Shari'a[152]. As seen from the controversy of the Shari'a debate, the implementation of Shari'a has been highly politicized.

With the introduction of Shari'a by Sani Ahmed Yerima (the then governor of Zamfara State) on October 22, 1999 in his state as a fulfilment of one of his campaign promises, a machinery was thus set in motion, and it marked the turning point in the history of Shari'a in Nigeria. To this effect, Kaduna like any of the Northern States with a significant number of Muslims, came under the pressure to do same. The Muslim community officially made a request to the State House of Assembly on December 14, 1999 for the implementation of Shari'a.

Consequently, an eleven-man committee constituted by Muslim members was set up and demanded all parties representing the interest for and against Shari'a to state their case in writing and submit it to the committee. This however did not go well with Christian members pointing to their complete absence in the composition of the committee membership. Although the Muslim members tried to justify their act by saying that it was purely an issue that concerned the Muslims and not Christians, this however, created room for suspicion and mistrust and thus polarized the State House of the Assembly along religious divide[153].

As the committee commenced its work, within the first three weeks Muslims were mobilized throughout the state and daily took turns demonstrating at the venue of the committee's sitting to submit a memorandum in support of Shari'a. This exercise got to its peak, when on February 14, 2000 Muslims decided on a five-day sustained peaceful demonstration in the state capital in a long procession that passed through all major streets demanding the outright introduction of full Shari'a law in the state and the appointment of an Emir in the city[154].

It was against this background that the Christians under the auspices of CAN, staged their own peaceful demonstration to communicate their stand on what they perceived as the forceful and constitutional attempt to impose Shari'a on a multi-religious and multi-ethnic society. As they marched to

---

[151] DICTIONARY OF ISLAM. Quoted in R.R. GOFWEN, *Religious Conflicts in Northern Nigeria*, 111.

[152] R.R. GOFWEN, *Religious Conflicts in Northern Nigeria*, 111.

[153] R.R. GOFWEN, *Religious Conflicts in Northern Nigeria*, 113.

[154] R.R. GOFWEN, *Religious Conflicts in Northern Nigeria*, 114.

the state house and the government house to officially register their stand, some Islamist in return staged a counter-protest. And while the Christians were returning from the government house, the two groups clashed and confronted each other. Hence, violence ensued.

The Shari'a violence was so deadly that it was described as a conflict of "ethnic cleansing from one neighbourhood to the other"[155]. Within three days many lives and properties were destroyed. It was so devastating that it became difficult to ascertain the exact number of deaths. This was as a result that Youths (both Christians and Muslims) had been taught how to handle guns and were eager to experiment with them. Muslim boys were allegedly given army uniforms and guns. Thereby setting in total confusion, since it became impossible to easily identify the fake army from the genuine Nigerian army. Hence, it took the military with armoured tanks to end the violence[156]. However, it is important to note that it was in this crisis that a priest of the Catholic Archdiocese of Kaduna (Rev. Fr. Clement Ozi-Bello) was killed.

The government reported a total number of 609 deaths, while Human Rights Watch reported those killed numbered 5, 000. However, a good number of other sources claimed that around 2,000 people were slain with the exclusion of victims of extrajudicial killings by the security agents while trying to bring the situation under control[157]. Against this backdrop, the existing fragile relationship between the Christians and Muslims in the state was all the more punctured. As a result, the Shari'a crisis spilled over to some local government areas outside the Kaduna town. Worthy of mention were the clashes between Gwagi and the Kataf in Birnin Gwari local government area, and Christians and Muslims in Federal College of Education, Zaria local government area in 2002[158]. It is, however, imperative to state that since the 2000 Shari'a crisis, the state remains vulnerable so much so that any slightest provocation could easily ignite violence. The indicative of this vulnerability is the fact that within the space of eleven years (2000 – 2011) over 23 cases of violence were recorded in the state[159].

7.5 *Boko Haram Insurgency 2009*

The insurgency of the Boko Haram is elaborately treated in the previous chapter. However, bearing in mind the frequency of the Kaduna religious crises, and the ethno-religious crises of Jos (1994, 2001), and Bauchi

---

[155] Cf., A.C. van GORDER, *Violence in God's Name*, 250.

[156] J.H. BOER, *Nigeria's Decades of Blood*, 67.

[157] J.H. BOER, *Nigeria's Decades of Blood*, 67.

[158] O.E. ALAO – A.G. MAVALLA, "Kaduna State Shari'a Crisis of 2000, 11.

[159] O.E. ALAO – A.G. MAVALLA, "Kaduna State Shari'a Crisis of 2000, 11.

(1994, 2000), majority of Nigerians were of the opinion that the menace of the dreaded Islamic fundamentalist group, the Boko Haram was but a continuation of the old Shari'a question operating under a new name[160]. But suffice it to say that while Boko Haram undoubtedly attack Christians, there were rogue elements who also acted on their own and attacked Christians using Boko Haram-style tactics especially in areas with a history of interreligious violence, either to stir up discontent or to settle scores due to intra-religious disputes. The case of Lydia Joseph and the "Miya Barkate Eight" in Bauchi State is a bolster to the fore.

On 29 August 2011, Lydia Joseph for instance, was apprehended while trying to burn St. John's Cathedral in Bauchi. Similarly, on 9 January 2012, eight young men, all Christians, were apprehended attempting to bomb the Church of Christ in Nigeria (hence COCIN) at Miya Barkate in Bauchi State[161]. If the above incidents were successful, the probability of the Boko Haram to have claimed responsibility would have been high since both incidents took place at the peak of their terrorists' activities.

Suffice to state here that in all the above described crises, there exist common factors that led to their emergence. In this regard, it is thus imperative to now examine some factors that could be responsible for the violence unleashed by the Islamic extremists within the northern geographical location.

8. Causes of Religious Violence

8.1 *The Principle of Absolutism/Religious Intolerance*

In the relentless effort in finding solutions to the continued religious violence, some scholars discovered that *absolutism* is one of the fundamental causes of most religious violence. The principle of absolutism demands for a "convergence to the centre" in pursuit of Islamic orthodoxy[162]. J. A. Atanda (a historian) refers to this principle as "horizontal intolerance" whereby it refers to the "holistic approach to issues of religion and politics"[163]. This was the principle that was adopted by the northern Nigerian Muslim leaders after the jihad of Uthman dan Fodio since the approach and the philosophy of this principle requires that:

Proselytization is not to be just a conversion of the people to Islamic religion. It must also involve the conversion of the ruler and of the political institutions to

---

[160] O.E. Alao – A.G. Mavalla, "Kaduna State Shari'a Crisis of 2000, 11.

[161] K. Mohammed, "The Message and Methods of Boko Haram", 20.

[162] Cf., M.A. Ojo, "Pentecostal Movements", 176 & 184.

[163] J.A. Atanda, "Conclusion – Paradoxes and problems of Religion", 187.

purely Islamic ones. In short, Islam must be a state religion and the state must be an Islamic one. It follows that only Muslims must rule the state and only Muslims can be proper citizens in such a state. At best, such other religions are to be tolerated, pending the conversion of their adherents to Islam"[164].

This principle seems to imply that it does not welcome any other religion. As a result, it promotes religious intolerance. However, if Islam must co-exist alongside other religions, it is to be tolerated for only but a short time during which the adherents of such religions are to be persuaded for conversion. In general, religious intolerance has been identified as the major source of religious conflict/violence in all societies, and permeating all forms of human civilizations, with attendant destructive tendencies[165].

People tend to hate and never tolerate others due to the level of their fanatical believe in their respective religious ideology. This is due to the obvious reason that fanaticism in general is incompatible with the commandments of justice and love. Love requires tolerance, and this noble virtue means respect for the opinions and beliefs of others, not out of religious or moral indifference, but, irrespective of one's own standpoint, out of respect towards one's neighbour as a free and equal person with the inalienable right to his own convictions[166]. Hence, religious intolerance breeds religious bigotry when the rights of religious freedom of members of other religions are out-rightly denied.

In the Islamisation of the northern Nigeria and the Conversion Campaign of the Sardauna of Sokoto, it is obvious that this principle played an important role. For although Christians were tolerated, their toleration however, was just for a little while. As a result, the religious intolerance exhibited of recent past by most Muslims against Christians in northern Nigeria cannot be isolated from this factor of absolutism.

Consequently, the totalizing philosophy of absolutism cannot be realistic in the pluralistic society of the northern Nigeria due to the fact the Christians today have become more conscious of their human rights that guarantee and ratify their right to life and a religion of their choice as fundamental to the tenets of a democratic nation such as Nigeria in the modern society. This is buttressed by the Council Fathers of Vatican II that the "Contemporary man is becoming increasingly conscious of the dignity of the human person"[167], and "Everyone has the right to worship God according to the dictates of conscience; and therefore, the right to private and

---

[164] J.A. ATANDA, "Conclusion – Paradoxes and problems of Religion", 187.

[165] R.R. GOFWEN, *Religious conflicts in northern Nigeria*, 50.

[166] U. SCHAEFER, "Religious Intolerance", 3.

[167] PAUL VI, "Dignitatis Humanae", §1.

public worship of God"[168]. As a result, such fundamental rights become the Christians sole civil obligation and pride to defend and assert without sacrificing them on the altar of religious absolutism.

8.2 *Islamic Reformation and Revivalism*

From the 19th century as already stated in the first chapter of this study, there arose a gradual development of the theory and practice of Islamism due to fast rise of modernization and its power of secularization. As a result, the birth of fundamentalist movements around the globe such as anti-colonialism was born. Against this backdrop, terrorist groups such as Al-Qaida (the first multinational terrorist group of the twenty-first century), emerged and confronted the world with a new kind of threat. Al-Qaida has, however, moved terrorism beyond the status of protest to a global instrument that challenges western influence within the Muslim world[169].

With this global rise of terrorism therefore, many Islamists associated with Islamic revivalism advocated for purely Islamic-based political agenda in place of principles of modern state introduced by European colonialists. To this effect, the twentieth and twenty-first centuries produced a number of these Islamists that include; Mawlana Mawdudi of pre-independence India, Ayatollah Khomeini of Iran, Sayyid Qutb of Egypt[170], and Osman bin Laden of Saudi Arabia (a disciple to Muhammad Qutb – the brother to Sayyid Qutb, and Abdullah Azzam – whom he later murdered alongside with his son on their way to the Friday prayer)[171]. Hence, Nigeria as a nation is not exempted from this global influence of Islamic revivalism.

It is interesting to note that at the core of the goal of Islamic reformation and revivalism is the search to use Islam to foster nationalist agenda and program, since for the revivalist or Islamists, the nation they sought to establish "was none other than the *umma* (holy community), the core of the promised Islamic state"[172]. This development eventually evolved in the Islamists completely objecting to the presence of Western cultural influence in their milieu and calling for people to go back to the roots of Islam and replicate the society of the first-century Islamic world. The desire to get back to the root of Islam hence, resulted in militant Islamist activities or fundamentalism[173]. As a result, there came into existence *Wahhabism* that

---

[168] POPE JOHN XXIII, "Pacem in Terris", §14.

[169] R. GUNARATNA, *Inside Al Qaeda*, 1.

[170] Cf., N.S.V. REZA, *Mawdudi & the Making of Islamic Revivalism*, 3.

[171] R. GUNARATNA, *Inside Al Qaeda*, 16-53.

[172] N.S.V. REZA, *Mawdudi & the Making of Islamic Revivalism*, 4.

[173] M. IWUCHUKWU, *Muslim-Christian Dialogue*, 66.

is manifested in the Salafi movement in Saudi Arabia, the Islamic Brotherhood in Egypt, the Mahdi movement in the Sudan, and the Uthman Dan Fodio cum Boko Haram in Nigeria.

In summary, by starting from the jihad of Uthman Dan Fodio, down to the 1980 Maitatsine first intrareligious crisis, and the Boko Haram extremism, the Islamic reformation and renewal of the twentieth and twenty-first centuries have been at the centre stage of their respective ideologies as reactions to the perceived domination of western secular ideologies over their Islamic culture and values in the northern region. To bring therefore into reality the promotion of the Islamic culture and values against the perceived dominated western secular ideologies in the region, the establishment of the Shari'a law becomes thus unavoidable, and all Muslims must rise up to show their support. Thus, the implementation of the Shari'a law in the twelve northern states exhibited the climax of the expression of the Islamic extremism in the northern region which has led us to where we are now.

Nevertheless, it is imperative to bear in mind that while we appreciate the peaceful and genuinely beneficial (from Islamic perspective) aspects of the principle of Islamic reformation and revivalism, we must also recognize the possible violent aspects of the principle which have been championed by the Islamic terrorist group like the Boko Haram. Thus, their link with international bodies such as Al-Qaida, Al-Shabaab, AQIM, MUJAO, and IS cannot be overemphasized in this regard.

8.3 *Political Emancipation*

Following the enforcement of the principle of the indirect rule[174] in the northern region by the British Colonial Administrators that paved the way for the Hausa/Fulani traditional rulers to lord it over the northern Christian minority group, and the selfish manipulation of the NPC political party for the promotion of Islamic agenda by the Sardauna of Sokoto, it is obvious that the northern Christian minorities were oppressed in all ramifications. As a result, political emancipation became the only option of their freedom. Hence the formation of Non-Muslim League (NML) that brought together the non-Muslim minorities of the northern region became necessary in 1952[175].

---

[174] The principle of the Indirect Rule had already been explained above in this chapter. See 4.1, footnote #45 above.

[175] M.H. KUKAH, *Religion Politics and Power in Northern Nigeria*, 7-8.

However, as NML lacked the economic patronage, organization and a cohesive base to gain political power, it was later metamorphosed to Middle Zone League (MZL) and finally to the United Middle Belt Congress (UMBC). It is against this background, that the resistance of the non-Hausa/Fulani ethnicities in the north to the dominance of the Hausa/Fulani oligarchy ended up in serious violence. For example, the 1960 and 1964 Tiv riots[176].

Nevertheless, the struggle for the emancipation continued as the Sardauna launched his conversion campaign in the northern region which was geared toward the islamisation of the northern region regardless of other existing religions outside Islam[177]. Consequently, the 1966 military coup in which the Sardauna was killed along with other top-ranking politicians, and the dissolution of the three major regions which were replaced by the creation of 12 states by General Yakubu Gowon in 1967 brought some relieve to the non-Muslim minorities[178].

Important to note is that this relieve did not end the oppression of the Hausa/Fulani. Hence, the fear of the Non-Muslim minorities persisted as they continue to face discrimination of various degrees by the ruling Hausa/Fulani majority. This include; discrimination in job opportunities, differential treatment based on religious affiliation as regards promotion and political appointments, discrimination in gaining admissions into higher institutions *et al.* To this effect, the resistance of the non-Muslim minorities over the dominance of the Hausa/Fulani majority continued and always resulted in major crises down the road that are described today as interethnic conflicts that often result into religious violence.

8.4 *Christian Fundamentalism and Exclusivism*

For the sake of objectivity and a good scholarship, it is fitting to also examine the excesses of the other major religion (Christianity) in question. By implication, the study will only amount to an incomplete and lopsided examination of factors that bred religious bigotry in northern Nigeria without a profound review of the dominant exclusive theology of salvation that is an entrenched component of Christian soteriology. There is no gain saying that Christian fundamentalism is a globally recognized bloc of Christians especially from the nineteenth and early twentieth centuries.

---

[176] M. IWUCHUKWU, *Muslim-Christian Dialogue*, 69.

[177] See 5.3 above.

[178] The 1967 newly created 12 states include; North-Western State, North-Eastern State, Kano State, North-Central State, Benue-Plateau State, Kwara State, Western State, Lagos State, Mid-Western State, Rivers State, and East-Central State.

Christian Fundamentalism insisted upon a number of doctrinal positions that it considered as the basic fundamentals of Christianity that needed to be reaffirmed in the midst of corrosive change and theological liberalism[179]. The doctrines included verbal inerrancy of Scripture, the virgin birth, substitutionary atonement, the physical resurrection of Jesus, and the bodily return of Christ as earlier mentioned.

Fundamentalists are not anti-intellectual but are enlightened apologists who counter liberal theology and skepticism by applying the same philosophical method and high criticism as their opponents.[180] To this effect, the Christian fundamentalists consider themselves as the most authentic and original followers of Christ. They grew and expanded from North America down to other parts of the world especially after the World War II. As a result, the Northern Nigeria was one of the places that the Christian fundamentalists extended their presence.

They came as independent Church missionary organizations and thereby established local Churches in different parts of northern Nigeria. They retained and spread their fundamentalist doctrines to their new converts. Some of the idiosyncrasies of Christian fundamentalism, like the concept of being the only saved people and specially privileged children of God, restored a sense of human dignity and pride to many of the marginalized northern Nigerian minorities, who had lived decades and perhaps centuries of imperial control and subjugation by the Hausa/Fulani oligarchy as earlier stated.

In like manner, the obsession and courage by Christian fundamentalists to evangelize and denounce some of the old myth perpetuated by former or present Muslim leadership only made it imperative that collision with Islamic fundamentalists was imminent[181]. However, it is pertinent to bear in mind that there exists a common thread that binds both Christian and Muslim fundamentalists. Being products of modernism, they both reject modernity.

Although this rejection of modernity becomes a common binding force among the Christian and Muslim fundamentalists, the Christian fundamentalists however see themselves as the only saved and privilege people while others are condemned. This became more complex with the presence of the US influenced type of Pentecostalism in northern Nigeria from 1960s. Its idiosyncratic theology of exclusivism and its characteristic minimalisation or condemnation of non-believers (Muslims inclusive) further brought religious bigotry to its full scale among the Northern Nigeria Christians and Muslims[182].

---

[179] O. KALU, *African Pentecostalism*, 250.

[180] O. KALU, *African Pentecostalism*, 251.

[181] M. IWUCHUKWU, *Muslim-Christian Dialogue*, 70.

[182] M. IWUCHUKWU, *Muslim-Christian Dialogue*, 70.

Nonetheless, it is imperative to note that the condemnation and trashing of non-members was not limited to non-Christians but also Christians alike who do not share their belief. According to the branding of people by this group of Christians, anyone whose doctrinal or theological presuppositions do not resonate with theirs belong to the large population of reprobates, and that group includes Catholics, Anglicans, and members of other mainline Protestant Churches who reject the theological assumptions of the Pentecostals[183].

Although not physically militant, but their public preaching is often inciting, hostile against non-members and other religions (Islam inclusive) thereby promoting the culture of hate among Nigerians. A good example is the inciting preaching of one Apostle Johnson Suleman (President and General Overseer of Omega Fire Ministries International - OFMI) who asked his Church members to kill any Muslim herdsman that is seen around his Church premises. His attempted arrest by the Nigerian government in January 2017 raised a public controversy[184].

8.5 *Sensationalism in Media Reportage*

In every given event in the sphere of human life, the role of the media cannot be underestimated because the media magnifies what it feels is sensational to its audience, and as well as reduces an event to nothing when it does not interest its audience. This principle of "media selected interest" as we may describe it follows suit in the event of crisis reportage particularly in northern Nigeria. It is a truism that when crisis is not well managed by the media, the possibility of its escalation and its devastating effects are always high.

A vivid example is the role of the media in the 1987 Kafanchan religious crisis as we have already seen earlier. Despite the efforts of the security personnel who brought the crisis under control, the news reports monitored on the Federal Radio Corporation of Nigeria (hence, FRCN), Kaduna, a day after the crisis in the campus, went viral in the state alleging that Christians were killing Muslims indiscriminately, burning their Mosques and copies of the Qur'an, and also banishing them from the town.

Further still, the broadcast alleged that an itinerant preacher had misquoted the Qur'an and blasphemed the name of Prophet Mohammed, urging Christians to kill Muslims and burn their Mosques[185]. It is obvious that

---

[183] M. IWUCHUKWU, *Muslim-Christian Dialogue*, 70-71.

[184] O. FABIYI – F. OLAKOR, "Apostle Suleman to Appear before DSS".

[185] ___, "Itinerant Christian Preacher", 10.

news reportages such as these add nothing to the crisis but escalation that often ends with more destruction of live and property. It is to this end that in the case of the Kafanchan crisis reportage, reprisal attacks were ignited by the Muslim youths first within the Kaduna metropolis and then later all over the state, causing an invaluable loss of lives and property[186]. It was this type of provocative and emotive reports that made most religious leaders in the country to accuse the media of fanning the embers of religious violence. CAN particularly called for the proscription of the New Nigerian Newspapers…, and the FRCN be probed for the sinister role and the editor of the New Nigerian newspaper be disciplined[187].

In like manner, the readily availability of the social media network to disseminate viral information in our modern era is also a factor to the fuelling of religious crisis. For instance, information (true or false, censored or uncensored) travels quickly worldwide within a twinkle of an eye, thereby generating intense hatred between belligerents and reprisal attacks in a cycle of violence. News headlines such as 'Islamic Assailants Kill Hundreds of Christians near Jos', 'Muslims slaughter Christians in central Nigeria', 'Christians hack Muslims and burn Qur'an' etc., are very common during religious disturbances[188]. Such alarming headlines, coupled with gory images of victims posted on the social media network, often trigger reprisal attacks.

8.6 *The Use of Religious Symbols*

The use of religious symbols in the public sphere is another salient factor that in the past was not taken into consideration. But today it has given rise to debate both locally and internationally on the scope of freedom of religion. In Nigeria for instance, it is increasingly becoming a source of religious conflict and violence. Nevertheless, it is interesting to note that among the most prominent of the religious symbols at stake in current debates is the Islamic headscarf, or *hijab*[189].

---

[186] R.R. GOFWEN, *Religious conflicts in northern Nigeria*, 91-92.

[187] M.H. KUKAH, *Religion Politics and Power in Northern Nigeria*, 194.

[188] Cf., I.T. SAMPSON, "Religious Violence in Nigeria".

[189] The headscarf is worn by a female over her head, generally covering her hair, ears, and neck. *Hijab* also has the meaning of female modesty in dress and, for some Muslim women, may involve wearing a large loose garment that can cover the hands and face – a *burqa*; or a veil that leaves only a slit for the eyes – a *niqab*. *Hijab* is an integral part of Qur'anic teachings for a large part of the Muslim world, but there is little agreement on whether it is absolutely prescribed. See L. BARNETT, "Freedom of Religion, 1.

With the implementation of Shari'a in the northern region, most Muslim women insist on the use of *hijab*, and in extreme cases, *Niqab* and *Burqa*, even where the regulatory regime prohibits their use.[190] A good example was the *fatwa* (Islamic death sentence) issued on a Christian lecturer (Dr. Andrew Akume) in 2005 for turning back a Muslim female student who wore a hijab from attending his lecture following the prohibition of the use of headscarves by female law students in the faculty of law, ABU, Zaria. This act did not only cause serious religious tension on the campus, but also ignited a diplomatic twist between the governments of Kaduna (home state of the university) and Benue (home state of the lecturer) states over Akume's safety.

In another development, while the inscription of the Arabic symbols on Nigerian currency denominations has been vehemently opposed by Nigerian Christians, who associate it with Islam and an overarching Islamisation agenda by northern Muslims, the Nigerian Muslims on the other hand, continue to oppose the use of the 'cross' as a symbol on public hospitals' bill/sign boards and other hospital accessories. Such a symbol is always perceived as imposition of Christian religious symbol on Muslims. These situations thus remain potential triggers of religious violence.

8.7 *Poverty and Ignorance*

The high level of poverty and ignorance in the Nigerian society particularly in the northern region where the *almajiri* form of education has been championed at the expense of the western education is becoming alarming and has thus become a source of concern and worry in the nation. As a result, underdevelopment, poverty and illiteracy rear their ugly heads in almost every sphere of life in the region. What is common in most cities of the region is the multiple streams of school age children roaming about the streets with begging bowls if they are boys and with tray loads balanced on their heads selling trifles if they are girls.

As per the youths within the age of 20 and above, while some of them are likely to be selling petrol measured in jerry cans in the black market as a source of livelihood, others on the other hand, prefer to loaf idly. For the female counterparts, they will have small or big basins (depending how well established and lucrative the business may be) doling out food to buyers in the streets. Those middle-aged or older, they recline tiredly on mats spread in the street corners as beggars with no discrimination to gender begging no matter the circumstances of the weather condition. The

---

[190] Cf., I.T. SAMPSON, "Religious Violence in Nigeria, 124.

following words succinctly recaps the level of poverty in the northern region thus:

> The United Nations Development Programme (UNDP), Human Development Report on Nigeria has consistently described Nigeria as a rich country with a poor population. The World Bank asserts this by estimating that 80% of oil revenues from 1965-2004, have accrued to only 1% of the population. This implies that the riches of our country are being cornered by a few people who have found themselves in corridors of power at the federal, state and local government levels. In 2008 UNDP estimated that 70% of Nigerians live below poverty line. That is, they earn less than US $1 (₦145) a day[191].

It is against this backdrop, that it becomes exigent to note that poverty and ignorance in northern Nigeria have always played a significant role in exacerbating religious crises and other socio-political unrests in the region. The presupposition is that the elites and most often the politicians buy off these youths easily that in most cases found loitering in the streets due to lack of job opportunities, drug addictions and the *almajiri* school system, for pittance and recruit them into conflicts, while the politicians and their families shy away or run from trouble spots to safe havens[192].

Nonetheless, it is important to note that ignorance here refers not only to the illiteracy of the western knowledge but also ignorance of one's religion. Since the majority of the youths are often brainwashed by their religious leaders, the truth of their religious tenets sometimes is not revealed to them. As a result, the values and tenets of such religion are hardly promoted. Hence, engaging into violent act at any given opportunity becomes easy as in the case of Boko Haram.

At this juncture, having examined the underlying factors that often trigger the intractable violence in the northern part of Nigeria it is fitting to now turn our attention to the challenges that often accompany such violence particularly with regard to the life of the Church. Although, the list of the above factors is inexhaustible, our next task therefore is to bring out the challenges that confront the missionary activities of the Church within the volatile region in question.

---

[191] D.J. GWAMNA – P.B. DAYIL, "Religious Fundamentalism in Northern Nigeria", 74.

[192] D.J. GWAMNA – P.B. DAYIL, "Religious Fundamentalism in Northern Nigeria", 75.

9. Challenges Confronting the Church's Missionary Activities in Northern Nigeria

9.1 *Islamic Fundamentalism*

From the above examination of Nigeria as a nation and the setting of the Northern region, it is obvious that the Northern Nigerian States are generally known to have a predominantly Islamic population, with a vibrant presence of Christian communities[193]. In the Southern region however, it is admitted that Christians are in the majority, but with a significant Muslim population. Interestingly, is the fact that Christians and Muslims for decades have coexisted peacefully in the country. In all the regions, there has been relative harmony and peace among the Christians and the Muslims despite their religious differences. But with the rise of Islamic radicalism in the Arab world in the late nineteenth century and early twentieth century which also influenced other Muslims around the world, the existing relative peaceful atmosphere was lost, and hence, religious intolerance is thus promoted.

Today there are several strong Islamic fundamentalists of various sects that are causing threat not only to the Church but also to the national unity of the country. Although each extremist group holds onto its ideology, they seem to however have a common desired goal that binds their common interest. That is the application of the Shari'a law to the fullest, and the islamisation of all Nigerians which is championed by the stricter Islamic radical groups such as the Boko Haram.

Since the implementation of the Shari'a law that was first championed by the then governor of Zamfara State Ahmed Sani Yerima on 27 January, 2000 in fulfilment of his promises made during his 1999 political campaigns in the effort to score cheap political popularity, the Shari'a law has been the core ideology of the Islamic fundamentalists who have been in existence since 2002 – prior to their first international appearance under the name Boko Haram in 2009. Hence, the impact of the expression of such religious extremism in the life of the Church cannot be overemphasized. It is against this backdrop that Ignatius Ayau Kaigama (the then Catholic archbishop of Jos archdiocese and a renowned peace builder), describes the Church's challenges in the following succinct words:

> In my opinion, it was not until the launching of what is now referred to as 'political Shari'a' in 1999 that much religious heat started being felt in Northern Nigeria. As observed earlier, Shari'a had already been in existence for decades without any problems, but its dramatic re-introduction not by Islamic scholars but by State political governors of some Northern States following the

---

[193] See Appendix F.

136

example of the Zamfara State Governor, Alhaji Sani Ahmed Yerima, opened the floodgates of mutual distrust, suspicion, intolerance and a paranoid fear that have since characterized Muslim-Christian relations. While Muslims saw the renewed attention to Shari'a and its application as commendable Islamic piety, Christians saw it as an attempt to create an Islamic society. It was seen to be more of a political move than a religious one; hence it was referred to by many Christians as a "political Shari'a". Muslims were at pains to explain that the Shari'a law such as the flogging of criminals or cutting off of the hands of thieves only applied to Muslims. Christians were unconvinced about it and insisted that the Shari'a affected them in many ways. For instance, in some States, there was the alleged attempt to enforce a particular dress code. It was forbidden for men to travel in the same vehicle as women, even though there was no adequate provision for transport facilities. Cinema houses, beer parlours, *et al* were forced to close and the consumption of alcohol was either restricted to certain peripheral areas or totally banned[194].

It is to this effect that the Shari'a policies in most of the twelve Shari'a compliance states, coupled with the existing strong religious intolerance in the northern region, hence, frustrates the activities of the Church's mission whereby public religious gatherings outside Islam, door to door evangelization, and other activities related to Christian religion are strongly opposed. This reality for instance, manifests itself in Sokoto diocese that was created in 1964. Being the seat of the Caliphate, the level of tolerance remains very low unlike other states especially in the Middle Belt. Hence, while its (Sokoto diocese) Catholic population continues to grow slowly with 39,767 in 2018, arch/dioceses like Kaduna (created 1953) and Gboko (created 2012) where there is high tolerance of Christianity, recorded the number of Catholic population as high as 581,950 and 772,702 respectively[195].

9.2 *Refusal of Land for the Building of Churches and Schools*

In most of the major cities in Northern Nigeria, Christians are unfortunately perceived as strangers, settlers and non-indigenes despite the efforts of some governors who tried to strike a balance in the issue. But this does not in any way reduce or prevent the act of discrimination against the Christians in Muslim dominated states. Hence, most of the Churches have remained locked in areas that the Colonial Administrators designated as *Sabon Gari* (strangers' quarters) and has thus slowed the expansion of the Church across the hinterlands.

---

[194] I.A. KAIGAMA, *Peace, not War*, 99.
[195] See Appendix O.

It is interesting to understand that these areas first housed a huge non-Muslim population of southern artisans, traders, and civil servants who laid the foundation for the postcolonial bureaucracy in the late 50s and 60s, and such areas were considered to be the habitats of non- Muslims whose cultural practices, such as music, consumption of alcohol and other social practices were considered un-Islamic[196]. But interestingly today, those designated areas (the Sabon Gari) have become residences of both Christians and Muslims due to fast development of urbanization thereby becoming overpopulated.

It is against this backdrop, that Christians are forced to spread around the cities without new places of worship. As a result, whenever efforts are made to acquire land for the building of Churches or schools such efforts are always mitigated by some prominent Muslims and even the civil authority. In some instances, even when land is purchased under the disguise of building a residential home, upon discovery that a Church is built instead, it is often destroyed by the Muslim radicals without compensations, and in most cases their actions always gain the support of Muslim clerics and those in authority.

In another development, since the taking over of missionary schools by the government in 1972 and worsened by the drastic down fall of education across the nation, the Church has been making concerted efforts to regain the seized schools and also to build new ones. But applications for the allocation of land by the government are often turned down in the Muslim dominated states. Instead, government funds are used for the building of Koranic schools and in most cases such schools are often underutilized. This is better summarized in the words of Kaigama:

> Churches continue to grow and expand there; the main problem is that in some States Churches are denied certificates of occupancy. Many of the Churches located in these States were issued certificates of occupancy by the colonial authorities, and even then, such Churches were usually located in areas which were considered on the periphery of the towns. Today it is very difficult to obtain permission for new Church buildings. Land is available for residential and commercial purposes but not easily for Church purposes, as indicated in this *Takadar shaidar cinikin fili* from the *Ofishin dagaci* (evidence of purchase of land from the village head's office): *"Ba choci, Ba gidan giya, Ba login tare da duk wani abinda hukuma ta hana"* (No building of Church, alcoholic parlour, hotel or any other thing forbidden by law). The teaching of Christian Religious Education is not allowed in primary, secondary, and tertiary institutions, while chaplaincy services are not provided for Christian students in State or Federal owned tertiary institutions[197].

---

[196] Cf., M.H. KUKAH, "Persecutions of Christians in Africa", 8.

[197] I.A. KAIGAMA, *Peace, not War*, 100-101.

This shows that the bitter experiences that confronted the Christian missionaries during the administration of the colonial administrators when they were prohibited from going to other hinterland of the Muslims dominated areas, is the same system that is still in practice till date in the northern region by the Hausa/Fulani in order to frustrate the activities of the Church in the region.

9.3 *Abduction and Forced Conversion of Christian Youths*

The issue of abduction in Nigeria is not a new development because people (both nationals and foreigners) have been kidnapped in the eastern region for a ransom. But this development is new in the northern region. Both men and women have been abducted not only by the Islamic militants but also by 'so-called direct relations' of the abductees such as uncles who belong to the Islamic fold not for a ransom as in the case of the Boko Haram, but for a forceful conversion into Islam in which the abductee is unwillingly given out for marriage to a distant Muslim young man. The case of the abducted 276 Chibok girls as earlier mentioned in the general introduction is just one out of many cases. For example, when I was working in a Catholic parish of St. Anne's Parish, Zongon Tama II (2006-2011), there was a case of a young girl called Hannatu and her brother who were kidnapped by the 'so-called' Islamic preachers group known as *Yan Adawa* of Giwa Local Government Area in which the said parish is located. The reason being that since their father agreed to be converted into Islam, his children *ipso facto* must be converted too despite their unwillingness.

With the intervention of the police, we were able to rescue the young man. But for the girl, all arrangements were already set for her to be forcefully given out in marriage to any of the Muslim young men in a distant land. It will interest you to note that prior to this case in question, there were similar cases that had taken place and they had succeeded in their evil agenda. But in the case of Hannatu, it was an eye opener to me and the Diocese of Zaria. Having reported the case to the Divisional Police Officer (DPO) of the Nigerian Police Force in charge of the area, it was later transferred to the Area Commandant (AC) and thereafter, it was taken to the court. Interestingly however, in every stage of the case, I was directly involved as a result of my position as the then pastor of the parish. After several hearings in the court, with the aid of the diocesan lawyer, we won the case and the young lady was allowed by the court to practice her religion of her choice according to the law of the land.

At this juncture, it is imperative to note that while the old traditional method of islamisation is maintained (as introduced by Sir Ahmadu Bello which we have already noted under subtitle 5.3 above), abduction and *hitherto* forced conversion of Christian youths particularly the girls are new organised trends that are being perpetrated by the 'so-called' *Yan Adawa* across the northern region, and interestingly, they often receive the maximum cooperation of the civil authority. Consequently, the Boko Haram's abduction of the Chibok and Dapchi girls respectively was just an iceberg of the reality on the ground. Although, in the case of the militants, the girls are not only forcefully married and converted but they are equally subjected to slavery, rape, and conscripted into Boko Haram militants as suicide bombers.

It is to this effect, that their modus operandi includes the capturing of a whole community[198] whereby the *crème de la crème* (the best of the best) of the community is forcefully taken into the Mambisa forest[199] which led to the massive movement of the people from the volatile areas to safe havens. Both Christians and Muslims have been forced out of their comfort homes and made refugees within their motherland and the neighbouring countries of Cameroon, Chad and Niger. In this regard, missionary activities have been frustrated and truncated.

9.4 *Poverty and Economic Hardship*

It is common that when people are forced out of their ancestral land and become refugees, agricultural activities, businesses and other economic endeavours stand still, and the end result is poverty and hardship. Hence, in whichever way we view poverty, either based on approaches such as the basic needs approach, the capabilities approach, and the human development approach, it however, finds its expression within the following dimensions of human development as viewed by the UNDP's Human Development Index (hence, HDI) that poverty encompasses (i) Life expectancy; (ii) educational attainment; and (iii) standard of living, measured by income in terms of its purchasing power parity[200]. Summing these dimensions, poverty within this context will thus connote material lack or wants, deprivation in human capacity development, lack of access to resource control, and social insecurity.

Confronted with this reality which most often is worsened by the constant perpetuation of violence, the Church's missionary activities are therefore

---

[198] For instance, the capturing of the town Busa and other sixteen local government areas in which they declared them as their caliphate. See D. BLAIR, "Boko Haram is now a mini-Islamic State".

[199] The Mambisa Forest is the hide out of the Boko Haram. It is being combed at the moment by the Nigerian forces as a way of putting an end to their existence.

[200] Cf., J. ADEYANJU – E.O. BABALOLA, "The Gospel and the Impact of Poverty", 25.

halted. For instance, the present situation particularly in Maiduguri where the expression of the Islamic extremism is highly recorded, and thousands of people were forced out of their homes serves as an example. Farms and businesses which were their main sources of livelihood were all destroyed, and as a result, people have been pushed below the level of poverty line whereby they live from hand to mouth.

Consequently, the above situation has influenced an overwhelming influx of Christians (Catholics alike) into the Prosperity Gospel Centres where prosperity is preached at the expense of the Gospel values. People prefer to frequent more often Christian business meetings for financial empowerment than attending catechism classes or Bible studies where their faith could be more strengthened and deepened. Churches are filled to the brim when sermons are more centred on prosperity than salvation. As a result, Christians move from one Church to another in search of solutions to their socio-economic problems.

In another development, due to economic hardship, there is of recent an increase of proliferation of Churches from one street to another. For instance, it is common to find over twenty Churches in one street[201]. Many people have become visionaries overnight and have established Churches in order to become General Overseers (GOs) or General Superintendents (GSs) *et al.* Pastors, Bishops, and Prophets are made after two or three months of Bible studies. As a result, such "so called" spiritual leaders undermine the fundamental teachings of the Christian Church through their erroneous canon of biblical exegesis where most sacred texts are not just superstitious and syncretistic but are also twisted to "fight" enemies/perceived enemies and to also raise "overnight millionaires" not minding the sincerity of the confessions of their worshippers[202]. This implies that in the search of quick solution to socio-economic problems, poverty and economic hardship have made a lot of people to commercialize the Church. As a result, the efforts of the Church in the promotion of its missionary activities are also frustrated.

9.5 *Forced Ejection/ Mass Exodus*

With the intractable violence of the Boko Haram within the region, many Christians have been forced out of their ancestral homes and unwillingly made refugees in their mother land while others fled to neighbouring countries of Cameroon, Chad and Niger. Against this background, it is interesting to note that within the peak of their terrorist activities (2012-

---

[201] Cf., M.H. KUKAH, "Persecutions of Christians in Africa", 8.
[202] M.H. KUKAH, "Persecutions of Christians in Africa", 28.

2016) most of the northern dioceses experienced a massive exodus of parishioners from violent states to safe zones.

S/N	ARCH/DIOCESES	ct		ba		yrc
		2010	2016	2010	2016	
1	Abuja	402,000	514,105	8,810	10,889	1989
2	Kaduna	532,155	581,230	7,282	13,397	1953
3	Yola	180,652	222,656	5,032	6,970	1962
4	Maiduguri	211,055	160,000	10,388	2,190	1966
5	Sokoto	45,569	31,500	2,252	1,391	1964
6	Zaria	71,550	55,594	2,440	1,839	2000

Table 2: Selected Northern Dioceses showing the effects
of Boko Haram Terrorist Activities on the Church[203]

From the above table (Table 2) it is obvious that the movement of parishioners affected a lot of the dioceses within the region. While some were positive developments, others were negative. For example, arch/dioceses such as Abuja, Kaduna, and Yola experienced an influx of Catholics while dioceses like Maiduguri, Sokoto and Zaria experienced the mass exodus of Parishioners. Maiduguri diocese (the headquarters of the Boko Haram) for example, had the total number of Catholics 211,055 in 2010, but in 2016 it was reduced to 160,000 Catholics. This was the same with Sokoto diocese which had 45,569 Parishioners in 2010 but in 2016 was reduced to 31,500.

Similarly, Zaria diocese experienced the mass exodus of Parishioners. It had 71,550 Catholics in 2010, but in 2016 it was reduced to 55,594. This reduction in the above affected dioceses was as a result of the sporadic attacks of the Boko Haram on Christians, their properties and Churches, and the capturing of some communities and making them Islamic States. Hence, most Parishioners relocated to safe zones which as a result, Abuja archdiocese for instance, experienced an influx of more Catholics from 402,000 in 2010 to 514,105 in 2016. The same influx was experienced in Kaduna and Yola as seen from the above table.

---

[203] The keys of the above table are; S/N – Serial Number, ct – Number of Catholics *per* Diocese, ba – Number of Baptisms *per* Diocese, and yrc – Year of creation of each Diocese. The Dioceses in blue colour experienced an influx of parishioners while dioceses in red colour experienced a drastic reduction of parishioners as a result of mass exodus triggered by the constant attacks of the Boko Haram. For more examples see Appendices O and P.

Consequently, the terrorist activities further reduced the administration of sacraments to Parishioners. Most Parish Priests could not reach their Parishioners because people were scattered. While some were abducted and forcefully ejected out of their ancestral lands, others willingly relocated to other places for safety. Hence, low reception of sacraments such as Matrimony, baptism, Confirmations and others. It is against this backdrop, that the above table for instance, shows dioceses in blue colour administered sacraments to more Parishioners as a result of the influx of Catholics experienced than the dioceses in red which experienced a drastic mass exodus of the Catholic faithful. For example, in 2010 Maiduguri diocese administered baptism to 10,388 parishioners (at the lower period of the terrorist activities of the Boko Haram), but at the peak of the terrorist activities, only 2,190 people were baptised. Thus, it is obvious that the presence of the terrorist group has undoubtedly posed a pastoral challenge on the Church.

10. Conclusion

The era of colonialism could be described as an era of mixed feelings because while we count the blessings we enjoyed as a result of the presence of the colonial administrators, we cannot also shy away from the bitter experiences of the aftermath of their presence. As we have seen from the foregoing in this chapter, this doubled-edge experience is better demonstrated more in the northern region of the country than other regions due to the obvious reason that the North is far more heterogeneous in nature than the South and West. Hence, the need to employ the principle of the indirect rule which was advantageous to the Colonial Administrators and their loyalists (the native authority), but disadvantageous to the minority tribe (the animists) became imperative.

In like manner, while we count the blessings of having new religions (Christianity and Islam) planted in the Nigerian soil by the missionaries, and the benefits that accompanied them such as schools, hospitals, enlightenment etc., the clash of these two religions also brought some bitter experiences whereby lives and properties are being destroyed at any given provocation. As a result, the nation's peace and stability is always put at risk. It is against this backdrop that we come to understand that it is as a result of the expression of religious extremism which manifests itself in varied ways that paves the way to the present intractable violence that continue to limit the socio-economic development of the region, and *vis-à-vis* the growth of the Church.

As highlighted above, the jihad of Uthman dan Fodio in 1804 set the pace for the expression of this extremism which later championed by his grandson Sir Ahmadu Bello during his conversion campaigns and the isla-misation programme of the northern region. Filled therefore with religious zeal, other Islamic radical sects began to spring up such as the Shiites, Izala, Maitatsine, and the present Boko Haram whose violent activities contributed greatly in soiling the relationship between Christians and Muslims, thereby creating a culture of intolerance, mistrust, hate and suspicion that led us to the present situation in the region.

As we examined some key religious crises that took place within the region, it is important to bear in mind that the list is inexhaustible. We further established that factors such as the principle of absolutism/religious intolerance, Islamic reformations and revivalism, political emancipation, Christian fundamentalism and exclusivism and others alike often ignite these crises. Notwithstanding, from these x-rays, we therefore established that the Church in northern Nigeria is confronted with the following challenges as regards her missionary activities within the region which include; Islamic fundamentalism, refusal of land for church and school buildings, abduction and forced conversion of Christian youths, forced ejection and massed exodus of Christians from their ancestral homes thereby leaving churches empty and frustrating its missionary activities within the region. From here therefore, we now turn our attention to the methodology employed for generating the data of the study which forms its third chapter.

CHAPTER III

Research Design and Methods

1. Introduction

Having presented the theoretical aspects of the study in the preceding chapters, at this point it is worthy to focus on the scientific methodology of the thesis. In this regard, chapter three is designed to give an elaborate account of the research design or rather the plan on how the research was conducted[1], and the justification for the choices made before and during the fieldwork. The chapter is divided into four broad sections that include; methodology, sampling, data collection, and ethical issues. While efforts are made to do justice to each of these sections, it is imperative to note that each of the section does not in any way stand independent of the others. They are however, interwoven with one another due to their interrelatedness.

2. Methodology

Describing methodology, as the principles, procedures, and practices that govern a research, scholars thus opine that, "methodology should be thought of as encompassing the entire process of conducting research (i.e., planning and conducting the research study, drawing conclusions, and disseminating the findings)"[2]. In other words, it is the overall description of the research procedures and strategies.[3] It is against this backdrop, that the main purpose of this section is to give the account of how the research was accomplished, that is what the data consist of and how they were collected, organized, and analysed.

Having therefore made this distinction, it is pertinent to distinctly state here that the topic "Islamic Extremism and its Challenges to the Catholic Missionary Activity in Northern Nigeria since 1999: A Missiological Study" is a sensitive one that always spurs the curiosity of the public to understand

---

[1] B.L. BERG, *Qualitative Research Methods for the Social Sciences*, 28.

[2] G. MARCZYK – *et al.*, *Essentials of Research Design and Methodology*, 22.

[3] B.L. BERG, *Qualitative Research Methods for the Social Sciences*, 271.

145

what the researcher intends to achieve, and *vis-à-vis* taking into account the composition of the northern region which is peculiar to its nature when compared with the other regions in the country. However, more will be said below about the northern region composition and its heterogenous nature under the choice of study population of the research as we progress.

Nevertheless, it is imperative to note that my choice of qualitative research methodology (interpretivist) over the other two traditional methodologies: quantitative (positivist), and mixed methodologies, is based on the following reasons. First, the theme of the research and the nature of its research questions raised in the study, owing to the fact that while the positivist (quantitative) tries to understand the subjective meaning of social action through experiment and prefers to work with numerical figures and quantifiable data that are analysed on the basis of variables, interpretivist (qualitative) on the other hand, tries to understand the subjective meaning of social action through an active interaction between the researched and the researcher. In other words, the exploratory nature of the investigation of the problem under study called for theorizing with the participants' point of view and not based on any known variable. Hence, qualitative methodology in this regard would help in generating explanations on the Islamic extremism and its challenges on the Catholic Missionary Activity.

Second, the problem under study is a complex and sensitive problem that cannot be reduced to a few quantifiable variables. Hence, the qualitative approach was considered appropriate in order to assist in analysing the various dimensions of the problem under investigation thereby paving the way for an in-depth insight of the problem. Third, the research questions of the problem under study do not seek to generate quantifiable data on predetermined instruments that would yield statistical data. But to generate data with the primary intent of developing themes from the data. Hence, the open-ended questions that began with "what", "why" and "how" are typical of qualitative approach[4].

Fourth, research that has to do with violence begs for emotions, feelings, and personal experiences of direct victims. Thus, face-to-face interviews are vital towards generating an in-depth data which is typical of qualitative approach. Finally, since the research aims at proffering possible solutions toward the realization of an enabling environment that will enhance peaceful co-existence among the Christians and Muslims in northern Nigeria, thereby boosting the missionary activity of the Church, engaging the study participants in the generation of the desired solutions thus, becomes expedient.

---

[4] Cf., J.W. CRESWELL, *Research Design*, 20-23.

3. Study Population

The motivating factor of the selection of my study population is based on the nature of the composition of the northern region, taking into account the theme of the study. However, I do not intend to repeat myself here because much has been said as regards the composition of the northern region and its teething problems in the previous chapters. Nevertheless, it is important to point out some obvious reasons of my choice.

First, from a cultural standpoint, the North is far more heterogeneous than any region in Nigeria. This could be as a result of the existence of many varied cultures that live side by side with the Hausa and the Fulani[5]. For instance, the Jukun and the Mumuye in Taraba State, the Hausa, Fulani, and Mahisiyawa in Kano, Sokoto, Katsina, Zamfara, Kebbi States, Birom and the Angas in Plateau State; Shuwa and Kanuri in Borno State; Gwagi, Baju, Kataf and Akurmi in Kaduna State; Tiv, Idoma, and Igede in Benue State, Igala and Gbira in Kogi State, to mention just a few. For each of these ethnics to survive therefore, the struggle for survival and emancipation becomes necessary.

Second, the North, although emerged as a monolithic bloc within the context of socio-political affairs in the country, it is however, composed of three major religious groups; Islam, Christianity and ATR which are made up of hundreds of linguistic and ethnic groups with conflicting historical legacies and the struggle for identity and survival[6]. Although, these three major religions in question are commonly found in other regions of the country, Islam is however, densely populated in the north. Owing to this co-habitual existence with one another, religious crises therefore are more recorded in the northern region than the others.

Third, the persistent terrorist activities of the Boko Haram, which continue to claim innocent lives on a daily basis, also presents to me a good reason for my choice. Finally, researchers who are conversant with Nigeria and particularly the northern region are aware that the complexity of the north is a representation of the complexity of Nigeria as a nation. Hence, it is within this complexity and the heterogeneous nature of the region in question that I considered it more suitable for the study population than any of the other two regions in the country. The next task then was to make the choice of the sampling techniques that could be used in order to generate the desired data.

---

[5] Cf., A.C. van GORDER, *Violence in God's Name*, 6.

[6] A.C. van GORDER, *Violence in God's Name*, 6.

4. Sampling

Bearing in mind that not all research studies that are carried out require human participants such as physics, biology, chemistry, and botany, whose unit of study may be atom, a cell, a molecule, or a flower, this research however, involves human participants because it is empirical in nature and not experimental. It is against this backdrop that sampling of the population to be studied becomes imperative. Taking into cognizance my personal experience and knowledge of the theme under research, the question then was who and what is worthy of inclusion in the sampling? This was a challenging task that must be carefully executed. Nevertheless, sampling is defined as "the process or technique of selecting a suitable sample, representative of the population from which it is taken, for the purpose of determining parameters or characteristics of the whole population"[7]. This implies that sampling paves the way for a researcher to draw a valid conclusion about the larger group under research without the need to study every unit in that group owing to the reason that the total population is often too large to study within a given limited time and resources[8].

Hence, Bruce identifies two types of sampling: (i) probability sampling and (ii) non- probability sampling and concurs by Kultar (a founding member and Director of Sambodhi Research and Communications, India)[9]. While the probability sampling is defined as a method of sampling that utilizes some form of random selection. Non-probability on the other hand, does not involve the process of random selection since the probability of selection of each sampling unit is not known. It is, however, interesting to note that while probability sampling is subdivided into simple random sampling, systematic random sampling, stratified sampling, cluster sampling, and multi-stage sampling, non-probability on the other hand, is subdivided into accidental or convenience sampling, purposive sampling, quota sampling, expert sampling, snowball/chain sampling, heterogeneity sampling, and maximum variation sampling.

I employed the use of the non-probability sampling method based on the following reasons: First, guided by the question of the sociologist, Martyn (a specialist in teaching research methodology at postgraduate level of Leicester University, UK) suggests that for those who wish to employ the use of purposive sampling: "Given what I already know about the research

---

[7] K. SINGH, *Quantitative Social Research Methods*, 102.

[8] Cf., P. LYONS, *The Dissertation*, 112.

[9] B.L. BERG, *Qualitative Research Methods for the Social Sciences*, 30-33. Also see, K. SINGH, *Quantitative Social Research Methods*, 102-108.

topic and about the range of people or events being studied, who or what is likely to provide the best information?"[10]. I employed the use of purposive sampling technique.

As the name implies, the purposive sampling technique is a sampling that is done with a purpose[11], and "the researcher uses his or her own judgement about which respondents to choose, and picks only those who best meet the purpose of the study"[12]. To this effect, I used the purposive sampling techniques since I had a targeted sample that I desired to generate my data from. Hence, interviewees such as the religious leaders (particularly the Catholic Bishops), leaders of CAN and JNI, Sociologists, Psychologists, Historians, and victims (both men and women) of the Boko Haram insurgence became my targeted respondents due to their respective positions, expertise, and life experiences. It is to this end, I did not consider random selection process to be my primary concern.

In addition to the purposive sampling, I equally employed the use of the quota sampling technique since its non-proportional quota sampling paves the way for me to select a minimum number of sample units in each category of the population (irrespective of the population size) in order to generate an even data that cut across all board.

Expert sampling (which involves a sample of persons who are known to have demonstrable experience and expertise in a particular area of study interest), is another sampling technique that I also used for the same reason stated above. Hence, sociologists, clergy, and those whom I considered to have had "privileged of information" due to their status/office in the society were also interviewed.

In the same vein, I further employed the use of snowball/chain sampling because of the need to have identified respondents who met the criteria of the selection and those who I was linked up with by few of the respondents. Considering the sensitivity of the research's theme, I needed to carefully identify respondents who have either academically dealt with such topic or have contributed immensely in the field of the study. In like manner, I needed to reach out to the victims who were directly affected by the inferno. Consequently, this necessitated my journey not only back home (Nigeria) but also to the crisis area (Maiduguri – Borno State) of the north-eastern Nigeria in 2016 for a fieldwork.

As regards the list of the respondents however, I was aware of its in-exhaustiveness. To this end, while in the field, I had to include the names of

---

[10] M. DENSCOMBE, *The Good Research Guide*, 17.

[11] K. SINGH, *Quantitative Social Research Methods*, 108.

[12] K.D. BAILEY, *Methods of Social Research*, 96.

the respondents (whom I was linked with) that were not originally included in the initial list. While some helped me to make the contacts on my behalf since I never knew them personally, others facilitated the contacts by providing me with the necessary information that I could make the contacts by myself and arrange the time and venue for the interviews. Nonetheless, it is worthy of mention that all interviews were personally conducted.

5. Fieldwork Planning

In planning, how to carry out the fieldwork research, there was the need to keep in mind certain factors. The first consideration was the time/season of the fieldwork which was essential to take into consideration bearing in mind that Nigeria is divided into two major seasons of the year: dry and rainy seasons – spring and summer experienced during the dry season, while, autumn and winter experienced during the rainy season.. This was a concern as accessibility to the participants was dependent on the season. For this reason, the fieldwork was carried out in the dry season of the year and lasted for three months, March 3 to June 9, 2016. This timing was necessary because the year 2016 was the year that the flashing areas started to experience stability, and the security of the people and their property was realized to an appreciable level following the efforts of the Nigerian government in clamping down the Boko Haram in 2015.

It is against this backdrop, that the Nigerian president announced publicly by December 2015, that "the Boko Haram has been technically defeated"[13]. Thus, movements of people in and out of the flashing areas became possible and relative peace was also realized for the first time since the inception of the terrorists' menace. To this end, the timing enabled me to travel as far as the volatile area of Maiduguri and conducted interviews with both victims and other respondents in the said area.

Second, the financial implications and my well-being during the fieldwork was another aspect to be considered. Having applied to Missio who were at the same time my sponsors for both licentiate and doctoral studies, I was set to go when they granted my request with some financial assistance. On my arrival back home in Nigeria, I was highly and warmly welcomed by my family members, colleagues, and all beloved ones and well-wishers. My Bishop (George Jonathan Dodo of the Catholic Diocese of Zaria) was very welcoming. He offered me an accommodation, a car as well as some monetary support as part of his contributions to the success of the fieldwork.

---

[13] K.D. BAILEY, "Nigeria Boko Haram: Militants 'Technically Defeated'".

During the period under review, I used the first month to concretize my contacts especially those I had previously tried to reach via emails, and I had not received feedback as regards to their consent of participation. In this regard, I bought a local mobile telephone line that could allow me to reach the intended participants and *vis-à-vis* to be reached too. The procurement of the mobile telephone line was important because I had to reach some respondents not only via emails but also through SMS messages and phone calls, even though, despite all the attempts made, some efforts proved unproductive.

Consequently, I had to travel to several different cities in order to meet with them one on one in order to obtain their consent of participation in the interview as well as to arrange the particular date, time and venue for the interviews based on their conveniences. Having established the needed contacts, the second and part of the third months were dedicated for the interviews. Find in appendix G a sample of the letter of request for participation in the interview to respondents.

Third, as the first set of appointments for the interviews was due, I procured the following needed materials: a laptop computer, an NVivo computer software package, a digital audio recorder, and a digital still camera (both with back-up batteries), field notepad, a set of headphones, a diary, interview request forms (both individual and group), interview thematic guide, interview recording sheets, letters of consent, a computer printer, pens and papers. Envisaging however, the erratic nature of Nigerian electric power supply, I also procured a rechargeable lantern that could assist me at night whenever the electric power went off. Despite this effort however, I still sometimes found myself constrained at night whenever the rechargeable lantern ran low of battery due to lack of the electricity that could power it.

Finally, bearing in mind the need of a research assistance, I also made contact with one of the Staff of the Catholic diocesan communication department of Zaria whom I worked with for five years while I was the communication director of the office. Knowing his skills in transcription, he became the rightful person to be contacted. All the conducted interviews that I considered fundamental to the research were fully transcribed by the research assistant except the less fundamental ones and those carried out in Hausa language due to the obvious reason that he was not fluent in it.

Nonetheless, despite his skilfulness in transcription, writing of articles, news reportage and editing, I still saw the ardent need to specifically instruct him on how I expected the interview data to be handled and transcribed bearing in mind that confidentiality in a fieldwork is a vital element that must be observed at all times.

6. Data Collection

As the name implies, this section sets to describe the strategies employed in gathering my data during the fieldwork. There are many existing strategies of data collection. As a result, the need to make the right choice of the appropriate methods became expedient. Marczyk and co-editors state four traditional techniques which include: i) interview, ii) global rating, iii) observation, and iv) biological measures. Hence, bearing in mind the nature of the questions raised in this study, I therefore employed the use of multiple methods of interview and observation since data collection are determined by the research questions of the study[14].

However, it is interesting to note that the process of gathering data by multiple methods is also referred to as triangulation approach. To this end, Martyn opines that triangulation is "the use of different methods, different sources of data or even different researchers within the study"[15]. The justification of my choice of this method therefore, is to enable me to gather data that will give me a deeper and a better understanding of the problem under investigation from different perspective, since the main principle of a triangulation approach is to enable the researcher to "get a better understanding of the thing that is being investigated if he/she views it from different positions"[16]. Hence, triangulation improves accuracy and authenticity since the alternative methods pave the way for confirmation of what had earlier been gathered. In the same vein, it gives the fuller picture of the problem under investigation since other alternative methods could provide complementary data[17].

6.1 *Interviews*

An interview as already mentioned above, is one of the methods used by a researcher in order to generate information in respect to the problem under investigation. Today, interviewing is the popular means of gathering information. For instance, the mass media, human service providers, and researchers are increasingly involved in the use of interviews as means of generating their data. Hence, an interview is a conversation initiated by the researcher in order to gain needful knowledge of the problem under investigation.

---

[14] G. MARCZYK – al., *Essentials of Research Design and Methodology*, 116.

[15] M. DENSCOMBE, *The Good Research Guide*, 134.

[16] M. DENSCOMBE, *The Good Research Guide*, 134.

[17] M. DENSCOMBE, *The Good Research Guide*, 138.

However, it is important to note that an interview, is something that is more than just a conversation because it involves a set of assumptions and understandings about a situation that is often dissociated from a casual conversation[18]. To this end, an interview can thus be said to be a special form of conversation whereby it is employed by the investigator in order to generate "empirical data about the social world by asking people to talk about their lives"[19].

Although, conversations may vary from structured to semi-structured and unstructured, all interviews however, are interactional because they require talking between the interviewer and the interviewee. Interviews differ from an ordinary conversation because in the interview, the interviewer/researcher listens intensely in order to pick up some needful key words, phrases, and ideas. In the same vein, it differs due to the kind of nonverbal cues that the interviewer watches for in order to effectively identify the interviewee's emotional state, deference or even lies[20].

Interviews are thus, common methods used especially in qualitative research methodology because of the following reasons: i) they produce a wealth of information, ii) they can cover any number of content areas, iii) they are relatively inexpensive, and iv) they are the efficient ways to collect a wide variety of data that does not necessarily require any formal way of testing[21].

Nevertheless, it is imperative to bear in mind that the effectiveness of any interview depends on how it is structured. That is, "the interview should be thought out beforehand and standardized so that all participants are asked the same questions in the same order"[22]. The following are the types of interviews: i) structured/standardized interview, ii) semi-structured/semi-standardized interview, iii) unstructured/unstandardized interview, iv) one-to-one interview, v) Group interview, vi) focus groups interview, vii) internet interview, and viii) online focus interview[23]. Describing each of these interviews, however, is beyond the scope of this work. Nonetheless, brief description can be made of the ones that are pertinent to this study. Hence, in this study, I used the semi-structured interview, the one-to-one interview, and the focus groups interview.

---

[18] M. DENSCOMBE, *The Good Research Guide*, 174.

[19] J.A. HOLSTEIN – J.F. GUBRIUM, "The Active Interview", 140-141.

[20] B.L. BERG, *Qualitative Research Methods for the Social Sciences*, 84-85.

[21] Cf., G. MARCZYK – al., *Essentials of Research Design and Methodology*, 117.

[22] G. MARCZYK – al., *Essentials of Research Design and Methodology*, 117.

[23] Cf., M. DENSCOMBE, *The Good Research Guide*, 175-188.

6.1.1 Semi-Structured Interview

Semi-structured interview is the interview that involves the implementation of a number of predetermined questions and topics in which the interviewer asks each of the interviewees in a systematic and consistent order. Unlike the structured interview that involves tight control and enclosed questions through the use of questionnaires, the semi-structured interview gives the interviewer some latitude of flexibility in terms of the order in which the topics are considered, thereby probing further beyond the answers to the prepared questions during the process of the interview in order to gain deeper insight of the problem under investigation.

In like manner, it also allows the interviewee to develop ideas and speak more widely on the issues (especially areas of interest) raised by the interviewer. It is therefore in line with the aforementioned, that I found the semi-structured interview suitable for my data collection. As a result, through the use of the semi-structured interview, I observed that most of the respondents were able to express themselves freely and elaborately narrated their life experiences thereby providing me with more information.

6.1.2 One-to-one/Individual Interview

The one-to-one or individual interview is also referred to as Individual Depth Interview (hereafter IDI). One-to-one interview is the interview that involves the meeting of the researcher/interviewer and the informant/interviewee on the basis of one-to-one. As the name implies, the interviewer gets only the attention of the interviewee, and it is conducted face-to-face. The individual interview is relatively easy to arrange and relatively easy to control because it involves only two actors; the interviewer and the interviewee. I found the IDI interesting because I had only the interviewee's ideas to grasp and interrogate, and to guide throughout the process of the interview.

Another interesting aspect that I discovered in the one-to-one interview is that it was fairly easy for me to locate specific ideas with specific informants since the opinions and views expressed throughout the interview originated from one source, that is the respondent. In like manner, during transcriptions of some of the interviews (especially the ones conducted in Hausa language), I realized that it was relatively easier to transcribe the one-to-one interviews when compared with the focus groups interviews because there was only one voice to recognize and only one person talking at a time without the interference of other informants as the case may be in the focus groups interviews.

Having all said and done, it does not imply that during the IDIs all went smoothly without problems. One of the most common problems I faced was the interference of telephone calls. Some respondents could not put off their phones due to their status in the society since people needed to contact them at all times. Although, some of the interviews were conducted in personal houses and some in the offices, the problem of phone calls kept on emanating in almost all the individual interviews.

In addition to the challenges faced, were the interference of office staff and family members during the process of the interviews in both offices and private houses respectively. In two incidents, the interviews had to be suspended for a little while. The first incident was in the house whereby the attention of the interviewee (who was the head of the house) was highly needed by a friend who popped in to see him briefly for about ten minutes. While the second incident was in an office whereby the respondent had to answer an incoming international telephone call for almost half an hour due to its urgency and importance. In such cases, I had to pause the interviews, and when resumed, I had to also remind the interviewees of the point they were making prior to the interruptions.

Important to note is that, despite the assurance of confidentiality, some interviewees were still uncomfortable with the issue of a recorded interview, even though I always ask for their consent to allow me the use of the audio recording. In one occasion for instance, the respondent asked me to put off the audio recorder. Unconvincingly enough, he insisted that I must remove the batteries of the audio recorder in his presence in order for him to be sure of not being recorded. It was after fulfilling his conditions that he granted me the interview.

At this juncture, it is pertinent to state that while in the fieldwork, I had wonderful experiences especially during the one-to-one interviews. The attitudes of some of the respondents increased my horizon of knowledge not only in the field of research but also in general. Hence, in total, I carried out eighteen (18) one-to-one interviews, evenly spread across the volatile areas within the region under study except for Maiduguri due to its high volatility. Seventeen (17) respondents were audio-recorded and one objected. The respondent that declined the audio-recording is noted in table 1. Find in the same table 1 the breakdown characteristics of the interviewees, while the list of the guiding themes used for the interviews is found in appendix I.

S/N	Pseudonym	Gender	Group	Occupation	Age	Date of interview	Duration of interview	Place of interview
1	Ajayi	Male	Christian	Retired Lecturer	66	20/05/2016	1hr 18 minutes	Zaria
2	Ankoyoyo	Male	Christian	Clergy	41	03/05/2016	1hr 21 minutes	Maiduguri
3	Ava	Male	Christian	Lecturer	47	02/06/2016	1hr 15 minutes	Jos
4	Bello	Male	Muslim	Lecturer	53	18/05/2016	1hr 12 minutes	Zaria
5	Chatsomen	Male	Christian	Clergy	50	16/05/2016	1hr 15 minutes	Kaduna
6	Chenda	Male	Christian	Civil Servant	25	02/05/2016	36 minutes	Maiduguri
7	Chokist	Male	Christian	Clergy	53	01/06/2016	45 minutes	Jos
8	Daccos	Male	Christian	Clergy	57	20/04/2016	1hr 02 minutes	Lafiya
9	Danjuma	Male	Christian	Clergy	43	02/06/2016	54 minutes	Jos
10	Dursa	Male	Christian	Clergy	33	04/05/2016	1hr 30 minutes	Maiduguri
11	Fuks	Male	Christian	Clergy	40	01/06/2026	45 minutes	Jos
12	Ipwuperjoh	Male	Christian	Clergy	33	01/05/2016	1hr 09 minutes	Maiduguri
13	Mallam	Male	Christian	Lecturer	51	02/06/2016	1hr 05 minutes	Jos
14	Muhammed	Male	Muslim	Civil Servant	65	16/05/2016	25 minutes	Kaduna
15	Nchok	Male	Christian	Clergy	56	06/06/2016	1hr 16 minutes	Zaria
16	Parangwom	Male	Christian	Clergy	55	28/04/2016	1hr 34 minutes	Maiduguri
17	Tampai	Male	Christian	Fisherman	62	30/04/2016	14 minutes	Maiduguri
18	Usman	Male	Muslim	Lecturer	54	23/05/2016	50 minutes	Zaria*

Table 1: The Breakdown of Participants in the one-to-one Interview.

* The respondent who declined audio-recording.

6.1.3 Focus Group Interview

The focus group interview is a way of generating qualitative data that essentially involves a small number of people in an informal group discussion which normally focuses around a particular topic or set of issues that are under investigation. The discussions involved in this type of informal group are usually based on series of questions to be focused on, and the researcher always serves as the moderator for the group by posing the questions, keeping the discussions flowing, and creating the enabling conditions for active participation of all members of the group.

Although, members are expected to participate actively in the discussions, the moderator however, also has a duty to monitor individuals who may dominate the conversation so that at the end the aim of having the group interview could be achieved. It is imperative to bear in mind that during the discussions in the focus group, the researcher does not ask the questions turn after turn of each respondent, but he/she, however, poses the questions to all while facilitates free interactions among the members.

I found the focus group interview technique suitable for generating my data due to the following reasons: i) it enabled me to bring together the victims of the Boko Haram terrorist activity to discuss their varied life experiences bearing in mind that some were directly captured and forcefully taken away from their beloved ones, while others especially the women, witnessed the brutal killing of their loved ones (husbands and children) right before their eyes. ii) it also provided the participants the latitude to refine what they have to say bearing in mind that they were all victims of the Boko Haram insurgence. To this effect, each could narrate his/her life experience. iii) through their different life experiences, the focus group interview provided the forum for participants to directly and vividly discuss their differences in respect to the respective issues raised. iv) As more than one person was interviewed at a time, through the focus group interview, the number and range of participants involved in the study were dramatically increased. With the increment of number of the participants at a time, it implies that a broader spectrum of the study population is covered by the research, and it added a greater variety of experiences and opinions that emerged from the investigation[24].

Important to note here is that my choice of using the focus group interview is not on the basis of a quantitative methodology which basically concerns about numbers and improved representativeness, but it is based on a qualitative methodology that is concerned with the way the group discussion can be more revealing since the focus group interview is traded on group dynamics. In other words, it did not only allow participants to listen to alternative points of view, but it also allowed them to express their support for certain views and *vis-à-vis* challenged others' views where they disagreed.

Noting that the standard of the focus group interview comprises 6-10 number of individuals[25], seven respondents were contacted and consented to the interview. However, on the day of the interview, only five were present arriving amongst great difficulties. Hence, I was left with the only option to make do with the available five.

As regards my experience during the focus group interview, it surprised me that I did not find it difficult to manage the group due to the reasons that the problem under investigation delves into the domain of violence that attracts emotions, feelings and empathy. Against this backdrop, there

---

[24] M. DENSCOMBE, *The Good Research Guide*, 175-188.

[25] Cf., S. KEEGAN, *Qualitative Research*, 74.

weren't many arguments as the case may be with other studies. Although participants could agree and/or disagree with certain views, the scenario was under total control.

This does not however, imply that the focus group interview was devoid of complications. As noted above, two of the respondents did not show up for the exercise. It was difficult at the beginning of the contacts, to agree on time and venue for all participants to come together. But with the efforts of keys actors that included the Catholic Bishop of the Diocese (Maiduguri), his Secretary and the Diocesan Vicar General, things later became much easier to handle.

Find below in table 2 the breakdown of the five participants of the focus group interview I conducted in Maiduguri on 30th April 2016. As earlier mentioned, the participants were all Christians and victims of the terrorist activity of the Boko Haram. The interview was conducted in Hausa language (a language that is generally spoken in the region) which I am very fluent in it. The focus group interview lasted for one hour nine minutes, and it was all audio recorded.

S/N	PSEUDONYM	GENDER	OCCUPATION	AGE
1	Asabe	Female	Self-employed	55
2	Ijagala	Female	Self-employed	35
3	Indagiji	Female	Self-employed	31
4	Jamada	Female	Self-employed	38
5	Ngoshinda	Female	Self-employed	40

Table 2: The Breakdown of the Participants of Focus Group Interview.

6.2 *Participant Observation*

Participant observation is one of the least structured methods of observation because the researcher neither puts much restriction on the type of information collected nor does he/she usually have a well-defined unit of analysis specified before entering the field. But it is however, commonly used in qualitative research. Participant observation is thus defined as "a field strategy that simultaneously combines document analysis, interviews of respondents and informants, direct participation and observation, and introspection"[26]. This implies therefore that "participant observation is not a single method, but it is a combination of methods and techniques."[27].

---

[26] N.K. DENZIN, *The Research Act*, 157-158.
[27] L. BICKMAN, "Data Collection I", 1976, 270-271.

Nevertheless, participant observation is understood as a process that is in two respects. First, the researcher is expected to become increasingly a participant and to gain access to the field and the informants. Second, the observation in like manner is expected to move through a process of becoming increasingly concrete and concentrated on the aspects that are essential for the research questions[28].

It is against this backdrop, that in addition to the interviews conducted, participant observation was also part of the investigation. This was necessary because it offered me the opportunity to gain more insight of the problem under investigation outside the usual official setting of the interviews. As a participant observer, my major role was to stimulate discussions that centre around my theme of research with particular attention to the research questions of the study. I listened to people's reactions and feelings on the issues and noted some of the grey areas that were not discussed during the process of the interviews.

In like manner, as part of the investigation, I also visited places such as: the Boko Haram praying mosque and *tafsir* (preaching) Centre, and some of the scenes that were bombed by the Boko Haram in the town of Maiduguri (Borno State). Importantly, bearing in mind the importance of photographs which often speak much more than words, and offer in a research such as this the potential for insights that are not accessible through interview methods alone, I decided to take photographs of some of the scenes I visited. Some of these photographs are found in appendices A & M.

7. Ethical Issues

Ethical codes on how to protect the interests of those who are ready to take part in a study have increasingly become issues of serious concern in every research that involves humans. The sensitivity for such ethical codes in research becomes high and essential due to scandals. For example, the gross "misuse of captives for research and experiments by doctors during the Nazi period in Germany"[29]. Hence, codes of ethics have been developed in several disciplines and several countries. On a general note however, these codes of ethics require that a research should be based on informed consent of the participant. In other words, the study's participants need to agree freely to partake in the study on the basis of information given to them by the researcher.

In addition, the researcher is required to avoid harming the participants, including the invasion of their privacy and not to deceive them about the

---

[28] Cf., U. FLICK, *An Introduction to Qualitative Research*, 220.

[29] U. FLICK, *An Introduction to Qualitative Research*, 45.

research's aims. It is against this backdrop, that before embarking on the fieldwork project, adequate steps were taken in order to keep to the expected norms of fieldwork research, and also to avoid trading on dangerous grounds bearing in mind the problem of residential segregations base on religious divide that have taken place in the past in the cities of Kaduna and Jos where Christians were forced to relocate from Muslim dominated areas, and vice versa. As Muslims do not freely go into the Christian neighbourhoods for the fear of being killed, *vis-à-vis* Christians do not dare to go to the Muslim neighbourhoods.

7.1 *Informed Consent*

An informed consent refers to the principle of respondents to understand the need of consenting to participate freely and voluntarily without coercion in a research. In other words, the researcher is duty bound to describe the research study to his/her potential participants and provide them with the opportunity to make autonomous and informed decisions as regards whether they desire to participate or not. To this end, potential participants should not be "forced or coerced" into providing data for research[30]. It is for this reason that informed consent has been characterized as the cornerstone of human rights protections. Hence, it is built on these three basic elements: i) competence, ii) knowledge, and iii) voluntariness[31].

Competence here refers to potential participants who are not under vulnerable coercion or undue influence, such as children, prisoners, or mental disabled persons. In the same vein, for the potential participants to be knowing means to be aware of the risks (if any) involve in a research, the ability to remain in the research or withdraw from it, and be aware of obtaining compensation in case of harm or injuries incurred as a result of their study participation (especially when the research involves risk taking). While in the aspect of voluntariness, it refers to the potential participants that are under duress. That is those who are disenfranchised and vulnerable to criminal justice system.

It is based on the aforementioned, that it is expected of every researcher (especial researches that are sensitive in nature, or those that involve direct participation of human beings) before going into the fieldwork, he/she must develop a consent form which must contain the following elements: i) identity of the researcher, ii) information about the research, iii) expecta-

---

[30] Cf., M. Denscombe, *The Good Research Guide*, 332.
[31] GE G. Marczyk – al., *Essentials of Research Design and Methodology*, 246.

tions about the participant's contribution, iv) the right to withdraw consent, v) confidentiality and security of data, vi) signature of the participant, with date, and vii) counter signature of the researcher with date[32].

Prior to my journey back home for the fieldwork, I ensured that I notified my potential participants especially those on the initial list and had their contacts. While few were reached through emails, others were informed through telephone calls. Although, I developed my informed consent form, none was use for the following reasons: i) some were not interested in it because a written proof of consent in Nigeria is not a common practice, ii) some clearly told me that, "I know who you are, hence, I don't need such a form". A sample of my consent form however found in appendix H.

It is imperative to further point out that, in every interview, I always introduced myself and my University of research. Thereafter, I introduced the title of the study, its brief description, and its aims. While I made them to understand the importance of their contributions to the research, I also assured them of the confidentiality of their information and their identity. In addition, I also made them to understand their right of withdrawal if the need arose. However, I did not encounter any issue whereby an interviewee wanted to discontinue the exercise. In fact, some were more than willing to give more than what they were asked for.

On the part of security agents, efforts were made to get them involved but all proved fruitless. On one occasion, I went to the DPO of Maiduguri central to have him interviewed but it wasn't possible because I was referred to the office of the Police Public Relation Officer (PPRO) whom I was told that he was not in town. Despite several visits made in order to reach him, all were unsuccessful. I was however, later told in confidence that he was only avoiding me because I was investigating sensitive security issues of public interest. Nevertheless, on a general note, I received maximum cooperation from the participants that I interviewed both individuals and the group interviewees.

7.2 *Confidentiality*

The principle of confidentiality is another important ethical principle of qualitative research especially in dealing with a sensitive matter of public interest. In the ethical principle of confidentiality, it is expected that the participants of the study are protected from any danger that may harm them because of their participation in the study. In other words, confidentiality is an active attempt that must be made by the researcher to remove

---

[32] Cf., M. DENSCOMBE, *The Good Research Guide*, 333-334.

from the research records of any elements that might indicate the participants' identities.

It is however important to note that confidentiality does not mean anonymity (that is the participants remain nameless) because anonymity is only common in quantitative research where questionnaires are administered. Although the researchers may know to whom the questionnaires were distributed, if no identifying marks have been placed on the returned questionnaires, the respondents in this case always remain anonymous.

But in most qualitative research, the participants are often known to the researcher, and consequently, the issue of anonymity remains practically non-existent. Hence, the need to protect the participants with a high degree of confidentiality cannot be overemphasized. This implies that the researcher must see the need to systematically change the real names of the respondents to pseudonyms.

In the fieldwork, I had to assure the participants of their right to protection. Thus, I conducted all the interviews by myself without employing the services of another person. And to ensure confidentiality, at the beginning of the interview, each participant was given a pseudonym in order to remain protected. A sample of this form is found in appendices J & K.

Although in some instances, participants consciously or unconsciously disclosed their names by way of introducing themselves or stressing a point that they had made. It remained however, my duty to protect them and keep their identity undisclosed. To successfully fulfill this, I completely avoided any occasion of using a video camera during the processes of the interviews. Nevertheless, photographs were taken in some cases, but that was done based on the consent of the respondents and those who desired it.

Another important ethical principle of confidentiality is the issue of careless or clumsy handling of records and data that could easily be accessed by a third party. In this regards, I took the intentional precautions to ensure that I did not let any information provided to me by the respondents to fall into the wrong hands. In addition, I was very careful not to discuss carelessly any of the data collected. All sensitive material such as interview information sheets, transcripts, record sheets, field notes and other documents that could lead to the identification of a respondent, were securely stored. Being conscious of the security of all the fieldwork materials, the audio recorder was kept separate from the recorded sheets, and *vis-à-vis* the transcribed materials. This was to avoid any accidental access of a third party to the materials. Importantly, it is worth noting that pseudonyms of participants were adopted based on cultural and religious affiliations.

7.3 *Dealing with the "Self"*

The issue of dealing with the "self" was an aspect I needed to be very careful with because imposing myself on the interviewees could affect the validity of the data generated. Hence, in dealing with the "self" the researcher is expected to adopt a passive and neutral stance in the interviews. This is necessary because when the researcher presents him/herself before the interviewee in a lighter way, especially through wearing conventional clothes and being as courteous as possible, it will give the interviewee some level of confidence and a sense of appreciation so that he/she can open up and provide the needed data.

However, if the reverse is the case, the interviewee can get distracted, upset, provoked and feel antagonized by what the researcher wears. Thus, he/she becomes hostile and defensive. Considering these factors, in most cases I conducted the interviews with simply conventional wears except in few occasions where I had put on my clerical wear as a Catholic priest because it is expected that all priests in Nigeria must appear before their Bishops in clerical wears especially for official meetings.

Although, knowing my status as a Catholic priest, some respondents felt more confident and safer to be interviewed. For example, one of the respondents, a professor and a Muslim, clearly confessed to me that he holds the Catholic priesthood in high esteem because they often express objectivity in their manner of approach to sensitive religious issues. As a result, he (the professor in question) opened up to me and at the end of the interview, he went further to assist me with some helpful materials and also referred me to some useful websites.

7.4 *Funding*

Funding is one of the key elements of a successful research because when funds are limited or not there at all, they always affect the success of any meaningful investigations. It is in this regard, that Missio (a Catholic agency in Germany) did not only sponsor all my study programme in Rome but also provided partial funds for the fieldwork, while the remaining part was provided by my diocesan Bishop (George J. Dodo) both in kind and in cash. The provided funds were able to pay-off my flight to and from Nigeria, and also took care of all the local logistics, from accommodations and transportation to the purchase of all the needed materials used during the fieldwork.

8. Data Analysis

In data analysis, transcription of the data is always necessary because it will enable the researcher to be able to analyse the generated data thereby eschewing from the loss of the richness of the data and the risk of a selective and superficial analysis. Nevertheless, there cannot be a perfect transcription of a tape-recorded data since it depends on what the researcher intends to do in the analysis[33]. Hence, in data analysis, it involves the separation of things into their component parts. In order words, the researcher is expected to discover the key components or general principles that underlie a particular phenomenon in order to be able to provide a clearer understanding of the thing in question[34]. With the growth of science and technology, the act of analysing data has been made easy. The use of computers for analysing qualitative data has been employed to this regard. It is generally known by an acronym *CAQDAS* which stands for "Computer Assisted Qualitative Data Analysis".

It is against this backdrop, that having conducted the first set of the interviews, I immediately swung into the process of transcription through the aid of my research assistance. Thereafter, I started the data analysis by employing the use of a computer software known as Nvivo. I used the eleventh version (i.e Nvivo 11). I found this computer software package appropriate to the study due to its features that are specifically designed for qualitative data analysis.

Through the help of the software, I was able to identify some bits in the data and the existing similarities among them. Hence, I coded them and categorized them into smaller units. Coding here refers to the act of assigning bits of the generated and transcribed data to particular categories[35]. In other words, it is the process of generating materials within the transcribed data by topic, theme or case. Hence, it simplified the data for me for easy analysis.

Generally, coding in data analysis, is one of the first stages that must be carried out. It is to this end, that my coding system was both descriptive and analytic. It is descriptive because the data were classified according to sex, religious, and cultural affiliations, and the type of the interview carried out. On the other hand, it is analytic because the data were coded based on their content and form. As a result, careful scrutiny was employed in understanding the implied meanings of the interviewees bearing in mind the ardent necessity in keeping to the originality of the message. This was nec-

---

[33] Cf., M. Bloor – *et al.*, eds., *Focus Groups in Social Research*, 56.

[34] M. Denscombe, *The Good Research Guide*, 97.

[35] M. Denscombe, *The Good Research Guide*, 98.

essary because some of the respondents spoke in bad English, and some spoke in a local language (Hausa).

Hence, to remain close to the original meaning of the interviewees' views, I noted down my observations in the recording sheet form immediately after each interview and later typed them and saved them in the Nvivo software package as memos (see appendices J & K for the recording sheet forms). It is imperative to note that the coded bits were saved as nodes which were the containers for my codes that represented the units coded. In the Nvivo 11 software, I found the nodes useful because they allowed me to gather all related materials in one place so that I could look for emerging patterns and ideas.

In respect to the transcription of the data as already noted above, I used the intelligent verbatim transcription method as against the true verbatim transcription in which every event of the interview is transcribed. Background noise, interruptions such as pause, coughing, laughter *et cetera*, are all inclusive in the true verbatim transcription. But in the intelligent verbatim transcription, the researcher is expected to avoid such interruptions, however, keeping closely to the originality of the interviewee's meaning. It is against this backdrop that, I found the intelligent verbatim transcription method appropriate to the study because some of the respondents could not speak good English and others even spoke in the local language as stated above.

Keeping these factors in mind, it would have been difficult for me to have claimed that I quoted them exactly in their words and expressions if the true verbatim transcription method were used. Nevertheless, I tried as much as possible to represent their views and not mine. It is against this backdrop, that I had to listen and listen again and again (wherever necessary) to the tape in order to understand while I remained faithful to the intended meaning of the interviewees. Hence, the going to and fro of the data cannot be overemphasized for a thorough transcription of the tape-recorded data in order to pave the way for a better detailed and rigorous analysis.

9. Exiting the Field

The common adage that says, "there is time to begin and there is time to end" expressed itself in this study. At the early stage of preparation, I was filled with enthusiasm and at the same time anxiety of what the experience and outcome of the field work might be. The beginning of a field work (from preparatory stage to the early stage of the commencement of the interviews in the fieldwork) and its end are important periods in every qualitative research. In this regard, the researcher is confronted with the reality of coming in close contact with the researched. The three months of my contact with the study population spurred in me the passion of finding immediate solutions to the problem especially having listened to the ordeals of the victims of the Boko Haram inferno. Exiting the fieldwork with this type of feelings and emotions, was therefore, highly challenging to me.

Although, other researchers might have come in contact with the same or similar study population, but the passion in me aroused the following questions. How did I manage the fieldwork? Did I do justice to the research questions or not? With respect to the respondents, did I make them (especially the victims) to feel that through my research, it will offer them a lasting solution to their predicament? How will my findings impact the life of the people and the Church in order to realize the enabling environment that will enhance mutual and cordial relationship among the northern Christians and Muslims, and *vis-à-vis* boosts the missionary activity of the Church? Can my research findings bring any attitudinal change between the Christians and Muslims of the northern Nigeria? How do I sustain my relationship with my research assistant, the respondents and particularly those who frustrated my effort by not granting me the opportunity to interview them? How successful was my fieldwork? These and other similar questions ran through my mind while I gathered together my belongings to return to school in Rome.

While in Italy, I kept contact through telephone calls with some of my respondents and those who were of great help to me during the fieldwork. It was through these contacts that on my arrival from the summer break, I was made to understand by one of my contacts that one of the victims whom I interviewed, died five months after the fieldwork as a result of the trauma experienced from the hands of the Boko Haram. In the same vein, in December of the same year, I also received the shocking news of the demise of one of my contacts. Though, trusting and believing in the resurrection, the two events were heart-breaking.

With regard to the dissemination of the research findings, at the end of this study, I hope to send copies of my thesis to some of the respondents especially those who declared interest in having it. Thereafter, a wider dissemination of the research findings will be done through the publication of articles in academic journals, presentations at conferences, and hopefully the publication of a book. In addition, copies of the research findings will also be placed in all the libraries of the three Major Seminaries of the three northern provinces. Seminars and workshops will be organized from time to time as possible ways that the findings could be shared with a wider audience of different strata in the society in order to bring its impact to a reality in the life of the people in the region.

10. Conclusion

The third chapter presented the detailed description of the research design and the practical accounts of the fieldwork. It began by describing the methodology of the thesis and thereafter it made clear distinction between methodology and method while exposing the type of the methodology employed. Bearing in mind the importance of sampling in qualitative methodology, since it involves the participation of human beings, the chapter went further to state the reasons for the choice of the sampling technique employed while noting the nature of the research questions raised in the dissertation, and its theme so that the needed data could be generated. In like manner, the same obligation also influenced the choice of data collection in which it described each of the techniques used.

Thereafter, it went further to elaborate on some of the importance of ethical issues while bearing in mind the sensitivity of the theme of the dissertation. Ethical issues that concerned particularly the researcher and the participants of the research, were adequately dealt with. This was necessary because such ethical issues contributed to the validity of the data generated and the trustworthiness of the respondents on the researcher.

The chapter drew its conclusion by analysing the data through the help of the computer software package Nvivo 11. It is however, imperative to note that, I found the use of the Nvivo computer software package helpful because of the following obvious reasons; i) it stores all my materials such as field notes and documents secured in text files, ii) all materials could easily be reached, and copies could quickly and easily be made, iii) coding was easily done, and iv) coded data could easily be located through the help of the software search facilities.

However, it is also pertinent to point out that while employing the use of CAQDAS, I discovered some limitations such as; i) not wholly relying on the software package for the data analysis because computers generally do not make the conceptual decisions, such as which words or themes are important to focus on, or which analytic step is to be taken, ii) I did not depend on the computer for understanding of the implied meanings of the interviewees because it cannot understand it, iii) being my first time of using the software package, extra time was spent in studying the software package in order to know it and understand better its potentials. But above all, the whole exercise was a worthy life experience.

CHAPTER IV

Data Presentation and Discussion

1. Introduction

In the previous chapter, I gave an account of the research design and methodology employed in gathering the data to be presented. To keep to the *status quo* of scholarly work, reasons were given as regards to why one method was preferred to the other. In this chapter however, its main concern is to present and discuss the data generated. It is important to clearly state that the chapter will present the opinions of the interviewees in a manner that their emotional and passional content of their statements maintain their originality. It is against this backdrop, that the chapter takes a narrative form and it will support the data discussed where and when necessary with quotations from the interviews conducted during the field-work, will be where necessary, references and also made to relevant available literatures in respect to the theme of the thesis.

Further still, the chapter will group issues to be discussed under nine main headings that include; witnessing, relationship between Christians and Muslims in northern Nigeria, factors responsible for the soured relationship between Christians and Muslims, forms of religious extremism, Boko Haram terrorism, causes of Islamic extremism, effects of Islamic extremism on the Catholic Church, and the ways forward. These main headings are hoped to give the reader a clearer picture of the volatility of the northern region, *vis-à-vis* the challenges that confront the Catholic Church especially in the area of fulfilling her missionary mandate.

2. Witness

Following the mission mandate of Jesus, in the gospel of Matthew, where he charges his disciples to, "Go therefore and make disciples of all nations, baptizing them in the name of the Father and of the Son and of the Holy Spirit, teaching them to observe all that I have commanded you; and behold, I am with you always, to the close of the age"[1], and his last farewell words to the disciples before his ascension into heaven, "But you shall receive power when the Holy Spirit has come upon you; and you shall be my witnesses in Jerusalem and in all Judea and Samar'ia and to the end of the earth"[2], it is generally expected of all Christians to bear witness to their master and saviour if this mission mandated is to be carried out. It is to this end that the Holy Father Pope Paul VI in his apostolic exhortation emphasizes witness as the first means of evangelization that must be carried out by a true believer. "The first means of evangelization is the witness of an authentically Christian life"[3]. Hence, the importance of witness cannot be overemphasized especially in our world today, for "mission means witness and a way of life that shines out to others"[4].

However, bearing in mind that the nature of environment, place, and the culture of the people could be contributing factors toward delimiting Christian witness, the interviewees were asked of their experiences within the northern region in respect to their call to be witnesses. To this perspective, there were different responses. Daccos (a Christian, age 57), however begins with the reality of the environment pointing out its hostility nature to the northern Christians in Nigeria. Thereafter, he further brings out the implications of witnessing within such a volatile environment. Hence, he says,

Witnessing is determined by environment. It determines what method can be adopted in other to suite the purpose. In the middle belt and northern parts of Nigeria we can say the situations here are quite different when compared to the one in the Eastern, or even Western part of the country. In the Eastern part of the country, Christianity first of all has existed for over two hundred years while in the northern part we are just celebrating a century of the existence of Christianity. This makes the difference between us in the north and the Christians in the south. Hence, the gap in the existence of Christianity tend to differentiate our understanding. But Witnessing has different dimensions to do. First, is actually to carry the gospel of our Lord Jesus Christ to the end of the earth and this can be done first and foremost which I think is the most effective one is by our life. If we live according to the teaching of Jesus, in itself, we will be great witnesses to him... The second is, to witness is to believe in the gospel of the cross. If Jesus who is God, saved the world by dying, who are we mere human beings to say we will save the world without the cross? The cross is necessary. Although, he says "carry your cross and follow me", it does not mean we have to carry wooden crosses like him, but the difficulties which you have seen that throughout the history of the Church[5].

---

[1] Mt 28:19-20.

[2] Acts 1:8.

[3] PAUL VI, "Evangelii Nuntiandi", §41.

[4] JOHN PAUL II, "Redemptoris Missio", §26.

[5] DACCOS, "Interview".

Ankoyoyo (a Christian, age 41) shares a similar view with Daccos by pointing out some instances of religious violence in the northern region even prior to the realization of the 1999 democracy.

> I think the issue of violence in Northern Nigeria has been there especially with the religious undertone even before 1999 to date. We know as far back as 1979, 1980 there were little skirmishes and signs that became manifest under the umbrella of the *Maitatsine* in 1980/81 of which some states, in the North had their fair share; Kano, Gombe, Yola and even here in Maiduguri in Wurinkutu. So, within those periods, there were conflicts and violence that somehow had the religious undertone. And since then, there had been also some violence in some states like Kaduna and all that. So, to put it bluntly, there have been violence even before we embraced democracy and then they have continued even after the democratic era[6].

Ankoyoyo goes further to establish that such violence in the region manifests itself in various ways such as physical, psychological and sexual.

> Psychologically, it has manifested itself in the prejudice and discrimination and the denial of basic rights of the Christian minority and so that has affected the Christians psychologically because what they are trying to impose is for them to accept the minority status. Physically, one can hardly keep the records be it in Kaduna, Kano, Sokoto, Bauchi, Gombe etc. It is almost all the states in the North. You know and of course if you talk of sexual violence and all that we know that there has been attempts to lure Christians girls into sexual practices with the use of money and other things to entice them. And in fact, in some places you hear people rejoicing that they have been able to sleep with Christian girls and all that. So, it manifests itself in all these aspects physical, psychological and sexual and don't forget the history of these forms of violence are well documented[7].

But interestingly, while Dursa (a Christian, age 33) agrees with both Daccos and Ankoyoyo to some extent, he however, holds a contrary opinion as regards the nature of the region prior to the 1999 realization of democracy. For him, earlier before 1999, the relationship between Christians and Muslims had been cordial not until 2006 when things took a dramatic change as a result of the Danish cartoon in Denmark which claimed the lives of many Nigerians due to the Muslims reaction in solidarity with the Muslim community across the globe[8].

Following closely the above accounts, it suggests that in the six geopolitical regions of the country as already stated in chapter two of this study, there exists a dichotomy between the former northern region that comprises of the north

---

[6] ANKOYOYO, "Interview".

[7] ANKOYOYO, "Interview".

[8] DURSA, "Interview".

central, north east and northwest, with the other regions in the south and west with regard to peaceful atmosphere that could enhance the act of Christian witness. Nevertheless, this does not suggest that the north is always at war. But as violence continues to gain momentum, even before and after the realization of democracy in 1999, the northeast however, only started to experience it from the attack of 2006 as a result of the Danish cartoon and the subsequently insurgence of the Boko Haram. Little wonder that prior to the democratic era, Borno State (whose state capital is Maiduguri – the epicentre of the Boko Haram) was popularly known among Nigerians as the "home of peace". But today it is a different story. This therefore suggests that Christian witness is more challenging in the northern region than in the eastern and western regions of the country due to its heterogenous nature. With the nature of the volatility of the north, it becomes imperative to hence, investigate the nature of the relationship between Christians and Muslims that exists before and after the independence.

3. Relationship between Christians and Muslims in northern Nigeria

As already mentioned in chapter two, prior to the Nigerian independence, Christians and Muslims have been living side by side with one another but the nature of the relationship between the two parties seemed to be characterised by suspicion and intolerance. It is to this end that Kukah noted that the hostile posture of many members of the ruling class towards Christian interests was summed in the total suspension of all missionary activities in the whole of the North on the grounds that the missionaries were causing confusion[9]. But in contrast, Isidore Nwanaju holds that the early Christians and Muslims were very tolerant to one another[10]. Nevertheless, efforts were made to understand the nature of this co-existence between Christians and Muslims in the region. Hence, interviewees were asked of their opinions.

In his opinion, Muhammed (a Muslim, age 65) concurs with Nwanaju that before the independence, the relationship was cordial but now is characterised by suspicion. He holds thus:

> The relationship has been very cordial but nowadays because of politics, selfishness of the ruling class, and the politicians, they have been able to put a wage in-between the two major religions. We now have a situation that a little problem will be turned into a religious or ethnic. We have been living together and during Christmas and Sallah festivities we share the joy together, but unfortunate today, the reverse is the case[11].

---

[9] M.H. KUKAH, *Religion, Politics and Power in Northern Nigeria*, 49.

[10] I. NWANAJU, *Christian-Muslim Relations*, 82.

[11] MUHAMMED, "Interview".

172

Similarly, Dursa and Daccos share the same opinion with Muhammed. But on the contrary, Ipwuperjoh (a Christian, age 33) agrees with Kukah when he holds that: "At present and even before Nigeria's independence the relationship has not been cordial and that leads us to the fact that there has been a mutual suspicion between the Christian religion and Islamic religion, but it is of a different dimension now"[12]. In the same vein, Asabe (a Christian, age 55) also concurs that the relationship has not been cordial, as a result, many Christians are being ejected by their landlords based on their religious affiliations. In her words she states:

> Some of the Christians residents have been ejected from their houses and their properties were thrown outside because they are Christians. "Move out of our houses they said, because we are going to bring our fellow Muslims who are homeless to occupy the houses"[13].

Chenda (a Christian, age 25) is also of the opinion that the relationship has not been cordial as he opines that:

> I was born and bred in their midst. But our relationship with them is uncordial because they don't love us the way we show them our love. By our house, there were both mosque and Church. During their feasts such as *Salla* celebration, when they bring to us their food, we collect, prayed over it and then we eat. But when it is our turn to take our food to them at Christmas, they do not collect. Sometimes they collect can-juice but most often they give it out. This shows that there is a problem among us. I will never forget on February 18, 2006, the new crisis that took place, in which they burnt down St. Augustine Church. It affected us because they entered our house and it was set ablaze by our neighbours. This was a proof that these people are not good neighbours[14].

From the aforementioned, it can be deduced that the relationship between Christians and Muslims in the northern region is characterized by mix feelings. While perhaps it was cordial before and after independence, but at some stage this relationship became soured. It is against this backdrop that interviewees were asked of the factors that are responsible for the soured relationship.

4. Factors for Soured Relationship between Christians and Muslims

All interviewees believed that there were certain factors that are responsible for the soured existing relationship among the Christians and Muslim. However, these factors vary, pending on the religio-cultural affiliation of interviewees. The followings are the common factors held by most of the respondents.

---

[12] IPWUPERJOH, "Interview".

[13] ASABE, "Interview".

[14] CHENDA, "Interview".

4.1 *Colonialism*

Some of the interviewees strongly believe that the seed of the soured relationship was planted at the time of the colonial administration whereby one group of the people was favoured by the Colonial Administrators over the others. The minority groups as we have seen in chapter two perceived to be second-class citizens by the majority group who are the Hausa-Fulani. Hence, relationship between these groups were built on hierarchical nature which paved the way for suspicion, mistrust and hatred. It is on this note that Ajayi (a Christian, age 66) states:

> Colonialism is the main factor because the foundation of hierarchical relationship between Christians and Muslims was laid during the colonial era. Christian missionaries were not allowed to go into the Muslim dominated hinterlands and schools were built toward empowering the Muslims pupils thereby ignoring the Christians community. A vivid example of this is the Barewa College in Zaria. Today we are reaping it because the Muslim is made to believe that in everything he must be on top while the northern Christians below. Hence, they most often openly say it that what God has given them is to be rulers. But this is not true because the bible says that we Christians should covet high places because that is where decisions are taken. The average Muslim knows these high places and that is why their effort is to occupy presidential seat, Bank managership, to occupy Vice Chancellorship and every important high place in the country, and through that they try to dictate or block, or make sure that Christianity does not have a breathing space, as long as they dominate and occupy these places[15].

Holding a similar view Ipwuperjoh who also blames the Colonial Administrators, observes that:

> When the British came during the colonial administration actually in the North, the tools for their governance were already set because the government here was already organized. So, they didn't want to actually interfere with the religion because they wanted to have a smooth government in the northern part of Nigeria and interpolate the other part of the country. They used indirect rule. You could see that they had preference for those who had already established their authority. So, there was dominance of Islamic religion in the north. So, when eventually the independence was given, there was a mock kind of war that took place in Sokoto. Nigeria was actually handed over to the Islamic Sultanate. So that is why when the official independence was declared in Lagos it was just ceremonial. When they had the mock battle, they accepted that Nigeria had defeated Britain as a result, they handed over the Sceptre of power that they seized when they came before independence which marked the fact

---

[15] AJAYI, "Interview".

that they were handing over authority to them and that is why this mentality of born to rule came because there was actually a support even from our colonial masters to them[16].

Along this pattern of thoughts are Ankoyoyo and Mallam. While Ankoyoyo blames the existing soured relationship on the Colonial Administrators due to their favouritism of the Muslims over the Christians, and their negligence over lack of structures that could protect the Christians as a minority group, Mallam (a Christian, age 51) on the other hand, blames the Colonial Administrators for the restriction of the Christians missionaries into the northern region hinterland to evangelise. In his words he opines,

"It started with restrictions especially in the colonial days when Christianity came in, move here, don't move there, regulations, but Christianity strived"[17].

4.2 *Cultural Tight*

Culture is one of the human realities that gives each human being his/her identity. In most cases, we are identified by our culture. Some, however, are engrossed in their culture so much so that the existence of the other cultures around them means nothing to them. It is against this backdrop that Ankoyoyo is of the view that due to cultural tight, relationships are difficult to be established particularly with people from the Kanuri culture. Given that such culture does not open up to strangers. As a result, such culture isolates itself from others. It is to this end, he thus observes:

When you are regarded as a second-class citizen and when you are denied certain rights that you know as a Nigerian citizen, they belong to you, how do you feel. To be frank with you, in Borno state for example, the Kanuri culture is a very closed culture. They hardly open up to others. I can tell you that the existence of Nigerian Inter-Religious Council (NIREC) in some states, in Borno state is not possible because they don't see the need, as long as you are not Kanuri, and even if you are a Muslim, but you are not Kanuri, you are not considered as a real Muslim. So, this kind of barrier makes it very difficult for people to blend mutually as it should be. Hence, I only hope that this reality that has affected all of us both Christians and Muslims, we will be able to see the need to come together to build this mechanism so that we can live together since we have no other place to go than wherever we find ourselves[18].

In the same vein, Ava (a Christian, age 47) observes that relationships suffer not only by those who are not of the same faith and culture, but also

---

[16] Ipwuperjoh, "Interview".

[17] Mallam, "Interview".

[18] Ankoyoyo, "Interview".

by those who are of same faith but different culture. As a result of such cultural tight, members of the same religion do not share the same place of worship. Hence, he states:

Of course, the nature of the average Muslim who is from the north is not the same with the average Muslim who is from the south. It will shock you to know that sometimes they don't use the same mosque for prayers because the average Hausa Muslim does not see the Yoruba Muslim as a good Muslim. So, they have different mosques even tomorrow. So, with that in mind you now discover that whatever…if they have a candidate… somebody even joked that if they bring one of their cows and made it a candidate, the average northern Muslim will vote for the cow. In this kind of situation, you will discover that because of this fanaticism, in whatever they do it plays itself out; their relationship with you even if you are neighbours, their relationship with you even at the market place, their relationship with you in every situation, and in politics even worse. It is therefore this kind of mindset that leads to extremism, that if it is not my own person that is not just a Muslim but a Muslim of northern extraction, and far northern extraction, nobody should support him and if eventually he is there, then frustrate him, that has been the situation, and that is how extremism plays itself out[19].

From the foregoing, it suggests that culture plays a key role in relationships particularly between Christians and Muslims. When a culture closes itself against others, it obviously discriminates, and hence sours the needed relationship to be maintained. However, it is important to stress that culture as we have earlier seen in the previous chapters, it goes beyond ethnic identity. But in wider scope, it covers values such as language, religion and others which serve as parameters of self-identity. Hence, religio-cultural tight paves way to a soured relationship. Owing to this reality, it thus buttresses Huntington's theory of "the clash of civilization" examined in chapter two that culture will be the fundamental source of conflict in the post-cold war rather than economy or ideology, although, this remains debatable.

4.3 *Politics*

Looking into the political arena, some interviewees pushed the blame to the Nigerian political system. The political elites in the north have the conception that leadership and politics belong to them. As a result, their domineering spirit always manifests itself wherever they find themselves. It is in this regard, Ankoyoyo holds that:

Muslims have come to say that leadership and politics is their birth right and all that. There is also an attempt to bring everybody into Islam, and this again

---

[19] Ava, "Interview".

176

is well documented especially the history of the campaign of Usman Dan Fodio and even Sir. Ahmadu Bello so that has been the reality since then[20].

Sharing a similar view with Ankoyoyo, Parangwom (a Christian, age 55) believes that the politicians have a big portion of the blame because "these politicians whether in military regimes or civilian regime have caused serious tension and divisions among the Christians and Muslims"[21]. Narrating her sad experiences however, Indagiji (a Christian, age 31) shares a similar opinion with Ankoyoyo and Parangwom as she observes that the relationship between Christians and Muslims has been a pretentious one arguing that facial expressions by the adherence of the other religion does not in most cases tally with their inner intention. As a result, there is little or no trust among the adherence of both religions in question. She thus observes:

> There is a problem because facially, somebody will pretend to love you but, in his heart, is hate. For example, whenever we are together, somebody will say all of us are one, we are all the same. But when he goes aside, he says a different thing. During the presidential elections, they were going about with axes, go-to-hells and clubs. Some of them were saying that, if Jonathan Goodluck, wins again, we shall sharpen these weapons and follow you all house after house and slaughter you. They said to me, if it were Buhari's tenure, your husband would not had been killed. One of them even said to me, is it not during Jonathan your husband was killed, and your son was abducted? Wait and see, when Buhari comes to power, by God's will, your son will be returned back to you after one week, if not, I bet you, change my name. Like a joke, it truly happened, as he said because it was during the Buhari time they brought back my son with other women and children. Hence, I come to believe that these people are criminals because what they say by the lips, is different from what they do[22].

4.4 *The Manipulation of Religion*

In establishing relationship and maintaining it, religion has a big role to play particularly among the Christians and Muslims in northern Nigeria. All the interviewees believe Nigerians generally are religious people. Both Muslims and Christians have a special sentiment in their respective religions. It is against this backdrop, all the respondents observe that knowing the importance of religion in the life of Nigerians, many politicians have employed the manipulation of religion in order to fulfil their political interests. To this end, relationship between Christians and Muslim is often

---

[20] ANKOYOYO, "Interview".

[21] PARANGWOM, "Interview".

[22] INDAGIJI, "Interview".

based on religious divide. To buttress the above point, Chatsomen (a Christian, age 50) holds that:

> The politicians know that religion is a good tool to divide the people in order to achieve their selfish ambitions. You see the politicians in most cases steal our money, they neither bring the money to the Church nor to the mosque. They use it on their family members and their selfish individual life. But anytime they want to fight for something that will bring money into their pockets, they bring religion into it because they discovered that religion is a viable tool, they could use in dividing the people in order to have whatever they desired to achieve[23].

Holding the same view is Bello (a Muslim, age 53) who believes that it is as a result of the manipulation of religion by the politicians, religion has become something else. For him, modern day preachers of both religions in question have missed the essentials of religion and promote most often their personal interests rather than the tenets of their respective religion. He observes:

> My thinking is that there is a manipulation of religion that breeds the problem between Christians and Muslims. Otherwise you will find out that hardly will you go around Nigeria as Christian and you don't have a Muslim friend or as a Muslim and say you don't have a Christian friend. Therefore, if not because of this manipulation, Christians and Muslims I believe can live peacefully without any fight... Due to politicization of religion which has turned religion to something else, people sometimes hide whatever their feelings are, and you don't know where people used to go and take their methods of preaching. Looking at the television nowadays is quite different from what we use to hear in those days. Preachers instead of preaching and teaching the tenets of their respective religion, they are busy attacking one religion or the other. My own submission is that as far as religion is concerned every religion accepts others. But out of people's attempt to attain certain positions or be acknowledged then you find out that certain things come in[24].

It is against this backdrop, that Ajayi opines that there is little or no line that divides religion from politics. The two realities work side by side with each other. While the Muslims accept this reality, the Christians on the other hand separate the two realities but find it difficult to reconcile their uniqueness especially by the Christians ruling class. Hence, he holds that:

> You can't divorce religion from politics in Nigeria because to a large extent everything is politicized in Nigeria. For the Muslims they don't hide it, they say that politics is their life, and that is their religion. But for us Christians we

---

[23] CHATSOMEN, "Interview".
[24] BELLO, "Interview".

try to say that you can separate them but the way we handle it when it comes to class interest you cannot see the difference between Christianity and Islam by most of our ruling class. That bothers me a lot[25].

From the above, is it obvious that religion has been a tool for many politicians who used it in order to divide Nigerians and thereafter achieve their political interests. This reality is distinctively made clear by one of the Nigerian historian scholars Yusufu Bala Usman when he observes in his book *The Manipulation of Religion in Nigeria 1977-1987* that most political violence in Nigeria are built around religious differences, and these can only be understood when seen within the context of socio-economic and religious life of Nigerians. For him therefore, the class of intermediaries who are being exposed of their incompetence employed the manipulation of religion by taking cover either as Christians or Muslims in order to blindfold Nigerians of the fundamental aspect of their reality[26].

4.5 *The Expression of Religious Extremism*

As we have seen the role of religion as regards the existing soured relationship between Christians and Muslims, all interviewees attribute the blame on religious extremism. However, I find the view of Ankoyoyo more interesting when he holds that religious extremism plays a big role because one religious group finds itself engrossed in its religion to the extent of ignoring the existence of other religions. It is the "too much attachment" to the religion that has led some of her adherents to express their beliefs to the extreme. As a result, such expression of religious extremism has deepened the existing distrust and has almost broken down the existing fragile relationship and cordiality amongst Christians and Muslims. To this effect, in his words he observes thus:

People have been living side by side, although the relationship has been suspicious and very fragile as I said perhaps because of some of these practices of discrimination and exclusion they have suffered. But the rise of insurgency has deepened that distrust, and almost broken down that fragile relationship and cordiality. Why? Because of the level of destruction that has taken place. And as I have earlier said at the beginning, all these were targeted on Christians alone not until when the narrative changed. But because these destructions were championed by some Islamic members, under the banner of Islamic war, many Christians have become suspicious, some would hardly have anything to do with Muslims in terms of relationship. Some would tell you that they can't live together. But I know some of these reactions are emotional reactions

---

[25] Ajayi, "Interview".

[26] Y.B. Usman, *The Manipulation of Religion in Nigeria*, 5-22.

because of the reality of the lost that many of them were faced with either the loss of a loved one, loss of properties and others[27].

Having directly been affected by the expression of religious extremism exhibited by the Boko Haram terrorist group, Jamada (a Christian, age 38) shares the same view with Ankoyoyo when she says that:

Prior to the inception of the Boko Haram, we used to share the joy of our respective festivities together. But at such moments any time they celebrate their festivity and share with us their meals, we eat but we in return, when we send to them our meals they collect and pour it to the dustbin. How I understood, was through their children. They abuse our children and say that "whenever you share with us your Christmas meals, we don't eat but pour it away, but you eat our own because you are infidels/pagans." Since then when I heard that, I stopped sharing my meals with them again. But I give only to those who accept it and eat it[28].

Sharing in the same opinion with others above, Parangwom holds that religious extremism has linked members of same religion all over the world as a unified family, so much so that, whatever happens to one in one part of the world, affects others in the other parts of the world. Hence, religious brotherhood supersedes family tights once you do not share the same religion. To this end, he goes ahead to expatiate his position by citing the 2006 Danish cartoon of prophet Mohammed which led to the death of innocent Nigerians and the destruction of property.

Although Bello shares a similar view with others as regards the expression of religious extremism by some fractions of the adherents of both religions, but he goes further to point out that Islam as a religion is accommodative in nature to other religions. Going down memory lane, he cited the accommodative nature of Prophet Mohammed when he lived in Medina with both Christians and Jewish community. However, living within an Islamic state as a non-Muslim, the state has a duty to protect you while in return you pay tax to the state. Hence, in his words says:

Who are you in Kaduna to say Christians must be Muslims or they shouldn't practice their own Christianity, when the Prophet lived with Christians and Jewish community in Medina when he started? That was the beginning of the constitution. They had a constitution on how to live, and that was how they live. As far Islam is concerned, you can live with other non-Muslims. But if it is your own state, then you can ask them to pay tax. That is *jizia* because you are giving them accommodation, protection and everything that they must pay for it. But in a situation like Nigeria, where it is not an Islamic State, because

---

[27] ANKOYOYO, "Interview".
[28] JAMADA, "Interview".

it is a state which came about people coming together not because of religion, so you have no right therefore to say that people shouldn't do this or must do that. Thus, Islam's principles are clear, if it is an Islamic State and you want to live in it, that Islamic State will give you protection and you also must be loyal to the State[29].

But regarding radicalism, he goes further to blame the Pentecostals as key actors on soiling the existing relationship amongst the Christians and Muslims. He states thus:

Pentecostal radicalism is what produced what we have today. As a result, Christians became the target of attacks at the beginning. Looking however at the development of the world, from the collapse of the Soviet Union the international politics became uni-lineal which also affected a number of our political development all over the world. That is how I see the Pentecostals coming in to the spheres of activity generally. For this reason, they become more political than religious. They came at the time when the world was just American world. Before then it was America and Russia so there were some checks here and there and it gave people the chance to think and compare. But now you don't have anything to compare. You just have to accept one kind of philosophy or thinking. American thing is an attack on Islam for one reason or the other. For example, the issue of Sadam, the 911 and Islam as terrorists. Pentecostals also have to come out and tell us that they have to also ascertain their Christian things as a defence. But the point is that to my understanding both the extreme Islam which are called the *Wahhabis* and the Pentecostals are not even the representation of the two religions. They are just a representation of certain understanding of the religions. So, there is no time when Islamic community will say let us come and target Pentecostals or whoever. What we are seeing now are just the expressions of certain people base on their own understanding and their own thinking of what they want to do[30].

5. Forms of Religious Extremism

In expressing religious extremism, it is obvious that it takes different forms. Efforts therefore were made to understand the nature of its expression. When asked what forms the expression of religious extremism manifest themselves, most of the interviewees opined that it is expressed in violence form, discriminatory form, and in the form of deliberate exclusion. However, before we examine these forms of extremism, it is imperative to state here that the expression of extremism was done in two phases as already noted in chapter one. While the first phase was focused on the demand for the implementation of Shari'a law in all the northern states, the second phase however

---

[29] BELLO, "Interview".
[30] BELLO, "Interview".

manifested itself in the demand for the creation of a theocratic state or rather the creation of an Islamic State (IS). In this regard, Mallam states:

> In the first phase was that of demanding the implementation of Shari'a law. What was wrong with the conventional legal system that we had. But you just went out of your way that look, we want Shari'a law. This is an extreme fold because there are issues even related to that that you can't even as for today explain within a certain circular setting and then even given our level of development, but you see it was the extremism that you are now saying that you want to go back. In the second phase, it was the same level of extremism that resulted in these people now deciding that they wanted to create a theocratic state and remember that it was at this stage that terrorism has now become a weapon and the means to this end, part of what they tell you is that they don't want anything western. We don't want western education, is an extreme form of behaviour. So, you have forgotten that you are leaving within the context where technology, knowledge, but you can see the way what they do to themselves. So, we don't use this, we don't use anything. The moment you are even associated with anything more than the western of course they know that you are not a member. These are extreme behaviours because you are denying a reality in the present. So, no schools, women must cover themselves in extreme forms and that is why the destruction of basic infrastructures from hospitals where everybody is benefitting from, to schools where is a necessity in the 21st century because we are leaving in a knowledgeable society but for them no, and then organs of structures of the state become the object of attack. So, these are extreme behaviours which have manifested in different ways but corresponding with the phases in which these conflicts have erupted[31].

5.1 *Violence*

As we have seen in chapter two, north as a region is known to be a volatile area because it is often prone to religious violence. Bearing this reality in mind, interviewees were asked of their experiences of religious violence. All (but with the exception of Usman who held that all violence he has witnessed are political) are of the opinion that they have witnessed religious violence from one stage of life to another especially from the year 1999 till date. In this light, Ankoyoyo points out this reality as he states:

> I think the issue of violence in Northern Nigeria has been there especially with the religious undertone even before 1999 to date we know as far back as 1979, 1980 there were little skirmishes and signs that became manifest under the umbrella of the *Maitatsine* in 1980/81 of which some states, in the North had their fair share; Kano, Gombe, Yola and even here in Maiduguri in Wurinkutu. So, within those periods, there were conflicts and violence that somehow had

---

[31] MALLAM, "Interview".

the religious undertone. And since then, there had been also some violence in some states like Kaduna and all that. So, to put it bluntly, there have been violence even before we embraced democracy and then they have continued even after the democratic era[32].

Going down memory lane, Chatsomen goes further to numerate certain religious violence that took place which resulted to the loss of lives and properties. In his words he says:

We have had quite a number of crisis; such as the Shari'a crisis in the year 2000 which started in Zamfara down to Kaduna state and other parts of the north. The Shari'a norms were contradicting the Christian faith; so, came a protest from the side of the Christians and from other Muslims who do not believe in the norms of the Shari'a law. This protest brought about bloodshed and thousands of people were killed. We had another crisis from the Miss World Beauty pageant in 2002 whereby the Muslims in Kaduna came out and protested against it. This also result to loss of lives and the destruction of Churches[33].

5.2 *Discrimination*

With regard to discrimination, all Christian interviewees opine that the expression of religious extremism of the other rival religion has discriminated against Christians in all ramifications of life, ranging from denial of land for the building of Churches, school, and cemeteries to the denial of job opportunities, promotion in the public offices, denial of admission into higher institutions etc. Expressing their dissatisfaction on the attitude of their counterparts, Parangwom observes:

Yes, our Christians here are seriously discriminated against by the Muslims, there is no doubt about that. This happens in many areas. Admission into the university or any other higher institutions here. You find out that some Christians whose results are excellent are not admitted until they do certain things, like conversion. They will tell you if you want to get this you have to be converted to Islam, otherwise they are denied such opportunities. What about promotion, even the employment there are some of our Christians who are not employed into certain areas as not for anything but because of their own faith. And even if they are employed, you find that when it comes to issue of promotion it doesn't happen. What of appointments whether into governmental or political offices. Here we also find out that Christians are discriminated against. We have a situation where we have a cabinet of twenty or more commissioners, and only to have may be one or two Christians, and the rest are Muslims. The same thing happens with the social welfare where it comes to

---

[32] ANKOYOYO, "Interview".
[33] CHATSOMEN, "Interview".

siting certain projects that would benefit the people generally like water, health facilities, or housing facilities and so on. The Christians areas are hardly noticed, let alone taken care of. When it comes to getting land for the Church, we are talking of freedom of religion in the country but in terms of getting land for the Church that hardly happens here. Once it is known that a piece of land is being purchased for a Church building, it will not be given. So, these are some of the areas that we get discriminated against as Christians in this part of the country[34].

Adding his voice, Ankoyoyo also observes:

You know that most of the Northern States Christians are denied pieces of land in order to build Churches. In some places they were denied land to bury their dead. Admission even to higher institutions and some courses appear to be reserved only for the Muslims. Our Christian boys and girls find it difficult even when they have the required credentials to study such courses, some will have to buy their way through. And even when it comes to political offices and appointments, our people also are being discriminated upon. It is difficult for you to rise to any political office. But it is very easier when you are a Muslim. Lack of promotion even in civil service. Many of our people have overstayed and their promotions are either delayed or denied. And if you talk of control of the media for instance, in some states like Borno State, Christians are only invited to air their programs at Easter and Christmas seasons but outside these periods, they hardly have access to the media. But you find yourself listening to *Tafsir* (an Islamic program) almost every day. Thus, they control the media. Politically, our people have been alienated and discriminated upon. Yet still, you go to Christian towns and villages where there are 95% Christians, the local Chief, be it *mai'anguwa* (head), or *emir* (chief/prince) is a Muslim, not minding the majority of the Christians. If you look across the north you can easily count the number of Christians who are either local Chiefs or Emirs, they are very few. These are some of the areas where Christians have been discriminated. Access even to economy, is also an aspect of Christians discrimination because there are no many Christians in politics, and they do not control the political machinery. If you go to any Northern town where they call "Sabon Gari" these are concentration of Christians or non-indigenes so to say and those places are always neglected especially in-terms of social amenities, roads etc. They don't benefit anything, and a clear example is here in Maiduguri, despite their contribution to the economy of the state, except in some Northern States where you have a good number of Christians who are in political offices. But in the core-North that is not applicable[35].

Dursa shares a similar view with Ankoyoyo when he says:

---

[34] PARANGWOM, "Interview".
[35] ANKOYOYO, "Interview".

The diocesan building engineer for example used to receive calls from the Shehu's palace asking him why he was building a pastor's house without permission. In the area of civil service, if you are a Christian from Borno state you are either denied or delayed promotion in your work place notwithstanding all your qualifications but a Muslim in that same position or even with less qualification is promoted and given due consideration while they cover up their deeds with other factors. So, Christians are always marginalized here. A good example here is one of the strong members of the Catholic Women Organization (CWO) who used to make Rosary beads. Prior to her retirement, while she was the headmistress of a school where she worked, she used to make Rosary beats during her leisure time in her office. At the time people picked interest in what she was doing, they reported her to the authority that she was teaching students in the class how to pray the Rosary. This false accusation earned her a very serious punishment. As a result, she was demoted from the position of a headmistress to a classroom teacher. Even the Church you visited yesterday, you could see that its sign post is written St. Michael Social Centre because when we asked for the license to build a Church, they refused but when we told them it was going to be a social centre, where both Christians and Muslims could go and rent for social activities, they accepted and later we slotted a Church there, which has become a parish now. So, you can imagine. Even in the market when a Hausa man is selling, if he knows you are an Igbo man or a Christian generally, he hikes the price but when the buyer is his fellow Muslim the price drops as low as possible. That's why they will tell you that they want to capture the economy of the state because they have allowed foreigners to come and hijack the economy of their state. These are all forms of exclusion if you like, forms of discrimination that confront Christians[36].

The expression of religious extremism particularly through discrimination, never spared even their own kindred, the *Masihiyawa* (the Hausa Christians) who never share the same belief with them. To this end, they deny them land for the building of their place of worship and even at market places they refuse money from them, and hence deny them of possessing what their money could give them due to the fact that they are simply Christians and not Muslims. It is against this backdrop that Nchok (a Christian, age 56) holds thus:

One of my greatest problems when I started work here was the issue of securing land with which we can develop and then have enough space and facilities that can contain us as a diocese. I realize that at that time I had wanted to use the Masihiyawa Catholics to penetrate and help us to get land since their culture is the same with that of the Muslims, for me it was shocking that while we recorded some successes, there were other instances that we suffered disappointments

---

[36] Dursa, "Interview".

when these Masihiyawa go into negotiations, even when discussions are maturing sometimes surprisingly they ask the question; hey wait a minute, tell me the truth, are you us or you are them? And when the Masihiyawa man does not understand what you mean by us and them, then they will further ask; are you a caftan wearer or you are a shirt and a collar wearer? Meaning that are you a Muslim or a Christian? In their way of doing things, being honest, they will say, 'if you want the truth, I am them', and thus they will tell you "end of discussion". But be it that as it may, it was surprising and shocking that much of the lands we have today that we succeeded in buying and developing some projects on we also bought them from Muslims. This means thus, there are those who are fanatical, and you may call them extremists who seem to qualify themselves to be the true Muslims who want to do things strictly according to the dictates of the religion – the Qur'an and the hadith. We had instances also where at a point Giwa local government was giving out loans to civil servants to buys motor bikes. Some of those who got those motor bikes as loans wanted to dispose of them. While we had some Muslims who joyfully wanted to sell those motor bikes to us (about two Muslims) others said God forbid for them to sell their property and be used to propagate Christ/Jesus/Isa as they may call him. Once you are a Christian, even if they were given the money and thereafter, they realized that it was money that came from a Christian, they would say no to it because it is against their faith. Whether it was the motor bikes or the lands, we needed them for the purpose of evangelization, and to work among them and for them in order to improve human relations through especially interreligious dialogue[37].

Even in the Internally Displaced Persons (IDP) camps, Christians especially the women suffer discrimination as regards the distribution of relief materials. Jamada narrating her life experience as a victim of the Boko Haram insurgence, she says:

One of the ways for example, when they bring gifts for the widows, in most cases when 100 Muslim widows get, hardly will you find two Christian widows. Sometimes, they will not give us at all. So also, in the area of education, when our children pass their exams and with good results especially in the field of medicine, they are not offered admissions because they are Christians. In the area of employment, if you bear the name Peter or John, they will not employ you, except names like Ali, or Mohammed. Truly speaking, their attitudes always expressed that they do not love us. Only God helps us[38].

Chenda also shares a similar view with the others. As a direct victim of the discrimination he states:

Surely it does because I am even a victim of such expression. In Ramat Polytechnic where I schooled in the department of Marketing, Maiduguri, prior

---

[37] NCHOK, "Interview".
[38] JAMADA, "Interview".

to my completion they gave me a carry-over in National Diploma (ND) 1 in Business Mathematics for the reason that I attended Chrism Mass celebration in St. Patrick. It happened that on that day we had lectures. The lecturer came into the class before his time and conducted a roll-call. Thereafter he gave out a test to the class and a home work. These affected me despite my appeals. On the part of their Muslim students, most often some of them will not attend lectures and even if they attend they come in with nothing even a jotter, but yet when results are released after examinations, their names are always in the leading list, and the Christian students' names (brilliant or not brilliant) are always pushed to the bottom of the list. In addition, during project writing, I was the group leader of five students (1 Christians and 4 Muslims). But any time I submitted a chapter of the work to our Muslim moderator he would not collect it except in the presence of the other four Muslim students. But any time they in-turn submitted part of the work, even if I am not there as a group leader, he collected it. In his action, I observed that the presence of Christian students in that institution is nothing to him. The issue of segregation among the Muslim and Christian students does exist[39].

5.3 *Deliberate Exclusion*

In many parts of the north, many Christians cry out for their deliberate exclusion from political offices where decisions are being taken for and against them and so also in higher places of civil service such as institutions and economic sectors. While some cry for violence and discrimination against them, others cry for deliberate exclusion from the hem of affairs. To this effect, interviewees expressed their views in the manner these challenges confront them. In his words Chatsomen holds that:

Exclusion from public offices is highly pronounced in Kaduna state. You have a Christian who is qualified for a post, but he is denied because he is a Christian. I give you an example; one prof. Andrew J. Nok was in the race for the Vice Chancellor of Ahmadu Bello University (ABU) Zaria. Among the contestants, he came out top and the most qualified. But he was denied because he was simply a Christian and no any reason. Quite a number of Muslims rallied round him and said to him, you better forget about this post. The Muslims look at ABU as their inheritance. They brought in an unqualified man from Katsina state and made him the Vice Chancellor. At the state level, you will discover that there are many Christians who are qualified for one job or the other, but they would not give them because they are Christians. You also find a situation where a Christian lady is looking for a job; they will tell her that before you are given the job you must marry me or convert to Islam. And many other stories of such kind. We have observed that most of the courses given to Christians

---

[39] CHENDA, "Interview".

today in ABU are petty courses even when they are qualified for professional courses, while the professional courses are given to the Muslims even if they are not qualified. This is sad; we claim to be one Nigeria but in reality, there some that are more Nigerians than others[40].

Ajayi also adds his own voice in a similar view with Chatsomen as he states:

Talking about particular religious crises, religious persecutions one has faced, I will say for any committed Christian in Zaria, in ABU and in the north, certainly we are on the battle field. It should be clear in our minds that persecution will come, and we have faced many. If for example, you take ABU where I worked, I believe that the labour of Christians was critical in building ABU. Many have come and gone, and I think we have paid our dues in ABU in helping to see to the growth of ABU and I have no doubt in my mind. I schooled in ABU in the 70s, and I started working in ABU in the 70s. ABU was a great university in the world, but what is ABU today? We are just living on past glory, and ABU is a good example where religious extremism, persecution has led us to where we are today. Is like the pharaoh of today does not know Joseph. The people that are coming up now don't seem to know that Christianity played a critical role in the development of ABU and all they are after now is what they called "we are taking over" and in every sphere they don't want a Christian at the hem of affairs. This is the persecution we are going through. They may say all sorts of things but is a persecution. But the point is that it reached a head at some critical junction when one of us contested for the Vice Chancellorship of ABU in the person of Prof. Andrew Jonathan Nok, and he beat them hands down with many of them as members of the council. But the truth was clear, but they came and scuttled it after they went to mosque to pray while the decision had already been taken. But thereafter they said before we come to sign and ratify everything, let us go to pray. They went for their 1.00 pm prayer but by the time they came back, they came with a letter and they say this letter was written by the chaplain of Redemption (the protestant Church within the campus) that this is their plan to this and that. They used that letter and scuttled the elections because it was just signing and declaration that was left to be done because the council was given the power. Like joke up to date Nok was never made a VC of ABU. Christians from all corners of the country intervened but nothing happened. Later we come to know that they have vowed that never to allow a Christian to become the VC of ABU again, since then that is the situation, we are now in. We have been praying and meeting but no good result. Because we are in an era of persecution and extremism. The thing is not reducing but is getting worse and worse every day[41].

---

40 CHATSOMEN, "Interview".
41 AJAYI, "Interview".

In the same vein, Nchok shares a similar view. Below is his opinion presented in its totality due to its relevance to this study:

We noticed also that this kind of attitude has also manifested in the schools setting to the extent that there are some departments like the institute of administration in ABU, Kongo, accounting section I was given the impression that for over twenty (20) years no Christian lecturer was employed to work in that department. Why? We can easily draw the conclusion that it was due to religious discrimination. We had a chapel there in the institute of administration, the Catholic community has been applying for permission from the University to pull down the temporary structure and put up a permanent structure that was also with difficulty until sometimes in June/July, 2007 when permission was finally given since around 1987 when the chapel was burnt during the famous Kafanchan crisis and then a temporary structure was put up, when later land was given to be shared between Catholics and Protestants. The Protestants had developed their own while our people were still managing the temporary one. But when the Catholics wanted to put on the permanent one there were some road blocks. This continued until 2007 when finally, permission was given. In 2008 I was told and even went and thanked the dean by then prof. Shoko and to let him know that soon we shall commence work, and he said, whenever we are ready, we should let him know. At the time we were ready for the work, we notified him, and he gave us the go ahead. The work started, and it was stopped. That the structure was going to block the administrative block they were going to relocate us. They relocated us to an empty space close to the staff quarters, part of it had been earmarked as part of staff children demonstration school. So, they used planning and physical unit section of the University to go and supervise the place and then map out the area they were to give the Catholic community to build their Church permanent structure. We went, they did excavation, we assembled materials and we were to start work but then I was in Lagos in the month of August in 2008 when I got a phone call from Fr. Lawrence who was by then in charge of the Catholic community that work has been stopped with orders from the University delivered by a Catholic. So out of respect for him, this was on a Friday. Meanwhile I had told them don't stop work. When I was told that this stop order was given, I asked, was it communicated in writing? They told me no. then I said, since the permission to build was in writing and was documented don't stop work until you see the stop order documented. When I came back, I was so disappointed to hear that the work had stopped, and it was out of respect for our member who was sent from the main campus that was prof. Omo, but if by Monday nothing happened, they will continue work. Like joke, that work has stopped up to now. That there was a protest letter by some members of Muslim community and just like joke that thing has dragged on up till now. There is no place I have not gone to; the community had done its own best written several times to the University but most of their writings are not attended to. I took the matter to the then governor of the state. Arch. Namadi Sambo, and during that period in October government issued a circular to all tertiary institutions in Kaduna state not to issue land and grant permission for the building of places of worship until they have cleared with the government. Meanwhile this is a Federal University, why should a state dictates what happens? We know that the school is located within the state, so anything happens the governor will be the first person to be called to know exactly what is going on. I got to understand too that there was some influence from the Emir's palace. When this thing happens, there were all series of meetings, committees that were set up both by the University and the state government, and all committees by the end of their resolutions the ruling will always be in our favour, but nothing has really happened. The last committee that was set up by the state government was in 2009 after we finally succeeded in seeing Namadi Sambo who said he was going to set up a high-powered committee to look into the matter and send its recommendations to the state government. That committee finished its work, submitted it in January 2010 and at that time the transition following Yar'adua's death came up. Thus, Namadi was taken over to Abuja as the Vice President, and it was late Yakowa who now continued as a state governor. Several times I met him on this issue until his death nothing happened. Then Lamaran Yero took over, until he left office nothing happened. With the present government, I have spoken with the present governor Nasiru in July or September last year, he said he will definitely look into it. I presented to him a resumé, a brief of the dossier, the executive summary of the fat document he said he will look at it, if he cannot solve the problem, he will meet Mr. President to see how these things can be taken care of. So that is another aspect. You try to apply for land sometimes in the local government but they will sit on those files that you are applying for land for things that will benefit the people of the area and yet they will sit on those files without doing what is required of them and then pushing them over to Kaduna so that government will now approve what you are looking for but nothing really has happened. Then we had cases of adoptions and forceful conversions. We had cases of young people who had gotten admissions into tertiary institutions but are denied indigene certificates simply because they are Christians. And, you remember of the experiences you underwent when you were in St. Anne's Zangon Tama II. Those experiences are still fresh in your memory, so I need not to go into details. In some cases, we had to threaten legal actions before the young people are granted their rights. Things of this nature are definitely bound to affect the spirit of evangelizing mission of the Church. Of course, the terrorists' activity targeted at Christians, I myself that I am speaking with you, I am a survivor because I would have been long buried in 2012 when we were attacked by a suicide bomber at the Cathedral on the 17th June 2012. It was God own doing that the planned attacked that was to leave a deadly and devastating impact on the worshipping community but God turned it into a child's play and the level of destruction was minimal compared to what they had planned as some of the things we heard as a rumour of how disappointed they were having invested so much money only to realize that the maximum causalities they expected were nothing[42].

---

[42] NCHOK, "Interview".

6. Boko Haram Terrorism

As terrorism has been a global phenomenon causing havoc and instilling fear on the minds of people, the Nigerian Boko Haram terrorist group is not in isolation. Its terrorist activities have brought Nigeria to the limelight as a terrorist country. Today, Boko Haram did not only instil fear on Nigerians, but has claimed the destruction of many lives and properties and has thus threatened the existence of the unity of Nigeria as a country.

6.1 *Emergence*

Bearing in mind the atrocities of the Boko Haram, the need to examine the emergence of the terrorist group cannot be overemphasized. To this effect, interviewees were asked of their experiences of the Boko Haram, its existence and how they emerge as a terrorist group. Hence, Dursa observes that:

The year 2009 was a very historical year in the whole world not only in Nigeria. It brought about the emergence and the first out-show of the Boko Haram insurgency. Later than 2009, they were still gathering members and harnessing energy. Those of us who have been here before 2009, we use to see the group like any other Islamic group who will gather round their spiritual leader in the mosque for religious teaching. They were very religious. They were always in the mosque, morning, afternoon and evening. But before we knew what was happening, they became dreaded with a goal to Islamize Nigeria and to enforce their religious teachings and practices to even their fellow Muslims and Christians alike[43].

Sharing a similar view with Dursa, Chenda states that:

Boko Haram started with their leader Mohammed Yusuf in the rail way quarters behind the St. Michael's Catholic Church Rail Way. The group started for a long period of time, but it was never suspected as a terrorist group. There was a mosque built by Mohammed Yusuf. Every day from morning till evening, activities used to take place there. People thought that it was a usual devotion of Muslim believers. They were busy initiating people into the group by force. This continued till 2009 when their violent activities came to the limelight. At that time, we were preparing for a national Catholic youth convention, in St. Thomas Kano. In August 2009, they started entering community by community, killing motor cyclists. Some of their members who were educated, took their certificates and burnt them to ashes saying that, "there is no need of schooling." Such members donated all their wealth to the group for the work of jihad. They kept on causing havoc in the town. Both Christians and Muslims never experienced peace since then. At the beginning of their insurgence, they neither targeted Christians nor government workers. But it started when

---

[43] DURSA, "Interview".

they loss one of their members and had to go to the cemetery for his burial. On their way, there was a traffic, and they became impatient and started harassing people and beating them up. Some of the people were hurt by their arrogance and made the effort to revenge. That was how a fight broke out. They started killing and there after they extended it to the government. But since, they could not withstand the wrought of the government, their attention was shifted to the Christians. That was how the whole inferno affected us Christians[44].

Narrating her painful experience of the atrocity of the Boko Haram, Ijagala (a Christian, age 35) holds that:

For me, at the time they started, it was small place in Markas (Railway community) just like other *almajiri's* (disciples) places. But gradually the place kept on expanding. Prior to the insurgence, the week before the insurgence, they paraded the town in army uniforms with guns, axes and planks each with nails at its edges[45].

6.2 *Terrorist Activities*

All interviewees hold the view that the activities of the Boko Haram were more terrifying than what one can imagine. Members of the group moved from one family to another, and from one community to another killing, maiming and destroying lives and properties. They also abducted people, forced them into denouncing their faith and embracing Islam and conscripted others into their terrorist group. Against this backdrop therefore, interviewees were asked of their experiences of the terrorist group. Hence, Ijagala narrates:

At the time it happened, they came to my house around 7 pm when I was about to lay down my mat outside by the door post. They started shouting *"Allahhu ak bar"* (God is great). My husband just ended his annual leave and took some evening outing with his fellow policemen (whom we are neighbours). I grew up in the midst of *farfare*, anything they said in farfaci I understood. I overheard them saying in farfaci that this house there is a force, once it is raining, we must enter it. When my husband returned, I told him this is what I overheard the Boko Haram members saying. Don't sleep tonight in this house but go to the Barracks and sleep there. But he retorted, "this your fear, will somebody enter the bottle and hide? If one is faithful to his God, is a thing of joy." That was what he said to me. Having had our night prayers, we slept. Around 2 am I woke up and went out to drop something, then I heard a gunshot. They had already entered our house through the fence in their military uniforms with guns and axes and had opened our house gate. We did not know when all these things happened because it was raining. I

---

44 CHENDA, "Interview".
45 IJAGALA, "Interview".

192

quickly ran back to the room and told my husband. But he said I should not worry, even if they kill him, I should look after the children and the unborn one too. Then he stepped outside and immediately they shot him on the head. There at the centre of the house they killed him. They went room after room killing all the males in the compound. When I was shouting on top of my voice, one of their members came and said to me if you don't stop crying, I will shoot you too. I went out to the Barracks and told the DPO of what happened, but he said he wasn't going out at that time. On my way back home, I saw the group near the house under a tree. One of them, entered the house again and told us to give him all the money that the government had paid our husbands. They ransacked the whole house and collected all the money and our telephone handsets. Before the arrival of the police in the morning, I had to dig a hole and buried the shattered brains of my husband lying in his pool of blood in the rain. I spent the remaining night outside my room in the rain praying the rosary by his death body. At the arrival of the policemen, they took all the corpses within the compound and deposited them in the mortuary. Then a day after, we took him to his town and buried him[46].

Narrating his personal experience with the terrorist group, Chenda states that:

In every year, we hold our deanery convention of all choirs in September and then we hold the diocesan convention in October. It happened that that year we were preparing for our choir deanery convention which I was their general choirmaster. Most often, I travel as far as Bauchi state or Plateau state to get new songs because I am connected with a lot of friends in those states. As the time for our convention was approaching, I left for Jos (the capital of Plateau State) in order to get more new songs. I spent almost a week in Jos. It was on my way back home on July 11, 2014, having passed Damaturu in Yobe State, we saw a checking point ahead of us manned by people in the military uniform. They were fully dressed in the military uniform and their guns. We thought that they were truly military men, but we all got it wrong. They stopped our bus, and as we slowed down to a stop, they immediately diverted our bus into the bush led by one group in a Hilux car and followed by another group behind us. On arriving the Sambisa forest, we met a lot of people in the camp, men, women and even children. Some of them were being trained. As new comers, they kept us separately from the old victims, men on one side and the women on the other side. There we slept that Friday till the following day Saturday. Prior to the arrival in the camp, they seized all our telephone sets. But before the seizure, I had already sent a text message to my family through one of my brothers telling them what had happened to us they should put us into their prayers. There in the camp, I spent four days crying all day long and night. They brought us food, but I never ate it, but kept on crying... The bus we don't even know where they took it to. But I had my file with me that contained all the songs I collected in Jos.

---

[46] IJAGALA, "Interview".

Among the songs, there was this song *"cikin tafin hannun Ubangiji, ba abin da zai yin mini rauni)* meaning, "Nothing will harm me, while in the hands of the Lord". That was the song I kept on singing at every moment that I am not crying. Some of them who were doing the services said to me, what is my problem, that I don't eat only singing. I told them that food is not my problem because I don't know how my family will be feeling since they do not know where I am now. Then, they further asked me, what am I holding in my hands? I told them it was a song. They said, which song looks like Chinese writing. I told them that was how the song was written because it was written in musical notes. They left me and never said anything again. Later in the day, they came back again and met me praying and singing, but they never bothered me. Every Sunday, they parked people in their Hilux van to an unknown destination. It was later, I was made to understand that when they parked them, they slaughtered them and abandoned the corpses along the roadside where the government security agent could see and deposited them in the mortuary. Whenever my family got such news, they would go to the mortuary and check for my corpse, but they would not see it. On Monday morning they came back again and met me singing. Then one of them said, my song is disturbing them, there was no need of my presence there, the others should know what to do with me. For me, I had already surrendered myself to God death or alive. That same morning, they came and took me in their Hilux van, with my face covered, and abandoned me by the roadside. Those that I left behind had concluded that I was also going to be killed like others. When they left me there by the roadside and there was no any sound of their car, I struggled and opened my face. Then on moving ahead a little I found myself at the main road. There I met with mobile police men on patrol. When they stopped, they started interrogating me. Where was I coming from? Immediately, I introduced myself to them and told them everything that had happened to me. Having been convinced of my stories, they got a free bus for me that took me to Borno express road, where I met with my tailor at Hausari who took me home in his car. On my arrival home, I met my family in a sorrowful mood, praying and fasting for my safety. On seeing me they all busted into cry. I immediately join them suit. It was after two days of my arrival having regained myself to a certain level that I was able to narrate to my family all my stories with the Boko Haram members from when I was abducted to the time I was liberated. Thereafter, we offered Holy Mass of thanksgiving with all the family members, friends and well-wishers. That was what happened to me. While in the camp, both men and women were used for different domestic services in the camp, and sometimes they would select some from both sides and trained them for the fight of the jihad. The victims were well fed. They gave them enough food and drinks. The food was prepared by the women who were there for a long time. There wasn't any act of beating. But we were never free. We lived almost a normal community life except the lack of freedom. We couldn't do what we wanted to do[47].

---

[47] CHENDA, "Interview".

Parangwom also shares a similar opinion with Ijagala but however, goes further to observe that the terrorist did not only abduct the Chibok girls as it attracted too much attention from both local and international media and organizations. But both men and women, and in like manner students who were not from Chibok were abducted in their various houses and wherever the ordeal befell down. To this end he states:

The Chibok girls are not the only girls that were taken away by the Boko Haram. We have some women and other girls that have been taken away before and after the abduction of the Chibok girls. And as you have rightly said some of them are used as slaves, suicide bombers and some of them are used even as cooks for the Boko Haram members. And of course, they are forcefully converted from their own faith to Islam. This is what happens. That is only in the area of the females. What about our young boys who have been forcefully conscripted into the army of the Boko Haram? So, that one is another angle. Of course, we have a situation even where our family members of our Church who are separated, some are taken away and some are killed, and of course these ones have devastating effects on the families. They also have some of their properties that have been destroyed whether houses, vehicles, crops or personal effects by the Boko Haram members… I am not saying that Chibok girls are not important but let us know that there are other women abducted. So, let them be equally included in the search[48].

Regarding the Boko Haram relationship with their female victims, some interviewees are of the view that they never spared them. They raped most of the women and the girls abducted and used them as sex machines. It is to this effect, Jamada says:

Here I strongly disagree with Indagiji for saying that the Boko Haram never had sexual intercourse with any of the women. My sister was taken right into the thickest part of the Sambisa, and they were kept in the big house there. She said each of the Boko Haram will have sex with them one after the other. Sometimes four men at a time. When one is tired, the other one takes over. Wherever they go, once they say lie down, there and then they have sex with the woman. It was when the Boko Haram slept off around 2 am they escaped and spent many nights in the forest before they could find their way home. On reaching home, her private part was already swollen, and she was looking terribly bad. We had to take her to the hospital. The fact is that, while some of them don't do it, a lot of them abuse our ladies and mess them up[49].

In the same vein, Ipwuperjoh holds a similar view with Jamada. However, he attributes such inhumane act to drugs. He observes thus:

---

[48] Parangwom, "Interview".
[49] Jamada, "Interview".

For the female gender based on the tenets and teachings of Islam according to what the extremists are propagating i.e. Boko Haram they believe that women actually should be protected even at war, but they could take them as captives to make them Muslims, to work for them and also to become their housemaids. But it took a different dimension eventually. We learnt that actually they are not only following the dictates of their teachings, they are also into drugs. So, whenever they take such drugs, there was the tendency to abuse women. We had a lot of instances of women who were liberated finally, narrated their ordeals on how they were used as sex machines, some married forcefully, some were used by them as sex objects from time to time. Series of men could line up to molest these women. It was so horrible for those who narrated their stories and those who were victims of this kind of abuse, it was touching, and it changed the lives of many of them especially as regards their perspective of men in general[50].

From the foregoing, it is obvious that a lot of abuses took place in the camps of the Boko Haram. Women were sexually abused, and men were recruited into the terrorist army. To this end, we may not eliminate the possibility of child soldiers since young boys were equally abducted during the raiding of communities.

6.3 *Sponsorship/Link*

There have been controversies about the sponsorship and link of the Boko Haram terrorist group. Their resilient to the Nigerian well trained security forces and their modus operandi raised some level of suspicion not only within the Nigerian citizens, but as well as among scholars, that they are possibly sponsored by certain individuals within the country and perhaps even outside the country thereby paving a way for the possibility of their link with other Islamic international terrorist groups such Al-Shabaab, Al-Qaida, and IS. To this effect, I tried to understand whether the terrorist group is being sponsored and linked with other international terrorist groups or not. In responding Ankoyoyo is of the view that there is no doubt about the group's sponsorship and linkage. He bases his argument on the obvious reasons of the nature of the Boko Haram's logistics before and after each attack, their quantity and inexhaustible nature of their weaponry, their finances, their ideology, and their modus operandi. For him therefore, if they were not sponsored and linked with other international terrorist bodies, Boko Haram would have been defeated ever since. In his words, he states thus:

Well one might be right to say that Boko Haram is a domestic terrorist group with an international face now. If you talk of the sponsorship and all that it is really amazing that up to now the Nigerian government or even the interna-

---

[50] Ipwuperjoh, "Interview".

tional community has not been able to point to even one person as a sponsor. But then if you look at the sophistication, the weapons these people use, if you look at the logistics in place, the way they carry out their operation then you know that definitely they might have sponsors locally and probably internationally. Now, internationally people will deny, but as I said the sophistication of this group, the logistics I don't think it's purely a domestic affair. One will be right to even ask, why were they able to cross to even the neighbouring countries and have their base like in the Cameroun, Chad and Niger and yet we know that the states where these things are happening border some of these Countries. Chad borders Libya and we know that since the fall of Gaddafi there were a lot of things that have happened because there was an inflow of arms and so many other things. So, the indications are clearly in the level of their sophistication, the finances they were even using to recruit new members. Where did they get all these things? If they are in the bush, are they manufacturing money? Are they manufacturing those weapons? So, some group must be responsible as sponsors? And of course, within the Nigeria circle, even within the Military some people have argued that some of the weapons that are being captured and being destroyed sometimes are from the Nigerian armoury. So, it means that some people within the military circle must have been selling some of these weapons to them. Granted in the course of their operation, they over-ran certain barracks and may be made away with all the weapons and the ammunitions there like Mongunu Barrack was over-ran twice, Bama Barrack was sacked and then there is one along Damaturu road. But the quantity and the inexhaustible nature of their weaponry and their ammunitions, is beyond imagination. You know there were times when they were claiming that they have better weapons that the Nigeria Military don't have. Where did they get all these things? These are things that people should think. Some people are slow in linking them but if you look at their ideology and their way of operations you can see the influences of ISIS, Al-Qaida and the others, they are so much in common. I believe that even if not directly but indirectly they have been sharing logistics and other amenities so that they can help them to organize and coordinate their activities[51].

Although he holds similar opinion with Ankoyoyo, Dursa however, basis his view on the fact that the leadership of the Boko Haram itself had made utterances via the social media that they have a link with the international terrorist organizations. So also, the Military while rampaging on the Boko Haram, have always spotted Arab nationals mounting on the heavy and sophisticated machineries of the group, and hard currencies are always found in their camps whenever the military overruns them. Hence, he observes:

There are always links; first, I think they themselves have come out on social media to tell us that they are now an Islamic State of West Africa and they are

---

[51] ANKOYOYO, "Interview".

coming to tell us their leader. That they have a link with some of these international terrorists' organizations in Iraq. Even at that, we have been in touch with some military men here who have confirmed to us that sometimes when the military men go on rampage, they tell us that the camp where Boko haram members are living, they often see white foreigners, Arabs mounting on their armour tanks and using some of their heavy weapons here in Nigeria. I have military soldiers who have confirmed that to me that on attack on the Boko Haram hideout or the Boko Haram attack on them as military, sometimes they spot few foreigners, who are not Nigerians. To them, such foreigners are among the Boko Haram as instructors, not only on indoctrination but also on how to use those heavy and sophisticated weapons. And even before now, in the social media we have seen how Boko Haram militia will overrun a particular community by using heavy and sophisticated weapons to overpower the security agents and take over the community. So also, in some of their hideouts you could get some hard currencies ranging from euros to dollars. So, all these are pointers that there is always a link with the international terrorists' organizations. And there was a time we travelled out of the country, I met a journalist who confirmed to me that before 2009 at the early part of 2000, he was somewhere around Libya and he was moving from Libya to Niger, Chad and around the boarder that he saw the quantity of machines, ammunitions and arms that were being shifted through the porous borders of Nigeria. So, he knew that in no distant time, Nigeria will be at the front of the war because those people who were responsible for the shifting of those arms were not Nigerian military officials. He saw that, but as a journalist, he was very careful. He saw them moving those heavy weapons and machines clandestinely mounted on the backs of camels and some of their caravans and shifted into Nigeria through the desert. In 2009 when the Boko Haram confronted the Nigerian security agents headlong, it was the confirmation of what that journalist saw. So, there is always a link with international terrorists' groups but that does not mean we do not have local sponsors too[52].

While agreeing with the above respondents, Chatsomen goes further to suggest that the terrorist group did not only publicly declared itself as having a link with the international terrorist bodies, but some of its members were also seen with the IS, and the manipulation of the heavy and sophisticated weapons goes beyond the capability of the local boys in Nigeria who most often when arrested, are always found with foreign currencies. Hence, he states:

I think it was publicly declared by them. It was not just an assumption. They are actually linked, that some of them were actually seen with the IS. So, it is not something that is hidden. The manipulation of the heavy and sophisticated weapons they used clearly suggests that these boys are not just our local boys.

---

[52] ANKOYOYO, "Interview".

They are sponsored financially both locally and internationally. The local boys recruited into this Boko Haram, cannot even feed themselves, but you find some of them flying out. Where did they get the money to fly? And sometimes when they are arrested, they are found with fat bank accounts and sometime huge amount of foreign currencies. So, where did they get it from? Somebody told me that sometimes those weapons we see them wasting cost hundreds of thousands of naira. But they waste them as if they were not purchased with money. It means that somebody is responsible for them. The locals also give them support. For instance, the foot soldiers are locally recruited[53].

It surprised me that Bello who is a Muslims by religion, did not shy away from the reality of the extremist activities of the Boko Haram and their link with IS and the like. Although he agrees with other respondents, but he goes further to establish that the Boko Haram's ideology of *Wahhabism* is the same with other international terrorists' organizations as it is proved by the manner of the group's preaching and attacks. He says:

My take here is that they all share the same fault because of the kind of interpretation of Islam promoted by the Wahhabis. They all preach *Wahhabi* Islam. They all say the same thing, and all share the strategy of attacks because is all clear in the methods of attacks and preaching. This is a serious link because sharing the same thought with somebody is enough evidence. Since you behave in the same way you don't need to be wherever the other person is. Whether officially they say they are IS or whatever, they are all the same because they share that same thought. You cannot understand this outside politics too because even this western world they contributed in financing some of these for certain reasons. For example, they want Asaad in Syria out of office and because of this they supported people who have now declared themselves as IS[54].

Mallam on the other hand, shares the same view with the aforementioned respondents but throws more weight on the local sponsorship as he *ipso facto* recognizes the influence of the international terrorists' organizations. He holds:

Yes, there is an international linkage and international funding. In fact, that is what has compounded the problem because *hitherto* these clerics here were depended on the local elites for sponsorship, for patronage, so he comes to your mosque, oh yes, the governor prays in my own mosque influence. Governor, these two boys please make them commissioners. It is done. Or this one wants this contract. It is done. That was the level. We had that influence, I will tell my supporters, this is who to vote. Now these people have move to the point that they now identify with these groups who have international fund-

---

[53] CHATSOMEN, "Interview".
[54] BELLO, "Interview".

ing and ironically because of the international connectivity they serve as role models, they are able to link up and they get funding. So, it is this funding that has given them the independence that they now come back and challenge the governor of the state. Once upon the time they were not challenging the governor of the state. Now he is telling you, governor leave it, with you or without you I can survive, and I am even telling you that I will take over. I have my men now, I have my soldiers well-funded, well kited. We have guns, you are my enemy, if I get you, I will kill you because I am telling you that I am now in-charge come and submit to me. All these are because of the international funding and remember that the international funding is not for nothing because even at the global scene the expansion of Islam and the desire to expand Islam beyond its original frontiers is an agenda. So, all you need to do is to hook up and ensure that you find a very firm mechanism of retiring the funds showing that you are progressing and of course attacking the infidels and whoever is a sign, you video tape, you are showing them what they are doing. Of course, funding continues to come because there is some wealth somewhere. Remember that Islamic states globally are the most richest because they are sitting on the black gold so arising from that they are getting access to these funds and that is why bin Laden like whoever we have on international organization that he funds and most of this wealth is coming from some of these individuals and that explains why you see them illiterates but they are well trained, exposed to sophisticated arms that you know under normal circumstances they cannot possess and manipulate them. So, there is an international linkage[55].

6.4 *Boko Haram Motive*

With the emergence of the Boko Haram terrorist group, there were speculations and counter speculations about the aim and motive of the group. What do they intend to achieve? As some were of the opinion that their main aim is political, others were of the opinion that it is religious. In order to understand the motive of the group therefore, interviewees were asked of their opinion as regards the aim of the Boko Haram atrocities unleashed on the innocent citizens. In his opinion, Usman (a Muslim, age 54) argues that the motive of the Boko Haram terrorist acts is nothing but political. As such, religion is only employed as a tool toward achieving political interest. Hence, he opines: "Religious extremism is more of politics than religion because it is employed by the extremist for the gain of power and fame. For true religious people don't go into extremism except those who pretend to be what they are not"[56].

While sharing similar view with Usman, Ankoyoyo goes further to argue that it will be unfair to base the atrocities committed by the Boko Ha-

---

[55] MALLAM, "Interview".
[56] USMAN, "Interview".

ram on politics *per se* because at the beginning of their attacks, Muslims and their places of worship were never targeted unlike the Christians. The reverse of the terrorism only took place when the narration changed. He, therefore, argues on both political and religious motives, as he states:

> You know anyone who understands or study Islam very well you will know that there is thin line between politics and religion in Islam. These are some of the debate that has been going on. But then if you follow the activities of Boko Haram, if you listen especially to the clips of Abubakar Shekau, and even listen to the clips of Mohammed Yusuf while he was alive, one cannot but to say that it is religious. Why do I say so? Some of us who live within the years that this thing became bad and so violent, we saw initially that these attacks were targeted at Christians and their properties but along the line the story changed. They were attacking and killing everybody. As I speak to you now, from Yobe State, Borno State, then Northern Adamawa State which comprise the Catholic Diocese of Maiduguri, we have lost over 250 Churches. We have lost over 10 Rectories, we have lost over 20 schools. We have lost over 5 Clinics. We have lost 2 convents. And then if you go to these places where these destructions happened, you see mosques standing. So how do you interpret this kind of reality. How do you name it? Is it religious? Or political? or is it both? So, people try to run away from calling this whole campaign a religious one because it has its own consequences. But now the narration has changed. But from the beginning it was clear. But since the narration has changed and that everybody is involved, they killed both Christian and Muslim. They destroyed both Mosques and Churches. So, no one is saved. But we must not run away from the fact that this war is being fought under a religious banner, and the banner under which this war is being fought is Islamic... So, in a nut shell my take is, it is both religious and political[57].

In the same vein, Muhammed and Ava share in the view that the motive of the group is political. While Muhammed argues that Boko Haram has nothing to do with religion it is basically political because for him a true Muslim cannot be seen killing his fellow Muslim no matter the circumstances. However, religion is used only as a tool toward the realization of the political motive. Ava on the other hand, argues that it is political because its aim of coming into existence was as a result of realizing a political career. They metamorphosed into whatever they become today because of the failure to fulfil the demand made by the group for the replacement of one of their members who was made a commissioner but later died in a ghastly motor accident. But on the contrary however, Dursa argues from the perspective of religious expansionism that the main aim of the terrorist group is to Islamize Nigeria and enforce their religious teachings and practices on both Christians and Muslims.

---

[57] ANKOYOYO, "Interview".

Debunking the idea of political motive, Dursa further opines that the agenda of other international terrorist groups is to Islamize the whole world and as such, Boko Haram cannot be isolated from this race. Citing from the group's principles of leadership, the practice of Christianity and any other religion was highly prohibited except Islam whenever they were in control of the few communities they captured and declared them caliphates. For him, if Boko Haram's main aim were political, at least Christians would have been allowed to practice their religion while they maintain the laws of the caliphates. It is against this backdrop, he states that:

> Looking at it from the global level, when you go through the social media, local news, you will see that there is always an attempt to Islamize the world. So, I think even in the northern part of Nigeria, probably through their Muslim leaders talked about this group to see whether they can forcefully impact their own Islamic theories and teachings. At the initial stage when we started hearing about Boko Haram in 2009, their main attacks were government establishments, government workers and Christians. At that point no Muslim or mosque was under attack. So, there was that attempt to forcefully convert Christians and forcefully promote Islam. So, I think, one of the major causes and the formation of Boko Haram is with the bid to Islamize the northern part of Nigeria, Islamize Nigeria, and at the end of the day, Islamize the whole world because of late you have also heard how they have also claimed allegiance to an Islamic terror group in Iraq IS which has almost the same ideology[58].

7. Causes of Islamic Extremism

With regard to the causes of the expression of Islamic extremism, all respondents are of the opinion that the root causes cannot be pinned down to a particular factor or two. They are numerous. However, I try to categorize them under following subheadings; radicalization, religion expansionism, political, poverty/ unemployment, ignorance, and cultural factor.

7.1 *Radicalization*

In his view, Danjuma (a Christian, age 43) argues that radicalization is one of the causes of Islamic extremism owning that religious leaders are not well trained in their religious beliefs who in turn transform such radical ideology onto their followers:

> One of the main causes is radicalization. Religious leaders that are not well trained in their religious beliefs will wake up and gather a group of people without being monitored and instil in them the message of hate, of segrega-

---

[58] DURSA, "Interview".

tion, of condemning the other in the minds of their believing members and over the years this group of people become highly radicalized, very harden, and taught very radical views that are contrary to the tenets of Islam. And at any given opportunity, you will see that coming out uncontrollable. Mohammed Yusuf had been into his program for years, he had been running a school and had been a wonderful preacher with good knowledge of Arabic and the Qur'an, but in-between this thing has been going on and no one took notice of it. So, as long as radicalization of people is not checked, we will continue to have similar kinds of Yusuf and Shekau of the Boko Haram all in the name of either purifying Islam or establishing Shari'a law. In Zaria for example, we have the problem of the Shiites led by Al Zak-zaki because people say whatever they want to say without being checkmated[59].

Sharing a similar view, Ipwuperjoh opines that those who teach faith do not teach the truth about the tenets of their religion, but rather teach especially the youths radicalized teachings. In like manner, Chatsomen and Bello hold a similar opinion. While Chatsomen observes that most Muslims believe that the Qur'an supersedes any other book on earth, as a result, it is more than enough once you have the sufficient knowledge of the Qur'an. Any other knowledge is not necessary and important. Hence, the pursuit of western education is a wasteful venture. Bello on the other hand, argues that radicalism is not a local movement but an international one, and it is being championed by the government of Saudi Arabi who promotes *Wahhabism* which is a stricter Islamic teaching of the Qur'an, taught by the *hanifi* school of thought. As a result, this stricter movement has permeated the nooks and crannies of the world and promoted radicalization that is in direct contrast to the teaching of the *malliki* school of thought practiced in Africa. In his words he observes thus:

There is also an external factor because what is happening in Islam internationally also influences the activity of the Boko Haram. Many of them studied in Saudi and when they return, they come back with this kind of extremism. This means that there is a kind of brand of Islam that they are teaching in Saudi. But to also understand that you must understand Islam. In Islam there are various kinds of *mashabas* which are schools of thoughts and Islam has permitted that each school of thought has a specific area which it is destined. Each school of thought has its interpretation. There is the *hanafi* school of thought, the *hambali* school of thought. There are about seven schools of thoughts. Each of the school of thought is guided by a respected Islamic teacher whose interpretation of the religion was accepted in those specific areas where he lived. The *hanafi* school of thought is a school of thought around Saudi Arabia, the middle east and others around them. The *hanafi's* understanding of Islam

---

[59] DANJUMA, "Interview".

used to be a very tough one. For example, his teachings provide the guidance such that people must do what he taught. In other words, he has compulsion in his teaching. In Africa, we follow the *malliki* school of thought which is a bit soft and accommodative. The part of the challenges is that most of these used to go and take books written on the basis of the *hanafi* school of thought that is very strict in his teaching and want to implement it here in Africa that is of the *malliki* school of thought that is not as strict as *hanafi's*. As a result, they feel that Muslims that are not of the *hanafi* school of thought are not Muslims. These factors therefore create the tendencies for people to be extremists in their attitudes[60].

7.2 *Jihad/Religion Expansionism*

Noting the nature of religiosity of Nigerians, some of the interviewees are of the opinion that the agenda of the jihad of Usman dan Fodio (as already noted in chapter two) is what is still at play in the modern society. In this regard, Ankoyoyo opines that there is a deliberate attempt by the Muslim community to see the realization of the jihad of Usman dan Fodio and the expansion of Islam across the six geo-political zones of Nigeria. Hence, he holds:

> There is also an attempt to bring everybody into Islam, and this again is well documented especially the history of the campaign of Usman Dan Fodio and even Sir. Ahmadu Bello so that has been the reality since then. I think that is what we are still going through up to this time[61].

In the same vein, Fuks (a Christian, age 40) holds that although causes of Islamic extremism hydra headed, religious expansionism cannot be isolated. He argues that Muslims need religious space and as such it has to be created. Islam must permeate the whole regions of Nigeria. However, wherever it does not work out amicably, forced is thus applied. In his own words he states thus:

> The factors as I have earlier mentioned cannot be tight down to one thing, but they are hydra headed. The first factor is religious expansion. They want the space, and where is not working they use force. They literarily said that the Qur'an must be dipped in the sea. By implications it means that from Sokoto state the far north down to the Niger Delta in the southern part of Nigeria must be Islamized because they want to control. So, the attitude to expand their frontiers is there[62].

---

[60] BELLO, "Interview".

[61] ANKOYOYO, "Interview".

[62] FUKS "Interview".

204

It is in line of this thought that Dursa contends that with the global events, there is a calculated attempt to Islamize the world. To this end, Nigeria as a nation cannot be isolated.

7.3 *Politics*

Examining the current trend of political movements globally, Mallam attributes the root cause of Islamic extremism to the international Islamic political movements that champion radical political figures such as bin Laden. The unexposed and uneducated are easily swayed by such movements in which the fight for jihad remains the central ideology. In this light, he states:

> Arising from the global trend in terms of Muslim revivalism which we could see fundamentalism, Islamic movements of course it became a fertile ground already because we are now seeing political movements, bin Laden political figures movement and of course the focus was the creation of a state, a theocratic state. For the non-exposed and uneducated minds, relating that way, the concept of the jihad became quite easy, to take over state power, take full charge. These politicians did business with them. Religious clerics became power brokers because they could all end all. They had a lot of influence, they control a lot of people in their mosques, they had of a lot of people in the reserve that they could use as mercenaries – the *almajiris* and whatever. Thus, they became a very important group. I was often heard that people had to go and see them, consult with them if they wanted political success. So, they became an interested party. They became an influential group. Arising from all these, the second phase was thus ushered in as the clerics became very power contestants. Since they could make and unmake. They can install you and can also threaten and by the virtue of that they were conscious of their weapons. So, terrorism now came in. Then the fundamentalism idea of taking over the state became a real issue. Thus, the foundation of Boko Haram was thus established. Of course, we were supporting you, we were still here whenever you did business with us, and we are now saying that look we want to be at the centre stage. Let's create a state and the *mallam* himself should now be the head of this government. Why not? So, the issue now became both at the initial stage their target was the non-Muslim population because they wanted to carry the support of their own fellow Muslims. So, it was only wise to move systematically. Christians, Churches were the targets. They would say look this is a Shari'a state, we don't want any Church here, we don't want any bear parlour here, we don't want any hotel here. That was it and nobody spoke. Nobody condemned it and said that this is anti-Islam or anything. Nobody said anything, and they made the move until Christians were at the receiving end[63].

---

[63] MALLAM, "Interview".

While Mallam examines the global politicking, Ava on the other hand, focuses on the local political trend. Christians and Muslims were living together and tolerating one another during the military regime, but as soon as politicians took over power, such existing cordiality was destroyed in order to score chief political points. It is to this end, he observes thus:

> Well, I have not failed to put it on the table of politics sincerely because if we begin to look at it from the micro level, you will ask yourself, these people where have they been all this while during the military rule. They lived together, they did businesses and interacted together, they intermarried etc., but immediately democracy came on board everything came to limelight. You know the kind of politicians we have are selfish. A politician can go to any length and get a position even if he is going to kill, slaughter, or sacrifice 99 people in order to get to that position, and then the easiest way to bring division in Nigeria is through religion. Ethnicity, people intermarried, people bear names that ordinary are not their tribal names etc. With that in mind, the big question people ask is that what actually went wrong? Just because politicians came on board and then they have to look at that thing that divide us more and capitalize on it so much so that if I am a Christian candidate I want to explore the fact that my Christian brothers and sisters will vote for me, and if somebody is a Muslim candidate, he too does the same thing. Therefore, when they bring up these religious sentiments saying look this is your right, I am your own man, I am of your own religion, I will protect your interest etc., and with the level of literacy especially at their own side you will now discover that look it is easier for them to change their mindsets to be influenced as it were. So, it is practically politics[64].

Chokist (a Christian, age 53) also shares a similar view when he argues that in Islam, only a thin line that divides religion and politics. For this reason, political interest always supersedes any interest in order to take control of power, and economy[65].

7.4 *Poverty/Unemployment*

Fuks attributes the causes to economy due to the ever-increasing population of the Muslims. He argues that with the geometrical growth in population, the control of economy becomes paramount for their livelihood. To this end therefore, he contends that "… but also for space for their economic and political control because their population is growing, and as a result, wherever they are, their source of livelihood must be made. Hence, they seek in all ways in order to control the economy"[66].

---

[64] Ava, "Interview".

[65] Chokist, "Interview".

[66] Fuks, "Interview s".

Similarly, Ipwuperjoh contends that in its entirety poverty is a cause because the perpetuators are within an area of limited resources. As a result, an offer of a token not minding how big or little it may be, can easily sway the poor youths into extremism. Thus, he says: "Poverty could be responsible for so many of those who are responsible and are involved in this violence because they take advantage of the fact that they are within the area of limited resources, they give them money to go out and carry out such acts"[67]. The view of Bello is not in isolation with the others as he argues that the nature of the environment provides a fertile ground. However, he feels that it is never enough reason for the destruction of lives.

7.5 *Ignorance*

Many respondents are of the opinion that ignorance of the religion and its Qur'an has a big role to play because a lot of wrong teachings emanate from the misinterpretation of the Qur'an and inculcating such false teachings on other illiterates. Against this backdrop, Ankoyoyo opines that:

So, you find that along the line, there are wrong interpretations that come from wrong understanding of what religion is and what even the text stands for. And when such interpretations, and misunderstandings are not corrected, it becomes an ideology. People now believe in it and then try to propagate it. I think all terrorist groups in the world today, be it IS, Al-Qaida, Al-Shabab, Boko Haram etc., they have their roots within the *Salafis* movement and this extremism as the word implies means they have gone overboard in-terms of interpretation and in terms of understanding it and then, they attempt to impose it on other people[68].

In the same vein, Muhammed holds that every member of a religion be it Christian or Muslim, ought to understand his/her religion better and promote the tenets of the religion and not personal interest. But when there is an ignorance of the tenets of one's religion, then extremism is eminent. To this end he holds:

As a Christian, I must understand what Christianity is all about. And likewise, as a Muslim, I must understand what Islam is all about. Anybody who knows his religion well, will not fight anybody. But because some people don't understand their religion well, that is why we have all these things happening, and the politicians now take advantage of the situation. In Islam they say we have three types of neighbours; A neighbour related to you, a neighbour in the same religion but not related to you, and your distant neighbour. So, it is encouraged that you love

---

[67] IPWUPERJOH, "Interview".
[68] ANKOYOYO, "Interview".

and respect one another and even share with those in need. So, if there is igno-rance in understanding our religion, extremism is eminent[69].

While Ava shares the same view with the above, he however argues along the line of total dependence on the *mallam*. Whatever the mallam says is unquestionable. Against this backdrop, such teachers/preachers who will deliberately misinterpret the Qur'an for their political or personal aggrandizement can easily lead others to extremism. Hence, he contends:

> I think, it bothers on lack of understanding, that is the way I look at. If you check a lot of people are living in a society where rumour thrive much more than truth, you are bound to have a situation like this because you can now see that the average Christian, I may say tends to move toward education very quickly, but the average Muslim is not in a hurry. So, this creates a kind of a divide whereas it could be easier for me to understand quicker. I give you a practical example. The last of my children is eight, he has a copy of the Holy Bible in his bag which he uses. But this is not the situation with the average Muslim's child because he relies on whatever knowledge he will get out of his own religion from the *Mallam* (Islamic teacher) and it is so done in such a way that whatever the *mallam* says, practically is what *Allah* has said. Whereas my son can look at a portion in the Bible and ask ques-tions for further clarification but on the other hand it is not the same with them. Their religion is holistically implanted unto them. So, they are guided by it and whatever comes outside what the *Mallam* has said is not acceptable[70].

7.6 *Cultural Factor*

As others view the causes of Islamic extremism in various ways, Mal-lam although, shares similar opinion with them, but he goes beyond the conventional ways and view it within the perspective of culture. For him, the average Muslim believes that the growth of Islam is by geometric pro-gression. The more children, the more the adherents of Islam. Hence, he continues to give birth to children that he cannot even account for believ-ing that God will take care of them. To Mallam therefore, this family bond-ing and community bonding pave the way to societal problems and most often leads to extremism. It is to this end that he states:

> ... I said the cultural factors because you see the situation where population itself is not controlled and is not unaccounted for, it becomes a problem. So, you have children, and you believe that well God will take care of them. So, you have so many children that you cannot even account for and so at the end of the day, you see the bonding. This bonding is very important. Bonding within the family, bonding within the community. But you see the issue of life and a lot of

---

[69] MUHAMMED, "Interview".
[70] AVA, "Interview".

things there is relatively more fluid, you find people moving and then children moving easier. I give you another example, there are blind people everywhere, they are laying people everywhere, the culture of begging is unknown to most of these societies. How comes? But you see if you move again to the extreme part of the north you will discover that it is like an order, nobody speaks against it. But when you look at other certain communities there are blind people and they go to the farm. So, the level of bonding is not there that is why I am saying that they are cultural factors. It creates room for this looseness and the control mechanism is surrendered to the religious clerics. The family bonding that look don't bring shame to us, don't do this, we cannot do this clan or family, you see, relatively it is lost as a control mechanism sociologically if you look at it. I have so many children so this one has now moved to go and stay with some over there. Of course, you see that bonding as a family and the control process had already been loss. These are the people that are recruited as armies by these religious clerics who become so powerful to the point that they make pronouncements that I invoke jihad on you. You see, it is so total that is why I said cultural factors will also come in. they are socio-cultural. In as much as we say yes, poverty, unemployment, inequality, hardship, but you see culture provides mechanism in which themselves are shock absorbers to these things, but some cultures are porous to the point that they don't have it and that is why it becomes a major problem, so these things rear themselves more than other societies. How comes then that nothing about jihad in the south, why? Very serious religious fundamentalists are there, but how comes they never talk about this jihad. But here is very easy. One young man will say... the next thing he is telling you that... tomorrow he has declared a jihad. So culturally as I said is diffused[71].

8. Effects of Islamic extremism on the Catholic Church

Many respondents are of the view that the excessive expression of the Islamic extremism by the Boko Haram terrorist group and other related violence unleashed on the Christians has affected them greatly and *vis-a-vis* the Church. The effects vary from destruction of life and property to abduction and forced conversion of victims. Against this backdrop, I categorize them into the following; destruction of life and property, mass exodus, abduction and forced conversion, economic hardship, Evangelism/vocation boom, and Enthusiasm.

8.1 *Destruction of Life and Property*

In narrating his experience of the Boko Haram, Daccos is of the view that the terrorist's operation was very devastating on the Church bearing in mind the number of people killed and Churches and other individual properties destroyed. Hence, he describes as follows:

---

[71] MALLAM, "Interview".

... their operation was very, very devastating and if you are talking of us as Catholics now, you know the whole diocese of Maiduguri, you know the Church as Vatican II describes it is the people, it is not just the building, but both have been affected, the people have been scattered and the buildings have been set ablaze across the places, even if the people come back will they go and start building their houses or be building Churches? So, in this way it has affected the Catholic Church heavily in this area[72].

Sharing in the above view, Dursa opines that the destruction of Churches was a result of the terrorists' conviction that the Church is in partnership; with westernization.

8.2 *Mass Exodus*

The sporadic bombings and the killing of innocent people saw the mass exodus of both Christians and Muslims. However, majority of Christians had to relocate from the volatile areas to safer zones. As a result, Churches were practically left empty. In view of the aforementioned, Parangwom observes that:

> There have been a lot of attacks taking place since 2009 up to date and because these attacks are often unleashed by the Boko Haram members, many of our Church members have fled from this axis and the Diocese to other safer places. This has reduced the number of the Catholics in the diocese[73].

Holding a similar view with Parangwom, Daccos opines that as people are scattered and priests are left with empty Churches, it will take the affected dioceses many years to reach where they were prior to the destructions. While expressing his view, Danjuma goes further to numerate certain vibrant parishes in some of these volatile areas such as Jos archdiocese, Pangshin, and Shendam dioceses that were in existence, but today have become mere shadows of themselves because they have been deserted. In this regard, he says:

> It has affected Christianity greatly. We have large number of Christians who have to leave the north in which some were born in, and some baptized because of this extremism. It has also affected the evangelization mission of the Church because we no longer worship freely, as a priest, you can't reach out to the rural communities for pastoral assignments. Big viable parishes in some areas have been abandoned. Ministers find it difficult to reach their members in order to minister to them. There in like manner, exists the atmosphere of hatred and suspicion. Both Christians and Muslims do not trust each other any

---

[72] DACCOS, "Interview".
[73] PARANGWOM, "Interview".

longer. In Konan Shagari for instance, you cannot find even a single Christian. In Angwan Rogo, an abandoned parish has now become a dumping ground because you cannot find a single Christian there again. This, however, can also be said of the Muslims especially where it is a Christian dominated area. The brand of Christianity we find ourselves today is a marginalized Christianity. There are some places you cannot get a piece of land to build a Church. Mission schools are hardly approved. It has also affected Christians through the availability of the sacraments. Some died without proper burial, some have stayed long without the sacraments of baptism, matrimony and confession... Yes, there is another place where we used to have a very vibrant parish in the diocese of Shendam called Wase. It was a huge Christian community, but what is left in it is just a small town where the local government and the headquarter are located, but the large chunk of its outstations that were inhabited by Christians are no longer in existence because of constant Fulani attacks by unknown gunmen. The parish is only serving few people that are left but no priest residing there. Yelwa parish in Shendam diocese is another vivid example. I was a curate there in 2000 when we used to go there and celebrate two Masses, but today, that town has become a shadow of itself. In my diocese in Pangshin we have cases of Fulani attacks and skirmishes in Bokos local government whereby the parish priest can hardly sleep in the night due to gun shots. Likewise, in Jos archdiocese, we have Riom local government where lots of outstations were lost due to constant attacks. It was there sometimes a whole community was macheted while they were sleeping by the Fulanis. Barakin Lahadi where the minor seminary of the archdiocese is located is another parish that is a shadow of itself. In Barakin Lahadi, everyday families are completely killed. The parish priest most often had to sleep in the minor seminary. However, the whole scenario, seems to be like a vicious circle because on the part of the Christians, some will go and rustle the Fulani cattle in the effort to sell them and buy guns for their protection, and by way of retaliation, some Fulanis will come in the night with their guns and wipe out almost a whole community and disappear before day break without any trace of them. But only to hear on the news that "unknown gun men" have committed such atrocities[74].

Narrating his ordeal with the Boko Haram, Tampai (a Christian, age 62) expresses his painful separation with his family and community. He narrates thus:

While in Baga, my ten-year daughter escaped to Chad, while her mother I don't know her where about. We have not yet met. In fact, back to my town, the story was that I was killed, not until when I met with one of my town's man who went back and told them I am still alive[75].

---

[74] DANJUMA, "Interview".
[75] TAMPAI, "Interview".

8.3 *Abduction and Forced Conversion*

Although the abduction of the 217 Chibok girls attracted the attention of the world, Parangwom is of the view that other women and girls were equally forcefully taken away from their ancestral home. This has also affected the Church because a lot of them were not only used as sex machines, suicide bombers and the like, but they were also forcefully converted from their faith to Islam.

> The Chibok girls are not the only girls that were taken away by the Boko Haram. We have some women and other girls that have been taken away before and after the abduction of the Chibok girls. And as you have rightly said some of them are used as slaves, suicide bombers and some of them are used even as cooks for the Boko Haram members. And of course, they are forcefully converted from their own faith to Islam… Of course, we have a situation even where our family members of our Church who are separated, some are taken away and some are killed, and of course these ones have devastating effects on the families. They also have some of their properties that have been destroyed whether houses, vehicles, crops or personal effects by the Boko Haram members. So definitely at the end of the day, it will affect the missionary activities of the Church in the sense that these crimes will not have been committed if peace were to be here[76].

Ngoshinda (a Christian, age 40) shares the same view with Parangwom when she contends that:

> At the pick of the menace of the Boko Haram, a lot of our people Islamized because of fear since when they come to Church they will be killed. But our priest advised us that when we stand firm in our faith with constant prayers, our mother Mary and her Son Jesus are always with us. We saw the effect of this encouragement especially we that we are from St. Michael, Railway because that was where the Boko Haram started the destruction. That was their headquarters in railway. But we are still there continuing because our Lord and Saviour is with us. We thank God for that[77].

8.4 *Economic Hardship*

Having being confronted with the reality of the destruction of Churches, rectories and schools, there is no doubt the Church is left with the challenges of rebuilding all bombed infrastructures. To this end, Church members are often overburdened despite the economic hardship of the country and the loss of their properties, businesses and farm lands. It is against this backdrop that Parangwom holds that:

---

[76] PARANGWOM, "Interview".
[77] NGOSHINDA, "Interview".

Economically, a lot of our structures have been raised down and even though things are calming down, we shall however face with the challenges of re-building these shattered structures because most of our Churches whether in the villages or cities have been raised down by the Boko Haram members[78].

8.5 *Evangelization/Vocation Boom*

The central point of terrorism generally is to instil fear on the people with the desire to achieve whatever may be their goal. Hence, the sporadic bomb explosions. As a result of this, a lot of Christians and members of the pious societies in the Church have been weakened by the fear of terrorism. They have been demoralized and the zeal to evangelize is weakened by fear. In like manner, young men who desire to join the priesthood or religious life are being discouraged by the fear of death. Hence, the activities of evangelization and vocation boom are being frustrated. It is in this light that Ajayi observes:

Certainly, it is affecting the Church in various ways particularly, the momentum, the commitment, the zeal for evangelism is slowing down. But probably for the Catholic Church, I think the momentum is probably going higher because I don't think you people are deterred, but there is no doubt that it is affecting evangelism, which is what our Lord Jesus says we should do, "go ye..." Increasingly what I see of the Church today because of that extremism and persecution and so on, the "go ye..." is going down. We are only consolidating and caging the Church, but we are no longer going as we ought to do... The few that are going are frightened, they are intimidated that let it not be heard and so on and so forth. If you take the case of Kaduna state for example, the current governor is even going the extra mile by coming up with the idea of a religious bill, that is the license for preaching. For those of us who are in the protestant arm of the Church, we feel it is a serious affront on us because for us I regard myself as a minister of God. So, if all of us at my lay level not ordained reverend and so on, will have to go and queue for license, how many licenses will you be obtaining and paying for. So, even at that level that religious bill cannot work. But it is an example of the extent which Islam is going[79].

Daccos shares similar view with Ajayi but within the perspective of the call to discipleship. In as much as the Church exists, the need for more labourers in the vineyard cannot be overemphasized despite the challenges of terrorism. It is against this backdrop, he opines that:

How many people would want to be seminarians and sometimes you will hear people who would say I want to come and be priest, and I will say oh! We are

---

[78] PARANGWOM, "Interview".
[79] AJAYI, "Interview".

looking for seminarians in Maiduguri and they say No they don't want to go. You know. Because they see Maiduguri as a place where people will go and die. These are the problems[80].

8.6 *Enthusiasm*

It is interesting to note that as respondents expressed their views with respect to the challenges that confront the Church, some of them however, went further to appreciate some of these challenges on a positive note. Surprisingly, the terrorist menace has become a booster to most of the faithful one who continue to persevere amidst all the hurdles. A lot of members have become more enthusiastic than ever before. Hence, Parangwom opines:

We also have the positive aspect which is the fact that the crisis has emboldened the faith of our people. Our people have become stronger in faith and some of them have gone to the extent of shedding their blood for the sake of the gospel and you know what that means as Tertullian would say "the blood of the martyrs is the seed of the gospel". So, these modern martyrs who have been martyred by the Boko Haram members are in heaven and what are they doing, they are championing our course there. They are praying for us… even though some people have left but the few that have remained hold onto their faith and that is a plus to the Church and as it is always the case the Church is definitely going to bloom from this very particular experience if these people eventually come back. They will come back and continually practice their faith despite any challenge that they will face[81].

Sharing the same opinion, Dursa also contends:

I will look at it from a very positive angle that the attacks by Islamic extremism has a kind of purified the faith of our people. The Christian community is vibrant now, even Jesus Christ himself will not be out for number but for quality and I bet you the quality of Christian faith that we have now, I think we have never recorded before. That people even in the midst of blasts on Saturday night are heading to the Church with their Holy Bible on the Sunday morning. People who have no place to lay their heads are seen very active and happy praising God… So, I think, the attacks of the Islamic extremists have brought out the best part of our Christian faith. It has also sent a lot of martyrs to heaven because we know there are few Christians who probably out of fear Islamized themselves but we have a large number of our Christian brethren who stood their grounds even before the so called Boko Haram terrorists to tell them that we are for Christ and we don't know Islam, even if you want to kill us, we are for Christ and because of this, some of them were killed and they are now a source of strength to us who are still alive in this front line[82].

---

[80] Daccos, "Interview".

[81] Parangwom, "Interview".

[82] Dursa, "Interview".

From the foregoing, it is obvious that the Boko Haram attacks really pose challenges to the Church but however, they are not totally setbacks as some may view them because their sporadic attacks spurred some of the Christians to an authentic call to be witnesses in all season. Hence, while the act of the terrorism is seen on one hand as a challenge to the Church, on the other hand it is a blessing in disguise.

9. Ways Forward

It is believed that in every problem there must be solution. It is in this regard that I tried to find the possible way(s) out of the stated problem. Hence, respondents were asked of their views in respect to finding lasting solutions to the problem. I group various suggestions into the following subheadings; government, Christians/Muslims efforts, and NGOs.

9.1 *Government*

All respondents were of the view that government has a big role to play as regards seeking for lasting solutions to the stated problem. However, all hands must be on deck since government cannot do it alone. The following points are championed by interviewees when asked of the ways out.

9.1.1 Creation of a Conducive Environment

The role of the government toward the creation of the needed enabling and conducive environment in living peacefully in a nation such as Nigeria cannot be overemphasized. The Nigerian constitution must avoid double standard and be very clear on the freedom of religion. Citizens must be free to worship the religion of their choice without intimidation. It is in this regard that Ipwuperjoh opines that:

> The Nigerian constitution should support the fact that there is a freedom of religion and not to have a double standard whereby it will say every citizen has the freedom to worship the religion of his/her choice and yet the same constitution will say Shari'a should be practiced in northern Nigeria if they want to. This gives a double interpretation of the same constitution. You know that for one to leave his Islamic religion and join another religion, the punishment is obviously death. So, for one to be able to leave his religion and join the other of his/her choice, the Church has to push for the establishment of religious freedom. If we work on that the Churches in the north will be able to work freely and be harmonized. This will go a long way to widen up the perspective of dialogue[83].

---

[83] Ipwuperjoh, "Interview".

Daccos shares a similar view when he argues that government must create the enabling environment that can bring violent young people (irrespective of socio-cultural and religious affiliations) in order to relate with one another with the view to understanding and befriending one another. He says thus:

> We need again to bring young people because for us to remove this distrust we need to create either some kind of things that will bring Christians and Muslims together where they will work together as a team in promoting and building relationship and sometimes it works wonderfully[84].

In the same manner, Ankoyoyo contends on the need for government to create the favourable environment that people could practice their faith freely without bitterness or discord. In his words, he opines:

> I think, for the citizens of a country, the government has a duty especially in creating the conducive environment for people to practice their faith. But when it becomes harmful, and when people are going to be very inciting and to preach things that will divide people rather than uniting them, I think the government has a responsibility[85].

9.1.2 Checkmate Excesses in Preaching and Teaching

As it is the responsibility for the government to provide the enabling environment, it is also necessary to checkmate excessive and inciting preaching by radical preachers. Laws should be enacted and be enforced with a sense of responsibility. In like manner, teachers in schools especially the *mahammadiya* schools must be monitored to eschew the inculcation of radicality on the young ones. It is to this end, that Daccos is of the opinion that government must adopt strategies that could help to checkmate inciting preaching by radical preachers. Those preachers who promote radicality and hate speeches both in schools and public places should be arrested and prosecuted without necessarily violating their fundamental rights as human beings. Hence, he observes:

> To adopt strategies like what France is doing or what Britain is doing. We go to all the schools whether they are *mahammadiya* or Christian schools, do they preach violence? Because this is where they groom these terrorists, and if you find anyone, anywhere, they are supposed to be banned otherwise if these people are not stopped when they mature and now youths, they are the ones who are going to carry arms and become terrorists[86].

---

[84] Daccos, "Interview".

[85] Ankoyoyo, "Interview".

[86] Daccos, "Interview".

Ankoyoyo shares the same view when he says:

So, it has been within us for a while in the north and I think the government must rise to its responsibility and checkmate some of these excesses, so that people who incite, people who provoke, and people who even teach the tenets of the religion wrongly can be called to order[87].

9.1.3 Transparency/Corruption

One of the characteristics of every good governance is transparency. When government is transparent in its dealings, corruption can easily be frowned at and it will build the confidence of its citizens. It is on this note that Parangwom observes that the fight against corruption which is the Nigeria's greatest enemy must be a collective effort and not only the government. All Nigerians must join hands in the fight. However, at all levels of government parastatals, transparency must be the watchword. Against this backdrop, he holds thus:

The first suggestion is that the government and all Nigerians should join hands to fight the greatest enemy of Nigeria and that is corruption. Corruption is the greatest enemy of Nigeria and with corruption; you have other branches of evil that take the place in Nigeria... The other way is to ensure that our political system be made in such a way that transparency should be the watchword. In other words, those elected should be credible and not people that are imposed on the masses[88].

In a similar way, Fuks contends for the need to tackle corruption head-long in order to create enabling environment for peace and prosperity in the nation. He argues:

One key factor that I have identified earlier which keeps on resurfacing from one stage to the other is the issue of corruption. If you look at the trouble that has plunged us into the mess, for me I have said something about economy, politics and religion, the unifying factor that destroys these elements is the issue of corruption. When we talk about dialoguing in a manner that will yield a sustainable peace, we must make a deliberate effort to unanimously say no to this dragon called corruption, because it has destroyed our communities because a lot of our youths are out there, they have nothing doing. Very few individuals have depleted the resources of this country to the point that the greater majority in terms of per centage nearly ninety per cent or ninety-five per cent of the population are in great danger of losing their source of livelihood or they cannot boast of any meaningful source of livelihood. When therefore, we talk about peace building, the issue should be brought to fore and educating our

---

people to be self-reliance, and those in the position of power or authority must make the wilful and deliberate effort to see what is due to the people it reaches them as when and at what it is due[89].

Sharing a similar view, Chenda argues that corruption must be fought headlong and justice and equity be promoted, and never politicize sensitive cases such as the Boko Haram insurgence. On this note, he sates thus:

> On the part of the government, efforts must be made to curb bribery and corruption. They must promote justice and equity. For example, some government may not desire to see the end of the Boko Haram, because the crisis has opened for them a way of survival through the diversion of relief materials and resources meant for refugees. Their hands must remain clean and wake up to their responsibility. If all these are done, I am convinced we can experience peace[90].

9.1.4 Provision of Basic Social Amenities

Creation of jobs for the teaming youths, the availability of power, education, health services, water, good road networks and the like are parts of the primary duty of every responsible government, and Nigeria is not in isolation. Nigerian government therefore must rise to its responsibilities and fulfill its campaign promises through the provision of the basic social amenities that could reduce the level of ignorance, suffering, mortality rates, and joblessness of its citizens. It is by so doing, crimes and radicality can be reduced to the minimal level. It is in this light, Muhammed argues that:

> The government should be up and doing in social responsibilities. There should be a way that the economic set up should encourage entrepreneurship. The youths should be engaged. We are not asking for white collar jobs. But when there is economic activity going on, no youth will be idle... Government should provide basic amenities for the citizens, reduce the level of poverty and engage the people in skill acquisition programs otherwise, Idleness is dangerous. There should be fairness and justice in her dealings[91].

9.2 *Christians and Muslims' Efforts*

As earlier stated, fighting terrorism is a collective effort, both Christians and Muslims must put their differences away and be united in achieving the desired peaceful co-existence. It is on this note, that issues such as; inciting preaching, hateful speech *et cetera* must be eschewed by all Christians and Muslims at all levels, and interreligious dialogue must be pur-

---

[89] FUKS, "Interview s".
[90] CHENDA, "Interview".
[91] MUHAMMED, "Interview".

sued with all sincerity of purpose not only by the religious leaders but also by all the adherents of both religions.

9.2.1 Love for One Another

Love for one another is the basic principle of our human existence. As every human being desire to be loved, so also, we must love others. Little wonder St. Paul will say that "faith, hope, love abide, these three; but the greatest of these is love"[92]. It is on this note that all respondents argue that both Christians and Muslims must embrace love, for sincere love heals the wounded heart. Parangwom contends that both Christians and Muslims belong to one human family, and both religions preach love. Thus, the need for the love of one another cannot be overstated among the adherents of both religions. In this regard, he notes:

> We should love one another you know the two religions, Christianity and Islam both speak about love, practical love. So, if from both sides we take ourselves as belonging to one human family. Yes, mode of worship may differ, but we belong to one human family then we should see ourselves as brothers and sisters and support one another rather than making statements that instigate violence[93].

Arguing in like manner, Muhammed contends that the proper understanding of the sacred book of each religion is of paramount importance bearing in mind that such books promote peace, love and equality. Hence, he observes:

> Let us go back and study our holy books of our respective religions very well. If we do that, there would not be any crisis. Our holy books all preach peace, love, equality, and accountability to one another. If we take each other as brothers and sisters, there would not be rancour and bloodshed. These messages are all contained in the holy books. We only need to go back to our religions and follow strictly the teachings of our religions. I believe there are pastors, Imams, and other religious leaders who get emotional and allow their emotions to overcloud their sense of reasoning, but if they strictly follow what the holy books say, that would not be a problem[94].

9.2.2 Dialogue of Life

Ankoyoyo argues for the need of having joint activities that will promote the culture of unity in diversity that should strengthens the existing relationship among Christians and Muslims. It is in this regard, he observes thus:

---

[92] 1 Cor. 13:13.

[93] PARANGWOM, "Interview".

[94] MUHAMMED, "Interview".

Well, I think this one calls for everybody's participation. The government, the religious leaders must be able to come together. We must learn to put away our differences and promote this culture of unity in diversity and peaceful existence, and that can be expressed through interfaith relations and dialogue. But more evidently, it should be found in cooperating joint activities, and establishing good relationship because that is the key to unlocking most of our existing differences. The government and the leaders must build and establish this good relationship and rapport among themselves and then encourage this culture of living together in peace which has been in existence in our various cultures even before we are Muslims or Christians[95].

9.2.3 Interreligious Dialogue

While Fuks contends on the ardent need for the mutual respect for both people's culture and religion, he is however of the opinion that deliberate efforts must be made to encourage a grassroot community approach, rather than a top-ranking approach. For when the commoners become the targets of peace building through interreligious, the desired lasting peace could easily be realized. He thus states:

When we look at the need for the respect for the people's culture and religion, the Christian understands that he as a Christian ought to respect the Muslim and respect him for his believe and vice versa. The orientation for the need of this approach must begin from the grassroot communities, because when we look at the aspect of peace building, let me compliment the high-level actors like Kaigama, Kukah, the Sultan of Sokoto, they are at the high level there. When they do it, the commoners in the communities don't feel the impact of what they are doing up there. How do they then step it down what they are doing up there to the commoners in the community? In this aspect, therefore, deliberate efforts must be made as regards the grassroot community approach. Hence while building the peace structure, it has to begin from the grass root communities because when the people in the communities value the religion of each other, we live in this village I value you as a Muslim, and you value me as a Christian, then when the trouble starts, it does not start with the top-ranking personnel in the society but begins usually from the grass root. Hence, the commoners must be the deliberate targets of the peace building approaches[96].

In same vein, Nchok is also of the opinion of the interreligious dialogue that will be pursued based on sincerity of purpose and not to be used as an avenue for money making. He thus states:

---

[95] ANKOYOYO, "Interview".
[96] FUKS, "Interview".

Interreligious dialogue and whichever shape or form, it needs to be pursued with the hope that one day it will be built on the foundation of sincerity of purpose because the dialogue that one sees today would have been more effective if the foundation were on a sincerity of purpose. Nigeria as a country has witnessed the flourishing of different layers, different degrees and approaches to this interreligious dialogue. There are NGOs that made a lot of money when the issue of dialogue came because of the crises in the country. One that would have helped the country very well it will seem the foundation and the quality of leadership does not have the amount of mutual trust and confidence that is required and that is the Nigeria interreligious council (NIREC) which was started by a few Christians, in fact among some few clerics who had a chat with Cardinal Onaiyekan who brought in some other Christians to see the need to create a forum that will bring together Christians and Muslims religious leaders at least let us begin to talk instead of staying on opposite camps... It started working and it was an instrument of giving positive advice to government. Issues of national interest that could either unite or tear this country apart are discussed and whatever resolutions are made, they go and advise the government. Government was also sponsoring the meetings as a result was dictating its tune. At a point as if NIREC was going to collapse but out of a sudden it resurrected but I want to tell you today this issue of the collapse of mutual trust and confidence in each other has badly affected NIREC...[97].

9.2.4 Common Grounds

It is believed that both Christianity and Islam have some similarities as they have dissimilarity. However, it is important to pay more attention on the things that we share in common rather than the things that divide us. It is against this backdrop that Ankoyoyo argues that both Christians and Muslims must be able to appreciate those realities that we share in common and shun those that divide us. Hence, he opines:

One reality is that we have so much in common as Christians and Muslims, but unfortunately, most often we dwell on the little things that separate us. But where on earth can you leave without diversity? So, we must be able to transcend those realities of diversity, because diversity is never a sin, and neither is it a course. It is actually a blessing if people understand because even in the Qur'an and the Holy Bible, these teachings are very clear. If God had intended, he would have created one people. But he created us differently, there is a reason and purpose for that. We would see the goodness of God in diversity and harness it for our good and the good of the society. But unfortunately, because of wrong understanding and wrong interpretations, we sometimes get it wrong[98].

---

[97] NCHOK, "Interview".
[98] ANKOYOYO, "Interview".

9.2.5 Prayer

Knowing the effects of prayer, many of the respondents agree of the need to embrace prayer with all honesty. Both Christians and Muslims must rise up and lift up their eyes onto God who answers in prayer. On this note, Chatsomen argues that prayer is the key to the Nigerian problem. Both Christians and Muslims must completely put their trust in God and believe in his power of providence as a creator. Thereafter, we will be able to see the need of seeking for forgiveness from one another and from God. In his words, he opines thus

> We should completely throw trust and our faith in God by prayer. Prayer is the key. But we must admit the fact that we missed this power of prayer some-where because in those days when people put their hearts together and offered their prayers God would always answer them. But today, the reverse is the case. Something is wrong somewhere else. We need to sit down as a family and as a people and seek for forgiveness from God and total restoration. Peo-ple that have backsliders need to come back because that is the only way to heaven. Their backsliding will not change God for God remains God. Only God can save us[99].

Daccos in the same vein argues that prayer is the real weapon that truly destroy evil. Both Christians and Muslims must continue to pray in season and out of season. Hence, he states that:

> The only way out is to continue with prayer. Prayer is the real weapon that can really destroy this because if the person that is evil and you are also able to convert him as St Paul was converted you don't need arm again isn't it? So that is why I say that they shouldn't stop praying[100].

9.3 *Non-Governmental Organizations (NGOs)*

Another aspect to curb the evil of extremism is through the help of meaningful, visionary and sincere non-governmental organizations (NGOs). Ankoyoyo argues that given the fact that they are experts in areas of human endeavours, NGOs could impact a lot on the citizens and assist in bridging reconciliation and peace. In his words, he observes thus:

> The NGOs are humanitarian groups and some of them have a long history. But you have to also know that sometimes they can be manipulated along the line especially in the discharge of their activities. Unless for those of them who are really grounded and tested in so many conflict areas, they will always have problems. They are stakeholders, in that they bring resources, manpower, and

---

⁹⁹ CHATSOMEN, "Interview".
¹⁰⁰ DACCOS, "Interview".

222

capacity. They have a lot to contribute. And given the fact that they are specialized in different areas of human endeavours, there are a lot that they can do in coordinating some of these activities because some of them are experts in bringing people together. Hence, they have values that they can offer and as such their importance cannot be overemphasized[101].

Dursa equally suggests that through the NGOs, people will become more aware of the need for peaceful coexistence and good relationship among Christians and Muslims. It is on this note he contends:

> The NGOs need to be part of the stakeholders. Let them go about counselling people and telling them the need for peaceful coexistence and good relationship among the adherents of the two major religions. This is very important toward reconciliation and healing[102].

10. **Conclusion**

This chapter presented and discussed the generated data from the fieldwork under eight headings: witnessing, relationship between Christians and Muslims in northern Nigeria, factor responsible for soured relationship between Christians and Muslims, forms of religious extremism, Boko Haram terrorism, causes of Islamic extremism, effects of Islamic extremism on the Catholic Church, and the ways forward. Under each of the heading, rightful portions of the interviewees were adequately quoted in order to present the correct argument of the respondents and to retain the originality of their expressions during the course of the interview.

Noting the extreme activities of the Boko Haram that brought Nigeria as a country to the limelight as a terrorist nation before the world, from the foregoing, the peculiarity of the heterogenous nature of the northern region therefore, was obvious when compared with the other regions of the country. Its volatility due to the presence of Islam cannot be underestimated. Hence, the Christians constantly live in fear and the uncertainty of whatever crisis may happen next. The presence of mistrust, suspicion and hatred were thus, readily elements that could easily spark up crisis at any given provocation.

To this effect, the chapter exposed the root causes of such extremism that manifested in the form of violence, discrimination and exclusion whereby each was subdivided into subheadings. Their multiplicity, however, explain the complexity of the problem of the northern region that could not be pinned down to a specific factor, owing that since military regime the region had been on-timed bomb waiting for any given opportu-

---

[101] ANKOYOYO, "Interview".
[102] DURSA, "Interview".

nity to explode. It is to this end that the realization of the 1999 democracy paved the way to the emergence of the Boko Haram terrorist group which has thus posed serious challenges to the northern Christians and has hampered the missionary activities of the Church.

CHAPTER V

Evaluation and Recommendations

1. Introduction

From the foregoing, we were able to establish the emergence of the Boko Haram and its effects on both the Nigerian state and the Church in particular within the northern region as a result of its terrorist activities. In this chapter, we shall evaluate the activities of the terrorist group alongside the implications of their violent actions that have brought Nigeria as a country to what it is today. In the same vein, we will analyse the missiological implication of the life of Christians within the volatile region under investigation bearing in mind the teachings of the Church as regards her mission mandate. Thereafter, we shall draw a conclusion by advancing few recommendations toward the realization of the desired enabling environment for a peaceful coexistence among Christians and Muslims. It is, however, important to note that this chapter presents the theological aspect of the study.

2. Boko Haram and the Nigerian State

In chapter one, we saw the emergence of the terrorist group who started like any other Islamic spiritual group who seeks to understand better the ways of *Allah*. With this impression in mind, it is obvious that no one would ever expect any violent activities outside the normal spiritual activities that are always known of any spiritual group. But with time the result turned to be the direct contrast, and surprisingly, the group's terrorist activities were ranked as one of the deadliest terrorist groups in the world[1]. The manner in

---

[1] In 2014 the Global Terrorism Index ranked Boko Haram as the deadliest terrorist group killing the total number of 6, 700 people within the year. Despite its suppression by the military and the Multinational Joint Task Force, the group still ranks today the third deadliest terrorist group across the globe as a result of the less deaths recorded in 2016 with a drop of 1,079 deaths. Cf., Iᴇᴘ, *Global Terrorism Index* 2017, 16.

which it began, did not only create confusion among the Nigerian citizens, but also among the government as well. Little wonder that the government first conceived and described the terrorist group as an insignificant group that was only seeking for a public recognition.

With time however, this narrative changed, and the common group hence became an eye sore to the government and the entire Nigerian people. Its intractable terrorist activities have been a teething problem that preoccupies every legislative discussion of the government. Taking into cognizance some of the theories numerated in chapter one, let us now examine the necessity of the emergence of the Boko Haram and thereafter establish the motive of their emergence owing to the varied existing narratives advanced.

2.1 *Boko Haram: Its Emergence*

At the early stage of the emergence of the Boko Haram, there existed numerous speculations of varied factors that could be responsible for its emergence. Such factors include; politics, economic, socio-cultural, and religion as noted in subheading 7 of the preceding chapter. But examining these factors closely, the readily disturbing questions that come to mind are; do these aforementioned factors provide enough reason(s) for the group to emerge and cause such a heinous havoc on innocent Nigerians and their government? Could it be an issue of individual choice and not based on any of the aforementioned factors owing that other youths (particularly within the same region) who are in like manner confronted with the same situation decided not to be part of the group? It is against this backdrop that we hereby examine the followings.

2.1.1 Radicalization

We have already established that radicalization is one of the root causes of religious extremism which is not only locally championed by the Boko Haram, but it is internationally promoted by the Saudi Arabian government through *Wahhabism* in which Mohammed Yusuf was schooled. It is therefore not surprising that the upsurge of the Boko Haram activities is intimately related to the spread of the international radical Islamist ideologies. Since *Wahhabism,* in particular, lends itself to the ideology of *Al-Qaida* and affiliated militant Islamist groups, it is undoubtedly that the characteristic of such fundamentalist doctrines imprint on the Boko Haram the notion that the Nigerian state is *taagut* (or evil), unworthy of allegiance on the part of a true Muslim[2]. Hence, it must be chastised or overthrown.

---

[2] Cf., H. SOLOMON, "Counter-Terrorism in Nigeria", 195.

226

It is also necessary to bear in mind that the nature of the Nigerian social welfare and the lack of basic amenities across the nation, paved the way to radicalism. For example, where the youths are not gainfully engaged in doing meaningful things in their lives, the possibility of such youths to become easy preys in the hands of radical bourgeoisies of the society, selfish politicians and radical preachers cannot be underestimated. The majority of the Nigerian youths are jobless, and many children especially those who reside in the northern region are left roaming about the streets. Even those who are in the school, cannot be guaranteed of quality education because many government schools (ranging from primary to tertiary schools) are left in a dilapidated stage. Social injustices are constantly perpetuated by those in authority against the masses. With the menace of corruption, the existing gap between the rich and the poor keeps widening on a daily basis. Above all, the national resources are not evenly distributed, and the dividends of democracy is not felt in the region.

In psychoanalysis model (as already seen in chapter one), we are made to understand that the psychological motivation of a terrorist is derived from his/her personal dissatisfaction with his/her life and accomplishments. While we note this theory, it however, left us with the question; are the youths in the north and particularly north-east the only dissatisfied youths as a result of the reality on the ground which cuts across all the six geopolitical zones of the country? If the answer is in the negative, it then goes to say that majority (if not all) of the Nigerian youths would have become terrorists because they in like manner are dissatisfied with the bad governance of the day. But they eschewed any act of terrorism. Hence, this model does not justify the acts of the Boko Haram owning to the fact that there are a lot of youths not only in Nigeria but particularly in the northern region who are dissatisfied with the situation of life that confronts them, but they are not lured into terrorism. Our ability to make free choice as human beings therefore plays a greater role in radicalization.

2.1.2 Poverty and Unemployment

There is a general recognition that poverty has made people eager for a change at all cost. Unlike the other regions of the country, the reality of poverty and joblessness in the northern region cannot be overemphasized. This is attributed to the massive deindustrialization of the region especially in early 2000s in which a large number of factories within the region were shut down as a result of an overflood of Asian textiles and other goods into Nigeria, and the high costs of power, water and maintenance. Worth of note are; Kaduna Textiles Limited (KTL), Arewa Textiles, United Nigerian Textiles Limited (UNTL), Nortex and the others. In the same vein, the region's largest media print houses – *New Nigerian Newspaper* and *Gaskiya Tafi Kobo* – were also shut down. Several sugar companies were privatized and eventually went out of production. To worsen the situation, the region's bank industry – *Bank of the North* – failed to meet the Nigerian Central Bank directive for all banks to reach a capital base of $15.3 million, as a result, it was assimilated into the Unity Bank (a Southern-based bank but with a nationwide presence)[3].

The massive number of children in the Quranic schools as against the secular schools who are most often left at the mercy of the exploitation of their *mallams* (teachers) who often send them out to the streets to beg cannot be left out. However, this does not mean that the northern youths are generally uneducated, but majority of them only receive informal training of the *almajiri* schools (as noted in subtitle 6.2 of chapter I) in which it lacks the ability to empower them for the challenges of the modern society that lie ahead of them. All these factors rendered millions of Nigerians, particularly the northerners jobless, thereby widening up the existing gap of poverty between the region and the other regions. Hence, the existence of the army of unemployed youths roaming about the streets in frustration.

Bearing this reality in mind, it is interesting to note that it was as a result of the poverty level in the region, that Mohammed Yusuf seized the opportunity to recruit and offered the teaming young men of the *almajiris* (who had been exploited while growing up and rendered homeless) food, shelter, security and alternative succour in their lives.

Against this backdrop, a one-time Minister of Women's Affairs and Youth Development, Aisha Isma'il once declared that it is the poor and the oppressed who are clamouring for change, because they are tired of exploitation[4]. Similarly, in response to the Kaduna 2000 Shari'a mayhem, the speaker of the Federal House of Representatives, Ghali U. Na'Aba, blamed it on to the prevailing poverty in the country[5]. Thereby suggesting an economic factor as against the common narrative of a religious factor. This reality was reiterated by one-time President of the United States of America, Bill Clinton that poverty is the key factor to the menace of the Boko Haram[6].

To buttress the above statements, it is pertinent to state that due to over-reliance on oil as major economic income of the country as already pointed

---

[3] Cf., L.K. HOFFMANN, "Who Speaks for the North?", 17. Also see DAILY TRUST, 2004.

[4] NEW NIGERIAN, 2000, 1.

[5] NEW NIGERIAN, March 2, 2000, 1.

[6] I. EKOTT, "Bill Clinton counters Jonathan".

out in chapter two (subtitle number 2), Nigeria went into its worst economic recession in 2016 after about 30 years ago as a result of downward trend witnessed by the country over a period of four years (2013-2017). In 2015, the annual average of Brent crude, the international benchmark for crude oil fell to $52.35 from $99.03 per barrel in 2014, and by 2016 it further dropped to $43.55 per barrel. But the situation degenerated when pipeline vandalism in the Niger Delta region reduced the oil output in the country from 2.03 million barrels per day (hence, mbpd) to 1.61 mbpd in third quarter of 2016 (Q3 2016).

Consequently, the Nigerian Gross Domestic Product (GDP) went as low as -2.34 per cent in the third and fourth quarters of 2016[7]. As a result of this development, in 2016 alone over 350,000 people were rendered jobless as opined by the Minister of State for Petroleum Ibe Kachikwu, and an estimated $7 billion in oil revenue was lost as stated by the group managing director of the Nigerian National Petroleum Corporation (NNPC) Maikanti Baru.[8] But with staggering success, Nigeria came out of the recession in the second quarter of 2017 (Q2 2017) following the slight economic growth of 0.55 per cent in that quarter as shown by the data from the National Bureau of Statistics (NBS). This rebound became possible as a result of the government efforts in improving performance in four key sectors; oil, agriculture, manufacturing and trade.

Although, poverty has no direct link to terrorism, it has contributed greatly to the volatile climate of the northern region, for it has made the people (particularly the youths) open to any empty promises by any selfish politicians who seem to offer any seemingly hope of improvement in their lives as a result of the frustrated situation that confronts them. It is against this background that the argument of the frustration-aggression theorists seems to hold water as championed by scholars such as John Chowing Davies, Randy Borum and Leonard Berkowitz. The inability of the massive youths to realize their economic dreams in particular as a result of joblessness and hunger in the land, for Davies that could lead to frustration, then anger that may gradually metamorphose to violence.

In the same vein, the theories of the structuralists and the economists who strongly opined that a society wherein its weak members are deliberately exploited by a certain group of the society it is obvious that conflict of interest abounds and can easily lead to violence. It is to this end that it is undoubtedly that poverty and unemployment are highly possible factors for the emergence of the Boko Haram owing that most membership of the group was drawn from

---

[7] CENTRAL BANK OF NIGERIA, "Nigeria GDP Annual Growth Rate". Also see Appendix L.

[8] O. BAYAGBON, "Oil Contribution to Nigeria's Gross Domestic Product (GDP)".

the massive uneducated, jobless, and undernourished *almajjiris* and some of the jobless youths who were already at the level of despair. Thus, the emergence of the Boko Haram was like a safe haven for such youths.

But the lacuna here is that if poverty and unemployment are the only reasons, we could as well presume that all the youths in the northern region are members of the Boko Haram, owing that within the same region, there also exists Christian youths and other moderate and well-behaved Muslim youths who are equally pushed below the structural lines of poverty and unemployment in the society and are confronted with the same economic frustration but they chose not to become violent or terrorists. In this regard, the question therefore that begs for answer is this, why is it that such youths (both Christians and well-behaved Muslims) are not terrorists?

Consequently, while we agree that poverty and unemployment expose the youths to be readily tools for violence and terrorism, it is also important to acknowledge that they are not sufficient reasons for terrorism as Randy Borum would hold that aggression can also occur even in the absence of frustration. To this end, poverty and unemployment *per se* are inexcusable factors for the emergence of Boko Haram.

2.1.3 Bad Governance and Failed State Institutions

While we blame the emergence of the terrorist group on poverty and unemployment, we must not turn a blind eye to the existing bad governance and failed state institutions and government policies[9] in the country that have bred corruption, social injustice, criminality, lawlessness and insecurity. Bad governance is the direct contrast of good governance, and good governance may be defined as:

> The running of the affairs of government in positive and progressive manner beneficial to the governed and which delivers the public goods. Its attributes include due process, transparency, responsiveness on the part of government, power sharing, rule of law, competence, separation and devolution of powers, a free press and a free virile civil society[10].

In bad governance all these attributes of good governance are either absent or they are not significantly felt by the people. Thus, it is undebatable that a

---

[9] An excellent study had recently been carried out on the Nigerian institutional design with regard to the regulation of ethnic conflicts within the country. Hence, for more details on Nigerian's institutional design, see the work of: P.C. Nweke, *The Role of Institutional Design in the Regulation of Ethnic Conflicts in Nigeria*: A Case Study of the Jos Conflict (2001-2012), Rome, 2016 (Thesis).

[10] S.O. Uhunmwuangho, "Challenges and Solutions to the Ethno-Religious Conflicts", 121.

nation where bad governance becomes the order of the day, there exist weak institutions and policies, and as a result, lawlessness takes over the stage where citizens decide to take the laws into their hands and no recourse to justice. This was buttressed by the then US Secretary of State, Hilary Clinton during her visit to Nigeria in August 2009, when she emphatically noted that:

> The most immediate source of the disconnect between Nigeria's wealth and its poverty is the failure of governance at the federal, state and local levels.... Lack of transparency and accountability has eroded the legitimacy of the government and contributed to the rise of groups that embrace violence and reject the authority of the state[11].

In this regard, it is an understatement to say that it was as a result of bad governance and *hitherto* corruption, that Nigerian's economy did not only go into recession, but it also slowed down drastically in its growth to the extent that after the coming out of the recession in 2017 the commoners on the streets could not and still not feel the impact of the positive economic growth. For instance, prices in the market are always on the increase, the strength of the naira gets weakened day by day, and corruption has not been eradicated. It is thus not out of place to state that from the immediate past administrator to the present one there is only little or no significant improvement in the global scores of the country's Corruption Perception Index (CPI) despite the fight against corruption by the present administration as Nigeria still scores between 26 and 28 per cent and ranks above 140 in corruption out of 180 countries in the world. The table below shows the ranking of Nigeria within a period of four years (2014-2017) alongside with the two least corrupt countries and the two worst corrupt countries in the world.

S/N	COUNTRY	CPI GLOBAL SCORES (%)				RANKING			
		2014	2015	2016	2017	2014	2015	2016	2017
1	Denmark	92	91	90	88	1	1	1	2
2	New Zealand	91	88	90	89	2	4	1	1
3	**Nigeria**	**27**	**26**	**28**	**27**	**136**	**136**	**136**	**148**
4	North Korea	8	8	12	17	174	167	174	171
5	Somalia	8	8	10	8	174	167	180	180

Table 1: Nigeria's Ranking and Scores amidst two least
and worst Corrupt countries in the world.

---

[11] THE NATION, August 14, 2009, 1.

In the northern region, the absence of good governance is obviously noticeable because those placed in authority do not put the nation's resources into proper use for the economic growth and development of the region and the entire country at large. Hence, poor infrastructures, poor governmental services of basic social amenities such as lack of good roads, schools, pipe-born water, scarcity of fuel, and bribery and corruption are at their peak. It is therefore not an over-exaggeration to say that the failure of the government to bring the dividends of democracy to the corridor of the people, necessitated the Boko Haram to demand for the establishment of the Islamic State within a state, believing that all these social vices will surely give way in their desired "theocratic" government of the Islamic State.

Although, the present government is fighting corruption, but corruption seems to be fighting back due to the presence of weak institutional designs and policies. Hence, the judiciaries where it is the bed rock of justice, have lost their credibility among millions of Nigerians due to the presence of corruption among some lawyers and judges. A vivid example is the present trial of the Nigerian chief justice – Walter Samuel N. Onnoghen — for non-declaration of assets upon his appointment as the chief justice of the country. A nation that is consumed by corruption, it is obvious that the majority of its citizens will languish in poverty amidst plenty despite its enormous resources which are often hijacked and enjoyed only by few individuals. The vacuum therefore, created by the failure of good governance and the existence of weak and failed institutions and government policies contributed enormously to the anger and frustration of the citizenry that provided the fertile ground for the emergence of the Boko Haram.

2.1.4 Ignorance of Religious Tenets

The ignorance of the tenets of religion is a salient factor that plays a great role in radicalism of any sect of any religion. It is a factor that receives less attention within scholarship as compared to common narratives of politics, religion and the others as stated above. From the fieldwork carried out, it is discovered that many adherents of both religions (Christianity and Islam) are ignorant of the teachings of their respective religions due to the shallow knowledge of the sacred books of the religions in question. Most often, religious radicalism is derived from the misinterpretation of the sacred books of the religion. For instance, when a particular sect either in Islam or Christianity misinterprets certain teachings of the sacred book of its religion and makes it an ideology, the possibility of such ideology to be imposed on others is high. To this effect, the radicalism of the Boko Haram emerged due to the shallow knowledge of their so-called leaders who most often misinterpreted the Qur'an and the Hadiths and tries to impose those erroneous teachings on others. To eschew therefore from religious radicalism, an in-depth knowledge of the tenets of both religions – Christianity or Islam – cannot be overstressed.

2.1.5 Boko Haram: A Political Uprising

Following the plausible narratives established in chapter one as regards the motive of the emergence of the terrorist group and the views of the respondents in chapter four, it is obvious that some of the narratives suggested a political motive. For instance, the narrative that holds that the Boko Haram wanted a share of the sliced cake of the amnesty programme granted to the Niger delta militias, suggests to be credible because, it was almost within the same time frame that the then late President Umaru Shehu Yar'adua signed an amnesty deal in which $68 billion was to be spent. But the unproductive invitation of President Jonathan GoodLuck to the group during his tenure for a dialogue between them (the terrorist group) and the Nigerian government proved the contrary. This is due to the fact that when the government – after persuasion from its citizens and concerned groups – decided to go into dialogue with the group, things did not go down well as presumed because the group was divided into factions. While some were for the dialogue, others were against it especially the key actors like Shekau and his loyalists[12].

Nevertheless, we cannot claim that the group is devoid completely of any political agenda despite its lack of political programme. The following reasons, however, suggest that the terrorist group forms an embryonic political group since its targets were initially on government institutions such as the police stations (which were most often the only effective presence of the state in remote villages), schools and prisons. Also, the rejection of western values equally suggests a political motive because such western values are not in conformity with the core values of an Islamic State. Hence, the contestation of a secular post-colonial state became obvious.

In another development, the group's manipulation by some northern politicians suggests strongly an interest in politics since Mohammed Yusuf and his cohorts could not resist the temptation of dining with some of these self-centred politicians. The appointment of Alhaji Buji Foi (one of the Boko Haram's members) for instance, as a state commissioner of religious affairs by the then governor of Borno state Alhaji Ali Modu Sheriff, as a reward to the group's effort toward his victory in the 2003 gubernatori-

---

[12] Cf., J. ZENN, "Boko Haram's Dangerous Expansion.

al re-elections of the state, and the release of an armed robber Abubakar Adam Kamba[13], are all bolsters to the fore. On this note, it is obvious that the Boko Haram got involved in dirty politics as soon as Mohammed Yusuf became popular and he was potentially able to gather votes from his members for the governor. This pay out at the time the Federal government reached out to the group for a dialogue.

Furthermore, the political interest of the group also manifested itself in the narratives of the local sponsorship of the group (as earlier established in 6.9 of chapter one) in respect to the belief of many southerners and some Christians in the north who perceived it as a political scheme in order to seize power from the then President Jonathan Goodluck who was a southerner and a Christian. This manifested itself in the 2011 Presidential elections in which votes were cast based on religious affiliation.

The narrative of the group's constant attacks on some Muslim scholars who contested its moral authority was also perceived as a political motive. For example, the killing of an Islamic scholar in Mifa village in Chibok Local Government Council of Borno state in the evening of February 14, 2017[14]. Although, this does not stop some well-meaning and fearless Islamic clerics to confront them on their misleading teachings and heinous activities in the name of Islam. A vivid example is the prophetic call of an Islamic scholar *Malam* Abdullahi Abubakar – a lecturer at Bayero University Kano (hence, BUK) – who cautioned the Boko Haram against the slaughtering of people and raping of women in the name of Islam which is against the tenets of the religion. *Ipso facto*, he vehemently condemned its ideology of establishing an Islamic State in the country and admonished his fellow Muslims especially the youths who are considering joining the terrorist group to have a re-think by stressing that the Boko Haram group is evil and must be rejected[15].

Despites the above stated reasons therefore, the question that continue to beat our imagination is this, is Boko Haram a purely political motivated terrorist group as claimed by such narratives, or is it "a wolf in sheep's clothing" that masquerades itself under political struggle? The answer is in the negative as there are also indicators that suggest the contrary. Hence, we now examine the other side of the coin.

---

[13] F. FALANA, "How Modu Sheriff Sponsored Boko Haram". Also see M.P. DE MONT-CLOS, "Boko Haram and Politics, 148.

[14] N. ONYEDIKA-UGOEZE – N. MUSA, "Boko Haram Terrorists killed Islamic Scholar".

[15] S. OPEJOBI, "Stop Killing, Raping Women, It's Anti-Islam".

2.1.6 Boko Haram: A Religious Uprising

Owning to the principle of expansionism, which remains the unfinished business of the 1804 jihad of Uthman Dan Fodio and the Islamisation and conversion campaign of Sir Ahmadu Bello as already mentioned in chapter two of this study, it is the desire of every average Muslim especially in the north to see the realization of the efforts of these two 'religious heroes' in question (Uthman dan Fodio and Sir Ahmadu Bello) who are held with great esteem and seen as models to the northern Muslims that are worthy of emulation. This explains the relentless efforts in the implementation of the Shari'a law which they believe was stifled by the Colonial Administrators. To this end, the clamour for the establishment of the Shari'a law in a secular democratic and multireligious nation such as Nigeria is obviously a vivid signal of a religious motive by the Boko Haram noting that it was done without taking into cognizance the fundamental rights and religious freedom of the other existing religious groups (the Christians and the African traditionalists) as stipulated in the Nigerian constitution.

Examining the trend of events therefore, the global influence of the Iran 1979 revolution[16] that saw the exit of Muhammad Reza Shah from power due to his reforms of modernism and westernization, popularly known as "white revolution"[17] which *hitherto* brought into power Ayatollah Khomeini (a profound charismatic and influential leader of the Iranian masses), cannot also be ignored with respect to the religious crises in Nigeria. Although revo-

---

[16] Between the transformative period of 1953 and 1975, Muhammad Reza Shah pursued an aggressive Western-oriented socioeconomic modernization programme, known as the White Revolution and vis-à-vis an aggressive expansion of the state as a continuation of his father's abandoned project when forced out of office in 1941. The presumed dividends of these reforms were not felt by most Iranians. Landlords lost substantial power and influence due to land reforms, peasant too did not benefit from the increase of state's oil revenues, and neither did the *ulama* (the educated class of Muslim legal scholars), nor the clerics who were demonised by Shah who went further to institute liberal dress codes and social norms which resulted in a widespread gulf between his secularized supporters and the conservatives of the society. Against this backdrop, Shah was confronted with a strong opposition that his security loyalists could not contend. Thus, it resulted to a revolution in 1969 that was intrinsically linked to religious ideology which saw finally the exit of Shah from power and the coming of Ayatollah Khomeini into power. See the works of: D.A. Brandis, "The 1979 Iranian Revolution"; M. Eisenstadt, "Iran's Islamic Revolution", 1-12; _ "Iran. Religious Elements of the 1979 Islamic Revolution", 1-19.

[17] It is imperative to note that the "White Revolution" was comprised of six reformation policies that include; land reform, nationalization of forests, sale of state-owned enterprises to the public, a worker's profit-sharing plan, female suffrage, and the creation of the Literacy Corps. See the work of D.A. Brandis, "The 1979 Iranian Revolution", 13.

lutions do not have religious causes but most often, they develop due to economic, social, and political crises, the Iranian 1979 revolution, nevertheless, legitimized itself with a religious ideology[18]. It is against this backdrop that, most of the religious crises in Nigeria were products of the Ayatollah's influence, since it paved the way to the wide spread rise of Islamic radicalism. The case of Muhammadu Marwa as already established in 7.1 of chapter two above (the charismatic leader of Maitatsine who was greatly influenced by the radical preaching of Ayatollah Khomeini) is a buttress to the fore.

Further still, the constant attacks on Christians whether at places of worship or in predominant Christian communities cannot be ignored. As the group began with the police and government institutions, the Churches and missionary schools, and all Christians and their properties became the next targets because Shekau through his spokesman declared a "war on Christians"[19]. Hence, at the peak of the insurgence, Christians were constantly killed on a daily basis. While some were killed during worships, others were murdered in their cold blood while asleep at night in their respective communities even when curfews were activated.

But quick to note is the killing of other fellow Muslims. Although, the common narrative to this effect was that the majority of the affected Muslims in question were killed because they were perceived by the terrorist group to have opposed the course of their "so-called jihad. Hence, they must pay the price. But it is, however, imperative to note that prior to the inception of the Boko Haram, due to too much bitterness and hatred, in many occasions, Christians were always at the receiving end even when the conflict was intra-religious (i.e between one Islamic sect and another).

Subsequently, following the five basic features that constitute a religious terrorist group as postulated by Ekaterina Stepanova in chapter one above, it is arguable that the Boko Haram's motive is nothing more than religious and not political because Stepanova's characteristics of a religious terrorism are commonly manifested in the terrorist activities of the Boko Haram. These features include; the presence of a religious leader for spiritual blessings and guidance, reliance on the sacred books by making direct references to the sacred texts such as (the Qur'an and the Hadith), the believe in self-sacrifice and martyrdom as an act of faith, the believe that the witness of God as the ultimate effect of the terrorist act, and the lack of a clear distinction between religion and politics. A good example is the role of the group's first leader Muhammed Yusuf which was transferred after his death to Abū Bakr Shekau.

---

[18] D.A. BRANDIS, "The 1979 Iranian Revolution", 3.

[19] Cf., J. ZENN, "Nigeria Al-Qaidaism", 110.

Advancing further, the credibility of this argument can also be deduced from the group's abduction of Christians' men and women, children and adults, and being forced to denounce their Christian faith and embrace Islamic faith. A vivid example is the case of Leah Sharibu the only Christian girl who is being held by the Boko Haram on the ground that she refused conversion to Islam, while her Muslim colleagues that were abducted the same day in Government Girls Science and Technical College, Dapchi were granted release[20]. In this regard, it is obvious that if Leah had accepted the conversion and denounced her faith by becoming a Muslim, she would have been released alongside with her colleagues and be reunited with her family and beloved ones. But the reverse was the case as she is still in captivity.

The questions then that demand answers are; if the Federal Government went into negotiation unconditionally as claimed by the Minister of information and culture, Lai Mohammed, why was Leah withheld and the government did not insist on all the girls to be released? With the case of Leah at hand, does it imply that she was the only Christian among the abducted 110 schoolgirls or there were other Christian girls, but they agreed to be converted to Islam and as a result they were freed? What was the religious affiliations of the so-called claimed five students who died as a result of trauma or were they deliberately killed due to their religious affiliations? Were their bodies handed over to the Federal Government? Was an autopsy carried out in order to ascertain the cause(s) of their death? Were the names of the deceased girls published? The questions may go on and on.

In the same vein, many Christians were killed on the grounds that they refused to denounce their faith in favour of Islam. If it were sorely political as some narratives may claim, why then the killing of Christians who refused to denounce their faith but spared those Christians who denounced their faith

---

[20] Apart from the ugly situation of the abduction of 276 Chibok girls on April 14, 2014 in Borno state whereby some of the girls are still at large despite the efforts of the Federal Government in securing the release of some of the girls, the unfortunate incident repeated itself in a dramatic way when the same Boko Haram went unhindered to the Government Girls Science and Technical College, Dapchi, in Yobe state on February 19, 2018 and kidnapped 110 schoolgirls between the ages of 11 and 19 despite the claimed phone calls made in order to avert the sadden incidence. Although, the Federal Government went into negotiation with the terrorist group for the release of the girls, only 104 regained their freedom in March 21, 2018 while five died on the day of their abduction due to trauma and fear (as claimed by the released schoolgirls) and one (Leah Sharibu) was withheld by the group on the ground that she refused to denounce her Christian faith and be converted to Islam which was confirmed by her freed colleagues. Cf., S. Ojeifo, "Dapchi Girls. Of Sham Release"; M. Sam-Ohuabunwa, "Leah Sharibu. Confirmation of the True Mission of the Boko Haram".

out of fear? Another important questions that must be asked too are; is the Boko Haram's main aim of existence to convert all Nigerian Christians beginning from the north to the other regions of the country, and where there is resistance, they should apply force and all kinds of threats? Or does it imply that with the abduction of schoolgirls and perhaps schoolboys, and communities (as the case may be), the mission of the Boko Haram's existence is accomplished? Reading therefore, in-between the lines of the activities of the terrorist group, the temptation to answer the above questions is in the affirmative. Hence, it suggests that it is purely a religious motive.

But we must apply precautions here because advancing the argument that Boko Haram's motive is purely political is not only turning a blind eye to the reality on the ground, but also it is a total denial of Christians' persecution in the region, and it also waters down the present reality of the constant killings, abductions and forceful conversion of Christians in the region (particularly in the northeast), and the recent killings of Christians within the Christian dominated communities in Taraba, Kaduna, Benue and Plateau states which are being perpetuated under the disguise of "herdsmen" or "unknown gunmen" that seem to suggest ethnic cleansing in disguise[21]. It is imperative therefore to quickly state here that the issue of the killings of the "herdsmen" and "unknown gunmen" in Nigeria, is beyond the scope of this study. Hence, it cannot be dealt with in this study in details. But it is, however, another interesting area that deserves research studies.

Nevertheless, on a balance scale of analysis, Schmid Alex argues that analysing terrorism from a religious perspective only showcases a partial exposition of the reality of the situation[22], and as it is already stated above that it is unfair to tie down the Boko Haram's terrorist activities to a particular factor, it therefore follows that religion *per se*, cannot be the only motive of the terrorist group as suggested by the above narratives. Consequently, confining the motive of the group's terrorist activities to religious terrorism could be misleading as some fundamental issues may be overlooked. Thus, all factors that contributed to the emergence and *ipso facto* the terrorist activities of the Boko Haram must be considered for the sake of objectivity.

---

[21] Of recent there have been series of sporadic killings by so-called herdsmen (or unknown gun men as often reported by the media) who are openly seen moving about with AK 47 guns instead of the traditional axe and cutlass they were commonly knwon with for the trimming of branches for enough leaves for their cattle to feed on. These killings continue in a systematic manner from one Christian dominated community or state to another. These states include Plateau, Kaduna, Benue and Taraba.

[22] A.P. Schmid, "Frameworks for Conceptualising Terrorism", 212.

Owning therefore to the above variances and the fact that there is little or no clear dichotomy between religion and politics in Islam since both intertwine, and both sentiments clearly exhibited themselves in the terrorist activities of the Boko Haram especially at the peak of their operations, we can safely infer that the motive of the terrorist group is neither political nor religious *per se* as some popular narratives may claim, but it is a combination of both because emphasis on one over the other is a blatant denial of the reality on the ground. Hence, it is religio-political. Although, one is often emphasized over the other as the situation permits. Hereafter, we examine the effects of the group's terrorist activities on the nation and the Church in particular.

2.2 *Boko Haram: Its Effects*

In every given circumstance of violence, there are always implications. These implications are often a double edge sword whereby both the perpetrators and the victims are affected in one way or the other. However, in this study we shall focus on the implications of the perpetrators over the victims being the prime focus of our study. Examining closely therefore, the activities of the Boko Haram, it is obvious that the intractable insurgency[23] and the sporadic bombings in the region, have enormous effects which left indelible marks of terrible experiences on the minds of the people. To say of the numerous loss of lives and property, the displacement of people and ever increased level of poverty and underdevelopment in the region, is an understatement. Let us, however, examine the following.

2.2.1 Destruction of Life and Property

The destruction of life and properties are always the end results of every violence. As a result, the Boko Haram terrorism has claimed a lot of lives and properties that cannot be imagined[24]. The use of sophisticated weapons such as AK 47 and other small armed weapons have destroyed an uncountable number of lives. For example, the constant sporadic explosions of the IEDs and bombs that destroyed not only lives and property such as shops, houses, cars, Churches and mosques as rightly observed by the interviewees, but they also have adverse effects on the ecology of the region and the missionary activities of the Church. For instance, there has been sharp drop of agricultural activities in the region bearing in mind that

---

[23] There are many sources that lay bare the frequency of these riots. See for instance: A.C van GORDER, *Violence in God's Name*, 230-293; J.H. BOER, *Nigeria's Decades of Blood*, 38-97; NIGERIAN TRIBUNE, 2001; TELL, 2001; THE PUNCH, 2002.

[24] Cf., M.A. MAMBULA, *Nigeria. Ethno-Religious and Socio-Political Violence*, 100-103.

both Christians and Muslims were forced to relocate to safe zones. This by extension adversely affected the economy of the country, and *hitherto* caused more hunger and hardship in the region.

2.2.2 Underdevelopment and Poverty

In every violence or public unrest that involves the loss of lives, the wanton destruction of property and structures cannot be overemphasized. At the peak of the terrorist activities of the Boko Haram every commercial activity came to a halt. Banks were closed, shops were shut down, all workers (both government and private) were locked at home. The Maiduguri Monday market for example, which is said to be the biggest market in the city is reported to have been seriously affected and closed as hundreds of shop owners are said to have closed their businesses and relocated to other safe areas. Movements of people for commercial and other purposes came to a still. The worse scenario was that agricultural activities were completely truncated because farmers could not go out to farm.

It is undebatable that all these deepen up the existing poverty of the region. To say of the malicious destruction of structures is an underestimation. It has contributed greatly not only to the underdevelopment of the region but also to the increased the number of joblessness. For instance, it is said that in 2009 alone, about 837 factories were shut down[25]. As a result, the number of jobless youths has thus been increased across the region and the country at large. To sum up, it is an understatement to say that the ease of doing business in the region has been made possible.

It is, however, interesting to note that due to the magnitude of the destruction, it will take a long period of time for the region to get back to its feet and compete confidently with other regions in the country as it is commonly said that where there is no peace, there is no development. It is with regard to this reality that the Borno State Commissioner of Information, Mr. Inuwa Bwala, observes that it will take Borno State 20 years to recover from the predicament it has found itself as a result of the insurgency[26].

2.2.3 Absence of Active Religious Freedom

While it is true that there is no longer general and systematic persecution of Christians as it were under the Roman emperors, it is also a fact that Christians still suffer persecution in isolated areas around the globe. Example is the case of the Egyptian Copts murdered by IS in Libya. Although, Nigeria is not listed

---

[25] Cf., I.Z.O SULE – al., "Governance and Boko Haram Insurgents in Nigeria", 41.

[26] I.Z.O SULE – al., "Governance and Boko Haram Insurgents in Nigeria", 41.

among the worst top 10 countries in the world where Christians are persecuted, it does not in any way suggest that Christians in Nigeria and particularly in the northern region do not face persecution. According to the statistics of the World Watch List (hereafter WWL), Nigeria is ranked the 14th out of 50 worst countries where Christian persecution takes place[27]. Most of these persecutions take place as a result of the denial of religious freedom whose foundation is found in the very nature of the human dignity that must be respected. It is to this end that the Council Fathers prophetically declared on the ardent need of religious freedom in the *Dignitatis Humanae* (henceforth, DH) that:

> The human person has a right to religious freedom. Freedom of this kind means that all men should be immune from coercion on the part of individuals, social groups and every human power so that, within due limits, nobody is forced to act against his convictions in religious matters in private or in public, alone or in association with others…the right to religious freedom is based on the very dignity of the human person as known through the revealed Word of God and by reason itself. This right of the human person to religious freedom must be given such recognition in the constitutional order of society as will make it a civil right"[28].

In this respect, it is imperative to therefore note that this paragraph 2 of DH presents the thrust of the entire declaration of the Church which parallels very closely the United Nations Universal Declaration on Human Rights (December 10, 1948) and the World Council of Churches (WCC) Declaration on Religious Liberty which was approved at its first Assembly in August 1948[29]. Nevertheless, in the Nigerian case this right is noted especially in its national constitution as suggested by the Council Fathers. In article 38, number 1 of the 1999 Nigerian constitution as amended, it states that:

> Every person shall be entitled to freedom of thought, conscience and religion, including freedom to change his religion or belief, and freedom (either alone or in community with others, and in public or in private) to manifest and propagate his religion or belief in worship, teaching, practice and observance.

However, it is interesting to note that this law in most cases is only in principle and not in practice especially in Muslim dominated areas. If for instance, the law of religious freedom is adhered to, why then is it that Christians in the north are segregated base on their religious affiliation, noting that the Qur'an clearly states that *"Lâ ikrâha fî d-dîn"*—No compulsion in religion?[30].

---

[27] OPENDOOR WORLD WATCH LIST.

[28] PAUL VI, "Dignitatis Humanae", §2.

[29] Cf., S.B. BEVANS – J. GROSS, *Evangelization and Religious Freedom*,179.

[30] Qur'an 2:256

But if we may ask further, is it not a form of compulsion when a group of Christians especially young girls (for example, the Chibok and Dapchi girls) are rounded up, forcefully taken away and made to denounce their religion? – as in the case of Leah Sharibu. Is it not compulsion when political and economic discrimination is practiced in favour of Muslims especially in areas that are predominantly Muslims? What happened to the Christian liberty to build Churches in Muslim dominated areas as Mosques are built in Christian dominated areas? In this regard, lands are out-rightly denied to them. How far have we gone in granting admission of all professional courses to Christian students as they are offered to their Muslim counterparts? What about the use of the media? Is it the same time allotted to Christian programmes as it is allotted to Islamic programmes in both state and federal media houses? How often is conversion to Islam the price to be paid for a job, a promotion, an appointment or a contract, while conversion of Muslims to Christianity becomes an automatic *fatwa*? The questions may go on and on. These of course, are indices where there is always a bridge of the law.

To this end, the effect of the Boko Haram terrorist activities on the infringement on the fundamental human rights of Nigerians cannot be over-emphasized. Today, in the bid to claim this right of freedom to religious worship, many Christians have paid the ultimate price with their precious lives. It is against this backdrop that the core missionary activity of the Church – to bear witness to the Gospel of Christ which is the Gospel of love, peace and justice[31], and to carry out other missionary activities have obviously been truncated. The absence of religious freedom in a multi-religious nation such as Nigeria is a deliberate attempt to deny the Christians or members of any religion (outside Islam) the right to profess their faith and live it accordingly[32].

2.3 *Government's Responses to Boko Haram*

Although, the Nigerian security agents were taken by surprise being the first time of such terrorist activities to bedevil the country, efforts were however made in curtailing the wide spread of the heinous activities of the sect to a minimal level. To this end, the Nigerian government adopted several measures ranging from deployment of special security forces, arrests and prosecutions of members of the sect, deportation of illegal immigrants and the temporary closure of some parts of Nigerian borders in the northern region, to capacity building of security forces on counter-terrorism

---

[31] Cf., Rm 14:17

[32] Cf., BENEDICT XVI, "World Day of Peace 2011", §5.

(henceforth, CoT), counter-insurgency (hereafter, COIN) operations, installation of surveillance equipment, and collaboration with international organizations.

Given the serious response by countries around the globe to tackling terrorism related offences, and the sporadic terrorist attacks in the nation, the Nigerian government passed its first anti-terrorism bill on the 17th February 2011 known as *Terrorism Prevention Act* (hereafter, TPA 2011)[33]. This act proscribes all manner of terrorist activities within the country. However, due to the inconsistencies in the modus operandi of the Boko Haram, the government amended this act in 2013 and expanded it in order to meet up with the current strategies and tactics employed by the terrorists in their attacks.

The establishment of a Joint Military Task Force known as *Operation Restore Order* (henceforth, JTORO) on 12th June 2011, with its headquarters in Maiduguri[34] – the flashing point of the Boko Haram – in order to counter the sect's growing terrorist potentials is worthy of note. The JTORO has been recording successes in their operations. However, a lot needs to be done as the terrorist attacks still take place although in a minimal level. It is, nevertheless, imperative to state that despite the recorded successes of the JTORO, its deployment however, received some criticisms for harsh tactics that have affected the civilians and damaged properties. Hence, the need for the collaboration of the security agents, the JTORO and the civilians in curbing and tackling the terrorists cannot be overemphasized.

Having discovered the porous nature of the Nigerian international borders in the northern region which paved the way for easy influx of weaponries by the sect, the Federal Government went into aggressive crackdown of illegal immigrants, by repatriating over 11,000 foreigners in February 2012[35]. But such action will only remain a camouflage if the government does not rise to its responsibility to provide adequate security to its citizens and the borders.

Nevertheless, it is pertinent at this juncture, to ask, amidst this insecurity and the terrorist activities of the Boko Haram, what are the missiological implications of Christians living within the region as regards their Christian vocation? In response to the above question, we now examine Christians' nature of "call to witness" in a volatile region.

---

[33] A.S.Y. BAGAJI – al, "Boko Haram and the Recurring Bomb Attacks in Nigeria", 72.

[34] F. ONUOHA, "Boko Haram and the evolving Salafi Jihadist Threat in Nigeria", 175.

[35] F. ONUOHA, "Boko Haram and the evolving Salafi Jihadist Threat in Nigeria", 176.

2.4 *The Call to Witness as the Foundational Mission of the Church: A missiological Implication*

Our call to be "witnesses" as Christians has been the foundational mission of the Church since by its very nature is mission[36] because "the Church originates from Christ himself, the author of mission and the mission of the Holy Spirit according to the plan of God the Father"[37]. It was out of the apostles' experience of their master's life from the beginning of his ministry to his passion, death and resurrection that they became matured in the faith and thus were commanded to go out and share those experiences with others[38]. St. Luke puts it more succinctly in the Acts of the Apostles as he recorded, "But you shall receive power when the Holy Spirit has come upon you; and you shall be my *witnesses* in Jerusalem and in all Judea and Samaria and to the end of the earth"[39]. This implies that by the reception of the Holy Spirit we are strengthened and become matured to share our Christian experiences with others. However, it is important to note that witness as we have earlier stated in the preceding chapter, has different dimensions.

The first dimension of witness has to do with the preaching of the gospel (kerygma). To be the disciples of Jesus means to be his true witnesses by bringing the message of the gospel to people thereby leading them to the vision of God[40] which is essentially the task of the Church. The Holy Father, St. John Paul II in his encyclical "*Redemptoris Missio*" confirms the above when he states:

> People today put more trust in witnesses than in teachers, in experience than in teaching, and in life and action than in theories. The witness of a Christian life is the first and irreplaceable form of mission: Christ, whose mission we continue, is the "witness" *par excellence* (Rev 1:5; 3:14) and the model of all Christian witness. The Holy Spirit accompanies the Church along her way and associates her with the witness he gives to Christ (cf. Jn 15:26-27)[41].

With respect to Jesus' mission mandate therefore, it implies that all Christians (persecuted or not persecuted) must rise to their responsibilities of being witnesses since the gospel is proclaimed by witnessing[42]. It is for this reason, that the Church emphasizes on the need for every member

---

[36] SECOND VATICAN COUNCIL, "Ad Gentes Divinitus", §2.

[37] SECOND VATICAN COUNCIL, "Ad Gentes Divinitus", §2. Cf., SECOND VATICAN COUNCIL, "Lumen Gentium", §17.

[38] Cf., Mt 28:19-20; Mk 16:15-18

[39] Acts 1:8

[40] BENEDICT XVI, "Africae Munus", §15.

[41] JOHN PAUL II, "Redemptoris Missio", §42.

[42] PAUL VI, "Evangelii Nuntiandi", §21.

to carry out this mission mandate as an obligation[43] by the virtue of our baptism.[44] But then for Christians within the northern region and other volatile areas in the world, the common challenge remains the hostility of the environment. How can Christians bear witness authentically in such volatile environment? To this end, the lived experiences of the martyrs in the second century become their source of strength and consolation. Consequently, this leads us to the next dimension of witness.

The second dimension of witness is, the belief in the gospel of the cross. St. Luke in numerating the cost of discipleship, makes us to understand that the great multitude which accompanied Jesus was not his (Jesus') main concern, but rather his main concern was the quality and authenticity of the disciples who would be willing to let go everything for his sake. Thus, he (Jesus) turned and said to them "If any one comes to me and does not hate his own father and mother and wife and children and brothers and sisters, yes even his own life, he cannot be my disciple. Whoever does not bear his own cross and come after me, cannot be my disciple"[45]. In other words, our call to discipleship involves self-denial and sacrifice. Hence, the cross becomes necessary for our salvation.

Nevertheless, it is imperative to note that prior to the edict of Milan in 313 AD Christians who confessed of Christ like Ignatius and Polycarp, and along with other martyrs such as Stephen, Perpetua, and Felicitas suffered great persecution. The edicts of Emperor Diocletian in 303 and 304 for instance, marked the apex of the early century persecution of Christians. In his imperial decree, Diocletian demanded the burning of all houses of Christian assembly along with their Scriptures. Any Christian leaders maintaining their practice of religion were to be imprisoned and tortured until they sacrifice to the Roman gods[46].

---

[43] The Canon clearly states that "All the Christian faithful have the duty and right to work so that the divine message of salvation more and more reaches all people in every age and in every land" (*CIC*, can. 211).

[44] Canon 204 - §1 The Christian faithful are those who, inasmuch as they have been incorporated in Christ through baptism, have been constituted as the people of God. For this reason, made sharers in their own way in Christ's priestly, prophetic, and royal function, they are called to exercise the mission which God has entrusted to the Church to fulfill in the world, in accord with the condition proper to each. §2. This Church, constituted and organized in this world as a society, subsists in the Catholic Church governed by the successor of Peter and the bishops in communion with him. While Canon 205 goes further to state that "Those baptized are fully in the communion of the Catholic Church on this earth who are joined with Christ in its visible structure by the bonds of profession of faith, the sacraments, and ecclesiastical governance".

[45] Lk 14:26-27; Mt 10:37-38;

[46] M. WATER, *The New Encyclopaedia of Christian Martyrs*, 351 – 352.

At this juncture, it is worthy of note that within the period of the sporadic persecutions, the early Christians lived with the knowledge that at any given moment they might have to pay the price for their baptisms. The truth of the reality of their situation, made them thus, to develop a theology of two baptisms. That is, the first was baptism by water, and the second was baptism by blood as a sign of martyrdom. It is against this background that the early Church was concretely connected to death[47]. St. Augustine would say in his book titled *The City of God* that "we offer thanks to God for their victories and by renewing their memory we encourage ourselves to emulate their crowns and victories..."[48]. Christians in the northern region of Nigeria, therefore, must be prepared for whatever challenges may confront them as a result of living out their Christian vocation and remain committed to their faith for Jesus clearly states without mincing words that; "If the world hates you, know that it has hated me before it hated you. If you were of the world, the world would love its own; but because you are not of the world, but I chose you out of the world, therefore the world hates you"[49].

Nevertheless, it is imperative to understand that the term "martyr" literally means "witness" which is an act of justice that establishes the truth or makes it known[50]. This reality is clearly manifested in the gospel of St. John in which he brings out one of its major characteristics of bearing public witness. For instance, the public witness of John the Baptist to Jesus and the crowd who witnessed Lazarus' coming back to life[51]. However, in the Acts of the Apostles, the term comes to signify those people, specifically the apostles, who will be witnesses to Jesus. "You will be my witnesses in Jerusalem, and in all Judea and Samaria, and to the ends of the earth"[52]. It is on this note that the term "witness" becomes one of the essential qualifications for the replacement of Judas Iscariot (when he denied Jesus and killed himself) with Matthias – "the eligible person must be a witness to the resurrection of Jesus"[53].

From the foregoing therefore, to authentically bear witness to Jesus within a volatile environment is to deny oneself to the extent of losing one's own live even when persecution seems inevitable. The courage and

---

[47] T. York, "Early Church Martyrdom", 20.

[48] Augustine, *City of God*, 255.

[49] Jn 15:18

[50] _ *The Catechism of the Catholic Church*, 566, §2471. _

[51] Cf., Jn 1:7,34; 3:32, 5:33,39 and 12:17 respectively.

[52] Acts 1:8

[53] Acts 1:21-26

246

the belief that good will surely triumph over evil as did the martyrs of the second century must be the watchwords of Christians in the north and in all volatile zones across the globe. Hence, the killings and sporadic detonation of bombs on Christians while at worship in their respective Churches is not an exemption from the above reality. Resilience therefore must be their watch-word for St. Paul admonishes Timothy while in the prison that "Indeed all who desire to live a godly life in Christ Jesus will be persecuted"[54]. However, this is not a call for martyrdom but a call to all Christians to remain resilient in their faith and never be discouraged despite the persecution while they remain constantly security conscious.

2.5 *The Role of the Church*

Amidst all these crises, the obvious question that comes to mind while reflecting on the reality of violence in our modern society is; what has been the role of the Church? Going down memory lane, with the emergence of Islam on the scene as one of the world competitive religions, its worldview before other religions becomes essentially important to be examined. In an attempt to answer the above question therefore, the first step is to examine the Church's perspective of Islam and thus her role amidst the crises. It is in this regard that, the Catholic perspective of Islam can be said to be characterized into two eras which include the era of confrontation and the era of respect and dialogue with each other[55].

2.5.1 The Era of Confrontation

The first era was the era of confrontation. In this era both religions (Christianity and Islam) claimed to possess the true faith while seeing other religion(s) in error. As each of the religion tried to convert and eliminate the other, confrontation thus became eminent wherein religious wars came into play. The crusades for instance, in which the European kingdoms invaded the Middle East with the intention to claim back the Holy Land from the control of the Muslim rulers could be said to be the high point of this confrontation. As a result, the phrase *extra ecclesia nulla salus* (Outside the Church, no salvation) became the main theology or philosophy that guided the life of the Church for many centuries owning that the Catholic Church is the only true Church in its strict sense and everybody outside it was in error.

---

[54] 2 Tim 3:12

[55] Cf., J. ONAIYEKAN, "The African Christian and Islam", 107-113.

To this effect, non-Christians were considered pagans and heathens that must be converted, and those Christians who could not agree with the Catholic position were considered schismatics (those who refused the discipline of Rome while maintaining the unity of dogmatic communion), and those who out rightly embraced dogmatic errors were considered heretics (protestants inclusive). This narrow attitude neither helped the relationship that existed among Christians nor did it improve the relationship of the Church with other religion(s).

But today we see both religions making efforts to tolerate each other by allowing the rightness of one's religion to coexist side by side with the wrongness of the other religion. Although, this may be "politically correct", but the problem of cordiality among the adherents of both religions still remains a problem since each of the religion is theoretically and theologically intransigent, claiming not only to possess the true faith but it is also duty bound to correct the error(s) of the other. This reality is acknowledged when the Holy Father Pope Benedict XVI in his apostolic exhortation *ecclesia in medio oriente* asserts that:

> We know that the encounter of Islam and Christianity has often taken the form of doctrinal controversy. Sadly, both sides have used doctrinal differences as a pretext for justifying, in the name of religion, acts of intolerance, discrimination, marginalization and even of persecution[56].

This implies that, for the existing relationship between the two religions in question to be strengthen, the need for the change of the Church's worldview of Islam in today's modern era cannot be overstressed. In other words, there is the ardent need of religious tolerance. This leads us to the second era of respect and tolerance of other religions as the Second Vatican Council (1962-65), led by Pope John XXIII came with a new spirit that led the Church to open itself to others (both non-Catholics and non-Christians) for better relationships.

2.5.2 The Era of Respect and Tolerance – Second Vatican Council (1962-65)

In more than two thousand years of history of the Church's existence, Vatican II Council was one of the outstanding Councils of the Church to have spoken positively of other religions, by recognizing the positive values that exist in them when the Church went through the providential revolution of an Ecumenical Council (the Second Vatical Council). As a result of this development, the Church opened her windows wherein the fresh air of tolerance, respect and dialogue with other great world religions (par-

---

[56] BENEDICT XVI, "Ecclesia in Medio Oriente", §19.

ticularly Islam) permeated her life. As result, the Second Vatican Council theologians were spurred to action and have been making immense effort to develop a theology that embraces other religions.

For example, Karl Rahner (a great theologian of the Church, and an influential voice during the Second Vatican Council – 1904-1984) developed an approach called *inclusivist approach* which gives a positive view of the other world religions. For Rahner, the members of the other traditions may attain salvation due to the fact that the grace of Christ is present in these traditions. But he, however, claims that the Christian tradition is "the absolute religion intended for all men, which can't recognize any other religion beside itself as of equal right". However, since God desires to save all human beings, "there are supernatural, grace-filled elements in non-Christian religions". Little wonder that Rahner considered a non-Christian to be an anonymous Christian[57].

Consequently, the Dogmatic Constitution on the Church – *Lumen Gentium* – gives an orderly theological framework of amending the Church's relationship with both non-Catholics and non-Christians as against the pre-Vatican II theology of *extra ecclesia nulla salus*[58]. Against this backdrop, the Church recognizes that she is linked in many ways with "those who, being baptized, are honoured with the name of Christians, though they do not profess the faith in its entirety or do not preserve unity of communion with the successor of Peter"[59]. This paragraph emphasizes the need of ecumenism that will enhance a better relationship between the Church and other Christians with the hope that Jesus' prayer will be realized. "That they may all be one as He and the Father are one"[60].

Then the next are the Jews "to whom the testament and the promises were given and from whom Christ was born according to the flesh"[61]. It was among them as we are reminded by St. Paul that Jesus as well as his Mother Mary and all the apostles, came into flesh[62]. This is to say that through the Jews, a new people of God, the Christian community was born. As paragraph 16 of the Lumen Gentium encourages interreligious dialogue, it thus becomes paramount for the Church to improve her relationship with not only the Jews, but also with the Muslims and other religions (ATR inclusive) who acknowledge God as the creator since they

---

[57] K. RAHNER, "Christianity and the Non-Christian Religions", 19-38.

[58] Cf., SECOND VATICAN COUNCIL, "Lumen Gentium", §16.

[59] SECOND VATICAN COUNCIL, "Lumen Gentium", §15.

[60] Cf., Jn 17:21

[61] SECOND VATICAN COUNCIL, "Lumen Gentium", §16.

[62] Rm 9:4-5

are equally included in the plan of God's salvation of human race. This is buttressed in the document *Nostra Aetate*.

> The Catholic Church rejects nothing of what is true and holy in these religions. She has a high regard for the manner of life and conduct, the precepts and doctrine which, although differing in many ways from her own teaching, nevertheless, often reflect a ray of that truth which enlightens all men[63].

With reference to Islam, the Council Fathers while acknowledging that God's plan of salvation also included Muslims as they also acknowledge God as the creator of the universe, who also profess to hold the faith of Abraham, and together we adore the one, merciful God, mankind's judge on the last day[64], a whole paragraph is devoted in respect to the Church's relation with Muslims. It goes thus:

> The Church has also a high regard for the Muslims. they worship God, who is one, living and subsistent, merciful and almighty, the Creator of heaven and earth, who has also spoken to men. They strive to submit themselves without reserve to the hidden decrees of God, just as Abraham submitted himself to God's plan, to whose faith Muslims eagerly link their own. Although not acknowledging him as God, they worship Jesus as a prophet, his virgin Mother they also honour, and even at times devoutly invoke. Further, they await the day of judgement and the reward of God following the resurrection of the dead. For this reason, they highly esteem an upright life and worship God, especially by way of prayer, alms-deeds and fasting. Over the centuries many quarrels and dissensions have arisen between Christians and Muslims. The Sacred Council now pleads with all to forget the past and urges that a sincere effort be made to achieve mutual understanding; for the benefit of all men, let them together preserve and promote peace, liberty, social justice and moral values[65].

Worthy of note is that since the mid-sixties, this text has been a guide to Catholics' perspectives regarding their approach to Islam. Consequently, with this new and fresh air injected into the Church, remarkable successes have been recorded and significant breakthroughs have been made particularly with respect to the Church's relationship with the Jews, Muslims and other religions. To this effect, the Assisi inter-faith gathering which was pioneered by St. John Paul II in 1986 set the ball rolling for the strengthening of the work of *Nostra Aetate*. Against this backdrop, the Catholic Bishops of Nigeria are not left out of the race. Nonetheless, it is pertinent to bear in mind that more will be discussed on interreligious dialogue as the work progresses.

---

[63] PAUL VI, "Nostra Aetate", §2.

[64] Cf., SECOND VATICAN COUNCIL, "Lumen Gentium," §16.

[65] PAUL VI, "Nostra Aetate", §3.

2.5.3 Catholic Bishops Conference of Nigeria (CBCN)

Since the independence of Nigeria as a nation in 1960, the CBCN has been the mouth piece of the millions of the Nigerian masses and the moral voice that continues to call on the government to remain committed to its responsibility to its citizens by providing the enabling environment that could promote social relations so that justice, freedom and peace are promoted and human rights are respected that citizens could realize their potentialities and attend the fullest of human development (social, political, religious and otherwise).

Against this backdrop, in 1975 the CBCN saw the need to call the attention of the government especially at the time when the nation was undergoing the processes of reconciliation, healing, rehabilitation and reconstruction after the long civil Biafra war. In her communiqué issued on 13 February 1975, the Bishops called on the government to remain committed to creating the enabling environment through the provision of the basic social amenities and other services that could better and improve the living conditions of the citizens. And these services must be distributed evenly as well as the most remote villages within the nation while giving priority to agriculture[66].

Subsequently, the moral voice of the CBCN was never muted by the political degeneration, corruption and violent activities of the nation's second republic era (1979-1983). Within this period, there was a transmission of power from the military regime to civilian government. Due to increase in oil prices and revenues, expectations from the government became high. But this was short lived because the oil boom ended abruptly at the peak of these expectations, and the existing animosity among politicians and the religious tension of 1980-85 Maitatsine crises, worsened the situation. While the Bishops voiced out the social evils perpetrated by some government authorities and those who siphoned the nation's treasure, they called on all Catholic faithful to continue to pray for peace and unity in the nation. Hence, the celebration of the first Eucharistic congress (November 19-21, 1982) became eminent with the theme: "Test and Fount of Faith, Unity and Love"[67].

In respect to the intractable terrorist activities of the Boko Haram, the CBCN strongly condemned such violence perpetrated against the innocent citizens of the nation especially in the northeast without mincing words. While extending condolences to all the bereaved and affected families, the attention of the government was drawn toward the prompt restoration of peace and the provision of relief materials to victims.

---

[66] Cf., CATHOLIC BISHOPS CONFERENCE OF NIGERIA, "Current Unrest", 9.

[67] CATHOLIC BISHOPS CONFERENCE OF NIGERIA, "Concern for the Political, Moral, and Educational Trends in Nigeria", 22.

We condemn violence on whatever excuse, and from whatever direction. We condemn it, above all, when the perpetrators blasphemously and fraudulently claim religious justifications for their actions. We deeply regret and condemn in strong terms, the wanton loss of life and property caused by the armed group called Boko Haram[68].

Every year after its deliberations, the CBCN sends out its communiqué to parishes, the presidency, the media and other concerned organizations, but the question remains, how much impact have such communiqués made especially with respect to the government? In most cases, it appears that the moral voice of the CBCN is not heard particularly by the government. It is to this end, that the need for the Nigerian Catholic Bishops to back up their words with action cannot be overstressed as demonstrated from time to time in its visits to the presidency.

But most importantly and worthy of praise was its action taken after the killing of two priests and seventeen parishioners in Benue state shortly after celebrating the morning Mass. The CBCN's call to all Nigerian Catholics and their supporters for a solemn peaceful demonstration across the nation May 22, 2018 (the same day the two priests and seventeen other parishioners were buried) in solidarity with the Diocese of Makurdi and against the incessant killings of innocent citizens across the nation, attracted not only the attention of the Nigerian government but also the entire world. This effort is thus worthy of commendation.

Having said and done, one of the most pertinent questions that must be asked is that, what are the possible ways forward? In attempt to this question, we now advance some suggestions that could help to pave the way to the realization of the desired enabling environment that will enhance peaceful coexistence, religious freedom and *hitherto* promote the missionary activities of the Church.

3. Recommendations

From the foregoing, we established that both Christians and Muslims bore the brunt of the Boko Haram extremist activities, as people were killed and property destroyed. With the maiming of people, abductions, raping, forceful evictions of communities and the killings of innocent citizens the search for possible solutions toward curbing the inferno is thus inevitable. Owing to this reality, this research seeks to advance forward few suggestions that could be essential to the realization of the desired peaceful atmosphere. Below are both short-term and long-term sugges-

---

[68] CATHOLIC BISHOPS CONFERENCE OF NIGERIA, "The Lord Comforts his People", 335.

tions. However, this does not suggest in any way that the followings are exclusive.

3.1 *Short-Term Recommendations*

These short-time recommendations are vital because of the immediate attention that in most cases victims must be attended to, bearing in mind that the basic immediate needs of the victims must be the priority of any serious government and its stakeholders. The short-term recommendations do not delve into the issue of investigations but is rather concerned with the immediate needed humanitarian services. Hence, its response must be prompt as the need arises. The following, therefore, are considered essential as regards the problem under study.

3.1.1 Immediate Relief for Victims

In every armed conflict, casualties are often inevitable. While few could be directly involved in the crisis, majority in most cases are often innocent victims. In whichever case however, victims of crisis must always be given immediate attention. For instance, in the preceding chapter, it is stated that some of the interviewees were made widows as a result of the loss of their husbands to the Boko Haram terrorism. Many were also made orphans, while some were lamed, abducted, raped, and psychologically traumatized as a result of either the witness of the brutal killing of their beloved ones or other bitter experiences suffered. In like manner, millions of people – as already noted – were forcefully displaced, and their sources of livelihood were destroyed. Against this backdrop, the need for adequate and immediate response to the plight of such victims by the government, religious and traditional leaders, NGOs, international bodies and all meaningful individuals cannot be exaggerated.

Relief materials such as temporary shelter (camps) for refugees, food and water, medical facilities, psychotherapy and other basic social amenities that could bring immediate relief to the victims must be promptly provided. While we note the efforts of the Catholic Church through the office of Justice, Development and Peace Commission (hereafter, JDPC), CAN, JNI, government and NGOs in this regard with respect to their respective prompt responses offered to the victims at various levels, however much is still desired to be done as some victims are still in the IDP camps and life becomes hard to bear every day.

Worth of note is that people with disabilities (hence, PwDs) often suffer neglect from the available humanitarian services. For example, they are sometimes ignored in evacuation and refugee situations, to the extent that their particular needs are overshadowed by the emergency needs of the population or the insufficient emergency responses. In like manner, the PwDs often have no access to relief services in refugee camps because of the difficulties in moving around, carrying, and queuing for relief materials. This reality is distinctively described by Arne H. Eide (a professor in rehabilitation) when she notes that PwDs are often invisible and excluded from accessing emergency support and essential services, such as medical care and water and sanitation facilities[69]. In this regard, government needs to establish special models such as the Disabled Peoples Organizations (hence, DPOs) who will assist in communicating the needs of the PwDs to the appropriate humanitarian organizations.

3.1.2 Reconciliation and Forgiveness

As part of peace process and healing the wounds between Christians and Muslims in the northern region, reconciliation and forgiveness are paramount. With the loss of loved ones, relations and friends, *vis-à-vis* the loss of the means of livelihood, many found it hard to forgive and let go bad resentments particularly those families whose bread winners were killed. Hence, the desire to revenge abounds. It is to this end that the need for forgiveness therefore is a *sine qua non* in the process of peace. For there can be no process of peace that will ever begin without an attitude of sincere forgiveness which takes its root in human hearts[70]. It is against this backdrop that both religious and traditional leaders have big roles to play while the government carries out its duties.

Members of the community must be reminded that both Christians and Muslims bore the brunt of the insurgences. Consequently, the need to come together and build a better relationship cannot be overemphasized, since the absence of forgiveness always paves the way for wounds to continue to fester, thereby fuelling in young men an endless resentment that produces the desire for vengeance which at the end of the day more harm is done than good. It is to this end that Robert Schreiter (a systematic theologian) argues that "without some measure of coming to terms with the past, the unhealed wounds will continue to fester, poisoning whatever the new society constructed, and poisoning the risk of victims themselves turning into the oppressors of others[71].

---

[69] A.H. EIDE, "Community-Based Rehabilitation" 100.

[70] Cf., BENEDICT XVI, "Message for the World Day of Peace 1997", §1.

[71] R. SCHREITER, "The Theology of Reconciliation and Peacemaking for Mission", 19.

In line with the above therefore, it is important to state as opined by Nchok (one of the respondents) that unhealed past wound is one of the factors that is often responsible for religious bigotry in the northern region. For him, the little children whose fathers were brutally murdered in their presence, might have found no reason to delete such unpleasant memories on their minds since there was little or no effort made to heal the past wounds despite the effort of the State government in curbing the crisis. While growing as adults, those children developed what is called a *trauma membrane*[72] that desired never to be intimidated again. Thus, the only way out for them was to seek for vengeance, which as a result, made the Kaduna Shari'a crisis of 2000 bloody. In his words he notes:

> Sometimes the poor woman and the children will take the man and hide him under the bed, but they will go from house to house even searching under the bed and whenever they find him under the bed, they will drag him out and slaughter him before his wife and the children. Imagine when these things started in the year 1987 to year 1991,92, 93 and up to the year 2000. That is why the crisis of 2000 was bloody because most of the children whose fathers were killed that way must have been living with the notion that if God leaves me alive to grow to the maturity and adulthood what was done to my dad I must avenge. I always say that I am not surprise that in the year 2000 and subsequent years that most of the responses to a violent attack, were responses from the young people which come from this age bracket because they would have said, look we have had enough, we cannot continue this way, and once the issue of revenge continues to manifest and rears its ugly head there is no way you can talk about mutual trust[73].

From the above view, it is obvious that the government failed in addressing sincerely the trauma membrane of both individuals and the community that was developed in the previous crises particularly within the Kaduna city. Hence, counter-conflicts abound.

This reality is well captured by the Holy Father Pope Benedict XVI in his post-synodal exhortation on the Church in Africa in service to reconciliation, justice and peace when he says that "Unless the power of reconciliation is created in people's hearts, political commitment to peace lacks

---

[72] A *trauma membrane* is a defensive protective layer that trauma survivors establish to protect themselves after experiencing a trauma as a result of experienced violence or armed conflict. The trauma membrane could be developed by either an individual or a society and its intention is to protect the individual or the society from an intrusive harm in the present and from harm that might occur in the future. See E. MARTZ, "Introduction to Trauma Rehabilitation", 61-62.

[73] NCHOK, "Interview".

its inner premise"[74]. The willingness to let go those unpleasant memories is the first step toward reconciliation. When victims are not willing to embrace reconciliation, and thereafter forgive the perpetrators, the realization of peace and enabling environment for robust missionary activities in the region is still farfetched. To facilitate the process of reconciliation and forgiveness therefore, the affected victims must be helped by appealing to their consciences to see reason(s) for reconciliation. It is in this regard that religion plays a vital role. For instance, after the 1945 World War II the Catholic Church in Europe played a big role in the reconciliation process which "laid the groundwork for what became the European community"[75].

Consequently, in the Nigerian society, the work of genuine reconciliation in most cases often involves the intervention of religious and traditional leaders of the affected community who are often taken with great esteem as the custodians of morals and cultures of the people. Hence, their words are always taken with utmost seriousness more than the politicians in government. It is to this end, that Cardinal Francis Arinze particularly called on religions to bring healing along the 'balm of Healing' in respect to the issue of physical violence, bearing in mind that physical violence often causes wounds on the minds of individuals, communities and nations at large which often leads to the development of trauma membrane. Against this backdrop, such condition of the mind, he argues, needs to be healed. Equating such affliction of violence with that of sin in the heart of Christians he notes:

> And sin is primarily an offence against God. It is often also an offence against one's neighbour. Jesus Christ, through His life, suffering, death, and resurrection, has redeemed humanity from the wound of sin and brought it healing. He has entrusted to His Church the dispensation of his ministry and his Gospel of healing and salvation…Other religions can articulate how they understand the role of religion in bringing healing[76].

This implies that, all Christians are urged to carry on the ministry of the healing mercy of Jesus, learning to forgive as the heavily Father forgives us[77], by putting away "all bitterness and wrath and anger and clamour and slander, and malice. And being kind to one another and tender-hearted[78]. For it is in forgiveness that we find reasons in building up new and better relationships owing to the fact that "reconciliation is not limited to God's

---

[74] BENEDICT XVI, "Africae Munus", §19.

[75] P. JENKINS, *God's Continent*, 42.

[76] F. ARINZE, *Religions for Peace*, 64.

[77] Cf., Mt 6:12

[78] Cf., Eph 4:31-32.

plan to draw estranged and sinful humanity to himself in Christ through the forgiveness of sins and out of love. It is also the restoration of relationships between people through the settlement of differences and the removal of obstacles to their relationships in their experience of God's love"[79]. The parable of the prodigal son is a good illustration to the aforementioned because the return of the younger son (his conversion) brought the realization of reconciliation between him and his father (whose wealth he squandered), and *ipso facto* between him and his elder brother through the mediation of their father[80].

Both Christian and Muslims must thus come together and be reconciled so that the dignity of every individual (irrespective of religion) could be restored, and new paths to development and lasting peace between them in the region could be opened at all levels. The case of South Africa is a boost to the above. After the era of apartheid, the South Africans realized that it was only by forgiving each other of the past transgressions that peace could be sustained, and a new nation could be built. As a result, the establishment of the Truth and Reconciliation Commission (TRC) in 1995 – when the then President of the country, Nelson Mandela passed the bill of the Promotion of National Unity and Reconciliation Act – became paramount[81].

3.1.3 Pursuit for Justice

Bearing in mind that the northern region is characterized by a host of challenges such as state fragility, weak institutions, social injustice, corruption, poverty and unemployment, which have contributed to the emergence of terrorism in the region, the need for justice becomes obvious as the clamour for peace becomes the order of the day by both Christians and Muslims. It is in this regard that the Holy Father John Paul II in his message on the World Day of Peace states that justice is essential because "there can be no true peace without respect for the dignity of persons and peoples, respect for the rights and duties of each person and respect for an equal distribution of benefits and burdens between individuals and in society as a whole"[82]. Where therefore justice exists, there abounds peace, and where peace exists there abounds development in all ramifications. But when these basic elements are lacking, they create the circumstances

---

[79] BENEDICT XVI, "Africae Munus", §20.
[80] Cf., Lk 15:11-32.
[81] Cf., J.B. HILL, *The Theology of Martin Luther King*, 18.
[82] JOHN PAUL II, "World Day of Peace 2002".

that permit oppression and exclusion, and *hitherto* create the fertile ground for violence and terrorism.

On a general note, it is argued that in any response to rule-breaking there are two objectives; (1) behaviour control (in the sense of securing future compliance with the rules), and (2) justice restoration. These objectives can be pursued by different means such as punitive and constructive means. While punitive justice or rather retributive justice brings into effect the need for meting out punishment where necessary, constructive or rather restorative justice brings into existence the need of re-establishing moral order and some sense of justice. In other words, "retributive justice is restoration of a sense of justice through the imposition of punishment, in form of adjudication or revenge; while restorative justice is restoration of a sense of justice through renewed value consensus"[83].

Nonetheless, in every given situation for the pursuance of justice, these two psychological concepts of justice must be considered bearing in mind that they are intertwined. But unfortunately, this is not the case as regards the Nigerian situation. Perpetrators of religious violence are often treated with impunity. Even when culprits are arrested, they are often released after some time without undergoing the meted punishment that is due to them according to the law. This is however, sometimes attributed to the presence of weak institutions and corruption owing that injustice and lawlessness come into existence when institutions that are meant to checkmate these social evils are weak or perhaps are absent.

Against this backdrop, the Nigerian Government must rise to its responsibility and call a spade a spade when and where necessary not minding whose ox is gored. Criminal offenses must be addressed with immediate effect and the perpetrators must be called to order according to the law of the state. This is necessary because when offenders are not punished, they continue to inflict pains on others and the prolongation of violence is often obvious. In the same vein, it is also important for government to make compensations of the damages caused when and where necessary. Although, this may not bring total healing of the existing wounds, but it will to some extent bring some relief to the victims. Hence, both retributive/punitive and restorative justices are essential in the effort of realizing peace in a violent society as in the case of the northern region.

It is in view of this that the Holy Father Pope Benedict XVI emphatically stated in his post-synodal exhortation on the Church in Africa in service to reconciliation, justice and peace that the "human peace obtained

---

[83] M. WENZEL – al, "Retributive and Restorative Justice", 379.

without justice is illusory and ephemeral"[84]. We must therefore embrace justice in order to realize a lasting peace for where there is no justice (as already noted above) there can be no peace, and in like manner there can be no any meaningful development. Nevertheless, it is important to state that while we make effort for reconciliation it does not mean that justice should be denied where necessary owing to the fact that justice is an essential requisite not only for forgiveness and reconciliation, which finds its ultimate foundation in the law of God and in his plan of love and mercy for humanity but also for a meaningful development. Both Christians and Muslims must therefore make a deliberate collective effort – irrespective of socio-cultural, political and religious divide – to see that justice prevails in all their dealings with one another within the region so that peace and development could be realized.

3.2 *Long-Term Recommendations*

The followings are categorized under the long-time recommendations owing to the fact that a lot of careful planning and execution are involved. Thorough social analysis, reorientation, and structural changes must be made. Furthermore, it also involves progressive procedures. It is often capital intensive because structures destroyed must be rebuilt, and experts from different fields of life must be engaged. Hence, the long-term recommendations, although they are more challenging than the short-term recommendations, they however guarantee lasting effects in as much as right steps are taking in the right direction.

3.2.1 Rehabilitation Intervention and Healing of the Past Wounds

In every post war, conflict, violence, crisis or whatever may be that inflict injuries and losses (both of life and property), there is always need for rehabilitation intervention by government, NGOs and other stakeholders. Rehabilitation, as a process, facilitates healing on multiple aspects of human life, which consists of interventions that help individuals and communities to regain their functioning, despite the incurred major traumas and losses. As noted by Erin Martz (an associate professor of counselling at the University of Memphis), rehabilitation refers to "the healing and repair on a human dimension (both psychological and physical)"[85]. The 'human dimension' here refers to both the individual and the community.

---

[84] Benedict XVI, "Africae Munus", §18.
[85] E. Martz, "Introduction to Trauma Rehabilitation", 14.

While at the level of the individual, interventions are geared toward the psychological trauma or physical injuries/disabilities of individuals, on the community level on the other hand, interventions are geared toward the economic, social, and political restoration of the community, and *ipso facto* the reintegration of groups of people within the affected community[86]. Hence, she describes post war/armed conflict rehabilitation in two aspects. While the first is called *individual-level rehabilitation* which refers to the responses to the stress created by injuries and disabilities. The second aspect of the rehabilitation is known as *community-level rehabilitation*. This refers to the responses to the destruction of a community or country's infrastructure after war or armed conflict[87]. Against this backdrop therefore, government must promptly intervene both at the individual and community levels of rehabilitation.

Worthy to note is the fact that the healing of psychological and emotional wounds of rape for instance, takes the Divine Grace of God to bring about a quick integration of the victims into the affected society. Enough resources must be devoted into the project. Likewise, the assistance of international bodies such as the World Bank, World Health Organization (WHO), European Union (EU), the United Nations International Children's Emergency Fund (UNICEF), International Committee of the Red Cross (ICRC), Doctors Without Borders, NGOs and other international humanitarian bodies, cannot be overstressed.

Nevertheless, bearing in mind that in every crisis no peace process has ever succeeded without the reintegration of former combatants, as well as the groups affected by the conflict, the conflict-to-peace transition programme such as Disarmament, Demobilization, and Reintegration (DDR) cannot be ignored by the Nigerian government, bearing in mind that the process of healing is all encompassing. Consequently, the government in collaboration with the religious and traditional leaders of the northern region must make deliberate efforts to see that those members of the Boko Haram who have denounced terrorism and repented are properly rehabilitated.

This could be better done when the DDR programme is rigorously followed by the government whereby the repented members are first, disarmed (by collecting all weapons in their possession), then demobilized (by gathering them in encampment area for proper orientation, deradicalization and training), and are finally reintegrated into the society (by settling them in selected communities with the aim to re-engage them in civil life). It is against this backdrop that while we applaud the effort of the present administration in its deradicalization programme in which 155

---

[86] E. MARTZ, "Introduction to Trauma Rehabilitation", 14.

[87] E. MARTZ, "Introduction to Trauma Rehabilitation", 10.

ex-members of the Boko-Haram were trained in different fields of life, sensitization and education, however, must also be made to the citizens (particularly the affected communities) in order to accept them as brothers and sisters and eschew stigmatization.

3.2.2 Effective Implementation of the Enacted Anti-Terrorism Law

The passing of the bill of anti-terrorism into law by the Nigerian law makers was a bold step taken by the government to curb terrorist activities within the country. But it must be noted that this singular action of the government was welcomed with mixed feelings. While others focus on the positive end result of the law, others on the other hand, pay attention to the contrary, having perceived that it was a continuous trend among the African countries who have manipulated the call for anti-terrorism across the continent to suit their personal political ambitions. Example is the outcry of Richard Downie (the deputy director of the Africa program at the Centre for Strategic and International Studies) who is recently reported to have said that "there is a growing tendency of governments to pass sweeping anti-terrorism laws and then to use them not only in legitimate efforts to arrest and prosecute terrorism suspects, but often as a weapon against regime opponents in general"[88].

By implication, the enacted anti-terrorism law will be used by the Nigerian government – if not checkmated – to witch-hunt its political opponents and the so-called perceived enemies. To buttress this point, were the governments of Ethiopia, Uganda, and other neighbouring governments who used the post 9/11 anti-terrorism laws to jail and silence journalists and discriminated against Muslims in their respective countries[89].

To guide against this and to curb the insurgency effectively, the provisions of the counterterrorism laws in Nigeria must be applied cautiously and legitimately devoid of any socio-political, religious or cultural sentiments. In like manner, it is imperative to balance the fight against terrorism with the protection of fundamental rights of the citizens. This will prevent counterterrorism measures from being counterproductive.

3.2.3 Legitimate use of Force

As it is the fundamental duty of every good governance to provide adequate security of life and property of its citizens, so also every Nigerian citizen has the fundamental right to life. The strategic implementation of the Nigerian government's policies must therefore be geared toward the

---

[88] J. GLASER, "Anti-Terror Laws in Nigeria Threaten Civil Liberties".

[89] J. GLASER, "Anti-Terror Laws in Nigeria Threaten Civil Liberties".

restoration of peace and security to the country, and above all the protection of life and property. From this point of view, it is imperative to stress that the efforts so far made by the present administration deserve commendation. But the reality of bringing to an end the insurgency is still much to be desired owing to the fact that the strategic policies employed by the government appear to have been mainly characterized by the use of force that sometimes leads to the destruction of what it ought to protect.

Although, national laws have developed the necessary control systems for the proper use of force, the growing importance of human rights has however, given rise to some additional international controls. A good example is the European Court of Human Rights which clearly states in articles 2 and 3 the need for the respect for human rights while engaging the rule of law in any given situation of government strategic policy. These articles read thus:

Article 2:

1. Everyone's right to life shall be protected by law. No one shall be deprived of his life intentionally save in the execution of a sentence of a court following his conviction of a crime for which this penalty is provided by law.

2. Deprivation of life shall not be regarded as inflicted in contravention of this article when it results from the use of force which is no more than absolutely necessary:

    a) in defence of any person from unlawful violence;

    b) in order to effect a lawful arrest or to prevent the escape of a person lawfully detained;

    c) in action lawfully taken for the purpose of quelling a riot or insurrection.

Article 3: "No one shall be subjected to torture or to inhuman or degrading treatment or punishment"[90].

While the court deals with cases that are explicitly as the lawful use of force under article 2, cases that are implicitly as the unlawful use of force are dealt with under article 3. The court therefore takes a solid stance by prohibiting the above-mentioned acts "in all circumstances, even in the fight against terrorism or organized crime, or in case of public emergencies threatening the life of a nation"[91]. It is against this backdrop that there has been an outcry from the residents of Borno state over the excessive use of force by the Nigerian security agents deployed to quell the insurgency

---

[90] EUROPEAN CONVENTION ON HUMAN RIGHTS, "As Amended by Protocols No. 11 & 14".

[91] CENTRE OF EXCELLENCE DEFENSE AGAINST TERRORISM ed, *Legal Aspect of Combating Terrorism*, 102.

in the region[92]. Bearing in mind that oppressive use of force as agued by experts may create a counter-effect of reprisal attacks thereby resulting, in the art of violence being reinforced in the region, government must therefore rise up to its responsibility in providing its security agents with necessary modern training and equipment particularly in the area of intelligence gathering and the use of modern technology.

3.2.4 Improved Security Intelligence

The obvious reality of our modern society today as observed by Douglas Pratt[93] is "the disquieting paradox of our time whereby we have so much information at our beck and con but so little knowledge. And without right knowledge there can be no right action"[94]. In view of this, the importance of intelligence gathering and sharing among the security agents cannot be overstressed. Nigerian government must, therefore, formulate the proper intelligence gathering plan and sharing among all the security agents in order to avert attacks before they occur or else there could be plenty information but very little or no action against the terrorists' activities. For example, there was plenty availability of information about Umar Farouk Abdulmutallab – the so-called 'underwear bomber' who attempted to sabotage, an American Northwest Airline flight on Christmas Eve of 2009, but there was little or no knowledge of what precisely he was up to, and as such there was no interception. Passengers were saved only by the divine intervention of God that the bomb failed to detonate. It was the same case with the Boko Haram, there was plenty of information about the terrorist group, yet the government never took any serious action to curb its excesses not until the scenario went out of control in 2009. For information therefore to become actionable knowledge, all the 'i'(s) and the 't'(s) as it is commonly said, must be dotted and be crossed, and the dots must also be joined for the issue of security is never a one man's show, but it is a collective responsibility that every stakeholder must be involved both within and outside.

While we commend the effort of JTORO which was a necessary right direction taken, the need of cooperation and intelligence sharing with the other neighbouring forces cannot thus, be overlooked. In this regard, mixed borders

---

[92] M.F. AJIBOYE-DARE, *Terrorism. The Nigerian Perspective*, 87.

[93] D. PRATT is Professor of Studies in Religion at the University of Waikato, New Zealand, and Adjunct Professor of Theology and Interreligious Studies at the University of Bern, Switzerland. He is also Adjunct Professor with the Global Terrorism Research Centre, Monash University, Australia. He is the New Zealand Associate, UNESCO Chair in Interreligious and Intercultural Relations Asia - Pacific.

[94] D. PRATT, *Religion and Extremism*, 100.

patrols in order to curtail the movement of armed groups and criminals, *vis-à-vis* the movement of weapons, must be intensified. In the same vein, Nigerian government needs to enter into international collaboration with countries such as the United States of America, the United Kingdom, France, Italy, Israel and others alike who have first-hand experience of terrorism and have thus over the years devised to a reasonable extent, credible and scientific means of dealing with situations of terrorism in their respective countries.

Furthermore, the issue of the welfare of the forces must also be taken seriously. To avoid nonchalant attitude from the forces in the front line of the fight against the terrorists, the government must promptly pay all security forces their salaries and allowances as when due. *Hitherto*, incentives from time to time should be encouraged as a way of boosting their morale in fighting the insurgency. More importantly, families of the deceased forces must be compensated as soon as possible in order to relief them from the pains of losing a dear one and perhaps the bread winner of the family.

3.2.5 Religious Freedom

In the preceding chapter, many of the respondents especially the Christians cried out of the challenges that confront them as regards their human rights to religious freedom. Christians are oppressed in almost every sphere of life in the northern region ranging from the oppression of lack of promotion in their working places to the denial of professional courses while seeking for admission into any of the higher institutions within the region. The denial of land for building of religious worship centres, schools and Christian cemeteries are always on the increase. Against this backdrop, the prophetic call of the Council Fathers made in the *Dignitatis Humane* cannot be overstressed. While the Council concentrates on the right of the human person in paragraph two of the above said document (as already quoted), paragraph four however, lays emphasis on the collective religious freedom of a religious group or community. It clearly states the rights of a religious group/community to be heard, to acquire and use property (land) for religious purpose, and to bear public witness to its beliefs both in spoken and written words.

Religious communities also have the right not to be hindered, either by legal measures or by administrative action on the part of government, in the selection, training, appointment, and transferal of their own ministers, in communicating with religious authorities and communities abroad, in erecting buildings for religious purposes, and in the acquisition and use of suitable funds or properties[95].

---

[95] PAUL VI, "Dignitatis Humanae" §4.

Bearing in mind the temptation of the misuse of these rights and privileges, the Council goes further to caution the religious group/community to be careful of not infringing on the rights of others while exercising its religious freedom.

Religious communities also have the right not to be hindered in their public teaching and witness to their faith, whether by the spoken or by the written word. However, in spreading religious faith and in introducing religious practices everyone ought at all times to refrain from any manner of action which might seem to carry a hint of coercion or of a kind of persuasion that would be dishonourable or unworthy, especially when dealing with poor or uneducated people. Such a manner of action would have to be considered an abuse of one's right and a violation of the right of others[96].

While Religious freedom remains a fundamental right of every human being irrespective of his/her socio-political, religious and cultural background as it is "based on the very dignity of the human person"[97], this fundamental rule of the social life of the human being therefore as noted by the Holy Father Pope Benedict XVI, "must find application and respect at every level and in all areas[98]. Although, religious freedom finds recognition in the Nigerian constitution as already seen above, however much is still desired to be done. Government, religious, and traditional leaders must rise to enjoin Nigerians to live in peace and harmony while respecting their individual cultural, ethnic and religious diversities, and as well as their political interests.

It is to this end that while we urge the government to remain committed to providing the conducive environment for religious activities to flourish at all levels by respecting the human and religious rights of all citizens, the religious leaders on their part (both Christians and Muslims) must remain resilient without religious sentiments in calling the attention of the government especially when these rights are violated by certain group of people or religious body.

More importantly, government must remain neutral on the matters of religion. It must stop the sponsorship of religious programmes particularly the sponsorship of religious pilgrimages (both Christians and Muslims), building of religious schools such as the *almajiri* schools, Churches or Mosques and the like in order to score political points. For such funds could be better used to alleviate the poverty level of the people. In the same vein, showing interest in one religion over the other by either the Federal, State or Local government can easily lead to anarchy and doom

---

[96] PAUL VI, "Dignitatis Humanae" §4.

[97] PAUL VI, "Dignitatis Humanae" §4.

[98] BENEDICT XVI, "New Year Address to Diplomatic Corps 2011".

bearing in mind that the Nigerian constitution explicitly states that "The Government of the Federation or of a State shall not adopt any religion as State Religion"[99]. Furthermore, government must eschew from the act of enacting a particular religion's law over the generality of Nigerians knowing that such action in a multireligious state such as Nigeria, surely provides the fertile ground for religious bigotry as we have noted in chapter two in 2.6.4 Kaduna Shari'a riot of 2000.

3.2.6 Poverty Alleviation and Creation of Job Opportunities

The welfare of the people is one of the paramount duties of every government. As millions of Nigerians are living in poverty, the Nigerian government must as a matter of duty and urgency rise to its responsibility to alleviate the suffering of the people amidst plenty. The nation's resources must be properly channelled in the right direction for the benefit of every citizen and not to be enjoyed by only few individuals. In the same vein, the nation's resources must also be equitably distributed across the regions without any region left out.

Also, economic policies must be put in place that will guarantee a sustainable economic empowerment and development across the nation. Institutions such as the *Economic and Financial Crimes Commission* (hence, EFCC), the *Independent Corrupt Practices Commission* (hereafter, ICPC), and other similar institutions must be strengthened and supported by both government and the Nigerian judiciary systems in order to nib to the bud all corrupt practices and related financial crimes, and *hitherto*, their charges. It is to this end that the effort of the present government is worthy of commendation for the fight against corruption. Nevertheless, the reality of its end is still farfetched as Nigerian's score is only 27 per cent and still ranks 148 in the 2017 global ranking of CPI.

While the fight against corruption continues, it is however essential to note that it must be holistic. For instance, the sale man/woman at the fuel station who having served the needed amount of fuel, often desires extra payment, must be stopped. The lecturers who molest their students and sometimes fail them when they don't offer them (the lecturers) a bribe or their bodies for sexual immorality (as regards female students), must also be stopped. Key officers who must receive bribe in order to offer jobs to qualified citizens must also be brought to book and face the wrought of the law. In summary, the fight against corruption, will only make more sense than ever, when no stone is left unturned.

---

[99] CONSTITUTION OF THE FEDERAL REPUBLIC OF NIGERIAN 1999.

Nevertheless, while we applaud the government's effort for providing a platform of economic empowerment like *the ease of doing business,* and its holistic diversification that is geared toward adding value to every stakeholder, particularly agriculture as the planned mainstay of the nation's economy, however, much is still desired, owing that the problem of unemployment in the country has plunged millions of Nigerians below the poverty line. In the same vein, millions of jobless and frustrated youths (both in rural and urban areas) are loitering in the streets without being engaged into meaningful activities that could benefit them and the society. As it is commonly said that *'an idle mind is the devil's workshop'*, the need to create job opportunities to this regard is paramount.

It is to this reality that the Nigerian government must, hence, make an urgent and aggressive effort in job creation strategies in order to eschew possible uncontrollable social tension and radicalism among the teaming populated jobless youths that may perhaps lead to another fresh break out of terrorism. The government must strictly adhere to and have the political will to execute the different strategies and policy framework that had been put in place in order to drive the employment drive in the country such as the National Employment Policy (hereafter, NEP) of 2002, the National Action Plan on Employment Creation (hence, NAPEC), National Youth Policy (hence, NYP) of 2009 as well as the National Policy on Education (hereafter, NPE).

Bearing in mind the wide existing gap between the northern region and other regions in the country in terms of socio-economic development, the Nigerian government needs to develop and implement a *Northern Region Development Commission* (hence, NRDC) that is similar to the *Niger Delta Development Commission* (NDDC), with a mandate that includes; the coordination of anti-desertification campaigns, large scale irrigation development, agricultural development, power development, road projects and the promotion of small businesses that could create job opportunities for the youths within the region. Nonetheless, check and balances must be put in place in order to avoid abuses so that at the end of the day the desired results could be achieved.

3.2.7 Educational Reforms

The role of education in the development of citizens cannot be overemphasized, particularly with regard to Nigeria, where ignorance plays a major role in creating fertile ground for violence. Although, education is not directly linked to terrorism, but its correlation manifests itself in the exhibition of the level of ignorance across board. In this scenario therefore, education is all encompassing because it includes both formal and religious education. The need for the formal education is essential because through the formal education, citizens are not only empowered but they also become aware of their rights and privileges, the "dos" and the "don'ts" within the society thereby bringing a transformation of the society from its level of ignorance to the level of enlightenment. This will pave the way for the millions of the youths to be gainfully empowered for the desired knowledge of the modern society particularly in the sector of labour and productivity, thereby reducing to a minimal level the number of mismatches between employment opportunities available in the labour market and the types of qualifications produced by the education and training systems in the country.

Bearing in mind that people without education are already preys in the hands of the educated elites, greedy politicians, and radical preachers (as already established in this study) who manipulate them for their selfish interest, governments at all levels, therefore, should as a matter of necessity reform the educational systems. Schools curricula must be updated, and government must ensure that qualified religious teachers of both religions are employed in all government schools for religious instructions.

Consequently, the Qur'anic educational systems should be reformed by all northern state governments by enforcing the introduction of a dual curriculum in which the *almajiris* will be better empowered with both religious and secular knowledge as it is obtainable in all Christian seminaries (both Catholic and Protestant seminaries) across the region. This is aimed at protecting the *almajiris* from the above miscreants and other means of exploitation, and thus grant them (*almajiris)* the ample opportunity to compete efficiently with their counterparts for the available job opportunities in the society while they maintain their religious beliefs.

Importantly, while we focus on secular education for the eradication of the enormous ignorance in the nation, we must also pay attention to religious education owing that ignorance of religious tenets is a factor for the emergence of the Boko Haram. Each religion (particularly Christianity and Islam) must fine-tune a better way to deepen the understanding of its religious tenets among its adherents. Both religious leaders and scholars must rise to their responsibilities to correct the doctrinal errors that are being promoted by radicals in the region thereby misleading a lot of young people into radicalism. To this end, catechesis of religious tenets must be intensified by both religions and never be left in the hands of half-baked religious teachers noting that we cannot give what we do not have.

3.2.8 Interreligious Dialogue

In a multireligious society such as Nigeria wherein there exists different interest in religious beliefs, the role of interreligious dialogue is very essential particularly in the Northern region. The truism is that while Christians face hostility and intolerance from Muslims, Muslims in like manner face hostility and intolerance from Christians. Both are hostile, and most often intolerant to each other. It is to this reality that having reflected on the relationship of the Church with other great religions, the Fathers of the Second Vatican Council opened a way for a new dialogue based on the ardent desire for a deeper understanding and respect of these great world religions.

To this effect, the Council's document *Nostra Aetate* – the Council's declaration on the Relationship of the Church to Non-Christian Religions – outlines this new approach of the Church's relationship with other religions which is reflected and has its foundation in *Dignitatis Humanae* – The declaration of Religious Freedom, and in *Lumen Gentium* – The Dogmatic Constitution on the Church. As a result, "the Church, therefore, urges her sons to enter with prudence and charity into discussion and collaboration with members of other religions"[100]. In other words, interreligious dialogue becomes indispensable for both religions to embrace while the Nigerian government makes the necessary effort to support and create the enabling environment for this noble course to prosper.

Interreligious dialogue is important particularly in the North because it is a *sine qua non* in the discovery of the truth that leads to the realization of the desired peace in a society. It is against this backdrop that the Holy Father Pope Benedict XVI notes in his message to the representatives of other religions on July 18, 2008, that "our quest for peace goes hand in hand with our search for meaning, for it is in discovering the truth that we find the sure road to peace"[101]. This is rightly said owing to the fact that both Christians and Muslims in the northern region are in search of a lasting peace in the region.

However, peace must be understood not within the parameters of disturbance, disorder, insecurity, and the absence of violence, war, and terrorism, but within the ambience of a harmonious coexistence of individual citizens within a society that is governed by justice[102], love and equity. For it is when the human heart is well disposed towards peace, and the individual is liberated spiritually, philosophically and culturally from evil dispositions and sin, that as individuals we can be better placed to promote

---

[100] SECOND VATICAN COUNCIL, "Nostra Aetate", §2.

[101] L. Coco, ed., *Interreligious Dialogue*, 6.

[102] Cf., L. Coco, ed., *Interreligious Dialogue*, 14-15.

peace in the society via interreligious dialogue, and subsequently, we can appreciate it.

We cannot however, shy away from the fact that religious leaders across the globe have long realized the importance of collaboration for the promotion of peace in our society. The World Conference on Religion and Peace (WCRP) for example which was established in 1968 by believers in various religions for the promotion of dialogue and collaboration between religions in favour of world peace has since been recognized by the UN as an NGO that contributes to the organization (UN) from an interreligious platform[103]. In like manner, the October 27th, 1989 World Day of Prayer for Peace in Assisi, Italy, convoked by the Holy Father, Pope John Paul II in which he invited representatives of the major world religions to come to Assisi to pray and fast for the promotion of peace during the International Year of Peace declared by the UN was the right initiative in the right direction.

But the question remains, how sincere and committed are the religious leaders in pursuing vigorously the path of interreligious dialogue towards the eradication of religious prejudices among the followers of the world religions? This is necessary to be noted because most often in Nigeria for example, religious leaders come together and discuss on meaningful issues that affect the generality of the people with respect to religious matters, important resolutions are made, but the implementation has always been the problem. At the end of the day, what is done sometimes by one religion is often a direct contrast of what is collectively agreed upon. Hence, sincerity of purpose from some religious leaders is lacking especially when it is not to their own advantage. It is this type of attitude of deceit that the Holy Father Pope Francis refers to in his encyclical letter *Evangelii Gaudium* (The Joy of the Gospel) as a "diplomatic openness which says 'yes' to everything in order to avoid problems"[104].

Convinced therefore, that interreligious dialogue is a path that can promote respect among members of different religions and help to bring peace and harmony to a world that is torn by conflict and war, poverty, and destruction of environment, a world that is captivated by materialism and secularism, and it is indeed in deep need of finding significant existence, the Holy Father Pope John Paul II distinctively stated in his message for the twenty-fifth Annual World Day of Prayer for Peace that: "It can be said that a religious life, if it is lived authentically, cannot fail to bring forth fruits of peace and brotherhood, for it is in the nature of religion to foster

---

[103] Cf., F. ARINZE, "Interreligious Dialogue at the Service of Peace", 91.

[104] FRANCIS, "Evangelii Gaudium", 251.

an ever-increasing fraternal relationship among people"[105]. How visible is this reality across the globe, and particularly in the northern part of Nigeria where radicalism has preoccupied the minds of many youths and religion has become an easy tool to manipulate for violence?

This reality can only be possible when we live out authentically the tenets of our respective religions. For religious beliefs "presuppose truth", and "the one who seeks truth, lives by it"[106] and hence, he/she cannot fail to bring forth fruits of peace and brotherhood/sisterhood. But where self-interest precedes the common good, then the fruits of our beliefs cannot be realized and hence religion becomes a mere tool of monopoly for our personal aggrandizement. It is to this effect that Muhammed re-echoes this reality when he opines that both Christians and Muslims must go back and study their respective holy books very well in order to avoid any religious violence.

> "If we do that (study the Bible and the Qur'an intensively), there would not be any problems. Our holy books all preach peace, love, equality, and account-ability to one another. If we take each other as brothers and sisters, there will no be rancour and bloodshed. These messages are all contained in the holy books. We only need to go back to them. I believe there are pastors, Imams, and other religious leaders who get emotional and allow their emotions to over cloud their sense of reasoning but if they strictly follow what the holy books say, that would not be a problem"[107].

From this point of view, religious leaders and all believers irrespective of one's religion must therefore see the need of seeking for the truth of his/her religion and lives his/her life by examples owing that every believer desires to know the truth as it is well captured in the words of St. Augustine "Lord, you have created us for yourself and our hearts are restless until they rest in you".[108] We must therefore remain committed in bearing witness to our respective religious truths.

Furthermore, leaders (both spiritual and temporal), and all believers must be seen in all ramifications of life promoting morality, unity, peace and justice, and shun every temptation to materialism and self-aggrandize-ment. By implication, the business of interreligious dialogue should not be limited only within leaders as shown in a survey which was carried out in 2004 as regards the effectiveness of dialogue in Nigeria. While the survey revealed that dialogue is effective in conflict resolution in Nigeria in which it could lead to peaceful coexistence among Nigerians and *vis-à-vis* help to

---

[105] JOHN PAUL II, "Message for the XXV Annual World Day of Prayer for Peace".

[106] Cf., L. COCO, ed., *Interreligious Dialogue*, 4.

[107] MUHAMMED, "Interview".

[108] AUGUSTINE, *Confessions*, 1.

break down walls of prejudices, it however revealed that dialogue is limited to just a clique in most organizations, whereby in most cases only the top administrators and top management cadre in such organizations often engaged in it[109]. This method of dialoguing manifests itself in like manner in interreligious dialogue. For instance, in situations of religious tension or violence, only the top religious leaders are often involved in interreligious dialogue[110].

Although, the effort of the Nigerian religious leaders (both Christians and Muslims) is worth noting by establishing a religious body in 2000 called Nigeria Inter-religious Council (NIREC) in collaboration with the Federal Government in order to explore the best ways of using religion as a tool that could guarantee justice, peace and democracy, and hence, put an end to religious violence and bigotry, the body has however remained a toothless bulldog. NIREC's inactiveness has unfortunately not yielded its desired results. Only very little has been achieved since its inception noting that religious violence and conflict still abound in the country.

Nevertheless, it is imperative to point out some realities on the ground that most often frustrate the efforts and effectiveness of a genuine interreligious dialogue in the northern region. These include; ignorance of religious tenets which mostly leads the youths to religious fanaticism and extremism. Lack of transparency among the adherents of both religions, suspicious and prejudice among both groups. As Christians suspect the Muslims, so also the Muslims suspect the Christians. While most Christians often feel that Muslims welcome interreligious dialogue only when they are at disadvantage at any given religious crisis, Muslims on the other hand, feel that Christians are always the champion of the interreligious dialogue because of their hidden agenda of conversion.

In the same vein, the patronage of government also plays a big role. Owing that Islam is a major religion in the region, government funds that are meant for the common good of every citizen in the state (irrespective of religious affiliation) are often used for the sponsorship of certain Islamic programme such as building of mosques, building of the *almajiri* schools, sponsorship of pilgrimage to Mecca, sponsorship of the *Yan'adawa* (Islamic group of preachers), and just to mention but few.

From the foregoing therefore, for an effective and genuine interreligious dialogue that will greatly have impact on the life of the commoners (both Christians and Muslims) in Nigeria and particularly in the northern

---

[109] Cf., P.B. TANKO, "The Effectiveness of Dialogue in Conflict Resolution", 45-52.

[110] More on the involvement of few in interreligious dialogue will be discussed below under "dialogue of life".

region, this study strongly recommends that government and politicians must stop the manipulation of NIREC's activities *ipso facto*, the manipulation of religion for their political interest. Also, government must remain neutral on religious matters by being an impartial umpire and not to be seen taking interest in one religion over the other.

Furthermore, NIREC members must be ready to open themselves to one another and enter into the interreligious dialogue with utmost sense of sincerity and transparency. Thereby call a spade a spade when necessary without minding whose ox is gored. *Hitherto*, religious leaders of both religions (Christianity and Islam) should as a matter of duty create avenues for the training of members in skills of dialogue and opportunism. This is emphatically emphasised by the Holy Father Pope Francis when he maintains that the training of members is essential because it will not only grant them the opportunity to be solidly grounded in their own identity, but they will also be able to acknowledge the values of others and appreciate them.

> "In order to sustain dialogue with Islam, suitable training is essential for all involved, not only so that they can be solidly and joyfully grounded in their own identity, but so that they can also acknowledge the values of others, appreciate the concerns underlying their demands and shed light on shared beliefs"[111].

Consequently, deliberate efforts must be made to step-down the act of doing interreligious dialogue. Let the commoners for instance, on their way to the farm, in the market places, at the squares, and at whatever level they meet together, be able to value and appreciate the gift of one another and the values of one's religion.

Owing that interreligious dialogue is a *sine qua non* to unity and peaceful coexistence in the region, courses of interreligious dialogue and peace education should be taught as compulsory subjects in both secondary and tertiary institutions with the view to inculcating into the Nigerian youths the virtues of patience, humility and respect to one's religion and its values through dialogue that gears towards unity in diversity. Finally, government at all levels must invest heavily in peace programmes, encourage peace movements, propagate peace messages via the media (both print and electronic), and *ipso facto*, encourage entertainment houses such as the Nigerian artists and filmmakers (the Nollywood) to also preach the message of peace.

---

[111] FRANCIS, "Evangelii Gaudium", 253.

3.2.9 Dialogue of Life

From the foregoing, it is obvious that Interreligious dialogue is essential but the most essential in the region under investigation is the Dialogue of Life. It is the most essential because majority of the Nigerian population and particularly in the north, are illiterates, and the common man on the street does not really understand what interreligious dialogue entails. Hence, interreligious dialogue must go beyond a mere comparative analysis of the two religions but be translated into dialogue in action.

As noted by the then Catholic Archbishop of Jos and the then CBCN president, Archbishop Ignatius Aya Kaigama that "a positive engagement in real life is what will bring about the genuine impacting of religion positively on a multicultural and multireligious society such as Nigeria"[112], hence, the necessity of dialogue of life in this regard cannot be undermined. But this positive engagement will become a reality when both Christians and Muslims realize that our common origin of being is from God and we are all God's children created in His image and likeness. But when carnage is unleashed on the adherents of the other religion, it indicates that we are yet to know genuine religion which is centred on the love of God and the love of neigbour which must thus express itself in a practical spirituality that respects and accepts the others' beliefs and way of life[113].

As already noted above, what is regarded as interreligious in most cases is the gathering of few privileged religious leaders that most often involves the Imams, Cardinal, Bishops, and the Sultan, who come together to interact, discuss sensitive issues that hinder the growth of both religions and unity of the country, exchange pleasantries, and thereafter photographs are taken which often go to the print media for publication. The general impression such gathering gives to the public is that Christians and Muslims are united and interreligious dialogue is effectively taking place. But this encounter has little or no impact on the life of the commoners who are directly involved in these religious crises. Hence, religious tensions still manifest themselves. This reality is succinctly captured by Fuks when he notes that:

> The orientation for the need of this approach must begin from the grassroot communities, because when we look at the aspect of peace building, let me compliment the high-level actors like Onaiyekan, Kaigama, Kukah, the Sultan of Sokoto, they are at the high level there. When they do it, the commoners in the communities don't feel the impact of what they are doing up there. How do they then step it down what they are doing up there to the commoners in

---

112 I.A. KAIGAMA, *Dialogue of Life*, 7.
113 I.A. KAIGAMA, *Dialogue of Life*, 8.

the community? In this aspect, therefore, deliberate efforts must be made as regards the grassroot community approach. Hence, while building the peace structure, it has to begin from the grass root communities because when the people in the communities value the religion of each other, we live in this village I value you as a Muslim, and you value me as a Christian, then when the trouble starts, it does not start with the top ranking personnel in the society but begins usually from the grass root. Hence, the commoners must be the deliberate targets of the peace building approaches[114].

It is to this effect that "the dialogue of life"[115] becomes expedient and must begin from the grassroot. Reason being that in Nigeria, there are many activities that bring both Christians and Muslims together in everyday life. Some of the events that provide the opportunities for interaction and the demonstration of genuine friendship include; weddings, marriages, graduation parties, naming ceremonies, festive periods such as Sallah and Christmas. In like manner, schools, business centres, and sports also provide the opportunities to gather together and pursue a common interest. These occasions provide the common ground for the commoners to share their joys and experiences together not minding the existing religious differences.

Importantly, it is worth noting that this reality of dialogue and collaboration of Christians with others is encouraged by the Council Fathers when

---

[114] Fuks "Interview".

[115] In emphasizing on the need for interreligious dialogue, the Pontifical Council for Interreligious Dialogue and the Congregation for the Evangelization of peoples clearly spelt out four types of the forms of dialogue which include; the dialogue of life (in which people strive to live in an open and neighbourly spirit, sharing their joys and sorrows with one another and vis-à-vis their human problems and daily challenges that confront them as a community. Nevertheless, this is expected to be built on the basis of mutual trust, understanding and respect for one another), the dialogue of action (which brings people together to collaborate with one another for the integral development and liberation of their community), the dialogue of theological exchange (this paves the way to specialists who seek to deepen their understanding of their respective heritages, and to appreciate each other's spiritual values with the aim to lay bare the spiritual richness of each other's religion that could lead to the need of a common action in the areas of morals and ethics in the society), and the dialogue of religious experiences (which allows people who are rooted in their own religious traditions to share their spiritual richness such as prayers and contemplation not with the aim to worship God in the same way, but to realize that the same God can be worshipped in different ways). It is however, imperative to note that all these forms are not in any way independent of each other. They are interwoven in a manner that with the contacts in daily life and the common commitment to action, they lead to the opening of the door for cooperation in promoting human and spiritual values, and perhaps, they may eventually lead to the dialogue of religious experience in respect to the great questions in our daily life that continue to seek for answers. Cf., PAUL VI, "Nostra Aetate", §2; W.R. BURROWS, *Redemption and Dialogue*, 104.

they call on all Christians to active collaboration and solidarity with those whom they live especially in the areas of social and economic life, education, justice, health care, and peace making.[116] This collaboration, however, involves even people of non-Christian religions.[117]

Against this backdrop, deliberate efforts must be made by both Christians and Muslims to seize those ample opportunities to include neighbours and friends who are of the other religion. For dialogue of life, is a dialogue of being together which does not involve the discussion of the great themes of faith such as whether God is Trinitarian or not, or how the inspiration of the sacred Scriptures is to be understood, but simply it is about the concrete problems of coexistence and shared responsibility for society, the state, and humanity at large. In this case, the existence of the Boko Haram is a concrete reality that confronts both Christians and Muslims and they must come together devoid of any religious sentiments, be united and thus fight it squarely. With this inclusivist approach, the problem of exclusivism can be reduced to a minimal level.

But the great obstacle of this reality is that in most cases, both Christians' and Muslims' parents and teachers indoctrinate the minds of the young innocent ones who grow up with the negative attitudes toward people of the other religion, thereby, frustrating the efforts of any genuine dialogue. *Ipso facto*, on doctrinal issues, we cannot shy away from the fact that there exist some fundamental differences between Islam and Christianity particularly in the area of the mystery of God. While Muslims for instance, believe in One God devoid of any attributes and Mohammed is the last prophet, Christians on the other hand, believe in the mystery of three Persons in one God (the Holy Trinity) and also in the mystery of the Second Person in God becoming man as Jesus Christ and saving all men. But interestingly to note is also the fact that both religions in question "believe in God who is Creator, Merciful, Compassionate, Sovereign, Almighty, Holy, Just, the One who pardons our sins, Transcendent yet close to the lives of his people, and the Judge at the day of judgment who gives reward or punishment according to our deeds"[118].

On the teaching about man, both religions hold that God is the source of human dignity, rights, values and duties, and that we are stewards of God's creation. He (God) calls us all continually to reconversion and to submit our lives to His Will[119]. Against these perspectives, deliberate efforts must

---

[116] Cf., SECOND VATICAN COUNCIL, "Ad Gentes Divinitus", §11.

[117] PAUL VI, "Nostra Aetate", §2.

[118] F. ARINZE, "Interreligious Dialogue at the Service of Peace", 93.

[119] F. ARINZE, "Interreligious Dialogue at the Service of Peace", 93.

be made by both Christians and Muslims to emphasize and pay more attention to the existing doctrinal convergences of both religions while they deemphasize and pay less attention to the existing doctrinal divergences. In other words, we must make concerted efforts to deemphasize our differences as Christians and Muslims while we emphasize greatly the common values that are found in our religions. We must all dwell more on what unites us as human beings than what divides us so that we can both see in one another that human being created in the same image and likeness of God, irrespective of our religious divides.

Finally, both Christians and Muslims must be ready to accept that each religion is unique, and it has its spiritual, doctrinal, historical and cultural foundations, and *hitherto*, must be respected at all levels. For it is the acceptance and respect for the religious beliefs of each religion that will surely lead us to a genuine dialogue of life with the intent to bring the realization of a harmonious and peaceful coexistence among the Christians and Muslims in the northern region.

3.2.10 Prayer

While the Psalmist reminds us that "In vain do the labourers labour if the Lord God is not on their side"[120], and prophet Jeremiah invites us to always pray to our God and He will hear us (Jer 33:3), both Christians and Muslims must see the need to turn back to God with sincere hearts and ask for His divine intervention. They must remain resilient in their prayers and trust in God, believing that the ugly situation at hand will surely come to pass one day. For the power of prayer cannot be underestimated. Prayer in the life of every believer whether Christian or Muslim is thus as important as the religion itself.

To all Christians especially those within volatile zone such as the northern Nigeria, they must bear in mind that there can be no mission without prayer. As they are called to bear witness to Christ, they must turn back to God in prayer because prayer connects intimately every believer with his/her God in spirit. It is to this end that they will be able to accomplish successfully their missionary mandate without despair despite the hostilities that surround them. For while Mary animates the mission of the Church by her quiet and reassuring presence, the Holy Spirit on the other hand, gives impetus and freshness to the missionary thrust to make believers proclaim the message of peace to all races, tribes and religions.

As every baptized is part of the pilgrim Church who offers prayers for the entire world, all Christians are therefore called to pray for the needs of

---

[120] Ps 127:1

the whole world while bearing in mind that their prayers must be extended to the very end of the world. In other words, their prayers must be extended to both believers and non-believers, to both well-wishers and those who do harm to them – Boko Haram inclusive. For Jesus prayed for the salvation of even those who killed him when he said: "Father forgive them for they do not know what they are doing"[121].

Knowing therefore the importance of prayer in our life Jesus did not only teach his disciples how to pray[122] but also admonished them to pray in season and out of season[123]. Consequently, both Christians and Muslims must sincerely pray to their God for a divine intervention because with Him "all things are possible"[124]. Nonetheless, we must not shy away from the fact that prayer is not an easy task to accomplish especially when a dramatic change is desired, but things remain the same or sometimes even worse. This can be highly frustrating and discouraging, and the possibility of giving up becomes high. But believing in the divine intervention of God in all situations, without relent, both Christians and Muslims ought to remain committed and resilient in their prayers.

4. Conclusion

Having evaluated the activities of the Boko Haram *vis-à-vis* the impact of its terrorist activities on the socio-economic, political and religious life of Nigeria, we went further to establish that its impact cannot be quantified owing to the loss of lives and properties recorded. As a result, the Nigerian government was spurred to action in search of solution to the insurgences. But what is interesting here is that, while examining the factors that led to the emergence of the group, we established that such factors which include radicalization, poverty and unemployment, bad governance which paved the way to corruption, ignorance of religious tenets, diverse political and religious interests are inadequate reasons for the emergence of the Boko Haram, even though, the motive of the group is politico-religious as established. To this end, we held that individual choice, played a great role owing that there are millions of youths within the same region who fall within the same situational life but eschewed the temptation of becoming terrorists.

The chapter further assessed the implication of the life of Christians within such volatile environment bearing in mind the missionary mandate of Je-

---

[121] Lk 23:34

[122] Cf., Lk 11:1-4

[123] 1 Thess 5:17

[124] Mt 19:26

sus. We established that as Christians, bearing witness to the values of the Gospel within the northern region is a moral duty, although, it is highly challenging. Nevertheless, they (particularly Catholics) must not be discouraged taking into cognizance the life of the early martyrs as their models. Hence, resilience must be their watch-word for St. Paul admonished Timothy while in the prison that Christians who must live to their vocation must be ready for persecution[125].

Thereafter, the chapter stated the role of the Church whereby through the effort of the Second Vatican Council, the Church opened its windows and was infused with the fresh air of fraternity thereby asking her members to enter into dialogue with other world great religions in other to establish better relations that would bring the realization of peace, love, justice and unity not only in the northern part of Nigeria but also across the globe.

However, bearing in mind that both Christians and Muslims desire for peace within the region, the chapter advanced few recommendations that could aid toward the realization of the desired enabling environment for a peaceful coexistence that would thus boost the missionary activities of the Church. For example, the immediate need of relief for victims, reconciliation and forgiveness, and the pursuit of justice as short-term recommendations, while rehabilitation intervention, religious freedom, poverty alleviation and interreligious dialogue just to mention but few were considered long-time recommendations due to the long-time planning and execution, and *hitherto*, the involvement of intensive capital and experts.

Although, these recommendations are not exhaustive, it is interesting to note that the fight of terrorism and the realization of peace is not only the sole responsibility of the government, but it is a collective responsibility that involves all stakeholders irrespective of religious, political, cultural or territorial divide. While we encourage interreligious with great attention to dialogue of life, prayer remains the strength that every religion thrives on. Hence, the Divine Creator must be invoked in prayer by both adherents in seeking for a divine intervention.

---

[125] Cf., 2 Tim 3:12

General Conclusion

From the foregoing, we established in this research that the northern region of Nigeria has been a volatile region when compared with the other regions (south and west) of the country. Not only as a result of the presence of the Boko Haram but also due to the long existing tension between Christians and Muslims within the region that has been responsible for the intractable crises ranging from socio-political to ethno-religious crises. However, the sporadic bombings and attacks of the Boko Haram on both Christians and Muslims has taken the region to a different level of violence experiences as it was the first time to experience the use of IEDs and detonation of bombs by killing massive number of people in order to instill fear on them. This was demonstrated when we evaluated the effects of the group's terrorist activities in chapter five.

To this end, we established that the terrorist activities of the Boko Haram did not only affect the Nigerian government as a state bearing in mind that one of the primary duties of any government is to protect the life and property of its citizens, but their (Boko Haram) terrorist activities also truncated the missionary activities of the Church within the region noting the challenges they posed on the Christians as stated in subtitle number 9 of chapter two. Hence, we demonstrated that the expression of Islamic extremism has posed challenges to the Church's robust missionary activities within the region.

It is, however, imperative to note that the work is divided into five broad chapters with a general introduction and a general conclusion, while we presented a comprehensive bibliography and appendices at the end of the study. In chapter one we attempted to explore a brief historical background of terrorism with the view to understanding the development of violent acts which gradually metamorphosed into terrorism. As we demonstrated in the chapter, the zealots who were referred to as the *sicarii* (daggermen) were first reckoned with the act of terrorism in the first century in the Middle East of Palestine.

This act however, was only based on "victim-selection" in which only individuals with political high profile, security figures, kings and presidents were the targets. But as time passed-by the act of "victim-selection" transformed into indiscriminate attacks from the early 20th century alongside with its classic ideology of radical revolutionary and anarchy. This change was necessary because the goal of the terrorists was to instill fear on a wider and distant scale than that of a targeted victim alone as we have earlier noted.

However, with the collapse of the Soviet Union and the end of East-West ideological confrontation the radical leftism was replaced by radical nationalism and religious extremism in the 1990s as the two most influential ideological pillars of terrorism. This development gave rise to the emergence of modern terrorism such as Al-Qaida which in turn gave birth to the proliferation of other terrorist groups across the globe, Boko Haram inclusive.

To understand the motive of these terrorist groups in relation to religion, we demonstrated a correlation between terrorism and religion. To this end, we established that a religious terrorist group must have the following features that include; the presence of a religious leader, making of direct references to sacred books, the believe in self-sacrifice and martyrdom as an act of faith, the effect of the terrorist act must be geared toward the witness of God and the lack of distinction between religion and politics.

Bearing in mind that Boko Haram formed the thrust of our research, we further demonstrated that the terrorist group has caused a lot of havoc to the Nigerian citizens thereby bringing the country into the limelight as one of the terrorist countries within the globe. Interesting to note is that this development did not only dent the image of the country but also affected its socio-economic and political life, and *ipso facto* its religious activities within the northern region particularly the missionary activities of the Church.

It is to this end that we examined the presence of the Boko Haram in the country from its emergence as a pious group to its terrorist activities while establishing that the terrorist group had a link with other Islamic international terrorist groups that include; Al-Shabaab, Al-Qaida, and IS. The meeting of the group's key figures with the leadership of Al-Qaida in AQIM in neighbouring Niger, is a booster to the aforementioned. Nevertheless, this became more clearer when the group officially pledged its allegiance to IS in March 2015 that led to its change of name from *Jamā'at Ahl al-Sunna li'l-Da'wa wa'l-Jihād 'ala Minhāj al-Salaf* (Association of the People of the Sunna for Preaching and Jihad According to the Salafi Method) to *al-Dawla al-Islāmiyya Wilāyat Gharb Ifrīqiyā* (The Islamic State, West African Province – ISWAP).

This link obviously granted them an international sponsorship in all areas of operations that ranges from finance to training as we demonstrated in chapter one. For instance, the group's claim to have sent its members for military training to Afghanistan, Lebanon, Pakistan, Iraq, Mauritania and Algeria gave credence to the speculation as regards the possibility of their international sponsorship. It was as a result of this training that the group's modus operandi of attacks sharply changed from the use of knives, machetes, bows and arrows, and petrol bombs to the use of suicide car bombers, IEDs, and the adoption of the Al-Qaida's tactics of suicide bombings which was never known in the history of Nigeria. Thereafter we established terrorism theories that served as parameters toward the understanding of the existence and activities of the terrorist group (Boko Haram).

Being the background of the research, we examined briefly in chapter two, the historical overview of Nigeria with the view to understanding the relationship that exists between Christians and Muslims being the adherents of the two major religions (Christianity and Islam) in the country. We also established that the existing relationship between the two actors in question has not been cordial. It has created a culture of suspicion, mistrust, hatred and intolerance of one another due to religious affiliation.

These social ills often manifest themselves in almost all spheres of life of the people that continue to breed the seed of violence which is often experienced in the northern part of the country due to the obvious reason that the Northern region is far more heterogenous in nature than its counterparts – the South and the West. But salient factors such as; Colonial Conquest of the Sokoto Caliphate, the Clash of Civilization, the rise of Pentecostal and Charismatic Movements, and the two Shari'a Debates of 1978 and 1998 are established as the factors that constituted the fertile ground of the present-day expression of Islamic extremism in the region. Further more, we established that the principle of absolutism, Islamic reformation and revivalism, political emancipation of the minority (other tribes who are mostly non-Muslims) from the hand of the majority (Muslims, particularly the Hausa/Fulani), Christian fundamentalism and exclusivism, sensationalism in media reportage, religious intolerance, poverty and ignorance etc., are the causes of the intractable violence that bedeviled the region.

While the presence of this violence slowed down the socio-economic and political development of the region, it also poses challenges to the missionary activities of the Church that include; the denial of land for the building of Churches, Christian cemeteries, and mission schools, the constant abduction of Christian youths and *de facto* their forced conversion particularly young girls etc.

In the third chapter, we presented the scientific methodology of the thesis. As the main thrust of this chapter, we described in detail the research design and presented the accounts of the fieldwork while stating the reasons that informed our choice of the sampling technique employed. Bearing in mind the nature of our theme and research questions, we also employed the use of qualitative method, and in generating the desired data for the study, we employed the use of non-probability sampling method that includes; purposive sampling technique, quota sampling technique, expert sampling, and snowball/chain sampling.

It is, however, interesting to note that while in the field, we employed the use of interviews that include; semi-structured interview, one-to-one/ individual interview and focus group interview for the generation of the data. We also used participant observation that offered us the opportunity to gain more insight of the problem under investigation outside the formal interview setting by stimulating discussions that centred around our theme of research, and also by visiting areas of importance with respect to our study while taking some photographs of the visited scenes.

The issue of ethics in in this research was of paramount importance. Hence, certain ethical issues such as informed consent, confidentiality, dealing with the "self" and funding were duly considered owing that in every research, the researcher has the duty to duly inform his/her respondents on the aim and objective of the research while allowing them to make the necessary judgement to either freely participate or not without coercion.

In the same vein, it is expected that the principle of confidentiality must be observed in order to protect the participants from any danger as a result of their participation in the study. It is to this end that we employed the use of pseudonyms in place of actual names of the participants for security reasons. *Hitherto*, we insured the protection of all sensitive materials such as interview information sheets, transcripts, recorded sheets, fieldnotes etc. Having collected the data, we went further to analyse it thereby avoiding the loss of the richness of the data and the risk of a selective and superficial analysis. Worthy of note is that in the data analysis we employed the use of CAQDAS through the aid of a computer software known as Nvivo (version 11).

Our task in chapter four was to present the data gathered and discuss it. In this regard, we presented the opinions of the interviewees while maintaining the originality of the contents of their statements. This was however done in respect to the essential areas of interest as regards the problem under study while bearing in mind our research questions. With regard to Christians living out their Christian vocation, the opinions of the respondents varied. While some held that the volatile environment does not permit the Christians to authentically bear witness to their divine call, others on the other hand opined that prior to the emergence of the Boko Haram, Christians could carry out their faith-based activities without opposition. But with the presence of the terrorist group, all religious activities outside Islam were put to a halt.

In like manner, opinions differed as regard the nature of Christian-Muslim relation in the region. While some respondents held that the relationship has been cordial, others however, observed that there has been mutual suspicion between the two groups whereby at any given provocation, violence could erupt. This was however attributed to the factors that include, colonialism, cultural tight, individual political interest, manipulation of religion, and the expression of religious extremism in public spaces.

With respect to the terrorist activities of the Boko Haram, all respondents unanimously opined that its presence in the Nigerian state is a total set back to both the socio-economic and political development of the country (particularly the northern region), and the religious growth of both religions in question, owing that the group neither spare Christians nor Muslims. However, interviewees attributed the emergence of the Boko Haram to the following factors; the wide spread of Islamic radicalism across the globe, jihad/religious expansionism, politics, poverty, ignorance etc.

In this chapter, we further investigated the effects of the expression of the Islamic extremism particularly on the Church. To this end, many respondents believed that the effects are enormous which vary from the destruction of life and property, forced ejection of people from their ancestral homes, to abduction and forced conversion of Christians. In each of these incidents, Christians were always the target. Hence, these posed serious challenges to the missionary activities of the Church within the region under study.

In the final chapter (chapter five), we made an appraisal of the study by evaluating the activities of the Boko Haram while noting the impacts of its terrorism on the Nigerian State and the Church in particular. However, in respect to the motive of the terrorist group, we established based on our findings that it was neither purely political nor purely religious as the popular opinions held, but it was politico-religious in nature bearing in mind that as there were political influences, so also there were religious sentiments.

Owing to the heterogenous nature of the region, in which both Christians and Muslims live side by side with one another, the existence of different ethnic groups, and *vis-à-vis* its volatility, we examined the missiological implications of the life of Christians in respect to their missionary obligation in bearing witness to the values of the Gospel and their Saviour (Jesus Christ). Against this backdrop, from our findings we demonstrated that the hostility of the environment is really a challenging one noting the nature of the persecution that confronted them. Since, it is the duty of every Christian (particularly the baptised) to bear witness which has been the foundational mission of the Church, the need to immolate the lifestyles of the martyrs of the first century on whose blood the Church thrived cannot be overemphasised.

Thereafter, we went further, to examine the role of the Church especially in respect to her relations with the other great world religions while keeping in view Islam. While we acknowledge that the relationship was not as cordial as it is now particularly with the inception of Islam, we however, appraised the courage of the Church, for the effort made by opening her doors and windows for the fresh air of tolerance and fraternal relationship to infuse into the life of her members through the teachings of the Second Vatican Council in which she emphatically stated that individual non-Christians can also be saved[1]. Consequently, she encouraged her members to enter into dialogue and collaboration with the other religions as we noted earlier in the second paragraph of *Nostra Aetate*.

At this juncture, it is imperative to note that while keeping in mind the present situation of religious extremism and violence across the globe, the Holy Father Pope Francis, expresses his conviction in his apostolic exhortation *Evangelii Gaudium* (The Joy of the Gospel) that interreligious dialogue and collaboration are necessary elements in the mission of the Church and of the world at large. In his words he says, "interreligious dialogue is a necessary condition for peace in the world, and so it is the duty for Christians as well as other religious communities[2].

With this pronouncement, the CBCN followed suit by strengthening the Nigerian Church relations with her Muslims brethren within the country through dialogue as it is believed that dialogue fosters not only peace, but it also spreads love and tolerance. But this is farfetched because of the inactiveness of NIREC and the lack of openness from the other religion despite the enormous efforts of the CBCN. As all hope is not lost, we therefore advocated the dialogue of life which is more practicable as regards the Nigerian situation bearing in mind that it brings both Christians and Muslims together at certain events of common interest. While we recommended that interreligious dialogue is an essential tool towards the building of the destroyed bridges of relationship among Christians and Muslims in the region, deliberate efforts however, must be made by the key actors of both

---

[1] Cf., LG 16, AG 7, GS 16.
[2] FRANCIS, "Evangelii Gaudium", 250.

religions to step it down to the level of the commoners so that its impact can be better felt by all.

Consequently, as our investigation revealed, it is undoubtable that the presence of the Islamic extremism and *vis-à-vis* the menace of the intractable violence of the Boko Haram in the northern region, have truly confronted the Church with enormous challenges with regard to carrying out effectively her missionary activities within the region. Thus, we argued that these challenges however, can be overcome if the necessary steps are taken in the right direction as we pointed out in chapter five. While it is understandable that the Nigerian government must necessarily rise to its responsibilities in providing adequate security and good governance to the Nigerian citizens, the spiritual leaders of both religions on the other hand, must also continue to make concerted efforts toward the promotion of interreligious dialogue while they encourage dialogue of life particularly among the commoners of both faiths.

This effort is vividly demonstrated by the Holy Father Pope Francis (and his predecessors) in all his pastoral visits across the globe and at various audiences and meetings with religious and political authorities. To this end, his constant efforts in promoting interreligious dialogue in our present time of Christian persecution across the world and the expression of religious extremism and hates in almost all spheres of life cannot be underestimated. For example, in his recent 3-day visit to the United Arab Emirates (hence, UAE) in February 2019, which was the first visit of its kind in the history of the Arabian Peninsula (the cradle of Islam) and since the inception of Islam in the Gulf, the Holy Father stressed the need for tolerance of other minority religion(s), and walk on the path of love and peace with particular reference to the wars in Yemen, Iran, and Iraq.

Notably, the visit of the Holy Father was not only historic, but it was also significant in the life of the Church, the UAE and the world at large. Hence, this singular act draws closer the entire Gulf to the Church and *ipso facto* it strengthens the existing fragile relationship of Christians and Muslims in the Middle East as it is demonstrated by the Emirate's Crown Prince Mohammed bin Zayed who ordered the building of an inter-faith Abrahamic Family House in Abu Dhabi while an agreement was also sealed in respect to building a Church and a Mosque in honour of the visits of the Holy Father Pope Francis and the Imam of Egypt's Al Azhar Mosque and University Grand Sheik Ahmed al Tayeb.

From the foregoing, we will agree that interreligious dialogue is not the quick solution to the enormous problems, conflicts and intolerance in the given geographical space called Nigeria, neither is it the quick answer to our investigated problem. However, it is a necessary tool that must be employed by both religions. It is against this backdrop that all hands must therefore be on deck. Consequently, Government as well as religious and traditional leaders, NGOs as well as national and international organizations, individuals and all stakeholders must make the deliberate effort toward the provision of the desired enabling environment for the realization of peace and harmony within the country which we hope it will lead to a peaceful coexistence of Christians and Muslims in the northern region wherein the missionary activities of the Church will once again thrive.

But importantly, we must seek for the divine intervention of God as the Psalmist reminds us that "in vain do the labourers work, if God is not on their side" (cf., Ps 127). We must therefore, "pray with all fervor for this peace which our divine Redeemer came to bring us. May He banish from the souls of men whatever might endanger peace. May He transform all men into witnesses of truth, justice and brotherly love. May He illumine with His light the minds of rulers, so that, besides caring for the proper material welfare of their peoples, they may also guarantee them the fairest gift of peace... and may the peace (long for in the northern region) for ever flow and reign (among people in the region and the world at large)"[3].

Finally, we hope that this research will not only serve in deepening our knowledge on the nature of Islamic extremism and the challenges it posed on the missionary activities of the Church within the northern region, but it will also contribute immensely to the missiological study of the Church at large.

Possible Suggestions for Future Research

In the course of this research, I was confronted with some disturbing issues that I could not address due to the scope and limitation of our study. To the best of my knowledge I feel that these issues deserve research attention in order to address the challenges of the Church in a wider scope that covers other parts of the country and the need to realise the enabling environment that will bring peace and harmony not only within the northern region of our study but also across the length and breadth of Nigeria. It is against this backdrop that I propose the followings for future research:

1. *The relationship between Christians and Muslims in the Western and Eastern regions of Nigeria*: Owing that this research only examined the relationship between Christian and Muslims in Northern Nigeria, the study of other regions in the country will widen the scope of

---

[3] JOHN XXIII, "Pacem in Terris" §171.

288

the study and will also bring out other realities in a more diverse and wider perspective across the country since a significant number of Muslims also live side by side with Christians in the Western region and few pockets of them are also found in the Eastern region.

2. *Herdsmen versus Farmers Clash*: In like manner, there has been incessant clashes between the herdsmen and farmers across the country and as a result, many lives and properties have been destroyed. Although, the Open Door World Watch List had carried out an extensive research on the problem, it however, focused only within the northern region particularly in the Middle Belt. But a more elaborate study that will cover a wider area across the other regions in the country will give a clearer picture of the problem owing to the fact that there were incessant killings of farmers in some parts of Western and Eastern regions by the Fulani herdsmen. However, these killings are not directly linked to the Boko Haram terrorist activities, but they contribute to the tension that exists between Christians and Muslims since the nomadic farmers are linked directly with Islam.

3. *The Presence of Bandits in Northern region*: During this research, there arose a new dimension of violence within the region under investigation. Many communities in the north (particularly in Kaduna, Katsina and Zamfara States) were confronted with the incessant killings and kidnaps of their members by bandits (popularly referred to as "un-known gunmen") whose origin is not known yet. However, speculations hold that they could be a fraction of the Boko Haram that took into banditry after the group's technical defeat as claimed by the Nigerian government. A research on this problem therefore will help in understanding the reality on the ground and how best the government can confront the situation in order to bring peace and stability in the affected states and the region at large.

4. *Residential Segregation*: The existence of Residential Segregation in the region was identified as one of the factors that militates the realisation of a cohesive unity between Christians and Muslims particularly in Kaduna and Plateau States, and other states within the region. As Christians for instance, continue to build houses and reside in a Christian dominated part of the city (Kaduna South) and in like manner, the Muslims continue to build houses and reside in a Muslim dominated area (Kaduna North), the realisation of peace, harmony and unity in the state and other similar states are therefore still farfetched. A deeper research on this problem will thus help in finding a better solution to the problem.

Appendices

APPENDIX A

The demolished headquarters of the Boko Haram in Maiduguri town – adjacent to the Maiduguri railway terminus, Borno State.

Source: Taken by the author during fieldwork 2016.

APPENDIX B

The Map of Africa showing West African Region in Yellow Colour.

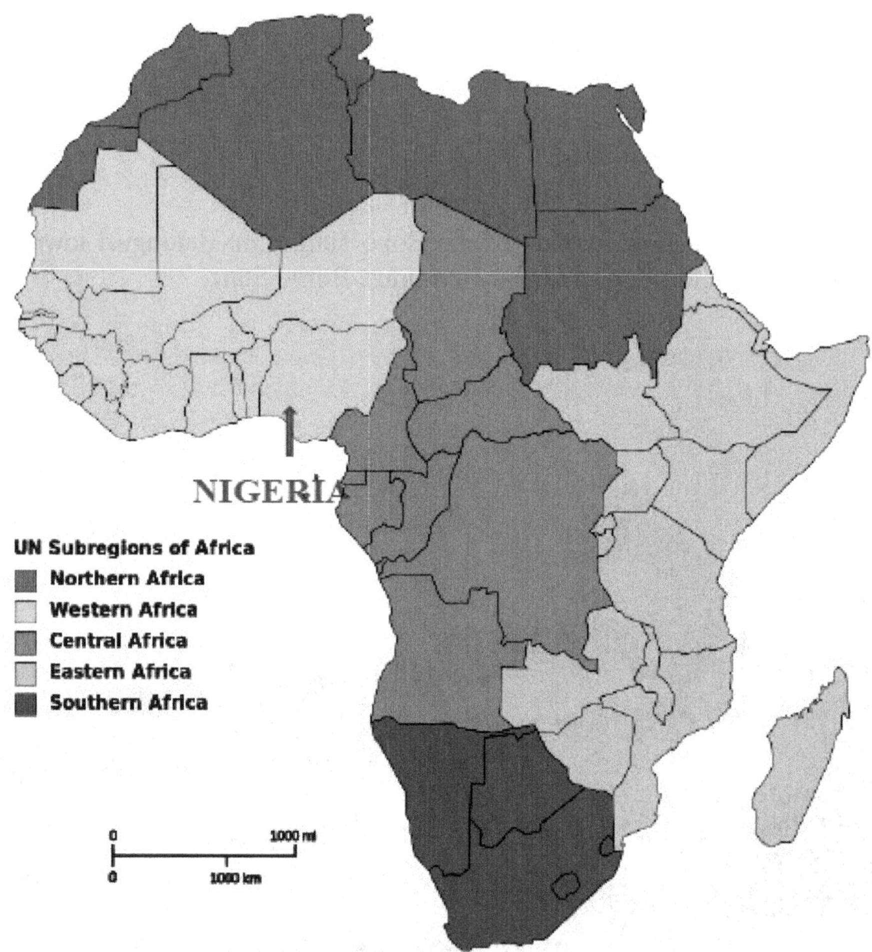

Source: www.upload.wikimedia.org/wikipedia/commons/thumb/f/f1/Africa_
map_regions.svg/749px-Africa_map_regions.svg.png, [accessed: 30.11.2017].

APPENDIX C

The Map of Nigeria showing its two major Rivers of Niger and Benue.

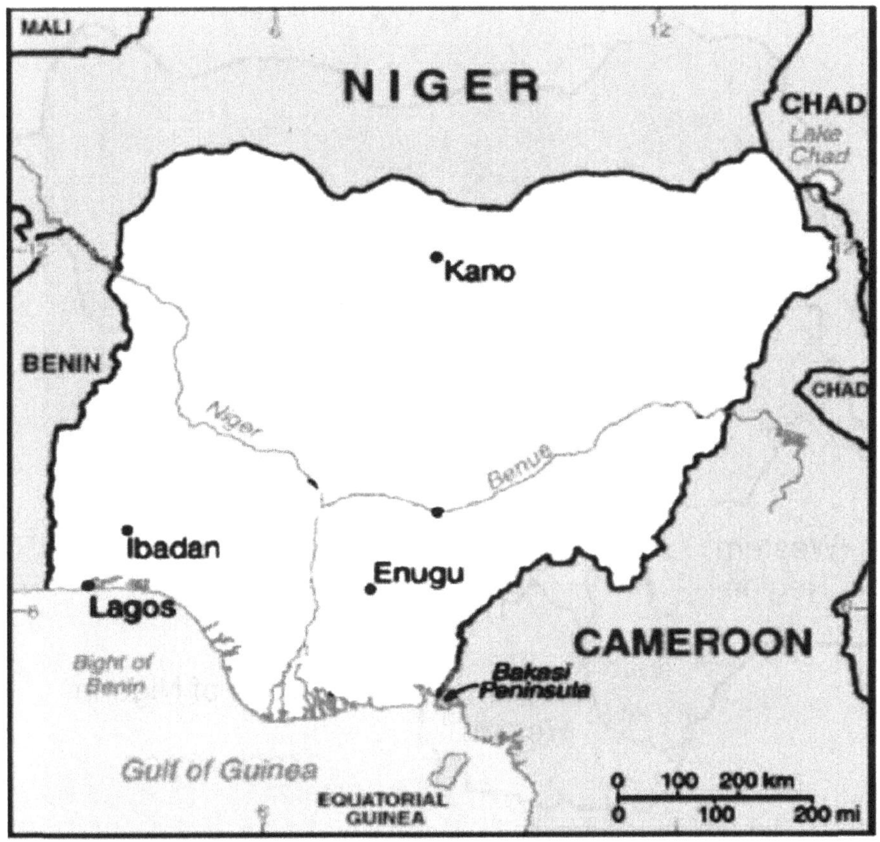

Source: www.researchgate.net/figure/Map-of-Nigeria-showing-the-36-states-and-the-Federal-Capital-Territory-FCT-Abuja_fig2_215800 573, [accessed: 14.04.2018].

APPENDIX D

The Map of Nigeria showing its former Three Major Geo-Political Regions.

Source: www.upload.wikimedia.org/wikipedia/commons/2/2b/Nigeria_ 1963-1967.png, [accessed: 30.11.2017].

APPENDIX E

The Map of Nigeria showing its Three Major Regional Dialects.

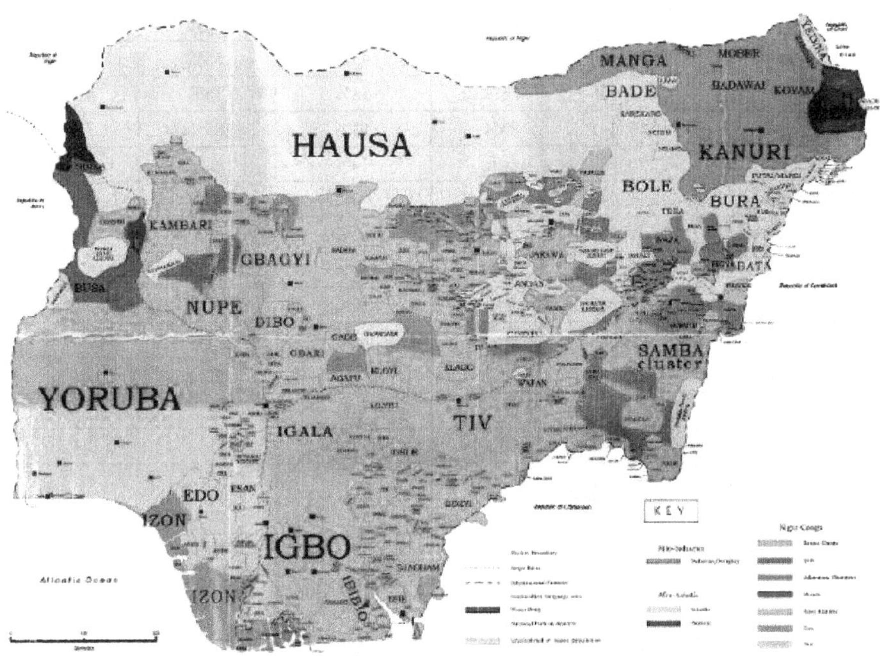

Source: www.nigerianmuse.com/wp-content/uploads/2013/10/Ethnic-Map-of-Nigeria.jpg [accessed: 30.11.2017].

APPENDIX F

Percentage of Christians per Northern State in 2014.

No.	State	Population per state[1]	Percentages of Christians (OD)[2]	Percentages of Christians (WCD)[3]	Percentages of Christians (Gaiya)[4]	Percentages of Christians (Final)[5]
1	Adamawa	3, 178, 950	75,9%	45%	55%	58.6%
2	Bauchi	4, 653, 066	35%	58%	35%	42.7%
3	Benue	4, 253, 641	85%	63%	85%	77.7%
4	Borno	4, 171, 104	40%	40%	30%	36.7%
5	Gombe	2, 365, 040	45%	40%	45%	43.3%
6	Jigawa	4, 361, 002	2%	19%	9%	10%
7	Kaduna	6, 113, 503	60%	38%	45%	47.7%
8	Kano	9, 401, 288	7%	20%	9%	12%
9	Katsina	5, 801, 584	10%	15%	10%	11.7%
10	Kebbi	3, 256, 541	40%	16%	22%	26%
11	Kogi	3, 314, 043	55%	60%	49%	54.7%
12	Kwara	2, 365, 353	40%	39%	40%	39.7%
13	Nasarawa	1, 869, 377	55%	45%	55%	51.7%
14	Niger	3, 954, 772	55%	37%	37%	43%
15	Plateau	3, 206, 531	80%	55%	80%	71.7%
16	Sokoto	3, 702, 676	1%	15%	7%	7.7%
17	Taraba	2, 294, 800	60%	46%	60%	55.3%
18	Yobe	2, 321, 339	5%	40%	5%	16.7%
19	Zamfara	3, 278, 873	1%	15%	1%	5.7%
20	FCT Abuja	1, 406, 239	45%[6]	45%	45%	45%
21	Northern Region	75, 269, 722 (53.6%)				26,194,969 (34.8%)
22	Nigeria	140,431,790 (100%)				

Source: A. MULDERS, "The Impact of Persistent Violence on the Church in Northern Nigeria" *Open Doors Research* (Unpublished work and made available to me by a colleague).

---

[1] Figures from Nigerian Population Commission, HQ Abuja internet link: http://www.population.gov.ng/ 2006 Census.

[2] Numbers based upon percentages given to Open Doors Field researchers by Church leaders, CAN Public relations officers, CAN Office of Northern states, Kaduna, CAN Officials (in some Local Government areas), and Pastors and Church workers in the Northern region.

[3] Numbers based upon the percentages of the World Christian Database in 2014, received by courtesy of Prof. Musa Gaiya, University of Jos, Department of Religious Studies.

[4] Percentages according to prof. Musa Gaiya, University of Jos, Department of Religious Studies, by email and telephone call March 2015.

[5] Numbers based upon average rate percentages of OD, WCD, AOAV and Gaiya.

[6] Due to lacking estimate figures for Christians in FCT Abuja we propose for calculation reasons 45% (Muslims 45% and ATR 10%); and this is in agreement with % WCD.

APPENDIX G

Letter of Request for the Participation in the Interview.

Via Arringo 44,
03010 Sgurgola, Fr.,
Italy.
Tel: 090 2593 2515/+39 351 048 6588
Email: nnangamo@ymail.com
26th January 2016.

TOPIC: *ISLAMIC EXTREMISM AND ITS CHALLENGES TO THE CATHOLIC MISSIONARY ACTIVITY IN NORTHERN NIGERIA SINCE 1999: A MISSIOLOGICAL STUDY.*

Dear --,
I am Rev. Fr. Bitrus Teneu Maigamo, a doctoral student of the faculty of missiology of the Pontifical Gregorian University in Rome, Italy. I was ordained a Catholic priest for the Catholic Diocese of Zaria, Kaduna State.

In view of this interview, it is conducted for the purpose of obtaining data for an empirical fieldwork on the challenges confronting the missionary activity of the Catholic Church in northern Nigeria due to Islamic extremism. The data collated will be used mainly for the analysis of the study as primary source that will assist me toward an objective evaluation that will lead to a logical conclusion and the suggestion of possible solutions.

The research is being carried out in partial fulfillment of the award of a doctoral degree in the above-named university. As the research is aimed at finding out the challenges posed to the Catholic missionary activity in the northern region by the Islamic extremists, your frank, free and open answers to the research questions will be of great assistance toward a successful study. In this regard, it is imperative to note that this interview will be conducted under the strict rule of anonymity. The data collated will be strictly used for only this scientific research, and any view expressed, observations and statements made will be treated with all sense of utmost confidentiality and respect without alteration(s).

May I therefore request for a personal interview between 30 minutes and one hour with you. The time, place and date of the interview are at your own disposal within the months of April and May 2016. I look forward to hearing from you. Kindly find above my contact of email and phone number.

Bitrus Teneu Maigamo (Rev. Fr.),
Researcher.

APPENDIX H

Letter of Consent for Participation in the Interview.

BITRUS TENEU MAIGAMO (REV. FR.)
Via Arringo 44,
03010 Sgurgola, Fr.,
Italy.
Tel: 090 2593 2515/ +39 351 048 6588
Email: nnangamo@ymail.com

CONSENT FOR PARTICIPATION IN INTERVIEW RESEARCH

I have been made known to be one of the interviewees to be interviewed in the research project to be carried out by Bitrus Teneu Maigamo (Rev. Fr.), a doctoral student of the Pontifical Gregorian University Rome, Italy. I am made to understand that the project is designed to collate data as regards the Islamic extremism in northern Nigeria and how it poses challenges to the Catholic missionary activity within the region. I wish to clearly state that:

1. My participation in this research project is voluntary, and I may decide to withdraw at any point in time without public notification.
2. Only the researcher is granted the right to conduct the interview within at least a time frame of 30 minutes to an hour.
3. Notes could be taken, and audio recording could be done during the interview, but video recording remains strictly by consent. Wherever contrary as regards the above, I will duly notify the researcher.
4. My identity must remain highly protected, and my views, observations and comments expressed must be treated with all sense of utmost confidentiality.
5. As a proof of participation, an undersigned copy therefore remains with me.

Having read and understood the explanations given to me, and have had my conditions accepted, I hereby freely volunteer and sign to participate in this research project as expected by its standard and policies.

_______________________________   ______________________   __________

Name of Participant   Signature   Date

_______________________________   ______________________   __________

Name of Researcher   Signature   Date

APPENDIX I

The List of themes as guides during the fieldwork in 2016.

1. GENERAL

TOPIC: ***ISLAMIC EXTREMISM AND ITS CHALLENGES TO THE CATHOLIC MISSIONARY ACTIVITY IN NORTHERN NIGERIA SINCE 1999: A MISSIOLOGICAL STUDY.***

A. Missiological Implications of Catholic witnessing.
1. Have you witnessed any instances of Islamic Extremism from 1999 to date that affected Christians in the northern part of Nigeria?
2. What is the nature of the Islamic extremism you witnessed? Violence? Discrimination? Deliberate exclusion from public office or services?
3. Can you please expatiate?
4. How does this Islamic Extremism affect the missionary activities of the Catholic Church in northern part of Nigeria?

B. Root Causes of Islamic Extremism
5. What are the root causes of Islamic Extremism in northern Nigeria?
6. Can you please mention some specific cases (if any)?

C. Christians – Muslims Relationship in Northern Nigeria
7. What is the relationship of Christians and Muslims in Northern Nigeria like?
8. Why is the relationship of Christians and Muslims in northern Nigeria not cordial?
9. Why the existing mutual suspicion between the adherents of the two religions in question?

D. Attitudinal Change of Christians to Muslims in Northern Nigeria.
10. Of recent, Christians in the north have become violent in their response to the Islamic violence, why this change in attitude.
11. How does this attitudinal change affect other Muslims outside the northern part of Nigeria?

E. Link between the Boko Haram and International Terrorists Groups.
12. What are the indications of a possible link of Boko Haram and the international terrorists' groups such as Al-Qaida, Al-Shabaab, IS etc?
13. What are the indications that Boko Haram intends to establish a government within a government in Nigeria?
14. Can you throw more light on this?

F. Catholic Pastoral Agents
    15. What are the responses of the Catholic Bishops and priests of the Northern Nigeria to Islamic Extremism?
    16. What is the role of Justice Development and Peace Commission (JDPC) in response to the uprising due to Islamic religious extremism?
    17. What is the position of the Christian Association of Nigeria (CAN) in respect to the constant menace of the Islamic extremism in the north?
    18. What do you think the Major Seminaries in Northern Nigeria should do to equip the seminarians as they are to face the challenges presented by Islamic extremism while in the pastoral field as priests?
    19. What Pastoral plans should dioceses in Northern Nigeria come up with in response to Islamic extremism?

G. Ways Forward Toward the Realization of a Peaceful Co-existing Society.
    20. What ways can you suggest toward the realization of a peaceful co-existing society in northern Nigeria and beyond.
    21. In what way can the government be of great help.
    22. What can both Muslims and Christians do in order to enhance the realization of a peaceful society in the northern Nigeria and beyond.

Any other Non-Governmental Organization (NGO) that can serve as a stakeholder?

2. CATHOLIC CLERGY

A. WITNESSING
    1. In your understanding of Jesus' teaching on the need of witnessing to his kingdom established here on earth, what ways and how best do you think Christians can bear witness to him in a volatile area such as the northern part of Nigeria?
    2. What are the implications of such witnessing within such a volatile terrain?

B. CHRISTIAN-MUSLIM RELATIONSHIP
    3. Before and after Nigerian independence, the relationship between Christians and Muslims was observed to be cordial and tolerant to some extent despite the experiences of the civil Biafra war and other ethno-religious crises, but of recent times especially from 1999 when democracy finally come to stay in the Nigerian political system, this relationship has been soured and characterized by suspicious, hatred and distrust particularly with the introduction of Shari'a law. In your opinion, what are the underlying factors responsible for the breakdown of this relationship and the intolerance among Christians and Muslims?
    4. How can such a soured and broken relationship be amended?

300

C. CHALLENGES TO CATHOLIC MISSIONARY ACTIVITY

5. What is your opinion as regards the Islamic extremism in northern Nigeria?
6. What are the root causes of this extremism?
7. How do Christians in the Northern part of Nigeria cope with such Islamic extremism?
8. What are the challenges confronting the Catholic Church particularly in the area of evangelization?
9. How can these challenges be tackled?
10. How can Catholic Pastoral Agents response to the Islamic extremism in northern Nigeria?
11. What Pastoral Plan do you think can be put in place in order to deepen the faith of the Catholic faithful that in return could enhance tolerance and realization of a cordial relationship with other religion(s)?
12. In your opinion, do you think there is need to introduce a course in the Northern Major Seminaries' Curriculum as part of the training that is needed to equip the Seminarians in dealing with Islamic extremism and insurgency while carrying out their pastoral assignments as priests in their respective canonical responsibilities?
13. What are your recommendations toward the realization of a peaceful co-existing society in northern Nigeria?

3. ELITE

A. CHRISTIAN-MUSLIM RELATIONSHIP

1. Before and after Nigerian independence, the relationship between Christians and Muslims was observed to be cordial and tolerant to some extent despite the experiences of the civil Biafra war and other ethno-religious crises, but of recent times especially from 1999 when democracy finally come to stay in the Nigerian political system, this relationship has been soured and characterized by suspicious, hatred and distrust particularly with the introduction of Shari'a law. In your opinion, what are the underlying factors responsible for the breakdown of this relationship and the intolerance among Christians and Muslims?
2. How can such a soured and broken relationship be amended?

B. CHALLENGES TO CATHOLIC MISSIONARY ACTIVITY

3. What is the nature of the Islamic extremism in northern Nigeria?
4. What are the root causes of this extremism?
5. How does the Islamic extremism affect Christians in Northern Nigeria?
6. How do Christians in the Northern part of Nigeria cope with such Islamic extremism?

7. What are the challenges confronting the Catholic Church particularly in the area of evangelization?
8. How can these challenges be tackled?
9. How did the government react to this extremism?
10. What are your recommendations toward the realization of a peaceful co-existing society in northern Nigeria?

4. REVISED GUIDES

A. Missiological Implications of Catholic witnessing.
1. Have you witness any religious violence from 1999 to 2015 that affected Christians in the northern part of Nigeria?
2. Can you mention any of the uprisings in question?
3. How does this religious violence affect the missionary activity of the Catholic Church in northern part of Nigeria?
4. Can you please expatiate

B. Root Causes of Islamic Extremism
5. What are the root causes of Islamic Extremism in northern Nigeria?
6. Can you please mention some specific cases?

C. Christians – Muslims Relationship in Northern Nigeria
7. Why is the relationship of Christians and Muslims in northern Nigeria is not cordial?
8. Why the existing mutual suspicious between the adherence of the two religions in question.

D. Attitudinal Change of Christians to Muslim in Northern Nigeria
9. Of recent, Christians in the north have become violent in their response to the Islamic violence, why this change in attitude.
10. How does this attitudinal change affect other Muslims outside the northern part of Nigeria?

E. Link between the Boko Haram and International Terrorists Groups.
11. What are the indications of a possible link of Boko Haram and the internal terrorists' groups such as Al-Qaida, Al-Shabaab, ISIS etc?
12. What are the indications of Boko Haram like international terrorists' groups intends to establish a government in Nigeria?
13. Can you throw more light on this?

F. Catholic Pastoral Agents
14. What are the responses of the Catholic Bishops and priests of the Northern Nigeria to Islamic Extremism?

15. What is the role of Justice Development and Peace Commission (JDPC) in the uprising due to Islamic religious extremism?
16. What is the position of the Christian Association of Nigeria (CAN) in respect of the constant menace of the religious violence in the north?

G. Ways Forward Toward the Realization of a Peaceful Co-Existing Society
17. What ways can you suggest toward the realization of a peaceful co-existing society in northern Nigeria and beyond.
18. In what way can the government be of great help.
19. What can both Muslims and Christians do in order to enhance the realization of a peaceful society in the northern Nigeria and beyond.
20. Any other Non-Governmental Organisation (NGO) that can serve as a stake holder.

APPENDIX J

Individual Interview Record Sheet.

Name of Interviewee _______________________________________

Pseudonym ____

Place of Interview ____

Age ____

Gender ____

Telephone Number ____

Occupation ____

Residence/Area ____

Date of Interview ____

Duration of Interview _____________________________________

Consent Form: YES ________________ NO _______________________

Recorded: YES ________________ NO _______________________

Observation(s):

APPENDIX K

Group Interview Record Sheet.

S/n	Name	Pseudonym	Date	Place	Age	G/der	T/phone	Residence	Occupation	D/ratn	C/sent	R/cded

Observation(s):

APPENDIX L

Nigeria's period of oil downward Trend 2013-2017.

Source: www.petrobarometer.thecable.ng/2018/02/14/oil-contribution- gdp-rebounds-four-year-fall/, [accessed: 15.12.2018].

APPENDIX M

Some photographs taken by the author during the fieldwork exercise 2016.

Catholic widows in one of the IDPs, Maiduguri

Debris of Catholic Bishop's House, Maiduguri

Battered gate of St. Michael's Parish, Maiduguri

APPENDIX N

Northern Nigeria Catholic Dioceses (Selected Statistics).

NUMBER OF PARISHES AND QUASI-PARISHES (pr)

S/NO	DIOCESE	1989	1993	2000	2005	2010	2015	2016	2018	YRC	YRC**
1	Abuja	24	12	23	36	39	66	74	81	1989	1994
2	Bauchi	-	-	-	12	16	23	23	23	2003	
3	Gboko	-	-	-	-	-	57	57	60	2012	
4	Idah	16	14	18	22	30	35	39	46	1977	
5	Jalingo	23	-	27	28	38	45	48	45	1995	
6	Jos	28	-	28	32	50	43	47	46	1953	1994
7	Kaduna	40	42	45	41	47	63	65	81	1953	1959
8	Kafanchan	21	-	25	30	33	44	48	51	1995	
9	Kano	-	-	20	28	33	36	30	36	1999	
10	Katsina-Ala	-	-	-	-	-	15	25	15	2012	
11	Kontagora	-	-	-	-	-	-	-	-	-	
12	Lafiya	-	-	-	15	21	19	17	14	2000	
13	Lokoja	15	15	15	15	24	37	39	39	1965	
14	Maiduguri	1	1	1	25	26	39	39	39	1966	
15	Makurdi	45	54	64	58	57	30	38	46	1960	
16	Minna	22	18	25	30	31	52	54	59	1973	
17	Otukpo	19	-	29	30	38	45	49	52	1995	
18	Pankshin	-	-	-	-	-	-	23	25	2014	
19	Shendam	-	-	-	-	-	-	28	28	2007	
20	Sokoto	9	9	9	14	16	24	27	27	1964	
21	Yola	18	31	21	24	26	34	34	34	1962	
22	Zaria	-	-	-	14	18	20	22	29	2000	

Source: Annuario Pontificio per l'anno, 1989, 1993, 2000, 2005, 2010, 2015, 2016 and 2018.

APPENDIX O

Northern Nigeria Catholic Dioceses (Selected Statistics).

NUMBER OF CATHOLICS (ct)

S/NO	DIOCESE	1989	2000	2005	2010	2015	2016	2018	YRC	YRC**
1	Abuja	42,793	46,708	200,000	402,000	558,115	514,105	599,750	1989	1994
2	Bauchi	-	-	68,699	78,000	79,000	80,600	84,680	2003	
3	Gboko	-	-	-	-	751,000	773,000	772,702	2012	
4	Idah	83,816	93,162	129,763	202,069	261,772	266,485	289,089	1977	
5	Jalingo	181,795	199,252	252,653	303,509	466,862	477,000	479,470	1995	
6	Jos	342,976	687,200	507,164	466,020	360,055	367,441	381,804	1953	1994
7	Kaduna	297,266	318,443	323,076	532,155	580,523	581,230	581,950	1953	1959
8	Kafanchan	227,687	233,781	250,000	285,868	308,000	309,000	320,000	1995	
9	Kano	-	105,913	123,984	181,000	198,000	202,000	212,590	1999	
10	Katsina-Ala	-	-	-	-	254,836	197,305	200,900	2012	
11	Kontagora	-	-	-	-	-	-	-	-	
12	Lafiya	-	-	189,686	190,893	421,620	421,520	245,600	2000	
13	Lokoja	29,250	35,792	36,507	30,869	33,105	33,345	38,640	1965	
14	Maiduguri	95,853	99,130	109,000	211,055	227,000	160,000	173,826	1966	
15	Makurdi	1,024,833	1,160,140	1,380,790	1,512,991	471,000	482,000	515,000	1960	
16	Minna	88,559	54,120	65,858	77,589	79,600	79,634	84,526	1973	
17	Otukpo	234,484	364,024	502,437	567,254	603,000	616,000	647,000	1995	
18	Pankshin	-	-	-	-	-	172,087	199,159	2014	
19	Shendam	-	-	-	-	173,307	179,601	172,770	2007	
20	Sokoto	31,937	43,721	60,554	45,569	30,883	31,500	39,767	1964	
21	Yola	95,553	96,083	156,890	180,652	215,786	222,656	228,000	1962	
22	Zaria	-	-	68,950	71,550	59,800	55,594	49,177	2000	

Source: Annuario Pontificio per l'anno, 1989, 2000, 2005, 2010, 2015, 2016 and 2018.

APPENDIX P

Northern Nigeria Catholic Dioceses (Selected Statistics).

NUMBER OF BAPTISMS (ba)

S/N	DIOCESE	1989	2000	2005	2010	2015	2016	2018	YRC	YRC**
1	Abuja	2,719	1	4,846	8,810	18,873	10,889	7,552	1989	1994
2	Bauchi	-	-	3,068	3,193	3,122	3,170	5,983	2003	
3	Gboko	-	-	-	-	21,976	22,062	23,663	2012	
4	Idah	3,914	4,561	5,120	6,977	4,594	4,713	5,057	1977	
5	Jalingo	12,970	10,038	12,259	10,329	10,569	13,319	17,410	1995	
6	Jos	19,066	22,697	22,367	11,650	11,436	6,891	7,505	1953	1994
7	Kaduna	20,810	13,300	12,532	7,282	17,429	13,397	14,131	1953	1959
8	Kafanchan	5,635	2,950	9,158	13,033	12,931	11,674	11,762	1995	
9	Kano	-	4,187	4,018	11,542	2,878	4,022	6,636	1999	
10	Katsina-Ala	-	-	-	-	10,357	8,974	5,916	2012	
11	Kontagora	-	-	-	-	-	-	-	-	
12	Lafiya	-	-	12,146	5,897	15,344	12,450	11,570	2000	
13	Lokoja	3,211	837	796	911	1,294	1,483	1,380	1965	
14	Maiduguri	5,019	3,880	7,002	10,388	3,777	2,190	3,503	1966	
15	Makurdi	38,347	35,945	49,927	14,980	7,916	11,203	15,876	1960	
16	Minna	2,343	3,414	5,330	3,608	5,689	6,294	9,859	1973	
17	Otukpo	9,542	16,623	19,748	9,862	8,577	9,558	9,081	1995	
18	Pankshin	-	-	-	-	-	3,781	5,235	2014	
19	Shendam	-	-	-	-	7,055	6,877	12,061	2007	
20	Sokoto	2,003	2,514	2,918	2,252	3,394	1,391	2,490	1964	
21	Yola	3,795	3,889	6,184	5,032	5,881	6,970	4,727	1962	
22	Zaria	-	-	2,057	2,440	1,565	1,839	2,133	2000	

Source: Annuario Pontificio per l'anno, 1989, 2000, 2005, 2010, 2015, 2016 and 2018.

Abbreviations

AAS	*Acta Apostolicae Sedis*
Acts	Acts of the Apostle
AECAWA	Association of Episcopal Conferences of Anglophone West Africa
AG	*Ad Gentes Divinitus*, Decree on the Missionary Activity of the Church of the Second Vatican Council (December 7, 1965)
al.	*allii* (others)
AnPont	*Annuario Pontificio per l'anno*
AQIM	Al-Qaida in the Islamic Maghreb
ATR	African Traditional Religion
BBC	British Broadcasting Corporation
BCW	Biafra Civil War
BJS	*British Journal of Sociology*
CA	Constituent Assembly
CAN	Christian Association of Nigeria
can.	Canon of the Code of Canon Law
CAQDAS	Computer Assisted Qualitative Data Analysis
CBCN	Catholic Bishops Conference of Nigeria
CCC	*Catechism of the Catholic Church*, 1994.
CDC	Constitution Drafting Committee
CE	Common Era
Cf.	Confer
CIC	*Codex Iuris Canonici* (Code of Canon Law), 1983.
CMS	Church Missionary Society
CNN	Cable News Network
COCIN	Church of Christ in Nigeria
COIN	Counter-insurgency
CoT	Counter-terrorism
CPI	Corruption Perception Index
CSN	Catholic Secretariat of Nigeria
CSTPV	Centre for the Study of Terrorism and Political Violence

CTC	*Combating Terrorism Center*
DDR	Disarmament, Demobilization, and Reintegration
DH	*Dignitatis Humanae*, Declaration of Religious Freedom of the Second Vatican Council (December 7, 1965)
DPO	Divisional Police Officer
DPOs	Disabled Peoples Organizations
ed.	Editor
edit.	Edition
EFCC	Economic and Financial Crimes Commission
Eng. Trans.	English Translations
EOKA	*Ethniki Organosis Kyprion Agoniston* – National Organization of Cypriot Fighters (Cyprus)
EU	European Union
etc.	*Et cetera* (and so on)
FAH	Frustration-Aggression Hypothesis
FCS	Fellowship of Christian Students
FCT	Federal Capital Territory
FLN	*Front de libération nationale* – National Liberation Front (Algeria)
FLP	Popular Front for the Liberation of Palestine
FRCN	Federal Radio Corporation of Nigeria
GDP	Gross Domestic Product
GJPLR	*Global Journal of Politics and Law Research*
GOs	General Overseers
GS	*Gaudium et Spes*, Pastoral Constitution on the Church in the Modern World of the Second Vatican Council (December 7, 1965)
GSs	General Superintendents
GTI	Global Terrorism Index
GWI	Global World Index
HDI	Human Development Index
ICPC	Independent Corrupt Practices Commission
ICRC	International Committee of the Red Cross
IDI	Individual Depth Interview
IDP	Internally Displaced Persons
IEDs	Improvised Explosive Devices
IEP	Institute for Economics and Peace
IFRA	*Institut Français de Recherche en Afrique*
IJRHSS	*Internal Journal of Research in Humanities and Social Studies*

IMU	Islamic Movement of Uzbekistan
IRA	Irish Republican Army
IS	Islamic State
ISIM	International Institute for the Study of Islam in the Modern World
ISPAC	International Scientific and Professional Advisory Council
ISWAP	Islamic State of West African Province
JASLWJ	*Jama'atu Ahlis Sunna Lidda'awati Wal-Jihad*
JDPC	Justice, Development and Peace Commission
JETS	*Journal of the Evangelical Theological Society*
Jn	Gospel of John
JNI	*Jama'atu Nasril Islam*
JHSS	*Journal of Humanities and Social Studies*
JOCRED	*Journal of Christian Religion and Education*
JORAS	*Journal of Religion and Society*
JTI	*Jamā'at Tajdīd al-Islām*
JTORO	Operation Restore Order
LG	*Lumen Gentium*, Dogmatic Constitution on the Church of the Second Vatican Council (November 21, 1964)
Lk	Gospel of Luke
LOC	Local Organising Committee
LSE	London School of economics and Political Science
Mbpd.	Million Barrels Per Day
Mk	Gospel of Mark
MSS	Muslim Students' Society
Mt	Gospel of Matthew
MUJAO	Movement for Unity and Jihad in West Africa
MZL	Middle Zone League
NA	Native Authority
NATO	North Atlantic Treaty Organization
NAPEC	National Action Plan on Employment Creation
NBS	National Bureau of Statistics
NCA	Northern Christian Association
NCE	*New Catholic Encyclopaedia*, B.L. Marthaler – al., eds., Thomson Gale, Farmington Hills, VI, 2003[2].
NCN	Nigerian Cable News
NDDC	Niger Delta Development Commission
NEP	National Employment Policy
NGOs	Non-Governmental Organizations
NIAS	Netherlands Institute for Advanced Studies in the Humanities

	and Social Sciences
NIREC	Nigeria Inter-Religious Council
NML	Non-Muslim League
NNPC	Nigerian National Petroleum Corporation
NOREF	*Norsk Ressurssenter for Fredsbyggin* (The Norwegian Peacebuilding Resource Centre)
NPC	Northern People's Congress
NPE	National Policy on Education
NRDC	Northern Region Development Commission
NSRP	Nigeria Stability and Reconciliation Programme
NYP	National Youth Policy
ODWWL	Open Door World Watch List
OFMI	Omega Fire Ministries International
OIC	Organization of Islamic Countries
PCID	*Pontifical Council for Interreligious Dialogue*
PIOOM	Interdisciplinary Research Programme on Causes of Human Rights Violations
PLO	Palestine Liberation Organization
PPRO	Police Public Relation Officer
Ps	Book of the Psalms
PwDs	People with Disabilities
Q	Quarter (of the year)
Rev	Book of Revelation
RF	Risk Factors theory
Rm	Letter of St. Paul to the Romans
RNC	Royal Niger Company
RSV	Revised Standard Version
SIM	Sudan Interior Mission
SIPRI	Stockholm International Peace Research Institute
SLATT	State and Local Antiterrorism Training
SMA	Society of the Missions of Africa
SUM	Sudan United Mission
TPA	Terrorism Prevention Act
Tr.	Translator
Trans.	Translation
TRC	Truth and Reconciliation Commission
TRI	Terrorism Research Initiative
UAE	United Arab Emirates
UMBC	United Middle Belt Congress
UN	United Nations

UNDP	United Nations Development Programme
UNICEF	United Nations International Children's Emergency Fund
UNODC	United Nations Office on Drugs and Crime
WAFF	West African Frontier Force
WCC	World Council of Churches
WCRP	World Conference on Religion and Peace
WHO	World Health Organization
WWL	World Watch List
1 Thess	First letter of St. Paul to the Thessalonians
2Tim	Second letter of St. Paul to Timothy
§	Paragraph
#	Number

Bibliography

I. **Primary Sources**

Fieldwork Interviews

AJAYI, "Interview with the author", Zaria, May 20, 2016.
ANKOYOYO, "Interview with the author", Maiduguri, May 3, 2016.
ASABE, "Interview with the author", Maiduguri, April 30, 2016.
AVA, "Interview with the author", Jos, June 2, 2016.
BELLO, "Interview with the author", Zaria, May 18, 2016.
CHATSOMEN, "Interview with the author", Kaduna, May 16, 2016.
CHENDA, "Interview with the author", Maiduguri, May 2, 2016.
CHOKIST, "Interview with the author", Jos, June 1, 2016.
DACCOS, "Interview conducted with the author", Lafiya, April 20, 2016.
DANJUMA, "Interview with the author", Jos, June 2, 2016.
DURSA, "Interview with the author", Maiduguri, May 4, 2016.
FUKS, "Interview with the author", Jos, June 1, 2016.
IJAGALA, "Interview with the author", Maiduguri, April 30, 2016.
INDAGIJI, "Interview with the author", Maiduguri, April 30, 2016.
IPWUPERJOH, "Interview with the author", Maiduguri, May 1, 2016.
JAMADA, "Interview with the author", Maiduguri, April 30, 2016.
MALLAM, "Interview with the author", Jos, June 2, 2016.
MUHAMMED, "Interview with the author", Kaduna, May 16, 2016.
NCHOK, "Interview with the author", Zaria, June 6, 2016.
NGOSHINDA, "Interview with the author", Maiduguri, April 30, 2016.
PARANGWOM, "Interview with the author", Maiduguri, April 28, 2016.
TAMPAI, "Interview with the author", Maiduguri, April 30, 2016.
USMAN, "Interview with the author", Zaria, May 23, 2016.

II. **Secondary Sources**

1. **Sacred Book**

___, *The Holy Bible*, RSV, Catholic ed., Ignatius Press, San Francisco, 2006².

2. The Documents of the Church

2.1 *Vatican II Documents*

SECOND VATICAN COUNCIL, "Ad Gentes Divinitus", Decree on the Church's Missionary Activity, *AAS* 58 (1966), 947-990, in A. FLANNERY, ed., (Eng. Trans.), *Vatican Council II: The Conciliar and Post Conciliar Documents*, I, St. Pauls, New Delhi, 2013, 715-758.

——————, "Lumen Gentium", Dogmatic Constitution on the Church, *AAS* 57 (1965), 5-71, in A. FLANNERY, ed., (Eng. Trans.), *Vatican Council II: The Conciliar and Post Conciliar Documents*, I, St. Pauls, New Delhi, 2013, 320-385.

——————, "Gaudium et Spes, Pastoral Constitution on the Church in the Modern World, *AAS* 58 (1966), 1025-1115, in A. FLANNERY, ed., (Eng. Trans.), *Vatican Council II: The Conciliar and Post Conciliar Documents*, I, St. Pauls, New Delhi, 2013, 794-879.

2.2 *Pontifical/Church Documents*

PONTIFICAL COUNCIL FOR INTER-RELIGIOUS DIALOGUE, "Dialogue and Proclamation. Reflections and Orientations on Interreligious Dialogue and the Proclamation of the Gospel of Jesus Christ," in *PCID Bulletin*, 77, Vatican City, Rome (1991).

AnPont, 2014, Libreria Editrice Vatican, Città del Vaticano, 2014.

BENEDICT XVI, "Africae Munus", Apostolic Exhortation on the Church in Africa in Service to Reconciliation, Justice and Peace, *AAS* 104 (2012), 239-314.

——————, "Ecclesia in Medio Oriente", Apostolic Exhortation, *AAS* 104 (October 2012), 751-796.

——————, "New Year Address to Diplomatic Corps 2011", January 10, 2011, Rome, [accessed: 25.11.2018], w2.vatican.va/content/benedict-xvi/en/speeches/2011/ january/documents/hf_ben-xvi_spe_20110110_ diplomatic-corps.html.

BENEDICT XVI, "World Day of Peace 2011", [accessed: 10.05.2018], w2.vatican.va/content/benedictxvi/en/messages/peace/documents/hfben-xvi_mes_20101208_xliv-world-day-peace.html.

——————, "World Day of Peace 2011", [accessed: 10.05.2018], w2.vatican.va/content/benedict-xvi/en/messages/peace/documents/hf_ben-xvi_mes_20101208_xliv-world-day-peace.html

——————, "Address to the Representatives of the Muslim Community of Cameroon, Yaoundé (March 19, 2009), Liberia Editrice Vaticana, 2009, [accessed: 01.06.2018], w2.vatican.va/content/benedict-xvi/

en/speeches/2009/march/documents/hf_ben-xvi_spe_20090319_
comunita-musulmana.html.

FRANCIS, "Evangelii Gaudium", Apostolic Exhortation on the Proclamation of the Gospel in Today's World, *AAS* 105 (2013), 1019-1137.

JOHN XXIII, "Pacem in Terris", Encyclical on establishing Universal Peace in Truth, Justice, Charity, and Liberty, *AAS* 55 (1963) 257-304.

JOHN PAUL II, "Tertio Millennio Adveniente", Apostolic Letter on the Preparation for the Jubilee on the Year 2000, *ASS* 87 (1995), 5-41.

——————, "Redemptoris Missio", Encyclical on the Permanent Validity of the Church's Missionary Mandate, *AAS* 83 (1991), 249-340.

——————, "Address Before the Angelus (November 18, 2001), [accessed: 01.06.2018], w2.vatican.va/content/johnpaulii/en/angelus/2001/documents/hf_jpii_ang_20011118.html.

——————, "Message for the XXV Annual World Day of Prayer for Peace Believers United in Building Peace", [access: 4.12.2018], w2.vatican.va/content/johnpaulii/en/messages/peace/documents/hf_jpii_mes_08121991_xxv-world-day-for-peace.html.

PAUL VI, "Evangelii Nuntiandi", Apostolic Exhortation, *AAS*, 68 (1976), 5-76.

——————, "Dignitatis Humanae", Declaration on Religious Freedom on the Right of the Person and of Communities to Social and Civil Freedom in Matters Religious, *AAS*, 58 (1966), 929-946, in A. FLANNERY, ed., (Eng. Trans.), *Vatican Council II: The Conciliar and Post Conciliar Documents*, I, St. Pauls, New Delhi, 2013, 703-714.

——————, "Nostra Aetate", Declaration on the Relation of the Church to Non-Christian Religions, *AAS*, 58 (1966), 740-744, in A. FLANNERY, ed., (Eng. Trans.), *Vatican Council II: The Conciliar and Post Conciliar Documents*, I, St. Pauls, New Delhi, 2013, 653-656.

PIUS XII, "Evangelii Praecones", Encyclical on the Promotion of Catholic Missions, *AAS* 43 (1951), 497-528.

——————, *Codex Iuris Canonici* (CIC),

PIUS XII, *The Catechism of the Catholic Church* (CCC), Paulines Publications Africa, Nairobi, 1995.

2.3 *Catholic Bishops Conference of Nigerian Communiques*

CATHOLIC BISHOPS' CONFERENCE OF NIGERIA (CBCN), "Current Unrest" in *Our Concern for Nigeria. Catholic Bishops Speak*, Chris Anyanwu – Otunba Jide Fadugba-Pinheiro (eds.), Catholic Secretariat of Nigeria (CSN), Abuja, 2015, 9-10.

——————, "Concern for the Political, Moral, and Educational Trends in Nigeria", in *Our Concern for Nigeria: Catholic Bishops Speak*, Chris

Anyanwu & Otunba Jide Fadugba-Pinheiro (eds.), Catholic Secretariat of Nigeria (CSN), Abuja, 2015, 21-23.

——————, "The Lord Comforts his People (Isaiah 40:1)", in *Our Concern for Nigeria: Catholic Bishops Speak*, Chris Anyanwu & Otunba Jide Fadugba-Pinheiro (eds.), Catholic Secretariat of Nigeria (CSN), Abuja, 2015, 333-338.

3. **Other Religious Books**

ALI, A.Y., tr., *The Holy Qur'an*. English Translation with original 'Arabic Text, Kitab Bhavan, New Delhi, 2011.

4. **Books**

ADELEYE, R.A., *Power and Diplomacy in Northern Nigeria 1804-1906. The Sokoto Caliphate and Its Enemies*, Humanities Press, New York, 1971.

ADIBE, J., *Nigeria Without Nigerians. Boko Haram and the Crisis in Nigeria's Nation-Building*, Adonis & Abbey Publishers Ltd., London, 2012.

AJAYI, J.F.A., *Christian Missions in Nigeria 1841-1891. The Making of a New Elite*, Longman, Green and Co. Ltd, London, 1965.

AJIBOYE-DARE, M.F., *Terrorism. The Nigerian Perspective*, LAP Lambert Academic Publishing, Saarbrücken, Deutschland/Germany, 2016.

AKINADE, A.E., *Christian Responses to Islam in Nigeria. A Contextual Study of Ambivalent Encounters*, Palgrave Macmillan, 2014.

ALLEN, J.L. Jr., *The Global War on Christians. Dispatches from the Front Lines of Anti-Christian Persecution*, Image, New York, 2013.

AN-NA'IM, A.A., *Islam and the Secular State. Negotiating the Future of Shari'a*, Harvard University Press, Cambridge, 2008.

ARINZE, F., *Religions for Peace. A Call for Solidarity to the Religions of the World*, Darton, Longman, and Todd Ltd., 2002.

——————, "Interreligious Dialogue at the Service of Peace", in *Interreligious Dialogue. Catholic Perspectives*, J.H. KROEGER, ed., Mission Studies Institute, Philippines, 1990, 87-94.

AUGUSTINE, *City of God* VIII, 27, 1, PL41.

——————, *Confessions*, Book I.

AYANDELE, E.A., "The Missionary Factor in Northern Nigeria 1870-1918", in *The History of Christianity in West Africa*, O.U. KALU, ed., Longmans London 1982, 133-158.

BAGAJII, A.S.Y. – al., "Boko Haram and the Recurring Bomb Attacks in Nigeria. Attempt to Impose Religious Ideology through Terrorism?", in *Annual Editions: Violence and Terrorism*, T.J. Badey, ed., McGraw-Hill Education, USA 14 (2013), 67-74.

BAILEY, K.D., *Methods of Social Research*, The Free Press, New York, 1994[4].

BALOGUN, K.A., "Religious Intolerance as a Source of National Disintegration" *Religion and National Unity*, B.S. Mala, ed., University Press, Ibadan, 1988, 153-172.

BECKER, H.S., *Outsiders' Studies in the Sociology of Deviance*, Free Press, New York, 1963.

BERG, B.L., *Qualitative Research Methods for the Social Sciences*, Allyn & Bacon, Boston, 2001.

BERKEY, J.P., "The Muhtasibs of Cairo under the Mamluks. Toward an Understanding of an Islamic Institution", in *The Mamluks in Egyptian and Syrian Politics and Society*, M. Winter – A. Levanoni, eds., Brill Leiden, Boston (2004), 245-276.

BEST, S.G., *Introduction to Peace and Conflict Studies in West Africa: A Reader*, Spectrum Books, Ibadan, 2006.

BEVANS, S.B. – GROSS J., *Evangelization and Religious Freedom. Ad Gentes, Dignitatis Humanae*, Paulist Press, New York, 2009.

BICKMAN, L., "Data Collection I. Observational Methods", in *Research Methods in Social Relations*, C. SELLTIZ – al., eds., Holt, Rinehart and Winston, New York, 1976[3], 251-290.

BLOOR, M – al (eds.), *Focus Groups in Social Research*, Sage Publications, London, 2001.

BOER, J.H., *Muslims: Why the Violence?*, Essence Publishing, Belleville, Ontario, Canada, 2, 2004.

——————, *Nigeria's Decades of Blood 1980-2002*, Essence Publishing, Belleville, Canada, 2003.

BORUM, R., *Psychology of Terrorism*, University of South Florida, Tampa, 2004.

BREMMER, J.N., "Religious Violence between Greeks, Romans, Christians and Jews" *Violence in Ancient Christianity. Victims and Perpetrators*, A.C. Geljon – R. Roukema, eds., Brill, Leiden, Netherlands, 2014, 8-30.

BRUCE, H., *Inside Terrorism*, Columbia University Press, New York, 1998.

BURROWS, W.R., *Redemption and Dialogue. Reading Redemptoris Missio and Dialogue and Proclamation*, Wipf and Stock Publishers, Eugene, 1993.

CAMPBELL, A., *The Assassins of Alamut*, Lulu Com, 2008.

CENTRE OF EXCELLENCE DEFENCE AGAINST TERRORISM ed, *Legal Aspect of Combating Terrorism*, IOS, Netherland, 2008.

CHALIAND, G – ARNAUD, eds., *The History of Terrorism: From Antiquity to Al-Qaida*, trans. E. Schneider – al., University of California Press, Berkeley, 2007.

COCO, L., ed., *Interreligious Dialogue. Pope Benedict XVI Spiritual Thoughts Series*, Eng. Trans., Libreria Editrice Vaticana, Roma, 2012.

COMMINS, D., *The Wahhabi Mission and Saudi Arabia*, I.B. Tauris & Co Ltd., New York, 2006.

CONTEH-MORGAN, E., *Collective Political Violence. An Introduction to the Theories and Cases of Violent Conflicts*, Routledge, New York, 2004.

CRAMPTON, E.P.T., *Christianity in Northern Nigeria*, Geoffrey Chapman, London, 1979.

————, *Christianity in Northern Nigeria*, Kaduna. Baraka Press and Publishers, 2004.

CRESWELL, J.W., *Research Design. Qualitative, Quantitative, and Mixed Methods Approaches*, 2nd ed., Sage Publications, London, 2002.

CROWDER, M., *The Story of Nigeria*, Faber & Faber Ltd, London, 1978.

DAFTARY, F., *The Assassin Legends. Myths of the Isma'ilis*, Tauris, London, 1994.

DE MONTCLOS, M.P., "Boko Haram and Politics. From Insurgency to Terrorism", *Boko Haram. Islamism, Politics, Security and the State of Nigeria*, M.P. De Montclos ed., African Studies Centre (ASC), Leiden, 2 (2014), 135-157.

DENNY, F.M., *An Introduction to Islam*, Macmillan, London, 1994.

DENSCOMBE, M., *The Good Research Guide. For a Small-Scale Social Research Projects*, Open University Press, Berkshire, 2007[3].

————, *The Good Research Guide. For Small-Scale Social Research Projects*, McGraw Hill, Open University Press, Berkshire, 2010[4].

DENZIN, N.K., *The Research Act*, Prentice Hall, New Jersey, 1989[3].

EIDE, A.H., "Community-Based Rehabilitation in Post-conflict and Emergency Situations", in *Trauma Rehabilitation after War and Conflict. Community and Individual Perspective*, E. MARTZ, ed., Springer, New York, 2010, 97-110.

EKECHI, F.K., *Missionary Enterprise and Rivalry in Igbo land. 1857-1914*, Frank Cass, London, 1972.

EZEH, M.E., *Archbishop Charles Heerey and the History of the Church in Nigeria 1890-1967*, St. Pauls, Mumbai, 2005.

FALETI, S.A., "Theories of Social Conflict", in *Introduction to Peace and Conflict Studies in West Africa*, S.G. BEST, ed., Spectrum Books Limited, Ibadan (2006), 35-60.

FALOLA, T. – HEATON M.M., *A History of Nigeria*, Cambridge University Press, United Kingdom, 2008.

FALOLA, T., *Colonialism and Violence in Nigeria*, Indiana University press, Bloomington, 2009.

——————, *The History of Nigeria*, Greenwood Press, London, 1999.

FERGUSON, J., *War and Peace in the World's Religions*, Oxford University Press, New York, 1978.

FITZGERALD, M.L – CASPAR R., *Signs of Dialogue. Christian Encounter with Muslims,* Silsilah Publications, Zamboanga, Philippines, 1992.

FLICK, U., *An Introduction to Qualitative Research*, Sage Publications, London, 2006³.

FREY, B.S., *Dealing with Terrorism – Stick or Carrot?*, Edward Elgar Publishing Limited, Cheltenham, 2004.

GBADAMOSI, T.G., *The Growth of Islam Among the Yoruba 1841-1908,* Oxford University Press, London, 1978.

GOFWEN, R.R., *Religious Conflicts in Northern Nigeria and Nation Building. The Throes of Two Decades 1980-2000*, Human Rights Monitor, Kaduna, 2004.

GUNARATNA, R., *Inside Al Qaeda. Global Network of Terror*, Columbia University Press, New York, 2002.

GUS, M., *Understanding Terrorism. Challenges, Perspectives, and Issues*, Sage Publications, Inc., California, 2006.

GWAMNA, D. – DAYIL P.B., "Religious Fundamentalism in Northern Nigeria. Towards an Interpretation", in *Religion and PostConflict Peacebuilding in Northern Nigeria* S.G. Best, ed., John Archers, Ibadan, 2011, 66-85.

HABERFELD, M.R., "Today's Terrorism – Introduction and Analysis. The Have Nots Versus the Haves" *A New Understanding of Terrorism. Case Studies, Trajectories and Lessons Learned*, M.R. Haberfeld – A. von Hassell eds., Springer, New York, 2009, 1-8.

HARMON, C., *Terrorism Today*, Frank Cass, London, 2000.

HARNISCHFEGER, J., *Democratization and Islamic Law. The Shari'a Conflict in Nigeria*, Campus Verlag, New York, 2008.

HEGGHAMMER, T., "Jihadi-Salafis or Revolutionaries. On Religion and Politics in the Study of the Islamist Militancy", in *Global salafism. Islam's New Religious Movement*, R. Meijer (ed.), Columbia University Press, New York, 2009, 244-266.

HICKEY, R., *The Growth of the Church in Northern Nigeria. An Historical Perspective*, Fab Anieh, Jos, 2010.

HILL, J.B., *The Theology of Martin Luther King, Jr. and Desmond Mpilo Tutu*, Palgrave Macmillan, New York, 2007.

HOFFMAN, B., *Inside Terrorism, New Revised and Expanded Edition*, Columbia University Press, New York, 2006.

HOLSTEIN, J.A. – GUBRIUM, J.F., "The Active Interview" in *Qualitative Research. Theory, Method and Practice*, D. SILVERMAN, ed., Sage Publications, London, 2004, 140-160.

HORGAN, J., *The Psychology of Terrorism*, Routledge, London, 2005.

——————, "The Search for the Terrorist Personality", in *Terrorists, Victims and Society. A Psychological Perspective on Terrorism and its Consequences*, S. ANDREW, ed., John Wiley & Sons Ltd., West Sussex, 2003, 3-27.

HUNTINGTON S.P., *The Clash of Civilization and the Remaking of World Order*, Simon & Schuster, New York, 1996.

IFEMESIA, C.C., *States of Central Sudan. Thousand Years of West African History – A Handbook for Teachers and Students*, J.F.A. Ajayi – I. Espie, eds., Ibadan University Press, Nigeria (1967), 72-112.

IKEIME, O., *The Isoko People. A Historical Survey*, University Press, Ibadan, 1972.

ISHAKU, J., *The Road to Mogadishu. How Jihadist Terrorism Tears Nigeria Apart*, I.M.P.A.C.T. Nigeria, 2012.

IWUCHUKWU, M., *Muslim-Christian Dialogue in Post-Colonial Northern Nigeria. The Challenges of Inclusive Cultural and Religious Pluralism*, Palgrave Macmillan, New York, 2013.

JENKINS, P., *The Next Christendom. The Coming of Global Christianity*, Oxford University Press, New York, 2002.

JENKINS, P., *God's Continent. Christianity, Islam, and Europe's Religious Crisis*, Oxford University Press, New York, 2007.

JUNG, C., *Civilization in Transition*, New York, Pantheon Books, 1964.

KAIGAMA, I.A., *Peace, not War. A Decade of Interventions in the Plateau State Crises (2001-2011)*, Hamtul Press Ltd., Jos, 2012.

——————, *Dialogue of Life. An Urgent Necessity for Nigerian Muslims and Christians*, Fab Education Books, Jos, 2006.

KHALIL, G., "Etiology of Deviant Behaviour", in *Theory and Politics of Terrorism*, J.L. Feldkamp, ed., I, USA 2014, 23-38.

KALU, O., *African Pentecostalism. An Introduction*, Oxford University Press, New York, 2008.

KANE, O., *Muslim Modernity in PostColonial Nigeria. A Study of the Society for the Removal of Innovation and Reinstatement of Tradition*, Brill Leiden, Boston, 2003.

KEEGAN, S., *Qualitative Research. Good Decision Making Through Understanding People, Cultures and Markets*, Kogan Page, London, 2009.

KUKAH, M.H., "Boko Haram. Some Reflections on Causes and Effects," *Boko Haram. Religious Conflict and Dialogue Initiatives in Nigeria*, S.O. ANYANWU – I. NWANAJU, eds., Edu-Edy Publications, 1, 2010, 1-13.

——————, *Religion, Politics and Power in Northern Nigeria*, Spectrum Books Limited, Ibadan, Nigeria, 1994.

LAMIDO, A.B., *The CMS in Wusasa. A Divine Mission to Hausaland*, Tamaza Publishing Co. Ltd., 2005.

LAQUEUR, W., *A History of Terrorism*, Transaction, New Brunswick, New Jersey, 2001.

LEAMAN, O., ed., *The Qur'an. An Encyclopedia*, Routledge Taylor and Francis Group, London, 2006.

LEMERT, E.M., *Human Deviance, Social Problems, and Social Control*, Pretence-Hall, Englewood Cliffs, New Jersey, 1972.

LEWIS, C., *The Functions of Social Conflict*, Free Press, New York.

LOPES, A., *The Popes. The Lives of the Pontiffs through 2000 Years of History*, Futura Edizioni, Roma, 2005.

LYONS, P., *The Dissertation. From Beginning to End*, Oxford University Press, New York, 2010.

MAKOZI, A.O. – OJO G.J.A eds., *The History of the Catholic Church in Nigeria*, Macmillan Nigerian Publishers Limited, Lagos, 1982.

MAMBULA, M.A., *Nigeria. Ethno-Religious and Socio-Political Violence and Pacifism in Northern Nigeria*, Page Publishing Inc., New York, 2016.

MAOZ, Z., *Paths to Conflict, International Dispute Initiation, 1816-1976*, Westview Press, Boulder Col., 1982.

MARC, R., *The Management of Conflict. Interpretations and Interests in Comparative Perspective*, Yale University Press, New Haven, 1993, 18.

MARCZYK, G. – al., *Essentials of Research Design and Methodology*, John Wiley & Sons, Inco., New Jersey, 2005.

MARTZ, E., "Introduction to Trauma Rehabilitation After War and Conflict", in *Trauma Rehabilitation after War and Conflict. Community and Individual Perspective*, E. MARTZ, ed., Springer, New York, 2010, 1-25.

MASLOW, A., *Motivation and Personality*, Macmillan, New York, 1970[2].

MCALLISTER, B. – SCHMID, A.P., "Theories of Terrorism", in *The Routledge Handbook of Terrorism Research*, A.P. SCHMID, ed., Routledge, New York, 2011, 201-271.

MOHAMMED, K., "The Message and Methods of Boko Haram", *Boko Haram. Islamism, Politics, Security and the State of Nigeria*, M.P. De Montclos, ed., African Studies Centre (ASC), Leiden, 2 (2014), 9-32.

NWANAJU, I., *Christian-Muslim Relations in Nigeria*, Logos Verlag, Berlin, 2008.

O'CONNOR, E., *From the Niger to the Sahara. The Story of the Archdiocese of Kaduna*, SMA Fathers, Abuja, 2009.

OJO, M.A., "Competition and Conflict. Pentecostals' and Charismatics' Engagement with Islam in Nigeria", *The African Christian and Islam*, J. AZUMAH – L. SANNEH, eds., Langham Monographs, Cumbria (2013) 147-175.

OLOMOJOBI, Y., *Islam and Conflict in Northern Nigeria*, Malthouse Press Limited, Lagos, 2013.

ONAIYEKAN, J., The African Christian and Islam. The Roman Catholic Perspective" *The African Christian and Islam*, J. AZUMAH – L. SANNEH, eds., Langham Monographs, Cumbria (2013) 103-121.

ONUOHA, F., "Boko Haram and the evolving Salafi Jihadist Threat in Nigeria", in *Boko Haram. Islamism, Politics, Security and the State of Nigeria*, M.P. De Montclos, ed., African Studies Centre (ASC), Leiden, 2 (2014), 158-191.

PRATT, D., *Religion and Extremism. Rejecting Diversity*, Bloomsbury Publishing Plc., London, 2018.

RAHNER, K., "Christianity and the Non-Christian Religions", *Christianity and Other Religions. Selected Readings,* J. HICK – B. HEBBLETHWAITE, eds., Oneworld Oxford, England, 2001, 19-38.

RASMUSSEN, L., *Christian-Muslim Relations in Africa. The Cases of Northern Nigeria and Tanzania Compared*, British Academic Press, London, 1993.

REZA, N.S.V., *Mawdudi and the Making of Islamic Revivalism*, Oxford University Press, Oxford, 1996.

SANNEH, L., "The African Christian and Islam. Historical and Religious Dimensions", in *The African Christian and Islam*, J. AZUMAH – L. SANNEH, eds., Langham Monographs, Cumbria (2013) 1-40.

SAUL, C.P., *Modern Social Theory*, Heinemann, London, 1968.

SCHAEFER, U., "Religious Intolerance as a Source of Violence" *World Without Violence*, Gandhi Arun (ed.), M. K. Gandhi Institute, 1999, 1-4.

SCHMID, A.P., ed., *The Routledge Handbook of Terrorism Research*, Routledge, New York, 2011.

SCHREITER, R., "The Theology of Reconciliation and Peacemaking for Mission", in *Mission, Violence and Reconciliation*, H. MELLOR – T. YATES eds., Sheffield, Cliff College Publishing, 2003, 1-29.

SCHUR, E., *Labeling Deviant Behaviour*, Harper & Row, New York, 1971.

SHAHZAD, S.S., *Inside Al-Qaeda and the Taliban Beyond bin Laden and 9/11*, Palgrave Macmillan, 2011.

SIDAHMED, A.S – EHTESHAMI, A., eds., *Islamic Fundamentalism*, Westview Press Inc., Cunnor Hill, Oxford, 1996.

SINGH, K., *Quantitative Social Research Methods*, Sage Publications Inc., New Delhi, 2007.

SOLOMON, H., "Counter-Terrorism in Nigeria. Responding to Boko Haram", in *Annual Editions. Violence and Terrorism*", T.J. Badey, ed., McGraw Hill Education, 14 (2013) 193-198.

STEPANOVA, E., *Terrorism in Asymmetrical Conflict Ideological and Structural Aspects*, SIPRI Research Report, 23, Oxford University Press, New York, 2008.

STIFTUNG, F.E., *The Rise of Religious Radicalism in the Arab World. Significance, Implications and Counter-Strategies*, Amman, 2015.

TANNENBAUM, F., *Crime and Community*, New York, 1938.

UMAR, M.S., *Islam and Colonialism. Intellectual Responses of Muslims of Northern Nigeria to British Colonial Rule*, Brill, Leiden, Netherland, 2006.

USMAN, Y.B., *The Manipulation of Religion in Nigeria 1977-1987*, M.O. Press, Kaduna, 2014[2].

van GORDER, A.C, *Violence in God's Name. Christian and Muslim Relations in Nigeria*, African Diaspora Press, Houston, Texas, 2012.

WHITTAKER, D.J ed., *The Terrorism Reader*, Routledge, New York, 2001.

——————, "Motivations for Terrorism" in *Theory and Politics of Terrorism*, J.L. FELDKAMP, ed., 1 (2014), Cognella Academic Publishing, USA, 9-21.

YORK, T., "Early Church Martyrdom. Witnessing For or Against the Empire?", in *Witness of the Body The Past, Present, and Future of Christian Martyrdom*, M.L. Budde – K. SCOTT, eds., Wm. B. Eerdmans Publishing Co., Michigan, USA (2011), 20-42.

ZENN, J., *Northern Nigeria's Boko Haram. The Prize in Al-Qaeda's Africa Strategy*, The James Town Foundation, Washington DC, 2012.

5. Encyclopaedia

ADOGAME, A., "Nigeria," *Encyclopaedia of Religion and War*, Routledge, New York, 2004, 329-330.

COLLINS, T. A., "Fundamentalism, Biblical", *NCE*, B.L. Marthaler – al., eds., Thomson Gale, Farmington Hills, US, VI, 2003[2], 29-30.

DULLES, A., "Fundamentalism", *NCE*, B.L. Marthaler – al., eds., Thomson Gale, Farmington Hills, VI, 2003[2], 27-29.

KENNY, J., "West Africa and Islam," *A Little Encyclopaedia of History, Beliefs, Practices and Christian Attitudes*, An AECAWA Publication, 2000.

WATER, M., *The New Encyclopaedia of Christian Martyrs*, Grand Rapids: Bakers, 2001, 351 – 352.

6. Articles

ADEYANJU, J. – BABALOLA E.O., "The Gospel and the Impact of Poverty on the Practice of Ideal Christianity in Nigeria" *IJRHSS* IV 2 (February 2017) 22-30.

ALAO, O. – MAVALLA A.G., "Kaduna State Shari'a Crisis of 2000. The Lessons and Challenges After Sixteen Years", *JHSS* XXI 10 12 (2016) 8-14.

BARNES, A.E., "Evangelisation where it is not wanted. Colonial Administrators and Missionaries in Northern Nigeria during the First Third of the Twentieth Century" *Journal of Religion in Africa* XXV 4 (1995) 412-441.

BARNETT, L., "Freedom of Religion and Religious Symbols in the Public Sphere" *Library of Parliament*, Ottawa, Canada, 2011-60-E (2013), 1-20.

BERKOWITZ, L., "Frustration/Aggression Hypothesis. Examination and Reformation" *Psychological Bulletin* CVI 1 (July 1989) 59-73.

BORUM, R. – al., "Assessing and Managing Violence Risk in Clinical Practice", *Journal of Practical Psychiatry and Behavioral Health* II 4 (1996) 205-215.

BRIGAGLIA, A., "The Volatility of Salafi Political Theology, the War on Terror and the Genesis of Boko Haram", *Diritto e questioni pubbliche* XV 2 (2015) 174-201.

BRIGHTON, M.A., "The Sicarii in Acts. A New Perspective", *JETS* LIV 3 (September 2011) 547-558.

CAMPBELL, J., "Boko Haram, Origins, Challenges and Responses" *NOREF Policy Brief* (October 2014), 1-4.

CORRADO, R., "A Critique of the Mental Disorder Perspective of Political Terrorism", *International Journal of Law and psychiatry* IV 3-4 (1981) 293-309.

EBWEREM, I.M., "A Dangerous Awakening. The Politicization of Religion in Nigeria", *IFRA-Nigeria* (2013) 75-100.

EISENSTADT, M., "Iran's Islamic Revolution. Lessons for the Arab Spring of 2011?" *Strategic Forum* 267 (April 2011) 1-12.

HACKETT, R.I.J., "Charismatic/Pentecostal Appropriation of Media Technologies in Nigeria and Ghana" *Journal of Religion in Africa*, XXVIII 3 (1998) 258-277.

HOFFMANN, L.K., "Who Speaks for the North? Politics and Influence in Northern Nigeria", *Chatham House – The Royal Institute of International Affairs*, Research Paper, July 2014, 1-28.

HORSLEY, R.A., "The Sicarii. Ancient Jewish 'Terrorists'", *The Journal of Religion*, LIX 4 (October 1979) 435-458.

HUNTINGTON S.P., "The Clash of Civilizations?" *Foreign Affairs*, LXXII 3 (Summer 1993) 22-49.

KASSIM, A., "Defining and Understanding the Religious Philosophy of Jihadi-Salafism and the Ideology of Boko Haram", *Politics, Religion & Ideology* XVI 2-3 (2015) 173-200.

MANTZIKOS, I., "The Absence of the State in Northern Nigeria: The Case of Boko Haram", *African Renaissance* VII 1 (2010) 57-62.

MCGARVEY, K., "Gender, Peace and Religious Coexistence. Insights from Nigeria", *JORAS* I (June 2011) 54-74.

MOUSSALLI, A., "Wahhabism, Salafism and Islamism: Who is the Enemy? *Conflict Forum* (January 30, 2009) 1-39.

OJO, M.A., "Pentecostal Movements, Islam and Contest for Public Space in Northern Nigeria", *Islam and Christian-Muslim Relations* XVIII 2 (2007) 175-188.

OKEMI, M.E., "Boko Haram: A Religious Sect or Terrorist Organization", *GJPLR* I 1 (June 2013) 1-9.

OKENE, A.A. – AHMAD S.B., "Ibn Khaldum, Cyclical Theory and the Rise and Fall of Sokoto Caliphate, Nigeria West Africa", *International Journal of Business and Social Science* II 4 (March 2011) 80-91.

PISCATORI, J., "Islam, Islamists, and the Electoral Principle in the Middle East", *ISIM* (2000) 1-64.

SCHMID A.P., "Frameworks for Conceptualising Terrorism", *Terrorism and Political Violence*, Routledge, London, XVI 2 (2004) 197-221.

SULE I.Z.O. – al., "Governance and Boko Haram Insurgents in Nigeria: An Analysis", *Academic Journal of Interdisciplinary Studies*, IV 2 (July 2015) 35-41.

TAIYE, A., "Religious Fanaticism and Fundamentalism in Nigeria since 1980: A Historical Perspective", *British Journal of Arts and Social Sciences* IX 2 (2012) 141-155.

TANKO, P.B., "The Effectiveness of Dialogue in Conflict Resolution. An Analyses of Findings from Four States in Nigeria" *JOCRED*, IV 2 (2006) 30-63.

THURSTON, A., "Nigeria's Mainstream Salafis between Boko Haram and the State", *Islamic Africa* VI 1-2 (2015) 109-135.

UBAH, C.N., "Problems of Christian Missionaries in Muslim Emirates of Nigeria 1900-1928" *Journal of African Studies* III 3 (1976) 351-371.

UHUNMWUANGHO S.O., "Challenges and Solutions to the Ethno-Religious Conflicts in Nigeria: Case Study of the Jos Crises", *Journal of Sustainable Development in Africa*, XIII 5 (2011) 109-124.

ZENN, J., "Nigeria Al-Qaedaism", *Current Trends. In Islamist Ideology* XVI (March 2014), 99-117.

WENZEL, M – al, "Retributive and Restorative Justice" *Law Human Behaviour* XXXII (2008), 375-389.

——————, "Boko Haram's Dangerous Expansion into Northwest Nigeria", *CTC SENTINEL* V 10 (October 2012) 1-24.

——————, "Iran: Religious Elements of the 1979 Islamic Revolution", *Religion and Conflict Case Study Series* (August 2013) 1-19.

7. Unpublished Works

BAKENI J.B., *Understanding the Enigma of Boko Haram,* Nigeria.

MULDERS A., "The Impact of Persistent Violence on the Church in Northern Nigeria" Open Doors Research.

8. Thesis

BAKENI J.B., *The Encounter of The African Traditional Religion, Islam and Christianity in Northeastern Nigeria. Towards A Contextual Theology of Interreligious Dialogue*, Pontificia Università di S. Thomas Aquinas, Rome, 2012.

BRANDIS D.A., "The 1979 Iranian Revolution. The Revolutionary Revolution" *Thesis*, University of Arizona, Arizona, 2009.

NWEKE P.C., *The Role of Institutional Design in the Regulation of Ethnic Conflicts in Nigeria. A Case Study of the Jos Conflict (2001-2012)*, Rome, 2016.

SALAMONE F., *Gods and Goods in Africa. Persistence and Change in the Fulani Jihad in the 19th Century Hausa Land*, McGill, 1976.

9. Dictionaries

AMERICAN HERITAGE DICTIONARY, 2000.

CONCISE OXFORD ENGLISH DICTIONARY.

LAST J.M., ed., *A Dictionary of Epidemiology*, New York, Oxford University Press, 2001[4].

WEBSTER'S DICTIONARY AND THESAURUS.

10. Magazines/Dailies

ABDULLA, "Nigeria Crisis A Threat to the Entire Country", *The Economist* (September, 2012).

DAILY TRUST (December 27, 2004).

NEW NIGERIAN (January 31, 2000).

————, (March 2, 2000).

NIGERIAN TRIBUNE (September 19, 2001).

QUALITY (1987).

THE NATION (August 14, 2009).

THE PUNCH (November 22, 2002).

TELL (August 10, 2009).

TELL (September 24, 2001).

ZIMMERMAN K., "From Somalia to Nigeria. Jihad", *Weekly Standard*, (June 18, 2011).

————, "A Taste of the Taliban: Islamist Attacks in Nigeria", *Economist* (August 1, 2009).

————, "Itinerant Christian Preacher", *Newswatch* (March 30, 1987).

11. Internet Materials

AL-BARNĀWĪ KSA, I., "I Pledge to Islam my Religion", [accessed: 20.12.2016], www. youtube.com/watch?v=y_X4v86Q3qs,.

ALLEN, K., "South Sudan. Women Raped under the Noses of UN Forces", BBC World News on Africa, [accessed: 25.10.2015], www.bbc.com/news/world-africa-27765898.

BARNES J.E. & COOPER H., "Trump Discussed Pulling US from NATO. Aides say amid New Concerns Over Russia", *The New York Times*, [accessed: 04.04.2020], www.nytimes.com/2019/01/14/us/politics/nato-president-trump.html.

BAYAGBON, O., "Oil Contribution to Nigeria's Gross Domestic Product (GDP) is on the Rise after Witnessing a Downward Trend over a four-year period-between 2013 and 2017", [accessed: 15.12.2018], www.petrobarometer.thecable.ng/2018/02/14/oil-contribution-gdp-rebounds-four-year-fall/.

BLAIR, D., "Does Nigeria's Taliban Have the West in its Sights?, *Daily Telegraph* (December 28, 2011), [accessed: 15.12.2016], www.telegraph.co.uk/ news/worldnews/africaandindianocean/nigeria/8980000/Does-Nigerias Talibanhave-the-West-in-its-sights.html.

————, "Boko Haram is now a mini-Islamic State, with its own Territory", *The Telegraph*, [accessed: 21.05.2017] www.telegraph.co.uk/news/worldnews/africaandindianocean/nigeria/11337722/Boko-Haram-is-now-a-mini-Isamic-State-with-its-own-territory.html.

BOLAJI, S., "Dapchi Girls Abduction. Some Unanswered Questions, [accessed: 30.01. 2019], www.punchng.com/dapchi-girls-abduction-some- unanswered-questions/.

BBC, "Boko Haram Declares 'Islamic State' in Northern Nigeria", [accessed: 04.12.2016], www.bbc.com/ news/world-africa-28925484.

————, Nigeria's Boko Haram Pledges Allegiance to Islamic State, [accessed: 04.12.2016], www.bbc.com/news/world-africa-31784538.

————, "Nigeria Boko Haram. Militants 'Technically Defeated' – Buhari", [accessed: 01.11.2017], http://www.bbc.com/news/world-africa-35173618.

CASPER, J., "More Martyrs. ISIS Executes Dozens of Ethiopian Christians in Libya" *Christianity Today,* [accessed: 06.05.2016], www.christianitytoday. com/gleanings/2015/april/more-martyrs-isis-executes-ethiopian-christians-libya.html.

CHANNELS TELEVISION, "Army Rescues 58 Women used as Sex Slaves, Others from Boko Haram", [accessed: 05.06.2018], www.channelstv. com/2018/06/04/army-rescues-58-women-used-as-sex-slaves-others-from-boko-haram/.

CENTRAL BANK OF NIGERIA, "Nigeria GDP Annual Growth Rate", [accessed: 15.04.2019], www.tradingeconomics.com/nigeria/gdp-growth-annual.

CHOTHIA, F., "Will Nigeria's Abducted Schoolgirls ever be Found?" BBC World News on Africa, [accessed: 15.10.2015], www.bbc.com/news/world africa-27293418.

CNN LIBRARY, "September 11, 2001. Background and timeline of the attacks", [accessed: 20.12.2016], www.edition.cnn.com/2013/07/27/us/september-11-anniversary-fast-facts.

CONSTITUTION OF THE FEDERAL REPUBLIC OF NIGERIAN 1999, [accessed: 25.11.2018], www.wipo.int/edocs/lexdocs/laws/en/ng/ng014en.pdf, 1-118.

CUDDIHY, M., "Kenyan University Attack. 149 Killed and 79 Wounded in Al-Shabaab Terrorist Attack on Garissa Campus", [accessed: 06.05.2015], www.abc.net.au/news/2015-04-03/147-killed-in-al-shabaab-terrorist-attack-on-kenyanuniversity/6369688.

DANIEL, "Persecution of Christians Reaches Historic Levels, Conditions Suggest Worst is yet to come", [accessed: 06.05.2015], www.opendoorsusa. org/newsroom/tag-news-post/persecution-of-christians-reaches-historic-levels-conditions-suggest-worst-is-yet-to-come/.

DANJIBO, N.D., "Islamic fundamentalism and Sectarian Violence. The 'Maitatsine' and 'Boko Haram' Crises in Northern Nigeria" *Peace and Conflict Studies Programme, Institute of African Studies, University of Ibadan,* [accessed: 13.07.2015], www.ifranigeria.org/IMG/pdf/ N_D_

DANJIBO_IslamicFundamentalism_and_Sectarian_Violence_The_ Maitatsine_and_Boko_aram_Crises_in_Northern_Nigeria.pdf, 1-21.

EKOTT, I., "Bill Clinton counters Jonathan, insists Poverty behind Boko Haram, Ansaru Insurgency", [accessed: 15.11.2018], www.premiumtimesng. com/news/122116-bill-clinton-counters-jonathan-insists-poverty-behind-boko-haram-ansaru-insurgency.html.

ENCYCLOPAEDIA BRITANNICA, "Rābih az-Zubayr", [accessed: 14.01.2017], www. britannica.com/EBchecked/topic/487969/Rabih-az-Zubayr.

ERO, C., "Bombing in Abuja. On Nigeria's Boko Haram", *International Crisis Group* (September 6, 2011), [accessed: 20.12.2016], www. blog.crisisgroup.org/africa/nigeria/2011/09/06/bombing-in-abuja-on-nigerias-boko-haram/.

EUROPEAN CONVENTION ON HUMAN RIGHTS, "As Amended by Protocols No. 11 and 14", [accessed: 23.11.2018], www.echr.coe.int/Documents/ Convention_ ENG.pdf, 3-62.

FABIYI, O. – OLAKOR, F., "Apostle Suleman to Appear before DSS with 30 Lawyers", *Punch*, [accessed: 21.05.2017], www.punchng.com/apostle-suleman-appear-dss-30-lawyers/.

FALANA, F., "How Modu Sheriff Sponsored Boko Haram", *Sahara Reporters*, [accessed: 08.05.2018], www.saharareporters.com/2014/09/04/how-modu-sheriff-sponsored-boko-haram-femi-falana-san.

GLASER, J., "Anti-Terror Laws in Nigeria Threaten Civil Liberties. The US Pushed Nigeria to Pass Legislation Giving Broad Powers to a Government Prone to Human Rights Abuses", [accessed: 23.11.2018], www.news. antiwar.com/2011/09/03/anti-terror-laws-in-nigeriathreaten-civil-liberties/.

IEP., *Global Terrorism Index (GTI), 2014. Measuring and Understanding the Impact of Terrorism*, [accessed: 06.05.2015], www. economicsandpeace. org/ wpcontent/uploads/2015/06/GlobalTerrorism-Index-Report-2014.pdf, 1-91.

————, *Global Terrorism Index (GTI), 2015. Measuring and Understanding the Impact of Terrorism*, [accessed: 14.12.2015], www. ECONOMICSANDPEACE.ORG/WPCONTENT/UPLOADS/2015/11/2015-GLOBAL-Terrorism-Index-Report.pdf, 1-107.

IEP., *Global Terrorism Index (GTI), 2017. Measuring and Understanding the Impact of Terrorism*, [accessed: 14.11.2018], WWW.RELIEFWEB. INT/SITES/RELIEFWEB.INT/FILES/RESOURCES/GLOBAL%20TERRORISM%20 INDEX%202017%20%284%29.PDF, 1-116.

INDEX MUNDI, "Nigeria Demographics Profile 2016", [accessed: 12.01.2017], www.indexmundi.com/nigeria/demographics_profile.html.

ISIZOH, C.D., ed., "Christianity in Dialogue with African Traditional Religion and culture," [accessed: 22.07.2014], www.afrikaworld.net/afrel.

JOHNSON, T., "Boko Haram", *Backgrounders, Council on Foreign Relations* (December 27, 2011) 4, [accessed: 18.12.2016], www.cfr.org/ backgrounder/ boko-haram.

HUMAN RIGHTS WATCH, "The Miss World Riots. Continued Impunity for Killings in Kaduna", *Human Rights Watch Africa Division*, Human Rights Watch, XV 13 (July 18, 2003), [accessed: 4.05.2015], www.hrw.org/reports/ 2003/ nigeria0703/2.htm.

KUKAH, M.H., "Persecutions of Christians in Africa. Context, Contents & Opportunities", (A Draft Text of Paper Presented at Conference on Contemporary Christian Martyrs) *Seed of the Church*, Notre Dame (November 2012), [accessed: 25.10.2017], www.icl.nd.edu/ assets/84236/persecutions_in_africa_contexts_contents_and_ opportunities_bishop_kukah.pdf, 1-16.

MOGAN, L., "Iraqi's Christians Persecuted by ISIS", [accessed: 6.05.2015], www.cbsnews.com/news/iraq-christians-persecuted-by-isis-60-minutes/.

MURTADĀ, A., *Boko Haram in Nigeria. Its Beginnings, Principles and Activities in Nigeria*, [accessed: 8.12.2016], www.SalafiManhaj.com, 2013, 1-61.

NCN., "Defend Yourselves or Die One by On, T.Y Danjuma tells Nigerians", [accessed: 06.06.2018], www.nigeriancablenewsonline.com/metro/ defend yourselves- or-die-one-by-one-t-y-danjuma-tells-nigerians/.

NIGERIAN POPULATION, [accessed: 12.01.2017], www.worldometers.info/ world population/nigeria-population/.

NSRP, "Policy Brief. The Niger Delta Amnesty Lessons Four Years on", [accessed: 05.12.2016], www. nsrpnigeria.org.

OJEIFO, S., "Dapchi Girls. Of Sham Release and Cynical Citizenry", *Vanguard*, [accessed: 05.05.2018], www.vanguardngr.com/2018/03/ dapchi-girls-sham release-cynical-citizenry/.

ONYEDIKA-UGOEZE, N. – MUSA, N., "Boko Haram Terrorists killed Islamic Scholar, Injure One Boy in Borno State", *The Guardian*, [accessed: 08.05.2018], www.guardian.ng/news/boko-haram-terrorists-attack-borno-village-kill-islamic-scholar-injure-boy/.

OPEJOBI, S., "Stop Killing, Raping Women, It's Anti-Islam – Scholar Advises Boko Haram", *Daily Post*, [accessed: 08.05.2018], www.dailypost.ng/ 2017/02/13/stop-killing-raping-women-anti-islam-scholar-advises-boko-haram/, [accessed: May 8, 2018].

OPENDOOR WORLD WATCH LIST, [accessed: 17.05.2018], www.opendoorsusa.org/christian-persecution/world-watch-list/.

SAM-OHUABUNWA, M., "Leah Sharibu. Confirmation of the True Mission of the Boko Haram", *Vanguard*, [accessed: 05.05.2018], www.vanguardngr.com/2018/04/leah-sharibu-confirmation-true-mission-boko-haram-2/.

SAMPSON, I.T., "Religious Violence in Nigeria. Causal Diagnoses and Strategic Recommendations to the State and Religious Communities, [accessed: 21.05.2017], www.ajol.info/index.php/ajcr/article/viewFile/78703/69042.

THE ARAB CONVENTION FOR THE SUPPRESSION OF TERRORISM, Cairo, April 22, 1998, [accessed: 05.12.2018], www.unodc.org/tldb/pdf/conv_arab_terrorism.en.pdf, 1-25.

THE UNITED NATION GENERAL ASSEMBLY RESOLUTION 49/60, December 9, 1994, [accessed: 05.12.2015], www.un.org/documents/ga/res/49/ a49r060.htm.

THE UNITED STATES FEDERAL CRIMINAL CODE, Definitions, [accessed: 05.12.2015], www.law.cornell.edu/uscode/text/18/2331.

- "Thirteen Questions About Northern Ireland" in *Passage-engelsk laereverk for Vgl*, [accessed: 07.25.2019], www.passage.cappelendamm.no/c104241/artikkel/vis.html?tid=120161.

UNITED STATES DEPARTMENT OF STATE, Diplomacy in Action, "Foreign Terrorist Organizations", [accessed: 27.11.2016], www.state.gov/j/ct/rls/other/des/ 123085.htm.

WIKIPEDIA, "Kaduna State', [accessed: 21.05.2017], www.en.wikipedia.org/wiki/ Kaduna_State.

Index of authors and subjects

Contents

Finito di stampare nel mese di Settembre 2020
presso Printbee - Noventa Padovana (PD)